NIGELLA
KITCHEN

Also by Nigella Lawson

HOW TO EAT
THE PLEASURES AND PRINCIPLES OF GOOD FOOD

HOW TO BE A DOMESTIC GODDESS
BAKING AND THE ART OF COMFORT COOKING

NIGELLA BITES
FROM FAMILY MEALS TO ELEGANT DINNERS — EASY, DELECTABLE RECIPES FOR ANY OCCASION

NIGELLA FRESH
(FORMERLY FOREVER SUMMER)
DELICIOUS FLAVORS ON YOUR PLATE ALL YEAR ROUND

FEAST
FOOD TO CELEBRATE LIFE

NIGELLA EXPRESS
GOOD FOOD, FAST

NIGELLA CHRISTMAS
FOOD FAMILY FRIENDS FESTIVITIES

NIGELLA KITCHEN

RECIPES FROM THE HEART OF THE HOME

NIGELLA LAWSON

PHOTOGRAPHS BY LIS PARSONS

HYPERION

NEW YORK

Design and Art Direction: Caz Hildebrand
Cookery Assistant: Hettie Potter
Editorial Assistant: Zoe Wales
Home Economics Adviser: Caroline Stearns
Props: Rose Murray
Layout/Typesetting: Julie Martin
Index: Vicki Robinson

First published in Great Britain in 2010 by Chatto & Windus

ISBN: 978-1-4013-2395-0

Hyperion books are available for special promotions and premiums. For details contact the
HarperCollins Special Markets Department in the New York office at 212-207-7528, fax 212-207-
7222, or email spsales@harpercollins.com.

First U.S. Edition

10 9 8 7 6 5 4 3 2 1

FOR MY FAMILY

Contents

Part II: Kitchen Comforts

NOTE FOR THE READER

♥ All eggs are extra large, organic

♥ Dishes containing raw or partially cooked eggs should not be served to those with weak or compromised immune systems, such as pregnant women, the elderly or the very young

♥ All bittersweet chocolate is minimum 62% cocoa solids

♥ All olive oil is regular (not extra-virgin), unless stated

♥ Flour cup measures are scooped and leveled. Almond flour meal measures are lightly packed. Light and dark brown sugar measures are firmly packed.

♥ Leftovers, if to be kept, should be covered and refrigerated or frozen as soon as cool, and kept no longer than indicated. Never reheat previously frozen or reheated food.

♥ Thaw frozen seafood gradually by placing it in the refrigerator overnight. If you have to thaw seafood quickly, either seal it in a plastic bag and immerse it in cold water, or—if the food will be cooked immediately thereafter—microwave it on the "defrost" setting and stop the defrost cycle while the fish is still icy but pliable.

♥ Where no suggestions are given, it is not advisable to make ahead or freeze.

♥ When making jam or syrup, be extra-careful, always watch the pan and do not stir unless advised.

♥ For suppliers of specialist items, see my website *www.nigella.com*.

♥ Always be sure to read a recipe right through before starting to cook.

♥ For quick recipes, taking 30 minutes or under, turn to the Express Index, **p.486**.

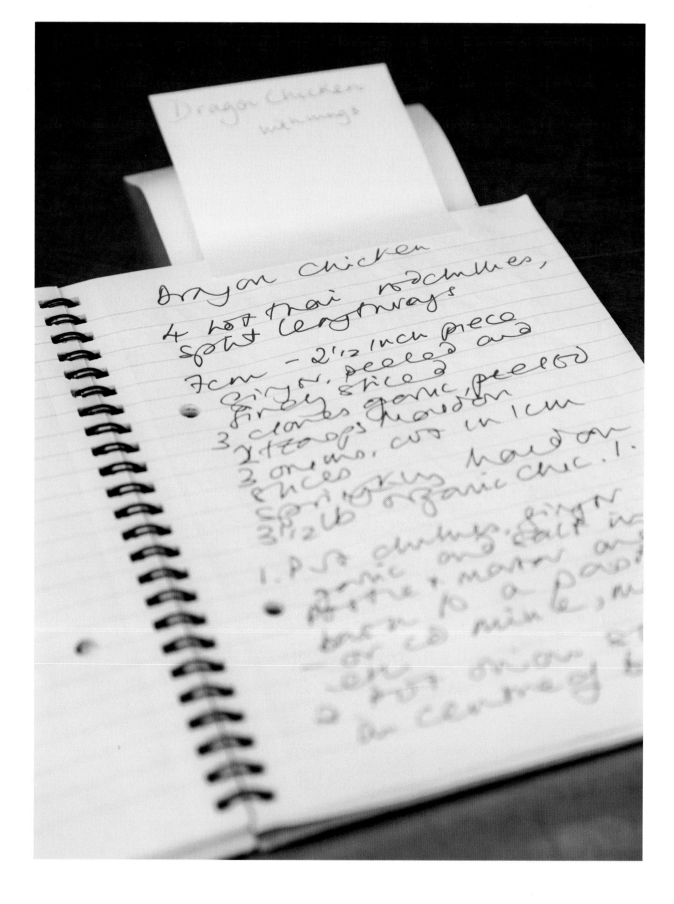

Dragon Chicken
Wings

Dragon Chicken
4 hot thai red chillies,
split lengthways
7cm - 2½ inch piece
ginger, peeled and
finely sliced
3 cloves garlic peeled
2 tbsps mustard
2 onions, cut in 1cm
slices mustard
3½ lb organic chic. l.

1. Put chillies, ginger
garlic and salt in
mortar and
bring to a boil
or 15 mins, m
2 tbsp onion or
the chilling b

INTRODUCTION

Or what the kitchen means to me, and why I live in it

This is a book I've been wanting to write for a very long time. The idea first came to me almost ten years ago and has been simmering away on the back burner ever since. Maybe I just needed to spend more time in the kitchen before I could write about it. And by "in the kitchen," I mean, rather, in a number of kitchens. They have all been different, but with one crucial element in common: they're where I feel most at home.

But, if this is the starting point of the book, it's not one I ever stray far away from. I know it's impossible to prove a negative, but let me start, about face, by telling you what this book isn't. It isn't a handbook or a manual. It isn't a lifestyle guide or aspirational treatise. It most definitely isn't intended as a work of social history, although I do believe that any cookbook ultimately ends up as one: the history of what we eat is indisputably the history of how we live and who we are. In fact, this book is simply the story of my love affair with the kitchen. Whatever the opposite of the currently still fashionable genre, the misery memoir, might be, this is it: a comfort chronicle.

Please, listen to me, though, when I say that my focus does not emanate from the belief that cooking holds any inherent moral qualities or reveals essential purity of purpose and congratulation-worthy virtue. Certainly not: it wouldn't occur to me to feel guilty about eating food I hadn't cooked – so long as I enjoyed it – any more than I ever have or would feel guilty about buying clothes rather than sewing something to wear myself. The born-again fervor and judgmental outlook of the status-conscious cook seem to me positively to preclude a happy life in the kitchen – or, indeed, out of it. I don't cook because I feel I ought to, but because I want to. And, of course, there are times when I don't want to. That's life. Sometimes reality has the edge over romance: albeit I have said before, and hand-on-heart declare again, that for me the kitchen is not a place I want to escape from, but to escape *to*, I will confess that there are times when the idea of cooking doesn't fill me with joy or make me radiate enthusiasm.

What I've discovered, after what feels like a lifetime's cooking, is that anything which holds true in the kitchen is just as true out of the kitchen. This is one of my mantras, and I fear it won't be the last time you hear me chant it. And I'm sorry if it reeks of homespun philosophy, but that's just what it is. So, while it may be the case that occasionally – at the end of a long day or when I'm so exhausted that just staying upright seems a challenge – I approach cooking with something less than my usual gusto, I nearly always find that just getting on with it can make me wonder what I was dreading in the first place, and why. But then, the same applies to so many obligations and undertakings that loom over us in life, outside of the kitchen, too. Fear – of disappointment, inadequacy, failure – seems to make fools of us, causing us to forget what we all unfailingly learn from experience: that not doing what frightens us makes us fear it more rather than less. Perhaps some day I'll write a book called "Feel the Fear and Cook it Anyway," although to some extent I suspect that this is, indeed, the subliminal message of every book I've ever written.

I understand why cooking can hold so much terror and the kitchen seem a place of stress, not solace. I'm sure this is partly to do with the contemporary cult of the chef, and is further fueled by the hysterical pursuit of perfection that defines the age we live in. I am not a chef, am horrified when thus defined, and resist, without a shred of disingenuousness, the miscast role of expert. Again and again, I say and can never seem to say enough: if we really needed qualifications and expertise before we stepped into the kitchen, human beings would have fallen out of the evolutionary loop a long time ago.

I remember being struck once by an episode in one of those (many) restaurant reality shows: the contestants were asked to make a mushroom risotto and were then castigated for having – each one of them – produced a dish quite unlike another's. I can see this makes sense in a restaurant kitchen: consistency is all. But for me, the fact that everyone makes a dish a little differently, that what comes out of our kitchens bears our own stamp, is precisely the essence of real home cooking. Not adhering to professional standards in the kitchen doesn't show our limitations, but is indicative of our liberation and individuality.

A real chef would have an apoplectic fit and a nervous breakdown – simultaneously – if forced to cook in my kitchen. The surfaces are cluttered, the layout messy and getting messier by the day (and, overall, I've no doubt my kitchen would fail many a food safety test and law of ergonomics). But I love it, even if it is more of a nest than a room. My kitchen is full of online bargains and the results of many serendipitous shopping expeditions – unusual china, cutlery, vintage bits and pieces, heavy-duty Dutch ovens that are left out because they won't fit neatly in drawers or cupboards – all of which I love particularly because they were bargains and are gloriously random. The clutter of a kitchen is part of its charm, so why worry that it isn't as clinically bare as a restaurant kitchen: it shouldn't be. I've still got, propped behind one of my hanging frames, a card clock that I used about eight or so years ago to teach one of my children to tell the time. I couldn't remove it now: it's part of our history; and that's what a kitchen means to me.

We all dream about the perfect kitchen with its well-appointed fittings, gleaming surfaces, and top-of-the-range equipment. It's both roomy and cozy at the same time, boasting lots of space and lots of light, but most of all it is the setting for our ideal life. This is a kitchen that I've never cooked in, let alone written about.

Whatever stove you have, it has to work for you, however haphazardly. However restricted the space, that has to work for you, too. However dated the design, it must work for you. And it will. Some of my fondest cooking memories are of producing mega-meals out of the rented kitchen of a holiday home in Cornwall. Not only did the electric cooktop never get very hot, but it kept turning itself off. One oven burnt like a furnace, the other ran insistently cold, and I often felt I was conjuring rather than cooking, as I juggled trays and ovens at regular intervals to stop one thing from burning while ensuring that another really was cooking. Knives and saucepans were sub-standard and in scant supply. But none of this mattered, because a kitchen, however inadequate or alien, has the ability to make you feel, once you've cooked in it a few times, as though you've marked out some safe and reassuring space of your own.

But there's more to it than that. The kitchen isn't just the room in which I cook, it's the place where I live. There's a dynamism to a kitchen that seems to draw people in.

Part hub, part haven, the kitchen is where, I've always found, people speak more freely than anywhere else. Maybe it's because when you're cooking, you can talk and listen without shining the light of your attention too closely on those who may need to talk or be listened to. I feel I am much more likely to find out what might be worrying a child, or to let an otherwise self-contained friend unburden herself, while I'm in the kitchen, gently busying myself with chopping a carrot or stirring a soup. There's a naturalness to the way one both carries on with the task in hand and listens, which seems to inhibit communication less than a more assiduous and fussy focus, however devoted.

Don't get me wrong: the kitchen is not just a sanctuary or some sort of warm and comforting cave. Its dynamism comes in part from the fact that, more than any other room in a house, the kitchen brings and welcomes the outside in. You may not add a new cushion to the sofa in the living room regularly, or hang new pictures in the hall every other week, but the kitchen relies on constant replenishment and continual refueling. I admit I am messier than the next person, but for me food shopping becomes part of the decor: the shape of a new bottle of oil on the counter, a jar of something too pretty to go into a cupboard, a bowl of fruit on the table; things constantly appear and disappear, making the kitchen look a little different, while staying reassuringly the same.

I've written before of the pull of paganism, and I rather relish having the seasons make their presence felt in my kitchen, if only in the way the fruit bowls fill – whether they're bulging with cherries or clementines, or presenting a darkly mellow Indian-summer tableau of grapes, figs, and blackberries – and the vegetable baskets are stocked. For me, fruits in season are both display and dessert; I can happily dispense with both flowers and dessert when the kitchen table is laden with harvest-home produce. And I regard nothing as beyond my remit: if I see some gorgeous vine tomatoes, I leave them on display (and, anyway, tomatoes should not really be stored in the refrigerator), letting them tumble on top of a cake stand or wooden board. Not that I'm against flowers – so long as they don't crowd out food or eaters, or interfere with the eyeline when you're sitting at the table. In fact, what does it for me is an ordinary, old kitchen pitcher filled with fresh herbs or unfancy flowers that look as if they have just been picked from the garden. I have no garden, so I must create the illusion.

And, unafraid as I am to put the kitsch in kitchen, it all gets a little more fanciful towards evening, when my weakness for a fairy light (and I run the gamut from pearl to

INTRODUCTION

chile peppers) turns the place into a magical grotto. It's a conceit I rather like. I need my kitchen to work, but I also want it to enchant.

I've tried to indicate, lightly, the way my kitchen works for me in the run of chapters that lie ahead. I've separated them into two sections, Kitchen Quandaries and Kitchen Comforts, although I feel strongly that the *answers* to such quandaries as dog the usual working week should offer comfort, too. And, please, bear in mind that the way I have grouped the recipes – whether suggesting a speedy midweek supper or a blow-out on Sunday – is essentially autobiographical rather than dictatorial: I write according to how I cook and live. But I don't confine myself, and nor should you. These are suggestions, not orders. I try to be practical, because advice in the kitchen (or, indeed, out of it) is of no use otherwise. To this end, I have often appended ideas for what to do with whatever you may have left over from a particular recipe, under the legend (and, please, just humor me here) *Making Leftovers Right*. For me, these rhythms of the kitchen are what mark the cook out from the chef, and make us feel purposeful and productive. What's more, this sort of greedy opportunism and thriftiness combined are essentially what real cooking is all about, and what this book is all about.

The life of a kitchen takes in many moods and many meals. The recipes in this book try to reflect and, more, to celebrate that fact. In common with my other books – those I wrote before and after I left the ideas for this book bubbling away on the back burner – this one is based on the premise that the kitchen is an enduring place of comfort and that the food which comes out of it provides essential sustenance not just for body, but for soul, too.

KITCHEN CABOODLE

When I was young, and even longer ago, cookery books used to contain counsel called, according to the French classical tradition, *"batterie de cuisine,"* in other words, a slightly panic-inducing list of all those pieces of kit and equipment that any cook worthy of the title should own. Don't worry, I shan't be visiting that kind of finger-wagging bossiness on you. I mean, really: how much or how little you buy for your kitchen is up to you. And even then, no one has a free rein. There are likely to be constraints before you even start: budget being one, space another.

Anyway, most kitchen items are a luxury, and a very pleasurable indulgence; all that is actually needed for the cooking itself is fire, a receptacle, and something to stir with. Still, I am hesitant about sounding too austere on the matter. As Imelda Marcos was to shoes, I am to the whole covetable arena of kitchen items and equipment (foodstuffs included). How then, could I advise too spartan an approach in you? For me, buying stuff for the kitchen is one of the great joys of life. While I'm not entirely innocent of extravagance, the truth is many gadgets cost a lot less than clothes, and what's more, you don't have to try them on.

Still, it is all too easy to clutter up a kitchen with stuff you want, or feel you might need, but cannot find room for, even without spending a lot of money. My advice is not to buy anything – even if you've found it on eBay for a dollar – if storing it is going to outweigh the advantage of using it; there is nothing more annoying than having to heave bowls and pans out of densely packed drawers and cupboards every time you need to prepare or cook something. If you can't house a piece of kit in relative comfort, it's better to make do without it.

Similarly (maybe this is just because I am a lazy wimp – though, in my defense, a lazy wimp with a history of back problems), I don't think it's worth having any piece of equipment, however brilliant, if you can never quite summon the effort and strength to lift it. Enormous unwieldiness can be my undoing. In the same way, equipment that needs too much care and attention defeats me in the end. I love cast iron, the high-maintenance male of the kitchen equipment world, but I have given away all my cast-iron skillets bar one, since their stagger-inducing weight, too much for my limp wrists, combined with the seasoning they require, make me end up resenting as opposed to cherishing them.

I make an exception for enamelled cast-iron cookware – although I sometimes feel I'm emitting the serve-accompanying grunt of a lady tennis player as I heave Dutch oven from cupboard to stove – simply because they cook so well and you can serve food in them, too, so you save on equipment and washing-up. That said, they are, I agree, eye-wateringly expensive. Over the years, I've built up a collection, and the small- and medium-sized round Dutch ovens (respectively 9 inch diameter/4½ quart and 10½ inch/5½ quart) are among a number of items that get enough usage to merit their being left helpfully by my stove. But if I had to choose just a single piece among this collection,

CAST-IRON
SKILLET

ENAMELLED
CAST-IRON
COOKWARE

it would probably be the one that's often referred to as a braiser and is wide, shallowish,
slightly dome-lidded and incredibly versatile. I mostly use the bigger of the two sizes (14
inch diameter/3½ quart), but if you were cooking more often just for two, the smaller one
(10½ inch/2¼ quart) would make more sense.

And, although the enamelled cast-iron ware is expensive, it is extraordinarily
enduring. In fact, one of my Dutch ovens – a legacy from my mother – had been a
wedding present to my parents, and they married in 1956. Not for nothing are such
sturdy beauties known as "heirloom pieces." There are two courses of action that follow
from all this: the first is that you save yourself money without sacrificing quality by buying
this type of cookware pre-owned. Regard it as vintage. And, as I say, since a Dutch oven
bought in the Fifties is still going strong *chez moi*, I don't see that it matters if the one you
buy happens to be old. The other corollary here is that you should either go for the good,
expensive stuff or buy cheap and be prepared to replace when necessary. The middle
ground – unless there is a particular design you can't resist – is not worth considering. This
is particularly apropos when it comes to sauce pans, frying pans, and roasting pans. In that
non-existent world without budgetary restraints, all would be copper-bottomed. The heat
really is more evenly conducted, so food doesn't stick as much; thus the benefits are reaped
in both the cooking and the washing-up. Still, I have quite a few cheapo-pans that I simply
know I must line with aluminum foil if the pan is not to need two days' soaking and a good
40 minutes' scrubbing later.

Don't make the mistake, either (and this goes with all purchases related to
cooking and eating, even the value you place on having a dining room), of concentrating
more on the times you entertain, overlooking how much more often – even as a profligate
socializer – you eat normally, that's to say, without flourish or company. To wit here: I find

a small roasting pan that comfortably takes a chicken makes a huge difference to everyday
cooking; what's more, I think the juices that run off are stronger, and the skin crisper and
the top more desirably caramelized, when the bird or joint being roasted is contained in
a pan that hasn't too much room to spare. Plus, it's easier to store and lighter to lift. My
particular preference is for an 11-inch round roasting pan that does a chicken wonderfully,
is perfect for cooking (in the oven) a hungry suppertime's allocation of sausages, a toad in
the hole, a good 12 lamb cutlets, a one-pan roast dinner for two, and so on. I always feel
less foolish when I'm not making more washing-up than the size of what's being cooked
warrants. If you feel it easier to find a more normal rectangular pan, then I'd go for one
about 9 x 13 inches. And do see the notes in Kitchen Confidential (**p.19**) regarding the
other option, pan-wise, which is the disposable aluminum foil pan.

Now to that modern necessity, the non-stick frying pan: I don't really believe
anyone can do without a good non-stick pan; but non-stick pans generally being as they
are, most people have to. It's true that over the years they've improved enormously, but
the reality is that even with the best non-stick pans, unless you are good about never using
anything metal or scrapey when you cook, and only clean with specially non-abrasive
scourers, their lifespan is limited. I've never bought a non-stick pan I haven't had to
replace, and although I'm prepared to believe my kit gets more of a battering than it might
in many kitchens, anecdotal evidence proves to me that I am not alone. Still, I don't give
up. I love a non-stick pan, and especially one that has either a removable or ovenproof

WOK

handle, so that I can sear on the stove before roasting, baking, braising or broiling. And I also need a non-stick wok; I know it's inauthentic, but I have never been able to make a proper Chinese iron wok work. I manage to make everything stick and the metal pitted. Plus, the virtue of a non-stick one is that you can use it to make pasta sauces and paella

GRILL PAN
AND GRIDDLE

and suchlike, thus giving it more flexibility in the kitchen. Other non-stick must-haves for me are a non-stick ridged grill pan (for meat) and a smooth griddle (for pancakes). But when I say must-have, I say it in the modern, consumer-society sense. None of the above is a necessity; they are that greedy contemporary creation, everyday luxuries.

BAKEWARE

I had a late start baking-wise, but as is so often the case, I have the evangelical zeal of the convert; and nowhere is that more obvious than in my baking supplies.
Every time I open a cupboard I risk being buried in an avalanche of madeleine molds, flan rings, springform and bundt pans, along with a fluttering confetti of paper muffin cups. Don't worry: I'm not going to suggest you follow suit and have a cake pan for every eventuality. Only you know how often you bake. If never, stop reading now and move to the next paragraph. Otherwise, I'd say a capsule collection would consist of a 12-cup muffin pan and a 2-pound loaf pan, and the paper liners to go with each (and see Kitchen Confidential **p.14–15** for further notes on stopping cakes from sticking), plus a pair of 8-inch round cake pans, a 9-inch springform cake pan, and, for deliciously little effort (it's the shape of the pan that does the work), a bundt pan. But watch it: this lark is addictive.

KNIVES

Proper chefs are most particular about their knives. Indeed, so particular, they carry their own set wherever they go. But I am no kind of chef, proper or otherwise, and while I have favorites among knives, am not prepared to make a fetish of them. Nor do I think you need many: a small vegetable knife, a medium-sized knife, and, if you want another, one that is somewhere between a hacking knife and a cleaver, relatively short and with a wide blade that tapers to a point, is enough. This last I use not for any kind of frightening butchery, but simply to cut through dense or large vegetables, to slice cheesecakes and carve meat. It makes such an enormous difference if your knives are sharp, it's like the feel of a car when it's just had a maintenance check, but I am hopeless at sharpening. The days are long gone when knife grinders came door-to-door, as I remember their coming to my grandmother's house (along with the Frenchman on his bicycle selling onions – and I'm not even joking), so I'm afraid I am easy prey for anyone bringing out a new-fangled knife-sharpener.

MEAT FORK

And, yes, a meat fork helps, but a normal one will do, too; better still, a pair of trident-like forks. I have a pair, bought in a department store probably twenty years ago, and I use them every time I roast meat, both to transfer the meat from pan to board and to hold it in place while I, clumsily, carve. You're not meant to puncture the skin of meat, as you want all the juiciness contained, but the only other way I can lift a heavy piece of meat

OVEN
MITTS

is to wear oven mitts and lift it without tools. That has its drawbacks, too. (Although now might be a good time to say that the most useful oven mitts, I find, are made of a kind of cushiony silicon and can be cleaned in the dishwasher.)

MEZZA-
LUNA

The one sort of knife I couldn't manage without (and I know this as I carry one with me when I stay in rented houses with unfamiliar equipment) is a mezzaluna. This half-moon-shaped (hence the name) double-handled knife has unfairly acquired

4

a reputation as some sort of expert-only piece of equipment. I admit it looks, initially, daunting – even dangerous – but if you think about it, you'll see it is the very opposite of the expert-only choice. I am very clumsy, what New Yorkers would call a complete klutz, and I know that when I chop – herbs, vegetables, chocolate, nuts – with the mezzaluna, both my hands are engaged and thus it is impossible for me to cut myself.

KNIFE STORAGE

And as to how you store your knives, I go for a heavy-duty magnetic strip, stuck to or hung on the wall nearest to the cooker; one of the advantages of this method is that you can stick your mezzaluna here, too. Anyway, I have never happily got to grips with the other options. Of these, the second-best choice would be a knife block, but I'm not particularly keen and one of my prejudices against them is that they clutter up the work surface, and there is never enough of that, as it is. The worst option as far as I'm concerned is possibly the safest, and that's the drawer. I can't be doing with keeping knives in a drawer. It is a real bore to keep putting the blade-cover that comes with each knife back on every time you've finished with it and so inevitably you (or I) won't, and as inevitably you'll end up cutting yourself (or someone else will). If you have small children, this will be of particular consideration. Of course, you can put safety locks on, but any drawer you keep knives in is a drawer you will want to be opening often, and it will drive you mad if you put catches on it.

No, a magnetic strip or two, extra-strong, that knives will stick to firmly, high up on a wall, accessible to you but not to anyone small, is the answer. It's true, at first I was a bit anxious; I didn't really like the idea of hanging potential weapons in welcoming reach of the first burglar, rapist, or serial murderer who happened to stroll into my kitchen, but I decided in the end that one really can't be worrying about such things. And anything's better than having to scrabble about in a drawer.

5

DRAWERS

Talking of which, my perfect kitchen, or best possible kitchen in an imperfect world (which is the most any of us can hope for) banishes drawers as much as is feasible. Truly, I believe the fewer drawers a kitchen has, the easier it is to work in. I find, almost infallibly, however well I know the contents of each drawer, I always open the wrong one to find whatever I'm looking for. And if it is the right drawer, it's the last thing I find in it. So my advice is to make those drawers you do have small, that's to say, shallow. Everyone thinks they need big capacious drawers to fit all manner of things in, but that just gives you more of a desperate rummage each time you need something, and the wonderfully roomy drawers become a disorganized disaster zone in no time. I can't even cope with a cutlery drawer: I stash knives, forks and spoons in separate hole-punctured containers, decorating my counter like three splaying, metal floral displays. The only drawer I actually put in on purpose is what I call my mug drawer: a large (but not deep) drawer expressly for keeping many mugs in one layer. I can't be doing with a mug-tree, and piling mugs up in cupboards is a nerve-racking business, so my innovation (a couple of kitchens ago) of a mug drawer is – and I speak as something of a tea-addict – invaluable.

CUPBOARDS

Otherwise – and to make matters on the surface (literally and figuratively) seem more complicated – I try to minimize the amount of cupboards in my kitchen, too. Having started off with fairly small (or, indeed, very small) kitchens, I always felt that cupboards would intensify the feeling of constraint and narrowness. Obviously, it would be pretty well impossible to do without cupboards altogether but in a small kitchen definitely, and in any kitchen preferably, it is better for those cupboards you do have to be below the work surface. I don't say that everything else should be spare and bare; no kitchen I have had has ever been that. So, above work surface level, why not just have open shelving? And I speak as a messy person: even a clutter of crockery looks better to me than an imposing wall of cupboard doors.

And then there is the hanging space. Any wall that can be used for the purpose, I fit with rails from which I hang all pots and pans, spatulas, measuring cups, colanders, strainers, scissors, indeed anything that can be made to hang. And if there are no walls available, and space allows it, then I suspend some rails down from the ceiling and hang these over the cooker.

I know that more practical people than me will immediately worry about the fat and grease and dust and dirt. The trick, and here we come full circle back to the beginning, is to keep only those things that you use often enough so that they will be regularly washed as it is. Besides, we live in the dishwasher age now, so a quick de-griming cycle is generally possible.

Of course, the main obstacle to my breezy planning is that we generally inherit kitchens and the shape they are in is thus often dictated by previous owners. Still, taking out some cupboard doors and making good the mess that ensues, or putting up some hanging rails is no great undertaking.

As in the kitchen, so in this book: space and time are at a premium; I don't think you would thank me for itemizing each and every piece of equipment I feel I need or wish

FOOD
PROCESSOR
6
to advise you to consider – or even to avoid. Perhaps that's just as well. Still, I would feel remiss if I moved on without listing some of the other props that make life easier for me in the kitchen. I start with the heavier-duty items, such as a processor and a free-standing

FREE-
STANDING
MIXER
mixer. Nobody can truly be said to need either, but a processor certainly makes chopping on a large scale easier, and a free-standing mixer makes anything to do with baking easier and has, furthermore, the advantage of being, unlike the processor, a beautiful entity in itself, to the extent that it may be left out on the kitchen surface – an adornment rather than an eyesore. A processor is usually kept out of sight, and yet has to be easily accessible: it is not worth having one if it's a huge upheaval to get it out every time you use it. And soup is much better liquidized in a blender than in a processor.

STICK
BLENDER

HAND MIXER
Cheaper alternatives to all three of the above would be, first, a stick- or hand-blender (which can do the work of the blender and processor and is indeed superior to both when dealing with small quantities) and, second, an electric hand mixer, which can – with your help – take over the tasks of the free-standing mixer. I have nothing against a knife, cutting board, bowl and wooden spoon, but there are times when a little bit of whizzing gadgetry can make the difference.

THERMOM-
ETERS
Less high-tech, but worth consideration – even if you think of yourself as a spontaneous, no-measurement cook – is an oven thermometer. You would be surprised to discover how out-of-true the thermostat on an oven can be. And all ovens vary: some really do burn hotter or cooler, whatever the gauge says. Certainly, experience is the best teacher, but it's worth being able to check scientifically as well. And it's not a bad idea to invest in an instant-read thermometer as well: it saves you having to slice into a joint before seeing if it's cooked to your liking. Although I tend to favor the pressing-by-hand method – if the

meat springs back readily, it's rare, if it has a little give, it's medium, and if it's unyielding, it's shoe leather – there are times you really want to know.

Otherwise, I do have a few other low-tech requirements: a food mill is in many ways superior to a processor or blender (of whatever kind) for those cooking occasions which require you to sieve and purée; it does both at the same time, and is very useful for making mashed potatoes. But my gadget of choice for making fabulous mashed potatoes is the potato ricer. In America there are many models of potato ricer available, although mine is, in fact – as I think many are – Italian. This object consists of a cylindrical cup with small holes in the bottom; it has a handle to hold it by and a hinged lever that presses a lid down into the cup, rather in the way of a garlic press. You put a potato in the container and push down with the lever and the potato comes out through the holes – more like vermicelli than rice. It may sound fiddly and slow to mash potatoes by putting a spud at a time into the ricer and squishing it through the small holes, but really it isn't, and here's the upside: you don't have to peel the potatoes before you start. The ricer extrudes the mashed potato flesh while the skin sticks inside the ricer, though you must lift it out (using the tip of a sharp knife for ease) and discard as you go.

Similarly, I find grating with the processor somehow an exhausting prospect: it's not that it's hard to do, but the washing-up generated seems disproportionate to the job. Hanging from my rails are a good supply of Microplane graters – fine grade for garlic, ginger and Parmesan, coarse for Cheddar-type cheeses – and stashed away in a drawer is an old-fashioned rotary grater, which I use when the amount of cheese needs to be weighed first, or exceeds my friction-grating patience.

I find I can't have enough whisks, and although I keep different varieties in the kitchen, the ones I use most (and even take with me to other people's houses) are the little ones sometimes known as vinaigrette whisks. At their most basic, these are little stainless steel handles with a loop of wire at one end, and further little loops wound round that loop, looking rather like a children's drawing of a beard. These basic whisks can be used to make sauces, emulsify dressings, remove lumps, whip up pancakes and so on.

The other two items I find it impossible to have too many of are scissors and teaspoons. However many I buy, I always run out or lose them. One day, I know I'll come across a mysterious, hidden cupboard in the house piled high with scissors and teaspoons; until then I am forced to restock constantly. None of this stuff needs to be expensive, however. I find bog-standard kitchen scissors up to all tasks I'll ever attempt, including spatchcocking a chicken. And I am more than happy with plastic or melamine teaspoons: in fact, I rather love them, and keep them in old-fashioned French terracotta yogurt containers, out on the kitchen surface (near the kettle since you ask), or in other odd little containers I pick up online or on my travels.

Another item you cannot, in my book (which this is), do without is a plentiful supply of plastic clips for sealing opened packages of rice, couscous, frozen peas, you name it. They're cheap, and save a lot of expensive and irritating spillage.

The last of my basic requirements is a timer, or rather several timers. These must be portable, or else you're stuck in the kitchen and this defeats the whole object, which is the freedom, perversely, that a kitchen timer gives you.

As someone who can be suckered into buying just about any kind of kitchen

FOOD MILL

POTATO RICER

GRATERS

WHISKS

7

SCISSORS AND TEASPOONS

CLIPS

TIMER

appliance, it is interesting how few I feel are actually worth buying. There is, however, a piece of equipment which, before I'd used one, I'd assumed might be another wasteful extravagance, but now wouldn't be without: an electric rice cooker. It isn't a coincidence that all rice-eating cultures have a version: these things, which range from basic to luxury, really do work. I wouldn't bother getting one, however, that didn't have a keep-warm facility as well as the usual steaming function. I cannot tell you how much easier it makes your life when you can come home, pour rice and water into the cooker, flick on a switch and just walk away without having to think about it again. And this makes a difference across the board: from feeding children to giving dinner parties. I promise you, it's so much better to club together with friends or colleagues to give someone who's just had a baby one of these than any sort of baby equipment. After my first child, I ate nothing but cheese and chocolate; after my second, and post-rice cooker, I managed to eat a little more healthily. And when my children were small, I'd put the rice cooker on before going out, and know that I could spend a few hours at the ball-pond, swimming pool, park, museum or wherever and come back knowing dinner was more or less on the table. All you need to add is some corn niblets or shredded chicken or grated carrots and you're done. And now, when I'm tired and know supper has to be cooked, I click on the rice cooker and am happy in the knowledge that not a potato needs to be peeled and there is one less pot on the stove or in the oven to keep an eye on. Similarly, leftovers can be – as the mantra of this book has it – made right, by that familiar, reassuring click of a switch.

But before smugness sets in, I feel I must list those greedily bought gadgets that, once home, languished gathering dust in a cupboard under the stairs before being sent, defeatedly, off to the thrift store. I'm ashamed to admit that some of the below went straight there – box-fresh, as used-goods sellers say – without even being granted temporary sanctuary in the basement.

My Kitchen Gadget Hall of Shame

Although I regard insomnia as an aid to recipe writing, I fear it is no friend to shopping sanity. When I look down the list below, it becomes apparent that all-too-many of what can only be labelled freak purchases have been made online, in the middle of the night and while under the influence of the derangement that comes from sleep deprivation as well as from the fixation on idiocies as well as anxieties which is the cause of that sleep-deprivation in the first place. It's a mess. And not just in my head: imagine the state of my cupboards!

Super-professional electric ice cream maker
Purchasing this was no act of midnight madness: I actually went to a proper commercial catering equipment outlet to buy this. In my defense, and its, this is more than a piece of equipment, it is a kitchen art installation. It is hugely beautiful, and makes ice cream just as you'd want it to. However, even though it's a commercial machine (which explains its

burdensome bulk) it still doesn't make very large quantities. Plus there is no detachable bowl, so washing-up is a nuisance. But a poor workman blames his tools; the truth is I just don't make proper ice cream often enough to have this monster of a machine gleaming reproachfully at me daily from the kitchen surface it dominates. Hence the no-churn ice cream on **p.180**, and the fact that this object has been in a dusty understairs cupboard for a couple of years and is about to take up residence in a touchingly optimistic friend's country kitchen.

Healthy-eating electric grill

I know, I know: what was I thinking? Who was I kidding? Myself, for starters. But just as (and here's an unlikely issuer of the utterance in question) Samuel Beckett said that "probably nothing in the world arouses more false hopes than the first four hours of a diet," so there is nothing that arouses more pleasurable self-delusion than those swollen, sleepless, post-prandial hours when, yes, actually a diet tomorrow seems positively welcoming. (But then, well full-up, the planning of a diet can seem excitably delicious.) I rather suspect that it was just such a night that ushered in this unwanted item. It's nothing personal, not as far as the grill is concerned, anyway; or rather, as the old Dear John letter goes, it's me not you. And while I was slightly embarrassed at giving just such a piece of equipment to a thrift store, I felt that the benefit to all parties outweighed the irony and poor taste.

Automatic bread maker

I would never have bought one myself, since (1) it is the kneading that I enjoy about bread-making, and (2) I don't think having a warm, fresh loaf of bread to eat around the clock is going to do me any favors, but my son – then around ten – came back from staying with a friend and begged for one, even to the extent of being particular about the make and model. Of course, it's my fault for giving in so easily, but I'll take any sort of enthusiasm in the kitchen. However, I can honestly say this had no more than three airings, despite a year in the kitchen before being dispatched to the Great Bakery in the Sky. The Irish Oaten Rolls – made without yeast, kneading or machinery – on **p.86** provide me with enduring justification for the finality of my decision, but if you're nervous about bread-making and like the notion of the machine baking away overnight, you may want to ignore my prejudices here.

Automatic jam maker

I have no excuses for this and no one to blame, either. I'm sorry but I am stumped as to why I even considered this, given that, while I don't mind kitchen gadgets that help me, I positively don't want machinery to do it *for* me – and what's more, I actually like a light spot of easy jam-making (and I cite the Jumbleberry Jam on **p.285** as evidence). But fellow addicts might have some sympathy for my weakness in the face of convincing cookery catalog copy. The genius of certain companies to make one feel, against the dictates of reason or even common sense, that one cannot live for one more moment without the nonsense they are selling is to be applauded rather than excoriated. The ability to invent an urgent feeling or need is the nearest thing to rhetoric that we get these days. Let's gloss over the fact that this machine didn't even make it out of its packaging before being turned into a charitable offering.

Automatic cheese graters

Another embarrassment, and actually quite an expensive one. I should have guessed by the price that this was intended for professional use. I imagined a device that would make endless teatime grating of Cheddar less laborious and time-consuming, and got instead something that turns wheels of Parmesan into powdery dust for a deli. The next version was more domestic in scale, but not as beautiful and entirely ineffective. Serves me right for my laziness, I suppose; and I am happy to pay the penalty for stupidity. I will never be disloyal to the rotary grater (see above, **p.7**) again.

Crock pot

I had one of these when I was young and enthusiastic and had to spend long days in the office. I remember startling some poor man who came to read the meter at 7.30 in the morning only to find me browning onions and stewing steak at the stove before leaving them to cook in their crock pot till late into the night, or whenever I was allowed home. Even then, when there was a reason why I needed to rely on this as a cooking method, I didn't really like the way the top of what was cooking turned dark and dried out – but what induced me to buy one recently, given that (1) I work at home and so can leave an actual oven on low for as long as I need without worrying about it, and (2) there is no necessity for leaving anything to cook for 12 hours when 3 would do nicely? Another one of my purchases to be sent box-fresh to a more deserving cause than me.

Automatic sauce maker

In my defense this was obtained in the line of a duty; I was testing out machines for a piece in *Vogue* some time in the last century. Still, this ludicrous piece of kit somehow stayed clogging up a kitchen shelf long after it was evident that it had no place in my life nor I in its. For all I know, it's still hogging space in whatever thrift store I shamefacedly donated it to.

Electric waffle maker

Now, I do know what lies behind the purchase of this: namely, the all-too-familiar combination of optimism and self-delusion that always turns the shopper into such easy prey. I can make pancakes for fifteen children at the weekend without it being any kind of big deal (although now they're teenagers, it has to be said, it's never early in the morning – or indeed morning at all) but just attempting waffles for my three was more stressful than you can believe possible. I know it's my failure – that it's my incompetence with the machine that's to blame – but who wants to pay to have that pointed out? And just to highlight my foolishness, I haven't yet implemented its move from cupboard to thrift store; I still delude myself that I am going to be that person who rustles up waffles for breakfast, one day.

Soup-making super-blender

I saw this once at a trade fair in San Francisco, and yearned for it for years. The fact that you couldn't actually buy one in the UK at that time, of course made it all the more alluring. Cut to many years later, just recently in fact, and I blew the huge amount this cost in a frenzy of enthusiasm. But ever since its arrival, I have been laid low with post-consumption *tristesse* (what the ad-men call post-purchase dissonance) and feel strangely alienated from it. And if truth be told, I am actually too frightened of it to use it or even understand the many instructions. But I like to pretend that one day I'll triumph, and what's more that the cost of the thing will be as nothing to the culinary rewards it showers upon me. So, it can be guaranteed long-term occupancy under the stairs.

Electric super-juicer

This purchase pre-dates the above, and I have long since given it to a friend who felt that a life and diet of non-stop juicing beckoned. I don't know why I got it in the first place (though it was very long ago, too long ago to recollect my state of mind, but I can infer it wasn't good) since I don't now see how it can make sense to have all the sugar of fruit without the fiber. (I think that's what led me later to the super-blender – all the fiber stays in.) Plus the mess the super-juicer makes is exhausting: there is a huge amount of skin and pulp that needs to be cleaned out between each use. And on top of that, it is not a machine that ends up paying for itself, so to speak: the amount you have to spend on fruit to keep this hungry beast fed is alarming.

Yogurt maker

I think this owes its shortlived presence in my kitchen to a combination of nostalgia (my grandmother had one) and internet-induced new-age fervor for the miracles of the bacteria to be found in real, home-made yogurt. It didn't stand a chance.

Electric carving knife

I didn't know that, if you were a bad carver, you became a dangerously bad carver when equipped with an electric knife. Or maybe I should rephrase this: I became a dangerously bad carver. Plus, the horrendous rasping buzz (I start off as a slightly noise-phobic person in the first place) is guaranteed to make every meal a headache. Still, I'm told such a tool is excellent for slicing frozen bread . . .

11

How would you like your tea?

KITCHEN CONFIDENTIAL

This is a compendium of my own shortcuts and practices, many of them inherited from my mother and, for the rest, innovations of my own, according to twin characteristics which in most of life could be considered flaws, but in cooking are a positive inspiration: greed and impatience. These characteristics, too, are inherited.

BOILING WATER ♥ When I have friends coming for dinner, or even when there is just a big pan of pasta to be cooked for everyday meals, I put the water on to boil before I need to start cooking, and then leave it at the back of the stove top, with the heat turned off but with a lid on, so that when I have to get food on the table, I don't then have to wait for half an hour for the water to come to a boil; this way it should be no more than a matter of minutes. It is also worth bearing this in mind for any type of cooking that needs – as pasta does – abundant water.

♥ If I'm cooking just a small amount of pasta – supper for a couple of people, say – or a quick boiled egg with toast for a midnight snack, I pour water from the tap into a sauce pan, just to about 1½ inch depth, and put it on the stove over a high heat, keeping an eye on it. While that's coming to the boil, I fill an electric kettle and let it do ditto. (It's important not to leave the kitchen while all this boiling is going on.) Thus, the pan and its contents are hot when you pour in the boiling water from the kettle (beware spluttering – you may prefer to do this off the heat) and you won't have to wait for it to come back to the boil.

BAKING ♥ I know I bang on and on about the fact that, when baking, all ingredients must be at room temperature, but I should add that it is important, too, that the bowl isn't icy cold. To take the chill off it, fill the bowl you're going to be mixing in with warm water from the tap and let it stand for 10 minutes, before emptying it out, drying it off and proceeding with the recipe.

♥ If you can't find baking spray to grease a cake pan, or whatever, simply dab some flavorless oil such as peanut oil onto a piece of paper towel and wipe that around the insides of the pan, re-dabbing and re-wiping until you feel you have safe coverage. Should you think you've overdone it and your pan is not merely greased but drippingly greasy, then put an old newspaper on the kitchen surface, sit a wire cooling rack on top of it and upturn the overgreased pan on to the cooling rack so that excess oil can drip onto the newspaper.

SILICONE LINING ♥ If you are a habitual baker – and I'm not trying to make it sound like a crime – then you would be well advised to buy a re-usable non-stick baking mat (in fact, it's made of a silicone material). Cut out circles to the diameter of your various cake pans and let

14

the lining just live inside them, so you're ready to go – bar a little greasing around the sides – when you feel the baking impulse come upon you. I have also cut out a couple of rectangular shapes to fit over cookie sheets. After each use, I just wash the lining, put it in the turned-off oven to dry, and then back it goes to its pan of origin, ready for the next outing.

♥ I don't bother to keep both all-purpose and self-rising flour in the house; if you don't use the self-rising flour regularly it'll probably lose its rising power before you finish the package, anyway. And it's also worth keeping an eye on the use-by dates on the containers of rising agents. If a cake doesn't rise, the usual culprit is an out-of-date container of baking powder or baking soda. My recipes tend to stipulate all-purpose flour (which is the flour you'll need for a bechamel sauce, say, as well) plus whatever is the necessary amount of rising agent; but my own rule of thumb to turn all-purpose flour into self-rising flour (though because it's not all-in-one, it isn't strictly *self*-rising) is to add 2 teaspoons baking powder for each cup of all-purpose flour. This can never be, however, more than a rule of thumb; the chemical process is affected by the other ingredients in the recipe. If whatever I'm baking contains cocoa, yogurt or buttermilk, I add ¼ teaspoon baking soda per 1 cup all-purpose flour along with the baking powder (which does itself contain baking soda in its mix, but in this case will need extra boosting power).

BAKING POWDER

BAKING SODA

♥ Not only is baking soda the best refrigerator and general all-purpose cleaner (just dissolve some in a little water and dab or scrub as the situation or stain demands, or leave a ramekin one-third full of baking soda in the refrigerator to banish smells), it is also the first thing you should take if you feel a bout of cystitis might be coming on. Dissolve 1½ teaspoons in a glass of warm water and knock back, wincing. This might just help until you can consult your doctor.

15

♥ Even if you are not a baker, do get a pastry brush. You can brush soft or melted butter in place of oil, to grease a pan, but it's also a good tool to oil steaks, help a chicken crisp up as it roasts by dipping the brush into the pan juices and daubing the top of the chicken with it. I advise a silicone brush rather than a bristle one: it can be cleaned in the dishwasher, and it won't molt onto whatever you're cooking.

PASTRY BRUSH

♥ Buttermilk keeps well, so it's worth stocking up with a couple of cartons when you buy it, but if you can't find any, you can turn fresh milk into a buttermilk substitute: pour 1 cup milk into a jug, add 1 tablespoon lemon juice (or vinegar), and let it stand for 5 minutes before using as directed in the recipe. Or just use, to make the same amount, ¾ cup plain yogurt plus ¼ cup milk; I never mind much whether it's whole, reduced fat, or completely non-fat here, but reduced fat or low fat are supposed to work best.

BUTTERMILK

♥ Always freeze slices of bread and slices of bacon in pairs (as well as in their packages), as you may find yourself without when you don't have time for a massive thawing session. And while we're on bread, if you have some – this time from an unsliced loaf – that's staling, then slice it, tear it into rough pieces and process it in batches to make

BREAD & BACON

breadcrumbs. Fill resealable bags with crumbs and clip or tie them tightly before stashing them in the freezer; they do not need to be thawed before use.

SCISSOR-
SNIPPING
♥ When cooking in a hurry, go full tilt with your scissors. Not only does it make life easier than getting out a chopping board and knife or mezzaluna for snipping herbs, but it's the best way to top and tail beans (and the best way, too, to teach children to do it) as well as to chop vegetables. Sometimes, though, it makes sense to scissor-chop once the vegetables have been cooked and are sitting draining in the colander. My abiding memory is of my mother standing over a steamy pile of spinach, attacking it furiously with her scissors. Very Hitchcock. (Perhaps it is that maternal frenzy which makes me so drawn to this primitive but threatening tool.) In fact, I use scissors for so much else, too: slicing bacon into strips to let them fall into a hot pan; cutting up cold chicken or ham to add to a salad; purée-ing the tomatoes in an opened can by plunging in my scissors and then snipping like mad.

VERMOUTH
♥ I don't like to open a bottle of wine when I need only a glassful for cooking, so I keep a bottle of dry white vermouth (for choice, Noilly Prat, which, at home when I was young, we used to call jokingly, English-style, "nolly pratt," as it remains for me to this day) by the stove and splosh into a pan in place of white wine. If I need more than, say, an espresso cup's worth, I tend to water it down a little as it has more bite than wine. Similarly, I am happy to use ruby port, diluted to make it less punchy, in place of red wine, although I more usually substitute dry marsala, a bottle of which is also kept in reach by my stove.

♥ Apropos of which, I once read an American chef in the *New York Times* who said that no serious cook would keep bottles of oil or anything else by the stove, as the heat would destroy their finer qualities. I must conclude, therefore, that I am not a serious cook. I find that it's having the ingredients to hand which makes me use them, and therefore makes what I'm cooking better. Thus, along with my regular olive oil, basil-infused oil, chile-infused oil and garlic-infused oil, I keep bottles of soy, Worcestershire sauce (such as Lea & Perrins), fish sauce, dry white vermouth, amontillado sherry, marsala, Chinese cooking wine, sake and mirin. If I can't cook with spontaneity, a lot of the fun and interest goes out of it for me, so this way I do cook enough for the contents of said stove-encircling bottles to run out before they spoil.

COLD-
PRESSED
CANOLA OIL
♥ There has been much talk about the use of local canola oil (well, local only if you're British) as a bio-fuel, but it's not often that being a Brit can make one feel culinarily superior. So now is the time to jump up and down about cold-pressed canola oil, which has a gorgeously mustardy and nutty flavor and beautiful golden color. I use it in place of extra-virgin olive oil more or less exclusively: it's much less expensive and, I'm beginning to think, even more delicious. I make dressings with it, dribble it on toast in place of butter, douse vegetables with it and take a bottle to people's houses (so evangelical is my fervor) in place of wine. My canola oil bottle of choice is Orphee's Optima, but there are one or two good ones out there now. The cold-pressed, golden viscous oil is worlds away from the paler, runnier, tasteless, expeller-pressed cooking oil.

♥ I couldn't live in a house without lemons, so it's easy for me to reach over and use the zest or juice as I cook without much, if any, forethought. Limes are a different matter: not only do they often start off mean and unyielding, but after even a small time in the refrigerator, and less time out of it, they become as hard as golf balls. I now make sure I have a stash of plastic lime juice in the house, which is to say, lime juice that sometimes comes in a violently green (often lime-shaped) squeezy bottle. This has been my practice for so long, I am enormously relaxed, even unapologetic, about it. Out of interest, I made some compare-and-contrast studies with side-by-side recipes using freshly squeezed lime and plastic lime: you couldn't have told the difference. Now, I may have been lucky with the brand I used, but it's worth giving it a go, to judge for yourself.

LEMON & LIME

♥ When I whisk egg whites, to make sure the bowl isn't greasy at all, I halve a lemon and wipe the cut half all around the bowl. The acid will get rid of the grease, and will help the whites whisk voluminously.

♥ I like to keep a packet of disposable vinyl gloves by my dishwashing paraphernalia. You can wear these before prodding hot pieces of meat or dismembering roast chickens as well as for shredding cold meat by hand. I wear them for peeling blanched tomatoes and while I chop these, too, as the gloves stop my hands getting sore from the acid. And they're a must for any beet preparation, unless you want a touch of the Lady Macbeths. Once you start using them, you'd be surprised how often you find them invaluable, not to say necessary.

VINYL GLOVES

♥ Without said gloves, if you are working with anything sticky – meatballs as much as cookies – keep your hands covered with a film of cold water: just dunk your hands at regular intervals under the cold tap. If what you're dealing with is very, very sticky (like say, the Rice Krispie Brownies on **p.312**), then work a small amount of flavorless oil into your hands as if it were expensive hand cream, and they will become non-stick baking utensils in themselves. Similarly, if you are using honey or syrup in a recipe, measure out the oil first (if there's some called for) or dab the spoon or cup with oil so that the goo doesn't stick as you're measuring it out. I like to oil, lightly, whatever I'm molding cookies with, too.

17

♥ I am a compulsive tea-drinker and the tea I like is strong, dark tea; to get rid of the brown that my mugs are inevitably stained with, I soak each mug in warm water to which I've added 1 tablespoon lime juice or – cheaper – vinegar.

TEA STAINS

♥ If you are a bread maker, keep the water you've used to boil potatoes in (or, indeed, pasta), as the starch in the water helps the yeast in your bread to rise. Though you can also just dissolve 1 teaspoon instant mashed potato flakes in a mug of water for the same effect.

STARCH

♥ If you've cooked a ham, and are not sure when you'll get round to using the stock for a soup, cool and chill the liquid quickly, then freeze it in 2 cup batches (in an airtight container for up to 3 months). The same goes for any other broth or stock you might have.

STOCK OR BROTH

It's too painful to leave any of it for too long in the refrigerator and then have to throw the precious liquid away.

♥ Similarly, should you have any wine left in an open bottle, or stout or cider, freeze that, too (in an airtight container for up to 3 months), to use in cooking at a later date. Alcohol does not freeze solid, but to a slush. I generally let anything fizzy go flat before I freeze it. And if you do happen to have some flat cola left by children too teenagery to remember to screw the top back on, use that (freezing it first, if you like) to cook a ham in.

FLOWERS ♥ This is an old lesson of my mother's, but it bears repeating, I hope: never put anything on the table that interferes with people's eyeline. So, no big bunch of flowers, but rather think of putting a bowl of lemons or aubergines, something beautiful that will get used and costs less than the blooms into the bargain. And if you do want flowers, keep them low. Even garage-forecourt flowers look pretty cut down in an old mustard jar or two.

DRESSING ♥ Talking of mustard jars, I am afraid I have just counted 7 empty ones near my stove. When they're all but finished I don't wash them out before making salad dressing in them, but use the mustard that's left clinging to the base of the jar to add flavor to the dressing. It's hard to beat a dressing made by pouring cold-pressed canola oil (and see **p.16**) into a bit of English mustard, sprinkling in salt and spritzing in lemon juice before shaking into a rich, gold ointment to dribble over a salad. If making a dressing from the leavings in a Dijon or wholegrain mustard jar, use olive oil and squeeze a little honey into it along with the lemon and salt.

18

♥ I also make dressings out of the dregs in a bottle of soy sauce: add a dot of sesame oil and fish sauce and a splosh of mirin and shake before using. If your soy sauce bottle is too narrow-necked, pour everything into an old screw-top jar to shake it up in.

SUSHI RICE ♥ Perhaps because I've got a rice cooker (and see **p.8**), I cook rice an awful lot, and my newest enthusiasm (though no more prized than my everyday favorite, brown basmati) is sushi rice. I adore its sweet stickiness, as do my children, so I always keep a sackful in the house. Now, I don't think I'd ever be able to make sushi – just don't have the patience or dexterity – though maybe one day I'll try. Until then, I am very happy to use sushi rice to mop up chicken teriyaki or sweet and sour chicken (see **pp.38** and **36** respectively) and just about anything else. I do use my rice cooker here, but if you're cooking manually, as it were, just follow the instructions on the package. And should your instructions be in Japanese, let me tell you that you need to allow ⅓–½ cup rice per person. And because rice is easier to cook by volume than by weight (in the sense that it is the ratio of rice to water that counts), in practice I use a 1 cup measure for 2 people. You need to rinse the rice until the water runs clear and then put it in a saucepan with 1¼ cups cold water. Bring it to a boil, then clamp a lid on, turn the heat under the pan to the lowest it will go, and leave it at a very gentle simmer for 20 minutes or until the water is absorbed. Fork through (rice of any kind should never be stirred with a spoon but with a fork) and serve.

I love sushi rice for supper with nothing more than some soy sauce and mixed seeds forked through it, though it is a special treat if there's some leftover chicken I can add, warmed through in a little chicken broth, too.

♥ I couldn't cope without a couple of sets of spoon measures and cup measures. The spoon measures – ¼ teaspoon, ½ teaspoon, 1 teaspoon and 1 tablespoon – are needed for baking, since in baking these measurements are precise, rather than referring to the size of your tableware.

CUP & SPOON MEASURES

♥ I weigh long pasta, such as spaghetti or linguine, by sitting a mug or tall glass, or similarly shaped receptacle, on my flat, digital kitchen scale (not as pretty as old-style ones, but better in action), pressing the button to reset to zero, and then putting the pasta in the mug as if putting flowers in a vase.

LONG PASTA

♥ I advise against using skewers to test whether cakes are cooked inside, but if you don't have a cake tester, do as the Italians do and use an uncooked piece of spaghetti.

CAKE TESTING

♥ I am never without a stash of supposedly disposable aluminum foil pans in my cupboard. I say supposedly only because they probably would survive a couple of uses with a cleanup in between; certainly, when I use them to set the polenta on **p.336**, I give them a bit of a wipe down and re-use. But where they come into their own is when you're baking something gungy and you're either frightened of getting it out of the pan or unenthusiastic about the dishwashing you'll have to do later, or both. In fact, I have largely dispensed with real metal pans for bars and pretty much whatever else I can get away with now: the sticky cocktail sausages on **p.418** are a case in point.

FOIL PANS

The disposable pans can be found in many supermarkets and I favor a "utility" size pan measuring 12¾ x 9 x 1²³/₃₂ inches (which says "suitable for 13 x 9 inch recipes"). If it helps further, anything that fits into a 13 x 9 inch rectangular pan can also be cooked in a 10-inch square roasting or baking pan. It's also useful to have slightly larger, or certainly deeper, foil pans for roasting rather than baking. I can't tell you how comforting a pan you don't have to wash up is if you're cooking for a party or during a particularly exhausting weekend. And as for eco-concerns, I always used to take the line that if you had to make a choice between saving the environment or your sanity, you have to go for your sanity; but since an actively Green friend of mine has told me how eco-friendly the foil is (easy to recycle *and* no harmful detergents have been used), you can smugly revel in your laziness as much as your virtue. I think that's what we'd call a result.

♥ I am a bit of a leftover queen – throwing away the scantest morsel is agony for me – but I cannot live successfully with those little Tupperware-type containers with their snap-on lids that I remember our refrigerator being filled with when I was a child. The shortcoming is entirely mine: I have never managed to go longer than a month without losing a lid. I have now moved into commercial catering take-out containers, which make me feel not only gloriously efficient as I stack them in refrigerator and freezer, but also as though I've got my own home deli. And many can go into the microwave, which is helpful; they aren't really reusable, but I do sometimes go twice round the block with them. Because they are sold wholesale only, and I buy mine online, they are not very expensive per piece; but you

PLASTIC CONTAINERS

may have to buy in bulk, which can be a problem. My advice to get round this is to club together with friends: you can order the minimum between you and share the containers out when the huge box arrives.

SALT ♥ I overwhelmingly prefer sea salt flakes (Maldon for choice) or kosher salt when I cook or eat, and because of its volume (you can get about twice as much table salt in a spoon of the same capacity) it is less salty than table salt. If you are replacing it with table salt, therefore, use half as much. And except for baking, I'd much rather you didn't . . .

FRYING ♥ If you don't want onions to brown when you fry them, sprinkle with salt; the salt makes the onion give off water, which in turn stops it frying too fiercely.

♥ When you're cooking in butter, add a drop of oil to stop the butter burning.

GRILL PANS AND GRIDDLING ♥ If you're using a grill pan or flat griddle, make sure always to oil the meat, or fish, or vegetables, not the pan, or everything will smoke like mad.

AND FINALLY ♥ This is so much easier to say than to do, but try, when you're cooking for people, not to apologize nervously for what you've made, alerting them to some failure only you might be aware of, or indeed, might have invented. Besides, it only creates tension, and although I do believe food is important, atmosphere matters so much more.

POSTSCRIPT ♥ I always buy a dish towel wherever I am on holiday, no matter how embarrassingly
20 touristy it is (or I feel), and the benefits are threefold: the souvenir is light to carry (to say the least) and will fit even if you're going hand-luggage only; every time you use it you will remember when and where you got it; and the mix of dish towels stops any kitchen from looking over-designed or styled. A kitchen should never look decorated; it just needs to feel lived in.

Part I

KITCHEN QUANDARIES

WHAT'S FOR SUPPER?

HURRY UP! I'M HUNGRY!

EASY DOES IT

COOK IT BETTER

MY SWEET SOLUTION

OFF THE CUFF

WHAT'S FOR SUPPER?

There are times when I, a food obsessive, a food addict even, find it difficult to think of what to cook. It doesn't happen often and I recover my greedy wits promptly enough, but I have to admit my weakest area, the one most likely to buckle under pressure, is the children's supper. If I don't get myself focused at the beginning of the week, I find that as suppertime approaches, which it rapidly does and daily (and I think my energy is at its lowest point at around 4:30 pm), I begin to flag and start opening and shutting freezer and refrigerator doors with more frenzy than enthusiasm.

My children are now of an age when they come back from school, pick at everything in the refrigerator, don't eat up all their dinner, and then pick again at bedtime. You understand, it can make mealtimes fraught. Plus, children are given so many assignments now, which can cast rather a pall on proceedings.

I suppose, too, I find this – I think many parents do – rather a sensitive issue. We all cherish that fantasy of the heart-warming family meal when everyone discusses their day and the table resounds with chat and loving laughter. Oh dear, please tell me it *is* a fantasy.

But it is what it is, as the contemporary wisdom has it, and from my very first book, which dedicated a whole chapter to weaning and feeding babies and toddlers, my recipes for children have taken a strictly autobiographical route. What other way is there of writing about food? My books can only ever be a record of what I cook. I remember when my daughter – sixteen at the time of writing – was little she asked me for "children's food." I was – and remain – quite adamant that there is no such thing as children's food, that food is food, and that's that. I'm not saying I don't sometimes indulge a childish taste or cook something I might not think of making if I were eating alone, but the recipes that follow are not ones that apply only to parents with children to feed.

Yes, it might seem a bit eccentric to serve up the Crustless Pizza for adult company, but my friends would probably be thrilled. The Chicken Fajitas make a perfect supper, and the Pasta alla genovese certainly earns a place in my Last Meal menu. But before I go on, I should address the salt and sugar issue. I admit that as my children have grown older, I have got more relaxed. But, those who wish to limit their children's intake can reduce amounts freely; and I myself have just discovered the joys of agave nectar, a natural, unprocessed syrup with a fashionably low GI, which you can use in place of sugar. I actually find it sweeter, so use about 25% less. But, as ever, you should go by taste.

I suppose my wish is that my children learn what a pleasure real food is, are not hedged about too much with can'ts and shouldn'ts and grow up understanding that eating is something to take pleasure in and not feel guilty about.

Mortadella and mozzarella frittata

In the great professional kitchens of old, French chefs would check a novice's ability by making him (and yes, it always was a him) cook an omelet. To ensure sufficient lightness of touch and swiftness at the stove, all the better to keep the omelet sufficiently *baveuse*, the chef would insist the pan be cooked on the back burner, while the front burner licked ferociously at the applicant's tender wrist. Yup, that's why I go for frittatas, not omelets. The Italian version is so much less stress-inducing: no flipping needed, either of pan or mind; you simply preheat the broiler and transfer the fat, eggy cake to it, once it's cooked halfway through on the stovetop.

This is a particularly voluptuous example of the Italianate version – the Marilyn Monroe of the frittata world.

24

Serves 4–8, *depending on age and appetite*

6 eggs
4 ounces mortadella, chopped
4 ounces fresh mozzarella cheese, chopped
1 tablespoon chopped parsley, plus extra for sprinkling

1 tablespoon freshly grated Parmesan cheese
salt and pepper, to taste
1 tablespoon butter
drop garlic flavored oil

♥ Turn on the broiler to heat. Beat the eggs in a bowl, then add the chopped or diced mortadella and mozzarella.

♥ Whisk in the tablespoon of parsley, along with the Parmesan, salt, and pepper, remembering that both mortadella and Parmesan will provide a certain saline hit.

♥ Heat the butter and oil in a frying pan (with ovenproof handle) or cast iron skillet approx. 10 inches in diameter and, once it's hot and foamy, add the omelet mixture.

♥ Cook for about 5 minutes over a gentle heat, *without stirring*, until the frittata is set underneath and golden.

♥ Transfer the pan to the hot broiler (keeping the handle away from the heat) and cook the frittata until it is set on top – *don't* leave the pan unattended, as this can happen quite quickly, and wear oven mitts to remove the pan.

♥ Let stand for a couple of minutes, then run a knife or flexible spatula round the edge of the frittata and ease it out of the pan, keeping it top-side up, onto a board or plate. Cut into 8 triangles like a cake, then sprinkle with the extra parsley and serve with green beans or salad.

Making leftovers right

*Leftovers should be covered and refrigerated as soon as possible, and eaten within 1–2 days. As with the Crisp Chicken Cutlets on **p.28**, think no further than sliding a wedge of this – cold – into bread or a roll, to make a sandwich, as offered under glass counters in bars all over Italy.*

FRITTATA
SANDWICH

Crustless pizza

I wouldn't want to go bandying about the name of this recipe in Naples, but this is what I call it. If it helps, think of it as a grilled cheese sandwich, only without the bread. Whatever, it makes a fast and easy supper on days when you're too tired to think about what to cook. This pretty well makes itself before you've even realized you're in the kitchen.

      Where I've suggested some sliced chorizo to adorn the top, you could just as easily sprinkle in some corn or snipped ham, or just about anything you fancy, and can get away with. But rest assured, there are plenty of times I've cooked this without any final addition: just egg, flour, salt, milk, and cheese. This is comfort: quicktime.

Serves 2–4, *depending on age and appetite*

1 egg	2 ounces small chorizo or
⅔ cup all-purpose flour	pepperoni slices, approx. ¾ inch
salt, to taste	diameter (optional)
1 cup whole milk	
butter for greasing	1 x round ovenproof pie dish, 8 or
1 cup grated Cheddar cheese	9 inches diameter

♥ Preheat the oven to 400°F. Beat the egg with the flour, salt, and milk to make a smooth batter.

♥ Grease a round ovenproof pie dish, then stir half the grated cheese into the batter, before pouring it into the dish.

♥ Bake for 30 minutes. Take the dish out of the oven, sprinkle with the remaining cheese, and add the chorizo or pepperoni (if using) – or anything else – now, too. Return to the oven and cook for another 2 or 3 minutes to make sure it's heated through.

♥ Once the cheese on top is melted and looks burnished gold on the crustless pizza, take it out of the oven and serve, cut into slices. A green or tomato salad on the side would not be a bad idea ...

LEFTOVERS NOTE
Leftovers can be reheated next day in a hot oven for 8–10 minutes, but sadly they won't be as nice as the first time around.

Crisp chicken cutlets
with salad on the side

I suppose these are really grown-up chicken nuggets, although it may make you feel better if you throw yourself into Italian mode and consider them *scaloppine di pollo*. But when I'm eating food like this – crisp coating, tender meat within – I don't think I care what it's called.

I'm not trying to strong-arm you into the salad I love to eat alongside – baby spinach leaves, or sometimes arugula, with some diced tomato and Parmesan – but such is my fervor that I feel I must append the recipe (such as it is).

The fresh breadcrumbs I specify are, as ever, really stale breadcrumbs, but I feel they must come from something that has been recognizably a loaf of bread rather than from a container. My freezer is full of crumbs that I've ground and stashed there, but if yours isn't, then you could use matzo meal instead, though you'll need to double the amount; it's so fine – even the coarser ground kind – relative to breadcrumbs, that you need to bolster quantities to ensure a sufficiently sturdy and crisp carapace.

Serves 4

4 chicken breast fillets, skinless and
  boneless
1 cup buttermilk
1 tablespoon Worcestershire sauce
  (such as Lea & Perrins)
2 cups fresh breadcrumbs (see
  introduction above)

1 teaspoon celery salt, or ½
  teaspoon for younger children
¼ teaspoon cayenne pepper
1 teaspoon dried thyme
½ cup grated Parmesan cheese
oil for frying, such as peanut
¼ cup chopped fresh parsley

♥ Unroll a large piece of plastic wrap, then open out the chicken breasts and lay them on the plastic. Cover the fanned-out chicken breasts with another piece of plastic wrap, and bash with a rolling pin until they are thin, but still whole. (If the underside sections come away, don't worry.)

♥ Whisk the buttermilk with the Worcestershire sauce in a shallow bowl, or put it into a resealable bag and squish to mix. Then add the flattened chicken pieces to the bowl or bag and leave out for about 30 minutes – or refrigerate overnight if you've got time – to marinate.

♥ Preheat the oven to 300°F, if you're using a smaller frying pan and want to keep the cutlets warm as you fry them. Mix the breadcrumbs, celery salt, cayenne, thyme, and Parmesan in a wide, shallow dish. Then, once the chicken has had its steeping, lift out the buttermilky pieces and press into the breadcrumb mixture one at a time.

♥ Coat the chicken on both sides with the seasoned crumbs and then lay them on a wire rack, the sort you'd use for cooling cakes.

♥ Heat the oil in a frying pan – using just enough to cover the base with about ¼ inch of oil.

♥ Once the oil is hot, fry the bigger pieces of chicken for about 3 minutes per side, and the smaller bits from the underside of the breast for about 2 minutes per side. As you remove the cooked pieces of chicken, blot them on paper towels and, if you wish, keep them warm in a low oven (on a cookie sheet) as indicated above, or serve them as you go. However you choose to dish up, serve these crisp chicken cutlets sprinkled with chopped parsley. You could consider a lemon wedge on the side, too, and the salad on the next page.

MAKE AHEAD NOTE
The chicken can be marinated 1 day ahead in the buttermilk mixture. Store in refrigerator until ready to breadcrumb and use. Leftovers should be refrigerated as soon as possible, and eaten within 1–2 days.

FREEZE NOTE
For ⅛-inch thick cutlets: the marinated and crumb-coated chicken can be put on parchment-lined cookie sheets, covered with plastic wrap, and frozen. When solid, transfer to resealable bags and store for up to 3 months. Fry direct from frozen over medium–low heat for 4–5 minutes each side. Check to make sure the chicken is cooked through before serving.

Salad on the side

2 tablespoons extra-virgin olive oil
2 teaspoons red wine vinegar
salt and pepper, to taste
2 good-sized tomatoes, seeded and
  cut into small dice
1 x 5-ounce bag salad spinach or
  arugula, or salad leaves of your
  choice
½ cup shaved Parmesan

♥ Whisk together the oil and
vinegar in a bowl and season with
salt and pepper, then add the tomato
dice.

♥ When you are ready to eat, add
the spinach and Parmesan and toss
to mix.

Making leftovers right

CHICKEN
CUTLET
SANDWICH

*There is no better way to eat a leftover breaded cutlet – whatever the meat, frankly – than
properly* all'Italiana, *that's to say, cold and stuffed together with some arugula leaves into a split
ciabatta roll, which may or may not be spread with mayo: think Mediterranean sub. I salivate at
the very thought. A few tomatoes alongside, as well as a glass of beer so cold it hurts, and you've
got yourself a simply heavenly snatched supper.*

Cheesy chili

I can't count how often I find myself stirring a pan with some ground beef in it, day to day. Not that this is anything to apologize for: it's easy, quick and comforting. I could probably measure out my life in chili bowls, and that's no bad thing either. This recipe draws again on a favorite time-saving practice of mine, which is to start off with some paprika-piccante chorizo sausages that give off a fiery orange oil in which to sear and season the beef.

Tex-Mex custom decrees that chili be eaten with – among other embellishments – a handful of grated cheese thrown on top. This is merely an impatient rendering of the same, whereby you simply chop or tear some mozzarella and stir it in to the chili in the pan, just long enough to let it melt into the meat.

If you've got the time, and have managed to think ahead, you could put some baking potatoes into the oven to provide a substantial vessel for the cheesy chili (it will also make the chili go further), but I don't think anyone would argue with a bowl of tortilla chips alongside, or indeed a beautiful loaf of bread, freshly sliced for dunking. All I'd add would be a crisp green salad, sharply dressed, and a small cup of chopped fresh cilantro for all-round anointing. My son, however, prefers to eat this with some steam-swollen barley, in which case the whole becomes, naturally enough, Charley.

Serves 4 *hungry teenage boys or 6 normal people*

4 ounces (2 sausages) chorizo, cut into fat coins and halved

1 pound ground beef, preferably organic

½ teaspoon unsweetened cocoa powder

1 teaspoon dried oregano

1 tablespoon tomato paste

1 x 14-ounce can diced tomatoes

½ cup water, to rinse out empty tomato can

2 teaspoons Worcestershire sauce (such as Lea & Perrins)

1 x 15-ounce can kidney beans, drained and rinsed

8 ounces fresh mozzarella, chopped

salt and pepper, to taste

handful chopped fresh cilantro, to serve (optional)

♥ Put a smallish cast iron Dutch oven or heavy-based pan (that comes with a lid) on the heat and add the semi-circles of chunky chorizo, cooking just long enough for them to start giving off a lucent orange oil.

♥ Add the ground beef, trying to break it up a little with a wooden fork and turn it in the oil to combine with the chorizo.

♥ When the meat has begun to lose its all-over raw color, sprinkle with the cocoa and oregano, dollop in the tomato paste and give a good stir before adding the canned tomatoes. Rinse the empty can out with ½ cup water, and empty that in turn into the pan, followed by the Worcestershire sauce and the drained, rinsed kidney beans, then let it all come to a bubble.

♥ Turn the heat down low, clamp on the lid and let the chili simmer gently for 20 minutes. I often remove it to a cold dish (for efficient cooling) when it's cooked, to reheat and eat later. (I've done that here, and reheated in a skillet, which is why you see the chili in what might seem an inappropriate vessel.)

♥ If you're moving seamlessly on, remove the lid now, turn up the heat until the chili starts to bubble vigorously again, then turn off the heat and stir in the mozzarella. Season and serve immediately, sprinkling with cilantro, if so desired.

MAKE AHEAD NOTE
The chili, without the cheese, can be made 2 days ahead. Cool, cover and refrigerate as quickly as possible. Reheat gently in skillet or large saucepan until piping hot, then add cheese as directed in recipe.

FREEZE NOTE
The cooled chili, without the cheese, can be frozen in airtight container for up to 3 months. Thaw overnight in the refrigerator and reheat as above.

Barbecued ground beef

For us, at home, this is barbecued beef sauce cowboy-style (well, we are all entitled to our delusions; indeed, we rely on them) which is to say it's a meat sauce either sandwiched inside a soft white roll to make a Sloppy Joe, or Sloppy José, or spooned just as it is, out of individual bowls, with a tray of toasted cheesy tortilla chips alongside for dipping and all-round augmentation of pleasure. There are many working days on which this and this alone is the crucial factor in staving off maternal meltdown. I've never served it with pasta, but it's a possibility – and if you were to, I'd advise a small, chunky-ish pasta, such as chifferi rigati or ditalini.

33

Serves 4–8, *depending on age and appetite*

1 celery stalk, cut into chunks
3 cloves garlic, peeled
2 onions, peeled and halved
6 ounces smoked sliced bacon
2 carrots, peeled and cut into
  chunks
2 tablespoons vegetable oil
1 tablespoon dark brown sugar
pinch ground cloves
½ teaspoon ground allspice
1 pound ground beef, preferably
  organic

to make up in a jug:
1 x 14-ounce can diced tomatoes,
  plus full can water
3 tablespoons Worcestershire sauce
  (such as Lea & Perrins)
3 tablespoons bourbon
2 tablespoons dark brown sugar
2 tablespoons tomato paste

to serve:
6 soft white rolls (such as hamburger rolls)
  or approximately 14 ounces unsalted
  tortilla chips
1¾ cups grated Cheddar cheese (for chips)

♥ To start the sauce, put the celery, garlic, onions, bacon and carrots into a food processor and process to an orangey mush.

♥ Heat the oil in a heavy-bottomed pan or cast iron Dutch oven (with a lid) and add the processed ingredients. Cook for 15–20 minutes, over a gentle heat, stirring every now and again, until soft.

♥ While the vegetables are cooking, mix together the liquid ingredients (and the 2 tablespoons brown sugar) in a measuring jug.

♥ Then stir 1 tablespoon brown sugar along with the cloves and allspice into the vegetable pan. Now add the ground beef, breaking it up with a wooden fork as you mix it into the pan of softened, spiced veggies, stirring until the meat begins to lose its raw color.

♥ Pour in the jug of liquid ingredients and stir gently into the meat. Put on the lid and turn down the heat to low. Simmer for 25 minutes.

♥ If you're serving as sandwiches to be messily chowed down (no other way, I'm afraid), you need do nothing but split the soft white rolls. If you're going for the toasted tortilla option, preheat the oven to 400°F, then scatter the chips in a jelly roll pan or lipped baking sheet (foil-lined for ease of cleaning later) and sprinkle the grated cheese over them before letting chips toast and cheese begin to melt oozily in the hot oven; 5 minutes should be enough but it may take 10. This is a contender for favorite home football food, which is to say watched on the TV, not from the stadium: the ultimate soccer succor.

MAKE AHEAD NOTE
The beef sauce can be made up to 2 days ahead. Transfer to non-metallic bowl, cool, cover, and refrigerate as quickly as possible. Reheat gently in large saucepan until piping hot.

FREEZE NOTE
The cooled sauce can be frozen in airtight container for up to 3 months. Thaw overnight in refrigerator and reheat as above.

35

Sweet and sour chicken

I am aware that this record of the recipes I feed my children may not chime resoundingly with the dietary wisdom of the day, but I have to say, I'm just grateful if they're not eating something smelly out of a supermarket package. Getting teenage children to eat what approximates to a meal is, as far as I'm concerned, an achievement to be celebrated. That this is a dish they actually request … well, I don't start worrying about a little bit of sugar and salt. Fresh food with some salt and sugar added knowingly seems better to me than processed food loaded with ingredients I don't even recognize (though if you're cooking for younger children, you could cut down the soy sauce here). And now that we know that ketchup can be positively good for you, I gladly dollop some in as I cook, for all that I am still fuddy-duddily opposed to universal application actually at the table. Its particular sweet vinegariness is what this dish is all about.

Serve with rice and a little baby bok choy to that most elusive of sounds: the appreciation of your children.

Serves 4–8, *depending on age and appetite*

2 tablespoons garlic flavored oil
1 red onion, peeled and chopped
2 red bell peppers, stalks removed,
  seeded and cut into rough ¾ inch
  square chunks
1 pound chicken thigh fillets (no
  skin or bones)
1 teaspoon Chinese 5 spice powder
3 cups (10 ounces) bean sprouts
1 x 8-ounce can sliced water
  chestnuts, drained (optional)

for the sauce:
2 tablespoons apricot jam
2 tablespoons soy sauce
1 cup pineapple juice
3 tablespoons ketchup
2 teaspoons rice wine vinegar (or
  enough to get the sour note right)
salt and pepper, to taste

♥ Heat the oil in a large wok or frying pan that comes with a lid, and cook the chopped onions, stirring every now and again, for about 5 minutes. Add the bell peppers and cook for another 5 minutes, or until soft.

♥ Cut each chicken thigh fillet into 4 pieces (I find snipping with scissors easiest) and add to the onion-and-pepper pan along with the Chinese 5 spice. Cook, stirring frequently, for another 5 minutes.

♥ Whisk the sauce ingredients together in a jug (tasting to check you have the right note of sweet and sour), pour into the pan with the chicken and other ingredients, and bring to a boil. Put the lid on and cook on a low heat, simmering gently for 15 minutes, until the chicken has cooked through.

♥ Stir in the bean sprouts, and water chestnuts (if using), check for seasoning, and let it come back to a boil. When you're sure it's piping hot right through, serve with rice.

MAKE AHEAD NOTE
The dish can be made 1 day ahead. Transfer chicken and sauce to a non-metallic bowl to cool, cover and refrigerate as soon as possible. Reheat gently in a saucepan, stirring occasionally, until chicken and sauce are piping hot.

FREEZE NOTE
The cooled chicken and sauce can be frozen in airtight container for up to 3 months. Thaw overnight in refrigerator and reheat as above.

37

Chicken teriyaki

I know the world is full of good parents who never give their children food with salt or sugar, and this recipe (among others) proves conclusively that I am not one of them. Oh, and on top of these dietary failings, the following also contains alcohol. There's really not much to be said by me if these infractions offend. Is it to the point that this meal seems to be both universally delicious and the work of lazy moments? If the answer is yes, cook on. However, should you be making this for younger children, halve the soy sauce quantity for under tens and quarter it for under fives, if you wish.

Serves 4–6, *depending on age and appetite*

2 tablespoons sake (Japanese rice wine)
¼ cup mirin (sweet Japanese rice wine)
¼ cup soy sauce
2 tablespoons light brown sugar
2 teaspoons grated fresh gingerroot
splash of sesame oil

1¾ pounds chicken thigh fillets (no skin or bones), preferably organic, cut or scissored into bite-sized pieces
1 teaspoon peanut oil
1¾–2½ cups sushi rice, cooked following package instructions (and see p.18)

♥ Mix the sake, mirin, soy sauce, sugar, ginger, and sesame oil in a dish that you can steep the chicken in. I use an 8-inch square Pyrex, but anything similar would do.

♥ Add the prepared chicken pieces and leave for 15 minutes.

♥ Heat the peanut oil in a large, shallow frying pan or Dutch oven (that has a lid) and, using a perforated spoon, transfer the chicken pieces from their dark marinating liquid to the pan, and sauté until they look cooked on the outside.

♥ Pour the marinade over the chicken pieces in the pan and bring to a bubble, then turn down the heat to a gentle simmer, put the lid on and cook for about 5 minutes – cut into a piece of chicken to make sure it's cooked through.

♥ Remove the cooked pieces with a perforated spoon (you could keep them warm in a bowl covered in aluminum foil) and turn the heat up under the pan to let the liquid boil down to a thick, dark syrup.

♥ Return the chicken pieces to the pan, stir well so that they are all coated in the sticky, savory syrup, then serve with a comforting pile of sushi rice and perhaps some steamed baby bok choy or green veggies of your choice.

40

Pasta alla genovese
with potatoes, green beans, and pesto

Children – who are perhaps more honest about their tastes than the rest of us – seem to have an overweening preference for carbohydrates, and I am more than happy to exploit this. If I've been working late, am feeling lazy, have forgotten to go shopping or suddenly find out that their friends are staying over and I don't know what they will or won't eat, I reach gratefully for a packet of pasta. I can honestly say I don't know how parents managed to feed their children in the days before pasta became universal culinary currency. Oh, yes I do, actually: they didn't care whether we liked what they cooked or not; we just ate what we were given.

My children wouldn't care if all I ever gave them was pasta with some bottled sauce poured over, and I don't deny that's sometimes indeed what they are given; but to please myself, and them, this is what I make when I get it together a little. Making this is hardly an effort; the potatoes cook in the pasta water – requiring a little extra time, nothing more – and the pinenut-less pesto is whizzed up easily by the processor.

If you're going to do this recipe, then do make the pesto yourself. Using pesto out of a jar is nothing I'd ever apologize for, but this is a dish in itself and needs to be kept distinct. For those who feel cooking potatoes with pasta is playing too much into the hands of kiddie carbomania, know that this is a Ligurian tradition. And it really works: the potatoes thicken into a sweet sludge to which the pesto adheres, to make a fantastically, elegantly comforting and fragrant strand-coating sauce. The green beans add to the verdigloriousness of the whole, making you feel good that you are getting the children to eat vegetables.

Serves 6–8, *depending on age and appetite*

1 pound large mealy potatoes,
  peeled and cut into ¾ inch slices,
  each slice quartered into chunks
1 pound linguine
7 ounces green or French beans,
  trimmed and cut in half

for the pesto:
leaves from 2 fat bunches basil
  (about 5 cups, lightly packed)
1 cup grated Parmesan cheese
1 garlic clove, peeled
scant ½ cup regular olive oil
scant ½ cup extra-virgin olive oil

♥ Put the prepared potato chunks into a large saucepan with enough salted water to take the pasta later, and bring to a boil.

♥ Cook the potatoes until tender, about 20 minutes, then add the pasta. Check the package cooking instructions, and at about 4 minutes before the end of the specified cooking time, add the green beans. If you are using an artisanal egg linguine, which takes less time, you will need to alter your strategy.

♥ While this is bubbling away, whiz the ingredients for the pesto in a food processor. Before you drain the saucepan, remove and reserve about ½ cup of the cooking liquid. Tip the drained potatoes, beans, and pasta back into the dry pan.

♥ Add the pesto from the processor and enough cooking water to give a runny sauce that coats the strands of pasta as you work it through with a fork or pasta server. Serve immediately.

MAKE AHEAD NOTE
The pesto can be made 2–3 days ahead. Make the pesto using only ¼ cup olive oil and transfer to screw-top jar or airtight container. Carefully pour the remaining oil over the top so that surface of pesto is completely covered with oil. Store in the refrigerator. Let stand at room temperature about 30 minutes before stirring and using.

FREEZE NOTE
The pesto can be frozen for up to 3 months in airtight container. Make the pesto and cover with a layer of oil, as above. Thaw for 2–3 hours at room temperature and stir before using.

42

Turkey meatballs in tomato sauce

I have been making meatballs for as long as my children have been eating solid food. But forgive me: solid food is such a ghastly term; besides, it doesn't come anywhere near evoking the melting tenderness of these supper treats. For strangely luscious they are. I say strangely, because I first made them out of ground turkey, rather than my usual preferred ground beef, when I suddenly and uncharacteristically fell victim to the ethos of the age and it came upon me to pander to the low-fat brigade. Obviously, my subconscious knew better and directed me thuswards for a reason. It turns out that turkey makes for a light and succulent meatball, which my children love despite the sudden change from what they're used to (that, too, is remarkable since children tend towards conservatism and are, as a rule, averse to change), and which has also been exuberantly greeted by Italian eaters, who no less vehemently value tradition over novelty, at the table at least.

All in all, this is quite a favorite in casa Lawson these days, and I can be found making a batch – half for supper and half to be frozen for future outings – regularly and pleasurably.

Serves 4–8, *depending on age and appetite*

for the sauce:
1 onion, peeled
1 celery stalk
2 tablespoons garlic flavored oil
1 teaspoon dried thyme
2 x 14-ounce cans diced tomatoes, plus approx. 3⅓ cups (2 full cans) water
1 teaspoon sugar
1 teaspoon kosher salt or ½ teaspoon table salt
pepper, to taste

for the meatballs:
1 pound ground turkey
1 egg
3 tablespoons breadcrumbs
3 tablespoons grated Parmesan cheese
2 tablespoons finely chopped onion and celery (from the tomato sauce ingredients)
1 teaspoon Worcestershire sauce (such as Lea & Perrins)
½ teaspoon dried thyme

♥ Put the peeled onion and the celery into a food processor and blitz to a mush. Or you can chop as finely as humanly possible by hand. Reserve 2 tablespoons for the meatball mixture.

♥ Warm the garlic flavored oil in a large, heavy saucepan or Dutch oven, add the onion and celery mixture, along with the thyme, and cook at moderate to low heat, stirring every now and again, for about 10 minutes.

♥ Add the cans of tomatoes, filling up each empty can with water to add to the pan. Season with the sugar, salt and pepper, stir and let it come to a bubble, then turn the heat down to simmer gently while you get on with the meatballs.

♥ Put all the ingredients for the meatballs, including the reserved chopped onion and celery, and salt according to preference, into a large bowl and mix together, gently, with your hands, wearing disposable vinyl gloves (see **p.17**) if you feel so inclined. Don't over-mix, as that will make the meatballs dense-textured and heavy.

♥ When all the meatball ingredients are just amalgamated, start rolling. The easiest way is to pinch out an amount about the size of a generously heaped teaspoon and roll into a ball between the palms of your hands. Put the meatballs on a rimmed baking sheet, lined with parchment paper, as you go. You should get about 50 little meatballs.

♥ Drop these gently into the simmering sauce; I try to let these fall in concentric circles, working round the pan from the outside edge inwards, in the vaguest of fashions.

♥ Let the meatballs simmer for 30 minutes, until cooked through. Serve with rice or pasta, or however you so please. I sometimes give them an automatic upgrade by serving with the Arugula and Lemon Couscous on **p.90**.

MAKE AHEAD NOTE
The meatballs and sauce can be made up to 2 days ahead. Transfer meatballs and sauce to a non-metallic bowl to cool, cover and refrigerate as soon as possible. Reheat gently in a saucepan, giving the occasional stir (be careful not to break up the meatballs), until meatballs and sauce are piping hot.

FREEZE NOTE
The cooled meatballs and sauce can be frozen in airtight containers for up to 3 months. You may find it handy to freeze in individual portions if making a large quantity. Thaw overnight in the refrigerator and reheat as above.

45

African drumsticks

I first ate this, under a slightly different guise, at a South African friend's house. The sauce was the same, but the meat marinated and cooked in it was pork. I prefer this version – the pork fat made the sauce a little too oily for absolute comfort, and I am no fat-phobe, as you know – and more pointedly so do my children.

My friend, who has since given in to my drumstick preference, says that apricot jam is an omnipresent feature of the cuisine of her native land, and I hope I do not offend by admitting that my only other alteration to her recipe is to lessen the amount of it. This way the sweetness is kept in check and there is enough warmth and spice to keep adult eaters happy without alienating the more childish palate, though for younger children, you might use less mustard.

Should you wish to be really authentic, I suggest you dollop your plate with a glossy heap of Mrs. Ball's chutney – *the* condiment of the continent.

Serves 4–8, *depending on age and appetite*

⅓ cup Worcestershire sauce (such as Lea & Perrins)	1 teaspoon ground ginger
¼ cup ketchup	1 tablespoon apricot jam
2 teaspoons English mustard, or to taste	1 onion, peeled and finely chopped
	8 chicken drumsticks, preferably organic
	1 tablespoon garlic flavored oil

♥ Preheat the oven to 400°F. Mix the Worcestershire sauce, ketchup, mustard, ground ginger, apricot jam, and chopped onion in a shallow dish.

♥ Dunk the drumsticks in this marinade to coat them all over. (If it helps, you could at this stage leave them to marinate, covered, in the refrigerator overnight.) Put the oil into a smallish roasting pan or ovenproof dish, in which the drumsticks will fit snugly, and tip the pan about so that the oil more or less covers the base. Arrange the drumsticks in the pan and pour over them any remaining marinade.

♥ Cook for 45 minutes to 1 hour, basting once or twice: the deeper the dish, the longer the drumsticks will take to color and cook through.

MAKE AHEAD NOTE
The chicken can be marinated overnight in a covered bowl in the refrigerator.

FREEZE NOTE
The chicken can be frozen in the marinade in a resealable bag for up to 3 months. Thaw overnight in the refrigerator (put bag in a bowl to catch drips) and cook following directions in recipe.

47

Spaghetti with Marmite

I came across this recipe in Anna Del Conte's memoirs, *Risotto with Nettles*. Now, there are so many recipes I could borrow from her, and many I have, but this is the one I have to show you here. She introduces it as "hardly a recipe, but I wanted to include it because I haven't as yet found a child who doesn't like it." The minute I read its title – once I'd got over my crossness that she hadn't told me about it during many years of friendship – I was charmed. Of course it helps that, being a Marmite addict, I knew it would work. And how it does. I have recently turned traitor and shifted towards the Vegemite side of the world, and this works as well, unsurprisingly, with the antipodean ointment.

I know the combination of pasta and Marmite sounds odd to the point of unfeasibility, but wait a moment. There is a traditional day-after-the-roast pasta dish, in which spaghetti is tossed in chicken stock, and I have eaten shortcut versions of this in Italy (recreated guiltlessly in my own kitchen) which use a crumbled bouillon cube, along with some butter, olive oil, chopped rosemary and a little of the pasta cooking water to make a flavorsome sauce for spaghetti. If you think about it, Marmite offers saltiness and savoriness the way a bouillon cube might.

I'm glad this recipe is here, and I thank Anna for it. But even when it's not an Anna-recipe, I think of her whenever I cook pasta, remembering her two ordinances: one, that the water you cook pasta in should be as salty as the Mediterranean; and two, that pasta should not be too officiously drained, but rather be "*con la goccia*," that's to say with some cooking water still clinging to it, as this makes it easier to incorporate the sauce. It was she who taught me to scoop out some of the cooking water just before draining the pasta, to help the sauce amalgamate later if necessary. Marmite can be found in gourmet stores, and also online.

Serves 4–6, *depending on age and appetite*

12 ounces dried spaghetti	freshly grated Parmesan cheese,
3 tablespoons unsalted butter	to serve
1 teaspoon Marmite, or more to taste	

♥ Cook the spaghetti in plenty of boiling salted water, following the package instructions.

♥ When the pasta is almost cooked, melt the butter in a small saucepan and add the Marmite and 1 tablespoon of the pasta water, mixing thoroughly to dissolve. Reserve ½ cup of pasta water; then drain the pasta and pour the Marmite mixture over the drained spaghetti, adding a little reserved pasta water to amalgamate if required. Serve with plenty of grated Parmesan cheese.

Chicken fajitas

I don't know if it is the male part of me or the child part (though the overlap is disconcerting, so confusion is to be expected) but I love a bit of DIY at the table. Fajitas offer occupation but no concentration, and this goes for cook as well as diner. These are, I guess, the Tex-Mex answer to the Chinese duck and pancakes, but more do-able at home. For one, you can buy the tortillas (and I would advise buying 2 packages rather than just the one specified, as I normally find that I could do with one or two tortillas more – you can always freeze what you don't use till next time), and the chicken is the work of minutes.

I am prepared to accept that this is an inauthentic gringo version. What do I know? Well, what I do know is that this is a cheering supper, and it doesn't, to me, taste very different to the fajitas I've come across in my travels. Here, I've made a kind of stir-fry, a juicy tangle of onion, bell peppers, and spiced chicken; at other times, I cook the onions and bell peppers together and the chicken separately. And when I've got leftover chicken, I often use this recipe as a first-stop user-upper, adding cold cooked shredded chicken to the bell peppers and onions and tossing altogether in the pan till piping hot all the way through.

The traditional salsa that should be part of the medley of accompaniments is not really to my taste, as it tends towards the overwhelmingly vinegary, so instead I bring out some Jumbo Chili Sauce (see **p.121**) that I always keep in my refrigerator (although if you were to dispense with the onions and bell peppers here, I suggest you make the tomato salsa I indicate for the Mexican Lasagne on **p.105**). I should add that it doesn't matter if you don't have any Mexican oregano; just use regular oregano. I happened to buy some of the former when I was last in the States, and rather love its earthy farmyard resonance. But I suspect that this is all in my head.

One final note: for a quick and cross-generational dinner, you could prepare the chicken pieces as below, but instead of turning them into fajitas, stir them through the Rice and Peas on **p.344**.

Serves 4, *but could be stretched to feed 8 smaller eaters*

2 skinless chicken breast fillets,
  preferably organic
1 teaspoon dried Mexican oregano,
  or regular oregano
1 teaspoon ground cumin
1 teaspoon kosher salt or ½
  teaspoon table salt
½ teaspoon sugar
1 tablespoon garlic flavored oil, plus
  2 teaspoons
2 tablespoons lime juice
2 tablespoons peanut oil or regular
  olive oil
2 onions, peeled, halved and cut
  into thin half-moons
1 red bell pepper, core and seeds
  removed, cut into strips
1 orange bell pepper, core and seeds
  removed, cut into strips
1 yellow bell pepper, core and seeds
  removed, cut into strips

8 soft flour tortillas (see
  introduction above)

optional accompaniments:
1 cup grated Cheddar or Monterey
  Jack cheese
½ cup sour cream or crème fraîche
1 x 7-ounce can corn niblets,
  drained (or ⅔ cup drained
  canned corn)
1 large avocado (or 2 small),
  finely diced and dressed with
  ½ teaspoon kosher salt and 2
  teaspoons lime juice
¼–½ head iceberg lettuce,
  shredded
1 ramekin chopped fresh cilantro
  (about ⅓ cup)
hot chili sauce, to serve (optional)

♥ Over a shallow bowl, cut the chicken with a pair of scissors into thin (½–¾ inch) strips lengthways, then halve the long strip across to give 2 shorter strips (to echo the bell pepper strips later). Don't get too hung up on precision, though; you're just trying to cut things into easily wrappable and munchable shapes.

♥ Once the chicken has been snipped into the dish, add the oregano, cumin, salt, sugar, 1 tablespoon garlic flavored oil, and the lime juice. Stir everything about and leave to marinate while you get on with the onions and bell peppers. And preheat the oven to 225°F if you wish to warm your tortillas.

♥ Warm the peanut or olive oil in a large frying pan or wok and fry the half-moon onion slices over medium heat, stirring occasionally, for 5 minutes.

♥ Spread the tortillas out on a cookie sheet and put in the oven to warm.

♥ Add the bell pepper strips to the onion pan and cook for a further 10 minutes. When both onions and peppers are tender, remove to a bowl.

♥ Warm the remaining 2 teaspoons garlic flavored oil in the pan and tip in the chicken with its marinade. Cook, stirring frequently, for 5 minutes. Check that the chicken is piping hot and cooked through, add the onions and bell peppers from the bowl, stir together, then decant to a serving dish.

♥ Take the warmed tortillas out of the oven and put on the table alongside the chicken tangled in onions and bell peppers and all the other accoutrements. Wrap what you fancy in the tortillas to eat straightaway.

MAKE AHEAD NOTE
The onion and bell peppers can be cut 1 day in advance. Cover tightly with plastic wrap and refrigerate. The chicken can be cut 1 day in advance and tossed with the oregano, cumin and garlic flavored oil. Cover tightly with plastic wrap and refrigerate. Add the lime juice and salt just before cooking.

HURRY UP! I'M HUNGRY!

It often seems tauntingly unfair that the occasions on which we need most urgent succour from food, tend to be those when we have the least amount of time to cook it. In the middle of a working week, when chores pile up, and the demands of my own deadlines and my children's (home assignments have been so much more the bane of my life as a parent than they ever were as a pupil) eat through the hours, and stress levels could be measured on a Geiger counter, I need to be sure that I can get food on the table before low blood sugar turns what is already a tense time into a traumatic one. I know I sound on the edge of hysteria here – or simply exaggerating for dramatic effect – when I say that going for too long without food can make me feel both suicidal and murderous, but it is a fact I have learned to accept in myself and to recognize in others. Accordingly, I have a pre-emptive strategy to avoid just such an unwelcome eventuality: namely, the recipes in this chapter, as well as others dotted around the book (and see Express Index **p.486**).

Since I have already written an entire book dedicated to food that's fast to make and good to eat, this is hardly a novel approach for me, but I am no less emphatic or evangelical on the subject. I still feel that many people are put off cooking because they think there is more to it than there actually is. I was making supper recently, just for me and a girlfriend (the Bloody Maria of **p.441**) and we were chatting, moaning, jabbering away and generally passing the time, as one does. I was at the stove, pontificating and pottering, occasionally pushing and prodding what was in front of me with a pair of tongs; she was facing me, at the kitchen table. After about ten minutes, if that, I presented her with her plate and she looked surprised, as she was sure she hadn't seen me actually cooking. In a way, I can see her point: this wasn't Cooking-with-a-capital-C, but the lower-case way which is always my starting point, and on busy days, I wouldn't think of going beyond. You put something on the heat, you take it off the heat.

Maybe this is too much of an oversimplification – but only by a whisker. Most of the quick suppers or snatched lunches which follow are variations on that theme: hot crisp cubes of bacon are turned into the basis of a dressing; lemon juice thrown into the pan juices once the meat's been removed becomes a vibrant sauce; it's a case of going with the flavorful flow.

Egg and bacon salad

I could eat breakfast at any time of the day, and often do, but this is a worthwhile variation on a theme. I know I'm showing my vintage here – egg and bacon salad was one of the party pieces of the late Eighties – but I'm unashamed. It's not so much that it's time for a revival, but that anything this scrumptious should never have been allowed to fall from grace.

Serves 4, *as a light lunch or starter*

4 eggs
1 head escarole or frisée or other
  bitter leaves of your choice
1 teaspoon garlic flavored oil
7 ounces (¾ cup) smoked lardons,
  cubed pancetta, or approximately
  14 slices smoked bacon, cut into
  chunks

1 teaspoon Dijon mustard
4 teaspoons cider vinegar
dash Worcestershire sauce (such as
  Lea & Perrins)
small bunch Italian parsley,
  chopped

♥ Put the eggs into a saucepan of water, bring to a boil, let boil for 1 minute, then turn off the heat and let the eggs sit in the pan for 10 minutes. I cook my eggs this way, as I love the yolks to be only just, or rather almost, hard-boiled, with the memory of oozy goldenness still evident at the center; it also keeps the whites amazingly silky. If, however, you prefer a proper, good and bouncy, reassuringly hard-boiled egg, cooked till the yolks are powdery and compact, keep the heat on under the pan for 10 minutes (and the same applies if you're making this for anyone with a compromised immune system, such as the old and frail, the very young or pregnant women).

♥ Meanwhile, tear the salad leaves into generously bite-sized pieces and drop them into a bowl.

♥ Heat the garlic flavored oil in a frying pan, and fry the lardons or bacon until crisp, about 5 minutes.

♥ Tip out the water from the egg pan and run cold water on the eggs. Once they feel cool to the touch, peel them.

♥ Turn the heat off under the frying pan, and transfer the lardons or bacon with a slotted spatula to some paper towels for a minute, while you make the dressing.

♥ Add the Dijon mustard to the bacony juices in the pan and whisk to mix, then add the vinegar and a dash of Worcestershire sauce, whisk again and pour this over the salad leaves, tossing to mix.

♥ Now add the lardons or bacon and toss again, then quarter the eggs and add them along with the chopped parsley, before giving the whole salad a gentle mix to combine but not disturb.

MAKE AHEAD NOTE
The hard-boiled eggs can be made up to 4 days ahead. Cool, leave shells on, then store in airtight container in the refrigerator. Remove shells just before serving.

59

Mussels in cider

The title explains simply what the key ingredients are, but doesn't begin to convey the luxe-for-less-time gloriousness of the feast. If you feel like it, you could tumble a handful of pancetta cubes in with the onion to crisp out and imbue the whole with its salty juices, but I rather love the naked sweetness of the mussels against the rasp of the cider.

Serves 2, *as main course, or 4 as starter*

4½ pounds mussels
2–3 tablespoons regular olive oil
1 onion, peeled and very finely
  chopped, or 3 scallions, sliced

2 cloves garlic, peeled and thinly
  sliced
3–4 tablespoons chopped fresh
  parsley
2 cups dry hard cider

♥ Soak the mussels in a sink or bowl filled with cold water. Clean the mussels by going at them with a knife to scrape off any barnacles, and pull off any beards. This may not be necessary, if you've bought them pre-packaged, but it's better to be prepared. Discard any cracked mussels, and tap any that are open on the side of the sink and, if they stay open, throw these away, too.

♥ Put the olive oil in a saucepan that has a lid and is big enough to take all the mussels later, put over medium heat and add the finely chopped onion (or sliced scallions), the sliced garlic, and about 1 tablespoon parsley. Stir about, cooking, for a minute or two, until just softening.

♥ Add the cider, then turn the heat up, throw in the cleaned mussels and clamp the lid on. Cook for a couple of minutes, giving the pan a shake occasionally.

♥ Peek in to see that the mussels have opened. If they haven't, cook for another minute; if they have, take the pan off the heat, and let it stand for a moment, so that the juices settle and any grit that might have been in the mussels goes to the bottom.

♥ Divide the mussels between your bowls and then spoon the juice over them, avoiding the gritty sediment. Sprinkle with the remaining parsley and serve with an extra bowl to put empty shells in, and a loaf of bread to dip into the ecstasy-inducing liquid. Don't force open or eat any mussels that have not opened during cooking or that have damaged shells – these should be discarded.

Lamb with rosemary and port

I love the sort of dinner that you can cook without any special effort, but without sacrificing gratification. That's the thing really: cooking is simple; you can choose to complicate it, but there's no need to. Even when you're at a low ebb, this is a manageable supper, and just what's needed to pull you out of a slump. It's comfortingly retro, too: I think it's the generous amount of – well – gravy that the juices and the de-glazing-action make. A steamed baby potato or two to help mop it up would be good, but I'm happy with canned, drained cannellini or flageolet beans, warmed with some garlic flavored oil and a little water and salt on the stove, or a pile of orzo, that rice-shaped pasta (though barley is what they should resemble) most often used in soups and in salads. But a good hunk of poised-to-dunk bread and some quick-to-cook green beans would provide a well-pitched accompaniment, too.

Serves 2

1 tablespoon olive oil
2 teaspoons Worcestershire sauce
  (such as Lea & Perrins)
2 boneless lamb leg steaks (center
  slice)

for the sauce:
1 tablespoon butter
1 sprig rosemary
1 fat clove garlic
¼ cup ruby port

♥ Mix together the oil and Worcestershire sauce in a bowl, then smear this over the steaks, either with a pastry brush or by dipping the steaks directly into the bowl.

♥ Heat a heavy-based frying pan, and cook the steaks for about 3 minutes per side, depending on the thickness of the steak and how you like it done. If you prefer to use boneless lamb sirloin or noisettes, I'd advise 2 per person, and less time for their cooking.

♥ Wrap them in aluminum foil to rest on a warm plate or in a warm place, while you make the sauce. With the pan still on the heat, but turned down low, add the butter and let it melt, then finely chop the needles from the rosemary sprig and add them to the pan.

♥ Peel and crush or mince the garlic clove into the pan, then pour in the port, letting it sizzle and reduce slightly. Unwrap the steaks and add any juices from the foil parcel to the sauce. Then put the steaks onto plates and pour the sauce over them.

Tarragon chicken

This is a quick-time version of the classic French *poulet à l'estragon* (though you could speed it up further by bashing out the chicken breast or by using a turkey cutlet in its place, which would make this dish pleasingly alliterative), and is an instant reminder of the comforts of old-school cooking. Tender chicken (it's the poaching early on that sees to this), aromatically fresh and insistently herbal tarragon, a generous splosh of vermouth, all rounded off by rich, pale cream: this has the nostalgic, yet robust, charm of that French bistro of fond memory or happy imaginings. If you can't get fresh tarragon, do not despair: just double the freeze-dried tarragon at the start and add some freshly chopped parsley at the end. And I can assure you it would be worth your while considering a teaspoon of tarragon mustard, too, along with the cream. About which, please don't wimp out on me: this is old-fashioned cooking which cannot be proscribed by new-age dietary concerns. But, if you insist, halve the cream, and add another 2 tablespoons of vermouth when you're pouring the rest in after the chicken's had its first 5 minutes' cooking.

Eat with a tumbled mixture of French or green beans and asparagus tips along with steamed baby white-skinned potatoes or, hard to beat for me, some white basmati rice forked through with a *soupçon* of butter and freshly ground white pepper.

Serves 2

2 teaspoons garlic flavored oil
2 fat scallions or 4 skinny ones,
  thinly sliced
½ teaspoon freeze-dried tarragon
2 chicken breast fillets, skinless and
  boneless
⅓ cup vermouth or white wine

½ teaspoon kosher salt or ¼
  teaspoon table salt
½ cup heavy cream
fresh white pepper, to grind over
2 teaspoons chopped fresh
  tarragon, plus a pinch more for
  sprinkling

♥ Heat the garlic flavored oil in a frying pan or Dutch oven that has a lid and in which the chicken breasts will fit pretty snugly. Add the scallions, stir, then sprinkle in the freeze-dried tarragon, stir again and cook them in the garlic flavored oil for a minute, stirring some more as they cook.

♥ Put the chicken fillets into the pan, curved side down, and cook for 5 minutes, watching that the scallions don't burn. If they look like they're beginning to, scrape them from the pan and let them sit on the chicken pieces.

♥ Turn over the breasts, and add the vermouth (or white wine). Let the vermouth bubble

64

up, then add the salt. Put the lid on, turn the heat down low, and leave it to simmer gently for 10 minutes. Check the chicken is cooked through by making a small cut into the thickest part and ensuring the juices run clear – if not, simmer for a few minutes longer and check again.

♥ Remove the chicken breasts to warmed plates. Bring the remaining liquid to a boil, add the cream and stir well, then sprinkle in the fresh tarragon, stir again and give a good grind of white pepper.

♥ Pour the sauce over the chicken breasts, and give a final scattering of tarragon to serve.

Red currant and mint lamb chops

My mother often used to make a kind of faux Cumberland sauce to go with lamb chops: she'd dollop some red currant jelly into a bowl, grate in a little orange zest and squeeze in a little juice, then stir in some freshly chopped mint, or dried mint if there were no fresh. Somehow, it worked, and this, which follows, is simply a development along the same lines. Impatience, I have learned from her and from the food I eat, can be an inspirational prompt to the cook. Laziness is accounted for, greed rewarded: that's a result.

I love these with some of my Rapid Roastini (see next page) and a tangle of peppery leaves.

Serves 2

1 tablespoon garlic flavored oil
6 small Frenched lamb rib chops
juice 1 clementine (approx. ⅓ cup)
1 tablespoon red currant jelly
dash Worcestershire sauce (such as
  Lea & Perrins)

dash red wine vinegar or sherry
  vinegar
salt and pepper, to taste
5–6 stalks fresh mint, finely
  chopped

♥ Heat the oil in a frying pan and cook the lamb for about 2–4 minutes a side, depending on how you like them and on the thickness of the chops.

♥ Remove the chops to a large piece of aluminum foil and make a baggy package, though sealing it tightly, and keep on a warm plate.

♥ Turn the heat down to low, then whisk in the clementine juice, red currant jelly, Worcestershire sauce, vinegar, salt and pepper. Take the pan off the heat.

♥ Unwrap the foil parcel, divide the chops between 2 warmed plates, and pour into the pan any juices that have collected under the waiting chops. Whisk well, then pour this over the chops.

♥ Sprinkle with about 2 tablespoons chopped mint, and offer more on the table to eat with the supper.

Speedy scaloppine
with rapid roastini

Well, I know it's true that an escalope can never take that long to cook, but when I make this for supper, I can never quite get over the near-instant gratification it provides. The scaloppine are cooked as the Italians do them so well, just kissed with some spiced flour and sauced with the pan juices de-glazed with a lemon. In Italy, you'd expect the meat to be veal; here I use either pork or – perhaps more frequently – turkey.

Serves 2

2 tablespoons all-purpose flour
shake mixed spice
shake cayenne pepper
4 small turkey or pork escalopes
(thin-sliced cutlets), about 12
ounces total

2 tablespoons garlic flavored oil
zest and juice 1 lemon
salt, to taste

♥ Put the flour and spices into a resealable bag, then add the escalopes, shaking to coat them.

♥ Heat the oil in a heavy-based frying pan and add the floured meat, cooking for 2 minutes a side or until the escalopes are just cooked through.

♥ Remove the escalopes to warm plates and take the pan off the heat.

♥ Grate the lemon zest into the (still warm) pan and squeeze in the lemon juice. Stir until the juices are golden and slightly syrupy. Season to taste, pour the sauce over the escalopes and serve with the rapid roastini below.

Rapid roastini

I am an enormous believer in instinct: whenever I allow myself to be deflected from what I think is right, I regret it, whether in the kitchen, or out of it. But here, in the kitchen, it went like this: I had, in the small hours, one of my bathetic revelations that if I fried some gnocchi, they might turn out like my *Express* sautéed potatoes. I mentioned the idea around and was met with, at best polite, grimaces. I insisted, tried it out, and luxuriated in how right I was. These are crisp on the outside, fluffy inside and totally scrumptious. And, in fact, rather than being like sautéed potatoes they are really more like miniature roasted potatoes, hence the title. If you want, you actually can roast them, and they'll need 10 minutes a side in an oven preheated to 400°F. I find more than 8 ounces is difficult to fry, so the oven's a good option (if a little slower) when you want to feed lots of people. I've allowed 8 ounces, that's half a bag (the other half will keep, sealed, in the refrigerator for up to 3 days) of gnocchi for 2 people, but I have a sliding scale: 4 ounces per head for children, 4–5 ounces for normal people, and 6 ounces per head for men and teenage boys. And I have to tell you how good they are as a quick kitchen appetizer, when they're piping hot, gorgeously golden and sprinkled with sea salt along with a cold, cold beer.

Serves 2

2 tablespoons regular olive oil

8 ounces fresh gnocchi from the chilled cabinet in the supermarket

♥ Heat the oil in a large frying pan.

♥ Put the gnocchi in, making sure you separate them, and fry for 4 minutes. Then turn them around and give them another 4 minutes.

♥ Or if you'd prefer to bake them, tumble the gnocchi into a roasting pan, add the oil, and put into a preheated 400°F oven for 20 minutes, giving them a stir after 10 minutes.

NOTE
I would not advise frying frozen gnocchi, as they could cause the fat in the pan to spit.

69

Golden sole
with tarted-up tartar sauce

Yes, this is made with gray sole, but the golden color comes – jubilantly – from the gold grains of polenta which coat the fish, in place of breadcrumbs, before a brief blitz in the pan. It is often worth cooking extra to leave a fillet to eat cold – yes – in a sandwich spread with leftover tartar sauce.

If there's time to steam some baby white-skinned potatoes, then go for it, otherwise know that these crunchy coated fillets make for a gorgeous dinner just with the slightly fiery tartar sauce, a green salad and maybe a pickled quail's egg or two. Well, I found a jar of them, and it did seem a match made in heaven ...

Serves 2

1 egg
dash garlic flavored oil
sprinkling salt and good grinding
  pepper
1 cup instant (quick-cooking)
  polenta
2 gray sole, flounder, or other flat,
  white fish fillets
peanut or corn oil, for frying

for the tarted-up tartar sauce:
zest and juice ½ lemon
½ teaspoon kosher salt or ¼
  teaspoon table salt

scant ½ cup crème fraîche or sour
  cream
2 teaspoons baby (nonpareil)
  capers, drained
1 dill pickle or 4–5 cornichons
3 rings (chopped) jalapeño peppers
  (from a jar or can)
1 tablespoon chopped fresh
  tarragon, plus more for
  sprinkling
2 tablespoons chopped fresh
  parsley, plus more for sprinkling

♥ Beat the egg, along with the garlic flavored oil, salt and pepper, in a shallow dish that will take 1 fish fillet, and leave it for a moment.

♥ Put the polenta in another, similar, dish.

♥ Dip the fish fillets, 1 side at a time, in the egg mixture and then put them into the polenta dish, press down, dredge, and turn to cover fully before leaving them on a wire rack to dry a little while you get on with the sauce.

♥ To make the sauce, zest the lemon into a bowl and squeeze in the juice. Stir the salt into the juice to help it dissolve.

♥ Add the crème fraîche or sour cream, capers, chopped dill pickle (or cornichons), jalapeños, tarragon, and parsley and stir to combine with a fork. Transfer to a ramekin or a small bowl and cover with a scattering of herbs.

♥ Heat enough oil in a frying pan to cover the bottom to approx. ⅛ inch, and cook the grain-covered fillets for 1–2 minutes a side, until the outside is crisp and the fish is cooked through. Then transfer the fish to a board or tray lined with some sheets of paper towel before plating up. Serve with the tartar sauce, some pickled eggs, and a lemony salad.

MAKE AHEAD NOTE
The coated fish can be made ahead but best frozen immediately, as below, and cooked from frozen.

FREEZE NOTE
Do not freeze if previously frozen. Coat the fish in polenta and set on a baking sheet lined with plastic wrap. Cover with a layer of plastic wrap and freeze until solid. Transfer to a resealable bag and freeze for up to 3 months. Fry the fillets direct from frozen, as directed in the recipe, adding 1–2 minutes to cooking time, and check fish is cooked through before serving.

Scallops with Thai-scented pea purée

I love the bouncy sweetness of scallops and, although you might think the equal sweetness of the peas would be too much alongside, the deep flavor of cilantro and chiles and the sharpness of lemongrass miraculously provided by the Thai green curry paste, make it a zingy and yet still comforting accompaniment. This is a real treat of a supper, both for the eater and the cook.

Serves 2

1 pound (3½ cups) frozen petits
   pois or peas
1–2 tablespoons Thai green curry
   paste
⅓ cup crème fraîche or sour cream
salt, to taste
2 teaspoons peanut or other
   flavorless oil
2 teaspoons butter

6 big scallops (such as sold in
   shell by fishmongers) or 10–12
   small bay scallops (such as sold
   in packages in the supermarket),
   preferably diver-caught
juice 1 lime
1–2 tablespoons chopped fresh
   cilantro or Thai basil

♥ Cook the peas in boiling, slightly salted water until tender, then drain and tip into a blender, adding 1 tablespoon curry paste and the crème fraîche or sour cream. Season to taste with salt and perhaps add more curry paste, depending how strong it is.

♥ Heat the oil and butter in a frying pan until foamy, then fry the scallops for about 2 minutes per side. If you are using big scallops, then it is sometimes easier to cut them in half across. When they are cooked, they will have just lost their raw look in the middle and be lusciously tender, while golden and almost caramelized on the outside.

♥ Lift the scallops onto 2 warmed plates and then de-glaze the hot pan by squeezing in the lime juice. Stir to mix well and pick up every scrap of flavor, then pour this over the scallops on each plate.

♥ Dish up the pea purée alongside the scallops, and sprinkle with the chopped cilantro or Thai basil. Serve with another wedge of lime, if you feel like it.

MAKE AHEAD NOTE
The pea purée can be made 2–3 hours ahead. Drain peas and immediately rinse with plenty of cold water. Purée when cold with 1 tablespoon of the curry paste and the crème fraîche or sour cream. Put in a bowl, cover and leave in a cool place or in the refrigerator. Reheat gently in a saucepan, taste and adjust seasoning before serving. If using sour cream, make sure that the purée doesn't boil, otherwise it will turn grainy.

Korean calamari

Never has a quick meal tasted so spectacular. Yes, you do need to hunt down this fabulous flavored paste – think chiles with a sweet and smoky hit of almost licorice intensity – but once you have it, the culinary kingdom is yours. In lieu of it, I suppose you could use any chili paste you like, to taste, but I could never allow myself to run out of my exuberantly colored gochujang – also stamped "Hot Pepper Paste (Chal)" – and so can't report from experience.

In fact, I am always ready to slide down the pole and have this at a moment's notice: the scallions are in the refrigerator; the squid is in the freezer; everything else is to hand; and if I don't have any fresh baby corn, I am more than happy to add whatever vegetable I do have.

Serves 2

1 cup sushi rice
5–6 ounces (6 baby) squid
2 tablespoons rice wine
2 tablespoons Korean gochujang
  paste
2 tablespoons soy sauce
2 teaspoons sugar

few dashes Asian sesame oil
2 teaspoons peanut or other
  flavorless oil
large handful fresh baby corn,
  or green beans, cut into ½ inch
  chunks
6 thin or 3 fat scallions, sliced

♥ Put the sushi rice on to cook following the package instructions or in a rice cooker following its instructions.

♥ Squeeze any tentacles out of the squid bodies, then slice the calamari into rings and put in a bowl with the tentacles and the 2 tablespoons rice wine. Leave for 15 minutes, then strain, reserving the liquid in a bowl.

♥ To this bowl add the Korean pepper paste, soy sauce, sugar, and few dashes of sesame oil, and stir to combine.

♥ Put a wok or large, heavy-based frying pan on to heat and, when it's hot, add the 2 teaspoons peanut or other flavorless oil.

♥ Add the sliced corn (or beans) and scallions and stir-fry for 2 minutes.

♥ Add the drained squid and stir-fry for another minute or two, until the squid turns opaque.

♥ Tip your sauce into the hot pan, stir-fry for 30 seconds or so, until piping hot, and then divide between 2 bowls of the sushi rice.

FREEZE NOTE
Fresh squid can be cut into rings and frozen with the tentacles for up to 3 months, in a resealable bag with as much air as possible squeezed out. But first check with your fish seller or supermarket that the squid has not been previously frozen. Thaw overnight in the refrigerator, on a plate to catch drips.

75

Korean keema

Keema is a fantastically hangover-salving dish of spicy (usually lamb) gound meat; this version uses ground turkey and, more significantly, its heat is provided by the gochujang, the Korean chili paste that I keep on hand (see Korean Calamari **p.74**) to pep up a jaded palate or a pallid-flavored ingredient. Being ground does not generally do turkey many favors, but the aromatic richness of the paste makes it sing. Dinner's on the table in a matter of minutes; if you wanted to make it speedier, you would have to buy rice that's already been steamed and needs no more than a few turns in the microwave to heat it.

Serves 2, *generously*

1 cup basmati or sushi rice
8 ounces ground turkey
6 thin or 3 fat scallions, chopped
1 cup frozen petits pois or peas
1 teaspoon vegetable or peanut oil
2 tablespoons rice wine
1–2 tablespoons chopped fresh
  cilantro

for the sauce:
2 tablespoons gochujang
1 tablespoon honey
1 tablespoon rice wine
2 tablespoons soy sauce

♥ Cook the rice following the package instructions, or in a rice cooker following the manufacturer's instructions. And put a kettle on to boil for the peas later.

♥ Whisk together the sauce ingredients, and stir in the ground turkey. Leave to steep for about 5 minutes, or while you are getting on with your next tasks, such as chopping the scallions and blanching the peas.

♥ Heat a wok or heavy-based frying pan on the hob. While this is heating up, pour boiling water from the kettle over the frozen peas in a strainer or colander, letting the hot water drain away, thereby thawing the peas. When the wok is hot, add the oil, then the thawed peas and chopped scallions. Stir-fry for 3–4 minutes.

♥ Add the turkey and its sauce, and stir-fry for 4–5 minutes until cooked.

♥ Add the 2 tablespoons rice wine with ¼ cup water to swill out the residue of the sauce from the meat-steeping bowl (so that nothing is wasted) and scrape and pour this into the pan, and stir-fry for about 30 seconds until it's all piping hot.

♥ Serve over rice, and with a good scattering of chopped cilantro.

The peas can be thawed in advance and the onions chopped. The turkey can be tossed in the sauce about 1 hour ahead (no more because of salt in the soy and acid in the vinegar). Leftovers can be covered and refrigerated as quickly as possible, then reheated in a saucepan or microwave until piping hot – but peas and scallions will be more olive in color than vibrant green.

77

Sunshine soup

There was a British singing outfit in the Seventies called Instant Sunshine, and this is it in soup form. The silkiness comes from the bell peppers which are quickly blitzed in a hot oven, then blended with the corn which is cooked in broth. There's nothing more to it, and it is health-giving and mood-boosting – providing sunshine on a rainy day.

I like this smooth and velvety with nuggets of the corn running through it, though you can make it as liquidized or as rough as you please. As for the bell peppers: it wouldn't matter if you used 2 yellow or 2 orange.

Serves 4 *as a starter, or 2 as supper in its entirety*

1 yellow bell pepper
1 orange bell pepper
2 teaspoons garlic flavored oil

1 quart vegetable or chicken broth
  (good-quality canned, carton or
  cube), preferably organic
1 pound (3½ cups) frozen corn
salt and pepper, to taste

♥ Preheat the oven to 450°F and cover a smallish lipped baking sheet with aluminum foil.

♥ Remove the core, seeds, and white membrane from the bell peppers, then cut the peppers into strips and place on the prepared baking sheet shiny-side down. Sprinkle with the oil and smoosh them about so that all sides are a little covered by oil, then leave them, shiny-skin-side up this time. Roast them in the oven for 25 minutes.

♥ Pour the vegetable broth into a large saucepan and bring to a boil. Add the frozen corn, bring back to boil, reduce the heat, cover and let bubble for about 20 minutes.

♥ Using a perforated spoon, remove about 1 cup of corn, and set to one side while you blend the rest of the corn along with all its cooking liquid and the blistered bell peppers, then toss the set-aside corn niblets back into the blended, but not too smooth, soup, and season to taste.

MAKE AHEAD NOTE
The soup can be made up to 3 days ahead: transfer to non-metallic bowl, cool, cover and refrigerate as quickly as possible. Reheat gently in a saucepan, stirring occasionally, until piping hot.

FREEZE NOTE
The cooled soup can be frozen in airtight container for up to 3 months. Thaw overnight in the refrigerator and reheat as above.

78

Lone linguine with white truffle oil

When the nights are cold, and the season tempts me, I can find myself buying a precious white truffle: stored embedded in rice, it infuses everything before the rice is made into a risotto, with shavings of white truffle on top. What remains, I keep among some eggs and then turn them into ridiculously flamboyant but heavenly scented scrambled eggs or a quick tagliolini bound with soft egg, melted butter, and the remnants of my white truffle. These are all most properly enjoyed when shared – and I'm not suggesting you go out and splurge on a white truffle for this recipe – but when I'm eating alone and want to feel gorgeously spoiled and almost criminally indulgent, I make this, my lone linguine, doused in melted butter and egg, whisked with grated Parmesan and a few heady drops of white truffle oil.

Serves 1, *happily*

4 ounces linguine
salt, to taste
1 egg
3 tablespoons heavy cream

3 tablespoons grated Parmesan
  cheese
few drops white truffle oil, or to taste
freshly ground white pepper
1 tablespoon butter

♥ Put on some water to boil for the pasta and, when it comes to a boil, salt it generously before adding the linguine and cooking for 2 minutes less than directed by the instructions on the package.

♥ In a bowl, whisk the egg with the cream and Parmesan, a few drops of white truffle oil and a good grinding of white pepper.

♥ When the pasta's had the time you've allocated, check to see if it's al dente. Just before draining it, remove ½ cup of cooking liquid.

♥ Return the drained pasta to the cooking pan and, on the stove but off the heat, add the butter and about 1 tablespoon of the cooking water and stir to mix.

♥ Now, stir in the eggy mixture and keep stirring so that the pasta becomes smoothly, softly and lightly coated. Taste to see if it needs any salt or any more truffle oil and act accordingly.

♥ Decant into a warm bowl and eat alone, and thrillingly.

Vietnamese pork noodle soup

I couldn't contemplate a section of speedy suppers without a noodle soup. Nothing can give succor as fast as a bowl of noodles in flavorsome broth. This is good for chowing down and for slurping and for keeping body and soul together when your stomach's empty and your day's been full.

In extremis, I am more than happy to use frozen chopped gingerroot and chiles, which are kept in my freezer for just such an eventuality (not so infrequent).

Serves 2–4, *depending how hungry you are*

10 ounces pork tenderloin, cut into thin discs and then fine strips
2 tablespoons lime juice
2 tablespoons soy sauce
½ teaspoon paprika
2 tablespoons fish sauce
8 ounces ramen noodles
1 tablespoon garlic flavored oil
6 thin or 3 fat scallions, thinly sliced

1 tablespoon chopped fresh (or frozen) gingerroot
1 quart chicken broth (good-quality carton, can or cube is fine), preferably organic
3 cups (10 ounces) bean sprouts
2 small baby bok choy, torn into pieces
2 teaspoons chopped red or green chiles

♥ Put the strips of pork tenderloin into a bowl and add the lime juice, soy sauce, paprika and fish sauce, but don't let this stand for more than 15 minutes.

♥ Cook the noodles following the package instructions and then refresh in cold water. Heat the chicken broth until almost boiling.

♥ Heat a wok or a deep, heavy-based frying pan, then add the garlic flavored oil and fry the scallions and ginger for a minute or so. Add the pork and its liquid to the wok, stirring as you go.

♥ Cook the meat in the pan for another 2 minutes, then add the hot chicken broth to the pan and bring to a boil.

♥ Check that the pork is cooked through, then add the bean sprouts and baby bok choy. Add water if the soupy base has evaporated too much – about ½ cup of freshly boiled water should do the trick, but you may not need it.

♥ Arrange the drained noodles equally in 2 large or 4 small warmed bowls, ladle over them the pork and vegetables, and finally the soupy stock. Scatter the chopped chiles on top and serve.

EASY DOES IT

There is nothing anyone could ever say that is more effectively guaranteed to make me snap than "Relax!" The more soothingly it's uttered, the more I tense up. So, I need to be cautious now, as I know just how irritating it can be to have someone tell you to calm down and stop your worrying. I'm not – not quite – about to do that. First, I promise you, there's not a person alive who doesn't feel the odd twinge of pressure when guests are coming over for dinner. And, secondly, I think that recognizing the pressure points, so to speak, allows you to plot a path to avoid them.

I know, now, what to do so that having people over midweek feels like a pleasant change rather than a menacing threat. Of course, I have my slip-ups and my off-days, when I long for my bed and wonder why I ever issued the invitation, or I start marching around the place hissing officiously and taking plates down from shelves with almost teenage levels of aggressive stroppiness. But at least I can relax (yes, relax) in the knowledge that it's not the food or the cooking that will be giving me grief.

I'm not talking about formal dinner parties, here. But then, I'm never talking about formal dinner parties, anywhere. Still, I need to know that I can have a gaggle of friends over for supper, even when mired in the usual weekday farrago, in a way which makes me feel that life is something to ease into and enjoy. This isn't about cooking, but about living.

Of course, it helps if the cooking is easy, and I wouldn't have it any other way. Or, more accurately, *couldn't* have it any other way. Not possessing the skills of a chef, I don't expect you to have them, either. Besides, it really is important to remember you are not taking part in some sort of reality cooking show: there is no call for complicated recipes, swanky techniques, or bravely novel ingredients; your friends are not coming to pass judgment on your food, but to eat it.

And at home, in my kitchen, I choose to cook what suits me. Yes, I want to please others, but I can't do that if I'm making my own life hell. Some days that means I'll defrost some home-made turkey meatballs I had planned for the kids' supper and partner them with lemony couscous and arugula. On others, it could mean a Spanish Chicken, Greek Herb Sauce, Mexican Lasagne, Indian-rubbed Lamb, Irish Oaten Rolls: for me, the kitchen is a great place to travel in.

But above all, it must be a safe place to travel in. There's enough turbulence out of the kitchen, without inviting it inside. The recipes that follow in this chapter, for all that I give many of them far-flung exotic tags, are exactly what I want to cook when I need supper to be special but not stressful.

Irish oaten rolls

This started off as an oaty Irish soda bread, and may return to that again (see below), but I find that when I haven't much time to cook, yet want to make a dinner feel cozy and special, these rolls are just the thing. You can have no more than 20 minutes and get these whipped up and baked, spreading their sweet and welcoming scent throughout the house. They certainly imbue my frenetic urban hub of a kitchen with all the reassuring warmth of the farmstead hearth of my yearning imagination.

   If you can find good organic flour and oats, so much the better: it does make a difference. You can let standards slip with the ale: I keep any opened Guinness by for this, since I am so impatient I don't much like waiting for the froth at the top to die down when I'm measuring it out.

   The only drawback (and it may not necessarily be one) with the quick-summoned rolls is that they aren't in the oven for long enough to bake up much of a crust; if you have the time to spare, though, you can turn this into a loaf by forming it into one large round, and baking it for 10 minutes at 425°F before turning the oven down to 375°F and giving it another 25 minutes; when cooked, it'll give a faintly hollow sound if you knock with your knuckles against the underside.

   This bread, whether made to form 1 big loaf or 12 rolls, is perfect with everything, but most of all still warm with some good butter slowly melting on top. But you

have to hope that some is left over, as it's hard to beat, too, when cold and smeared thickly with butter and jam.

Makes 12 rolls

2⅔ cups whole wheat flour, preferably organic stoneground
1 cup quick-cooking oats (not instant), preferably organic, plus 2 teaspoons
1 teaspoon table salt

2 teaspoons baking soda
1¼ cups Guinness
⅔ cup buttermilk
¼ cup peanut oil or other vegetable oil
¼ cup honey

♥ Preheat the oven to 425°F.

♥ Line a cookie sheet with parchment paper.

♥ In a bowl, mix the flour, oats, salt, and baking soda.

♥ In a jug, mix the Guinness, buttermilk, oil, and honey. For ease, measure out the oil and then do ditto with the honey, as the oil lining will stop the honey from sticking to the cup measure. Stir the liquids together with a wooden spoon.

♥ Add the liquids to the dry ingredients and stir with the wooden spoon to combine – you will get a sandy oatmeal, rather than a dough: at first, it will seem too runny but then, as the baking soda goes to work, it will become first mousse-like and then heavy like damp sand.

♥ Pat into small handfuls to form 12 mounds on the lined cookie sheet; don't bother to shape them until all 12 are laid out and you can see which rolls need to have dough pinched off and which need to be bulked up, so that they are more or less of even size. When you've finished, pat each into a rough round roll shape about 3 inches diameter by 1–1¼ inches high.

♥ Sprinkle the remaining 2 teaspoons oats over the rolls (a fat pinch each) and pop them into the oven for 15 minutes then transfer, 1 by 1, to a wire rack to cool just a little. Eat warm, or leave to reach room temperature. Soda bread is always best eaten on the day of baking, though reheating or toasting can revive a roll or slice of bread a day or two later.

MAKE AHEAD NOTE
Best eaten on the day they are made but the rolls will keep for 1–2 days, wrapped in a clean kitchen towel in an airtight container in a cool place. Reheat in oven preheated to 350°F for 5–10 minutes (best for the day after making). The rolls can also be split in half and toasted (best for 2 days after baking).

FREEZE NOTE
The rolls can be frozen for up to 1 month in tightly sealed resealable bag. Thaw for 2–3 hours at room temperature and reheat as above. The rolls may be slightly crumbly after thawing.

87

Arugula and lemon couscous

This is what I add to turn a batch of everyday meatballs (see **p.44**) or, indeed, anything from lamb chops to a chicken stew into a spring-like, simple, and chic dinner. And, as elsewhere (see **p.119**), I take the quick couscous route, rather than any slow soaking and steaming.

Serves 4–6

3⅓ cups chicken or vegetable broth (carton, can or cube), preferably organic

3 tablespoons garlic flavored oil

2¾ cups couscous

zest and juice 1 lemon

4 scallions, thinly sliced

4 ounces (about 3 cups) arugula leaves

salt and pepper, to taste

♥ Heat the broth until boiling.

♥ Heat the oil in a medium saucepan that comes with a lid, then add the couscous and fry, stirring all the time, for about 2–3 minutes.

♥ Pour in the hot broth, still stirring, and keep stirring over a very gentle heat until the stock is absorbed into the couscous, about 5 minutes.

♥ Turn off the heat, leaving the pan where it is, with a tight-fitting lid, for another 10 minutes. (If you cook on gas, you could leave it on the lowest setting with a heat diffuser under the pan, if you have one.)

♥ Fork through the couscous, turning it out into a big bowl. Keep working the couscous with the fork to make it lump-free. Sprinkle in the lemon zest and juice, sliced scallions, and salt and pepper, to taste, before adding the arugula leaves and tossing together carefully to mix.

Indian-rubbed lamb chops
with butternut, arugula, and pine nut salad

There is something about the scented heat of the spices here that intensifies the tender sweetness of the lamb, and since you do no more than make a rapid rub, and the chops themselves need only scant cooking, this is as undemanding to cook as it is rewarding to eat. On top of that, the earthy fragrance, as you cook, gives you all the effects of a high-end spa's scented candle without the added expense. There's all upside here. With one proviso, that is: make sure you don't let my impatience rub off on you. Cook these choplets at too high a heat, and the air will be acrid and smoky rather than aromatic.

The butternut squash salad is not an obligatory accompaniment, but it is a fitting one, not least for its radiant Bollywood coloring. If it makes life easier, by all means cook the butternut cubes ahead, though make sure they're at room temperature before you assemble your salad. Between you, me and the gatepost, I wouldn't actually refrigerate them in the first place, but I am all too aware that food safety strictures would command me not to advise you to follow suit. Your call.

But if you're in a mad dash, then a salad made with colorful mixed leaves of any sort would be delicious; and be advised that you could make an even more rapid rub for the chops by simply mixing the salt specified below with 3 teaspoons of Madras curry powder.

Serves 4, *with the salad*

1 teaspoon ground cilantro
1 teaspoon ground cumin
1 teaspoon ground ginger
¼ teaspoon ground cloves
½ teaspoon cayenne pepper
½ teaspoon ground cinnamon

3 teaspoons kosher salt or 1½
  teaspoons table salt
12 small Frenched lamb rib chops
  or 8 larger lamb loin chops
2 tablespoons garlic flavored oil

♥ Measure out the spices into a wide, shallow dish along with the salt, and mix to combine.

♥ Dip the lamb chops into the spice mixture, dusting them well on all sides.

♥ Warm the oil in a frying pan, then fry the chops for about 2–3 minutes a side, depending on thickness, over medium heat. They should look darkly burnished – but still juicily pink within – when cooked.

The spice rub can be mixed together up to 1 month ahead. Store in airtight container or screwtop jar in a cool, dark place.

FURTHER NOTE
Leftover lamb can be stored in the refrigerator, tightly wrapped in aluminum foil, for up to 3 days, and can be frozen in an airtight container for up to 2 months.

93

Butternut, arugula, and pine nut salad

I know the whole bowl thing below sounds as though I am trying to save myself as much dishwashing as possible. While this is partly true, it is also the case that I can't bear to waste any of these glorious ingredients as I proceed.

Although I am happy to do the rubbing-cum-dusting for the chops with naked fingers, I feel vinyl disposable gloves (see **p.17**) are necessary for the salad. Too much unprotected handling of a butternut and I end up looking like I've got a 60-a-day habit, unfiltered at that.

1 butternut squash, approx. 2¼ pounds
1 teaspoon kosher salt or ½ teaspoon
  table salt
1 teaspoon ground turmeric
1 teaspoon ground ginger
2 tablespoons cold-pressed canola
  oil (see Kitchen Confidential, **p.16**)
  or olive oil, plus 2 tablespoons for
  dressing

⅓ cup golden raisins
¼ cup water, from a freshly boiled
  kettle
1 teaspoon sherry vinegar
4 ounces (about 3 cups) arugula
  and other salad leaves
⅓ cup pine nuts, toasted

♥ Preheat the oven to 400°F. Don't bother to peel, but halve and seed the butternut squash, cut into ½ inch thick slices, then cut each slice into four.

♥ Put the butternut pieces into a bowl with the salt, spices, and 2 tablespoons oil and smoosh them about, then tip into a lipped baking sheet (lined with aluminum foil). Don't clean the bowl yet.

♥ Cook the squash for 30–40 minutes. Check to see if it is cooked through by the time the ½ hour's up by piercing with a fork; some squashes cook faster than others.

♥ Add the golden raisins to the spice-smeared bowl and cover with the freshly boiled water; once cooled, whisk in the vinegar and the 2 tablespoons oil that remain.

♥ Put half of the salad leaves over a large plate or bowl and arrange the butternut pieces on top. Sprinkle with the remaining salad leaves and the toasted pine nuts. Scrape the raisin-studded dressing out of the bowl to dribble over it all, and toss gently before serving.

MAKE AHEAD NOTE
The butternut squash cubes can be roasted 1 day ahead. Cool completely, then cover and refrigerate until needed. Remove from the refrigerator about 1 hour before serving, to allow to come to room temperature.

94

Making leftovers right

It may well be that you end up with a wee bit of salad over. Frankly, you can eat this just as is (perhaps with a little lime juice spritzed over to freshen it up) or else cook some rice and stir this through just in time to warm through properly at the end of the cooking.

Spring chicken

This is really a tweaking of a fairly traditional rabbit recipe, and if you consider yourself something of a bunny boiler, then feel free to substitute rabbit pieces for the chicken thighs itemized here. The chicken is easier to come by in a grocery store, though, and more likely to please generally. You can leave the skin on or off the thighs, as you wish, but I think it's important that the bone be left in. This is just my preference (I think it boosts flavor), but bear in mind that this is a pretty easy-going recipe, and you could use thigh fillets if that's easier, or indeed – at the other end of the spectrum – a whole chicken, portioned.

If there is a proper dessert planned for afterwards I think 2 thighs each, while a modest portion, would not be a mean one; if you're planning a one-course dinner, I'd consider the 12 pieces a safer bet for 4 rather than for 6 people. And as for what you serve it with: I veer between rice and baby white-skinned potatoes (plain steamed in either case) and every now and again go for some other grain: spelt or barley or some such are all delicious for offering carbo-comfort and soaking up the flavorsome juices.

Serves 4–6

1 teaspoon vegetable oil
5 ounces (½ cup) cubed pancetta (Italian *cubetti di pancetta*) or lardons, or 10 slices bacon, chopped
12 chicken thighs (bone in, with or without skin), preferably organic
1 leek, cleaned, quartered lengthwise then thinly sliced
1 celery stalk, quartered lengthwise then thinly sliced
3 cloves garlic, peeled and chopped

2 teaspoons freeze-dried tarragon
1 teaspoon kosher salt or ½ teaspoon table salt
good grinding white pepper
2 cups dry hard cider
2⅓ cups frozen petits pois or peas
1 tablespoon Dijon mustard
1 small romaine lettuce heart, cut into strips or roughly shredded
2 tablespoons chopped fresh tarragon

♥ Heat the oil in a large, wide Dutch oven that comes with a lid (and can be taken to the table) and add the cubed pancetta (or lardons or bacon), cooking them until they begin to give off their juices and start to color.

♥ Add the chicken thighs (skin-side down if yours have skin), tossing the cubes of pancetta on top of the meat (to stop the pancetta burning and to make space) as you put the poultry in the pan, and cook for about 5 minutes over medium heat.

♥ Turn the thighs over and tip in the prepared leek, celery, and garlic. Season with the dried tarragon, salt, and pepper, then stir everything around a bit, letting it cook for another 5 minutes.

♥ Pour in the cider, then sprinkle in the frozen peas. Bring the pan to a boil, then cover, turn down to a very gentle heat, and cook for 40 minutes. Do check after 30, though, to see if the chicken is cooked through, and if you are disobeying me and going boneless, then 20 minutes should do it.

♥ Remove the lid, stir in the mustard, and then toss the shredded lettuce over the chicken, letting it wilt in the hot sauce for a couple of minutes.

♥ Scatter the chopped tarragon over the dish and take the steamily fragrant pan to the table with quiet pride.

MAKE AHEAD NOTE
The chicken, without lettuce, can be cooked 1 day ahead. Transfer to non-metallic bowl, then cool, cover, and refrigerate as quickly as possible. To reheat, return to Dutch oven, cover, and reheat gently, for around 20 minutes, until chicken is piping hot all way through. Add a little water or chicken broth if pan becomes too dry. Add the lettuce and continue as directed in recipe.

FREEZE NOTE
Cook and cool the chicken as above, then freeze in airtight container for up to 3 months. Thaw overnight in the refrigerator and reheat as above.

Making leftovers right

PASTA
SAUCE

If there are any leftovers, remove the bones from the chicken, shred the meat, and refrigerate as soon as possible. Reheat in a saucepan until piping hot and turn into a sauce for pasta, adding a little chicken broth, water, or some heavy cream as you reheat. Even if you have only a ladleful of cidery, bacony peas, it's worth keeping to reheat likewise. But do use up any leftovers within 2 days.

Spanish chicken with chorizo and potatoes

Much as I love to have a pan bubbling away on the stove, I often feel that the most stress-free way to feed people is by taking the oven route. When I'm frazzled, I firmly believe that a "tray-bake" is the safest way to go. Enjoy the easefulness of the oven: you just throw everything in, and you're done. I think I'd go to the supreme effort of laying on a green salad as well but, other than that, you may kick up your flamenco heels and enjoy the fiesta.

Serves 6

2 tablespoons regular olive oil
12 chicken thighs (bone in, with skin)
1¾ pounds chorizo sausages, whole if baby ones, or cut into 1½ inch chunks if regular-sized

2¼ pounds baby white-skinned potatoes, halved
2 red onions, peeled and roughly chopped
2 teaspoons dried oregano
grated zest 1 orange

♥ Preheat the oven to 425°F. Put the oil in the bottom of 2 shallow roasting pans or quarter sheet pans, 1 tablespoon in each. Rub the skin of the chicken in the oil, then turn skin-side up, 6 pieces in each pan.

♥ Divide the chorizo sausages and the baby potatoes between the 2 pans. Sprinkle the onion and the oregano over, then grate the orange zest over the contents of the 2 pans.

♥ Cook for 1 hour, but after 30 minutes, swap the top pan with the bottom pan in the oven and baste the contents with the orange-colored juices.

Making leftovers right

CHICKEN
QUESADILLAS

*You can reheat what remains (removing the bones from the chicken first) within 2 days, maybe with some canned diced tomatoes, sherry, and orange juice, but my absolute favorite final destination for this dish is a quesadilla. When I was last in Kansas City, that shining city of lights, I breakfasted on a chicken, pepperjack, and potato quesadilla (as one does) and it inspired me. So, just get as many soft flour tortillas as your leftovers command, take the bones out of the chicken, dice the meat along with the chorizo and potatoes, and stir in some diced, shredded, or grated cheese (Cheddar, mozzarella, Monterey Jack, all are possible), dollop some of the mixture into each tortilla, fold, then griddle or fry. Make sure the chicken is piping hot. And do see **p.433** for more in-depth instruction. This makes for a splendid hangover-banishing breakfast or near-instant dinner, the sort you chow down on while watching something compellingly bad on TV.*

Chicken with Greek herb sauce

This is, many years down the line, a variant of a recipe spawned in my first book and cooked regularly ever since. Cooking, too, follows the law of natural selection, and this version has evolved to become a fallback of choice. It is not widely different from the *Ur*-recipe but there are, chiefly, two things in its favor: one, it uses chicken thighs rather than breast, which cost, as I can't stop myself reiterating, about half the price but have twice the flavor; and they are cooked in the oven rather than on the stove.

And if there's time, light the oven earlier and give some baking potatoes 45 minutes to 1 hour before the chicken goes in. Yes, it's easy, but that's not all: I can't tell you how divine a baked potato is when heaped with this herb-flecked yogurt.

Serves 4–6

12 chicken thighs (bone in, with or
  without skin), preferably organic
juice 1 lemon
¼ cup regular olive oil
salt and pepper

for the Greek herb sauce:
2 cups plain Greek yogurt
4 fat or 6 thin scallions

1 green chile, seeded
1 clove garlic, peeled
½ cucumber (preferably English/
  hothouse), peeled and finely diced
3 tablespoons each chopped
  fresh cilantro and mint, or
  2 tablespoons each plus 2
  tablespoons dill
salt and pepper, to taste

♥ Preheat the oven to 400°F. Place the chicken thighs (skin-side up if yours have skin) in a shallow roasting pan or ovenproof dish, then pour the lemon juice and olive oil over them and season with a little salt and pepper.

♥ When the oven's up to heat, put the chicken in and roast for 45 minutes.

♥ Meanwhile, get on with the sauce. Tip the yogurt into a large mixing bowl and scissor in the scallions and the seeded chile, cutting both as finely as you can.

♥ Now mince the garlic into the yogurt and add the diced cucumber and most of the chopped herbs, reserving a little to sprinkle on top later. Mix all these ingredients together.

♥ Remove the chicken pieces from the oven, and transfer to a serving dish. Season the sauce to taste, then scrape it into a smaller bowl to serve, sprinkling the remaining herbs over the top, and put a spoon in the bowl for dollopping at the table.

Mexican lasagne
with avocado salsa

I feel I am careering about like some giddy traveler with Air Miles to spare here. The thing is, I cook instead of traveling – a kitchen rather than armchair tourist – and it's less tiring, so it stands to reason that I can cover more ground.

Still, the notion of a Mexican lasagne might seem a fantastic voyage too far; let me just say that here this is a shorthand for Mexican-inspired ingredients piled up in lasagne-like fashion – in other words, Tortilla Pie! In place of pasta layers, there are soft tortillas and in between them a riotous assembly of tomato, red bell pepper, onion, chiles, corn, and cheese.

I like to make a last-minute avocado salsa (see **p.107**), which is no more than a kind of unmushed guacamole, but it's an embellishment rather than a necessity.

You can see from the picture how snug the "lasagne" is in its dish. If you can totter toward the oven without spilling it, you're halfway there; but I advise you to put a cookie sheet or sheet pan in the oven as you preheat to catch any drips that might fall later.

And talking of later, one of the joys of this is that it reheats, by the slice, so wonderfully on the days that follow. So do think about cooking this even when you don't have so many to feed first time around.

105

Serves 8

for the sauce:
1 tablespoon garlic flavored oil
1 onion, peeled and chopped
1 red bell pepper, seeded and chopped
2 green chiles, chopped, with seeds
1 teaspoon kosher salt or ½ teaspoon table salt
2 tablespoons finely chopped cilantro stalks
2 x 14-ounce cans diced tomatoes, plus 1⅔ cups water to rinse out empty cans
1 tablespoon ketchup

for the filling:
2 x 15-ounce cans black beans, drained and rinsed
3¼ cups drained canned corn (from about 1½ x 15-ounce cans)
2½ cups grated mature goat's Cheddar, or cheese of your choice
8 soft flour tortillas (approx. 10 inch diameter)

1 x round ovenproof dish, approx. 10 inches diameter x 2¼ inches deep

♥ Preheat the oven to 400°F, slipping in a cookie sheet at the same time.
To make the sauce, heat the oil in a saucepan on the stove and fry the onion, bell pepper, and chiles. Add the salt and cook gently for 15 minutes and, once soft, add the chopped cilantro stalks.

EASY DOES IT | KITCHEN QUANDARIES

♥ Add the canned tomatoes, then rinse the cans out with water and add this too. Spoon in the ketchup and let things come to a simmer, leaving the sauce (or salsa, in keeping with the Mexican mojo) to cook while you get on with preparing the filling – about 10 minutes.

♥ **To make the filling**, mix the drained beans and canned corn in a bowl. Add most of the grated cheese, reserving some to sprinkle on the top at the end, and mix together.

♥ Start to assemble the lasagne by spooning about a third of the salsa into the bottom of your ovenproof dish and smearing it about, then layer on 2 tortillas so that they cover the sauce overlapping slightly, like a Venn diagram.

♥ Add a third of the beans and cheese mixture, covering the tortillas, and then about a quarter of the remaining salsa and another 2 tortillas.

♥ Repeat with another third of beans and cheese, and some more salsa before layering on another 2 tortillas.

♥ Finally, add the last layer of beans and cheese, nearly all of the remaining salsa, and cover with the last 2 tortillas. Spread the very last bit of salsa over the tortillas and sprinkle with the remaining cheese.

♥ Bake in the oven for 30 minutes, and let it rest for a good 10–15 minutes before slicing like a pizza, and eat with the avocado salsa opposite.

106

MAKE AHEAD NOTE
The lasagne can be assembled 1 day ahead. Cool the tomato salsa before assembling. Cover dish tightly with plastic wrap and refrigerate until needed. Bake as directed in recipe, allowing an extra 5–10 minutes' baking time and checking the lasagne is piping hot in center before removing from oven.

FREEZE NOTE
The assembled but uncooked lasagne can be frozen for up to 3 months. Wrap dish tightly in double layer of plastic wrap and a layer of aluminum foil. Thaw overnight in the refrigerator and cook as above.

FURTHER NOTE
Leftovers should be covered and refrigerated as soon as possible. To reheat, put individual slices in ovenproof dish, cover with foil, and reheat in oven preheated to 350°F for 15–20 minutes. Check that the lasagne is piping hot before serving. Wedges of leftover lasagne can be frozen for up to 2 months, tightly wrapped in plastic wrap and then either in foil or in a resealable bag. Thaw overnight in the refrigerator and reheat as above.

Avocado salsa

Now I've started salsa-ing, it seems I can't stop, but what I mean here is not so much a sauce as a pile of spice-puckering cubes. The vinegary heat from the pickled jalepeño peppers is perfect alongside the soft, smooth flesh of the avocado, and the combination sings with the melody of a mariachi band alongside the bean-pebbled, cheese-rich tortilla bake.

Serves 8, *as a condiment to eat with the Mexican lasagne*

2 avocados
1 scallion, thinly sliced
3 tablespoons chopped green
  jalapeños from a jar or can

salt, to taste
1 tablespoon lime juice
¼ cup roughly chopped fresh
  cilantro

♥ Halve the avocados, remove the pits, and then, using the tip of a sharp knife, cut lines down the flesh of each half, about ¼ inch apart, and then the same across.

♥ Turn the avocado halves inside out, or otherwise release the pale green cubes into a bowl, then tumble in the scallion, chopped jalapeños, salt to taste, lime juice, and most of the cilantro and toss gently to mix.

♥ Taste to see if more salt is needed before scattering with the remaining cilantro and taking to the table.

107

Tomato curry
with coconut rice

Not being a vegetarian, I have a rather indelicate lack of faith in meatless main courses; I worry all too readily about whether it's going to be filling enough. I suppose this is habit, which in turn is largely cultural conditioning, but, beyond that even, my fear is to do with balance: I need to feel sure that everything on the table provides a true marriage of tastes and textures; I can't abide the one-note meal. Here I'm happy: the acid brightness of the tomatoes is met with the sweetness of peas and the rich creaminess of the coconut rice, which is itself pricked with the sharpness of lime, while its Carrara-whiteness is punctuated by the gritty blackness of the seeds (not there just to satisfy culinary egomania).

Serves 4, *as a main course with the coconut rice that follows*

2 tablespoons cold-pressed canola oil (see Kitchen Confidential **p.16**) or regular olive oil

2 large onions (approx. 12 ounces total), peeled and chopped

1 teaspoon kosher salt or ½ teaspoon table salt

4 cloves garlic, peeled and chopped

3½ pints cherry or grape tomatoes, halved

2 teaspoons turmeric

1 teaspoon English mustard

1 teaspoon hot chili powder

1 teaspoon garam masala

1½ cups frozen peas

♥ Heat the oil in a wide Dutch oven or saucepan that comes with a lid, and add the chopped onions, sprinkling with salt, and stirring frequently as you cook them over a low to medium heat for about 7 minutes.

♥ Stir in the chopped garlic, then add the halved tomatoes, before stirring in the spices, and cook for 20 minutes with the lid on over a low heat.

♥ Cook the peas in another pan (in boiling salted water as usual), drain, and add to the tomato curry for the last 5 minutes' cooking time. By all means cook the peas directly in the tomato curry, but be prepared then to sacrifice both the vivid red of the tomatoes and the bright green of the peas.

MAKE AHEAD NOTE
The tomato base (not the peas) can be cooked 1 day ahead. Transfer to non-metallic bowl, then cool, cover, and refrigerate as quickly as possible. To reheat, return to saucepan and heat gently until piping hot. Cook and add peas as directed above.

FREEZE NOTE
Cook and cool the tomatoes as above, then freeze in airtight container for up to 3 months. Thaw overnight in the refrigerator and reheat, adding the peas, as above.

Coconut rice

Serves 4, *with the tomato curry above*

1 tablespoon garlic flavored oil	1 x 14-ounce can coconut milk
4 scallions, thinly sliced	2½ cups freshly boiled water
2 teaspoons nigella seeds or black mustard seeds	1 teaspoon kosher salt or ½ teaspoon table salt
1½ cups Thai or basmati rice	juice of 1 lime, or to taste

♥ Warm the oil in a heavy-based saucepan that has a lid, add the scallions and nigella seeds (or black mustard seeds) and cook for a minute or so, pushing this way and that with a wooden spoon.

♥ Stir in the rice, letting it get slicked with oil and thoroughly mixed with the black-dotted green shreds.

♥ Pour the coconut milk into a measuring jug and top up to the 4 cup (1 quart) mark with freshly boiled water, then add this to the rice, stirring it in with the salt.

♥ Bring to a boil, then turn the heat down to low and put on the lid. Cook for 15 minutes, by which time the rice should be cooked and the liquid absorbed.

♥ Fluff up with a fork as you pour in the lime juice, and taste to see if you need either more salt or more lime.

Quick calamari pasta

In one of my favorite parts of Tuscany, not the cypress-studded hills of Chianti, but by the coast, up a steep and squiggly lane behind Porto Santo Stefano, is a restaurant called La Fontanina. And there, I ate this, or rather its inspiration: a flat bowl of calamari-shaped pasta, almost indistinguishable – until that first tender bite – from the actual squid rings which, glistening with garlic-infused wine, comprised the sauce. I thought about this when I came back, but it wasn't until, in a favorite deli (some years on from that first sampling), I stumbled across a packet of pasta called "i calamari" – in a powder-blue paper packet, made by Voiello, shape no. 142 – that I determined to make it myself. It's silly really, as the heavenly taste doesn't rely on the culinary pun, but the delight we get from food is complex. The more universally stocked De Cecco range does have a mezzi rigatoni shape that would stand in respectably; and, of course, you are free to use any pasta shape – I sometimes feel a counter-intuitive pull toward fusilli.

Serves 4–6, *as a main meal*

1 pound pasta, as close to calamari-
  ring shape as possible
salt, to taste
1 pound baby squid (cleaned weight),
  sliced, tentacles left whole
2 tablespoons regular olive oil
4 scallions, thinly sliced

1 clove garlic, peeled
1 fresh chile, seeded and diced
½ cup dry white vermouth or
  white wine
¼ cup pasta cooking water
1 tablespoon unsalted butter
handful chopped parsley

♥ Put a large pan of water on to boil for the pasta. Once it is boiling, salt the water and add the pasta to cook following the package instructions. Then get on with your squid sauce.

♥ Cut the squid into approx. ½ inch rings. Heat the oil in a pan and fry the scallion for 1 minute, then grate in the garlic and add the chopped chile, stirring well.

♥ Add the squid rings and cook, stirring, for about 2 minutes. Pour in the vermouth (or white wine) and cook for another 2–3 minutes or until the squid is tender and the wine boiled down quite a bit. Lower in a cup measure to retrieve some water from the pasta pan and stir about ¼ cup into the squid pan along with the butter; it will look liquidy, but do not panic.

♥ Drain the pasta and add to the squid, tossing everything together well. Sprinkle with the parsley and work that through, then serve.

Clams with chorizo

Seafood, pork, and sherry: three ingredients, one fantastic but simple Spanish-inspired meal. I adore the plain sweetness of some steamed baby white-skinned potatoes alongside – each small, pebbly potato to be pronged by a fork and dipped into the headily aromatic liquid – but am happy, too, with nothing more than some bread to tear off and dunk into the rich juices.

Serves 2–4, *depending whether it's part of or a whole meal*

2¼ pounds clams
1 pound chorizo sausage, cut into
   fat coins

½ cup amontillado sherry
3 tablespoons snipped chives

♥ Put the clams to soak in a big bowl of cold water, or directly in the sink.

♥ Fry the sliced chorizo in a dry, large, cast-iron or heavy-based saucepan or wok that comes with a lid.

♥ Once the chorizo is colored a little and has given up some madly orange oil, remove the crisp coins to a piece of aluminum foil and wrap them up to keep them warm.

♥ Drain the clams – throwing away any that remain open or whose shells are broken – then add the closed clams to the layer of chorizo oil oozed in the pan. Turn the heat up high, splosh in the sherry, and clamp on the lid.

♥ Cook for 2–3 minutes, by which time the clams should have opened. Discard any that have not. Take the pan off the heat.

♥ Return the coins of chorizo to the pan with the chopped chives, and stir through.

Salmon and sushi rice
with hot, sweet and sour Asian sauce

This started off as Japanese-inspired, what with the sushi rice, the sake, and the mirin. But then it moved a little south-westerly, as I encompassed the notion of the Vietnamese dipping sauce, using – for fire – a Thai chile. I think we are altogether safer, then, to embrace this as pan-Asian, thanks to an impetus that is in part fridge-foray, in part fusion.

Perhaps because I've got a rice cooker (and see **p.8** for full apologia for its existence in my kitchen) I am always readily inclined to base dinner around a bowl or three of sushi rice (see, too, **p.18**). I adore its comforting stickiness and the way it offers itself up so sweetly to sharpness and heat and even – when the simplest of sauces feels like too much – just the deep saltiness of soy sauce. But for me, the true joy of this is that it is both filling and chilling (in the contemporary sense) at the same time.

Serves 4–6

2½ cups sushi rice
1 x 1 pound slab skinless salmon
    fillet (in one piece)
2 cloves garlic, peeled and minced
2 red or green chiles, finely chopped
2 tablespoons minced gingerroot
¼ cup fish sauce

2 tablespoons sake (Japanese rice
    wine)
2 tablespoons mirin (sweet
    Japanese rice wine)
2 tablespoons lime juice
2 tablespoons water

♥ Cook the rice following the package instructions, or to suit a rice cooker, if you're lucky enough to have one. The quantities may be reduced if you are 4 rather than 6.

♥ Sear the salmon on a flat griddle or frying pan for 4–5 minutes on one side over a medium heat, then turn it over and cook for 1 minute on the other side. The salmon should be just opaque and cooked in the center. Remove it to a large piece of aluminum foil and make a baggy package with tightly sealed edges to keep it warm.

♥ Mix all the other ingredients together, and put in a bowl to serve alongside the salmon and the cooked rice; then unwrap the fish and put it on a plate.

♥ I like to use small bowls, and let people flake the fish themselves onto their rice, before dribbling over it the chile-flecked sake sauce.

MAKE AHEAD NOTE
The sauce ingredients can be mixed together 1 day in advance. Store in a screw top jar in the refrigerator and shake well before using.

Lemony salmon with cherry tomato couscous

This is one of those recipes that is easier to follow than to write: that's to say, there are many bowls involved, which might make this look troublesome and fiddly, but the actual process involved is almost insultingly simple.

Now, I know that it is not strictly right to indicate that you cook couscous by pouring boiling water over it. In an ideal world, I accept, one should soak the grains in cold water before steaming them over hot, but I take the shortcut, and repeatedly (see also **p.90**), and I apologize to those whom I thereby offend.

Serves 4

heaping 1 cup couscous
3 teaspoons kosher salt or 1½
  teaspoons table salt
½ teaspoon paprika
1 tablespoon grated fresh gingerroot
1 cup freshly boiled water
½ small red onion, finely chopped
  (about ¼ cup)

zest and juice 1 lemon
1 tablespoon garlic flavored oil,
  plus 1 teaspoon
1 pint cherry or grape tomatoes
4 salmon fillets
¼ cup chopped fresh cilantro

♥ Put the couscous into a Pyrex or similar heatproof bowl, with 2 teaspoons kosher salt (or 1 teaspoon table salt), ¼ teaspoon of the paprika, and all the grated ginger. Give everything a bit of a mix before pouring over it the freshly boiled water. Cover the bowl, either with plastic wrap or a plate, and leave to one side.

♥ Into another bowl, put the finely chopped onion.

♥ Now get out a wide, shallow dish, big enough to take the salmon fillets later, and zest the lemon into it.

♥ Now, back to your onion bowl, and squeeze in the lemon juice.

♥ Over to the "zest" dish, and add the remaining salt and the paprika and stir in the 1 tablespoon garlic flavored oil.

♥ Halve the cherry or grape tomatoes and put them into yet another bowl; pour the extra teaspoon of garlic flavored oil over them, mix about a bit, then leave to one side.

♥ Heat a large frying pan for the salmon fillets. While the pan's getting hot, turn them, both sides, in the "zest" dish to coat them with the zest, paprika, and oily salt.

♥ Place the fillets in the hot pan and cook for 2–3 minutes a side – depending on thickness: you want these still juicy and a vivid coral color in the middle, so do check as you cook.

♥ Meanwhile, uncover and fluff up the couscous, which should have absorbed all the water, then tip the tomatoes with lemony onion, juice and all, into the couscous, mixing with a fork.

♥ Add nearly all the cilantro to the couscous, and stir it through, then taste for seasoning, adding more salt if you need to.

♥ Spoon some couscous onto each plate and place a salmon fillet alongside, sprinkling with a little more cilantro as you hand out each plate.

The salmoriglio solution, and other short sauces

It's always worth having up your sleeve some quickly got-together sauce or dressing that can turn a plain cooked chicken, chop, or fish into something special. Here are a trio of my favorites:

SALMORIGLIO SAUCE
This is a fantastically punchy herb-fragrant sauce that can be dribbled over plain grilled lamb chops or a breast of poached chicken, or used to enliven a fillet of flounder or salmon. And when you've got to the end of the bowl (I stash it in the refrigerator between servings), whisk in some more oil and make a glorious dressing for some steamed or tender boiled cauliflower.

Makes generous ¾ cup

2 garlic cloves, peeled
1 teaspoon kosher salt or ½ teaspoon table
  salt
small bunch oregano (approx 10 sprigs)

1 cup (lightly packed) Italian
  parsley leaves
¼ cup lemon juice
½ cup extra-virgin olive oil

♥ Put the peeled garlic cloves into a bowl with the salt, leaves stripped from the bunch of oregano, parsley leaves, and then the lemon juice.

♥ Process these ingredients to a paste, with a stick blender or in a processor, and then pour in the oil, blending until it emulsifies into a richly green, slightly runny pesto-like sauce.

MAKE AHEAD NOTE
The sauce will keep in the refrigerator in covered container for up to 1 week. Stir before use.

JUMBO CHILI SAUCE
This chili sauce is big – big flavor, big kick, big reward. The name, however, derives from the fact that the recipe was given to me by my brother-in-law, Jim–Jimbo to me, but often known as Jumbo due to his compact size.

    My son is completely addicted to this sauce, and I cannot have enough of it, either. I love it with shrimp, with cold chicken, with fries, with everything.

Makes scant 2 cups

1 x 12-ounce jar fire roasted red bell
  peppers
3 red or green chiles
1 small clove garlic, peeled
zest 1 lime and 1 tablespoon juice

3½ cups (lightly packed) cilantro
  leaves
2–3 teaspoons kosher salt or 1–1½
  teaspoons table salt, to taste
½ cup peanut or other flavorless oil

♥ Drain the jar of roasted bell peppers and put them into a food processor or into a bowl.

♥ Pick the stalks from the chiles, and seed them, wearing disposable gloves, if you don't like it really hot. Add to the processor or bowl.

♥ Tip in the garlic clove and lime zest and juice. Cut the stalks from the cilantro and add these, too. Process or whiz with a stick blender until paste-like.

♥ Add the cilantro leaves and salt and process or blend again, then pour the oil down the funnel of the processor as the motor is running, or pour the oil into your bowl and whiz again with a stick blender. It will make a sauce that is more liquid than a salsa, but soft and spoonable rather than a pouring sauce.

MAKE AHEAD NOTE
The sauce will keep in the refrigerator in covered container for up to 1 week. Stir or shake well before use.

122

PARSLEY PESTO

There are two main ways I eat this: one is dribbled over a quickly and simply fried fillet of turkey or chicken breast or to add edge to a roast sweet potato; the other is, as you might expect, as a sauce for pasta. And to eke it out at the end, I add a bit more oil and some lemon juice and use it to dress a romaine heart salad. It's also exquisite with broiled sardines, but I don't cook those often due to in-house complaints about the smell. If you have a garden and an outdoor grill, you're laughing.

For all that I use Italian flat-leaf parsley, I think of this rather as an English pesto: it smells to me like the country on a windy, sunny afternoon.

Makes 1⅓ cups

scant ½ cup grated Parmesan
   cheese
1½ cups parsley leaves
1 clove garlic, peeled

½ cup walnut pieces
1 cup extra-virgin olive oil
½ teaspoon kosher salt or ¼
   teaspoon table salt (optional)

♥ Put the Parmesan, parsley leaves, garlic, and walnuts into a processor and, with the motor running, slowly pour the oil down the funnel until the fragrant mixture has emulsified, or put the ingredients in a bowl and whiz with a stick blender, adding the oil as you go.

♥ Taste to see how much, if any, salt you want and duly add it, giving the sauce a quick final blitz.

MAKE AHEAD NOTE
The pesto will keep in the refrigerator in covered container for up to 1 week. Cover surface of pesto with a thin layer of oil to prevent pesto from turning too dark.

FREEZE NOTE
The pesto can be frozen for up to 3 months, preferably with a thin layer of oil covering surface. Thaw overnight in refrigerator before using.

124

And one more for luck

UNIVERSALLY USEFUL BLUE CHEESE DRESSING

I promised a trio of sauces, but I just had to get this in under the wire. If you like blue cheese – as I, swooningly, do – then know that this, dribbled over sliced, sweet tomatoes along with a torn-off log of baguette, is a perfect enough supper just as it is. And you can make a fabulously retro steakhouse-style starter, by cutting a head of iceberg lettuce into wedges and dribbling each crunchy wedge with this plus, perhaps, a scattering of crisp-fried bacon crumbles. And it makes a fabulous dressing to dribble over leftover rare roasted beef.

Makes 1 cup

6 ounces (1½ cups) crumbled blue
  cheese
1 teaspoon Worcestershire sauce
  (such as Lea & Perrins)
1 teaspoon steak sauce (such as A1)

⅓ cup buttermilk
3 tablespoons whole milk
1 teaspoon apple cider vinegar or
  good white wine vinegar or white
  balsamic vinegar

♥ Put the crumbled cheese into a bowl, add the Worcestershire sauce, steak sauce, buttermilk, milk, and the vinegar and mix gently until well combined. Thin if necessary with a little iced water. Chill until needed.

MAKE AHEAD NOTE
The dressing will keep for 3–4 days in covered container in the refrigerator – store in cold part of the refrigerator rather than in the door.

125

COOK IT BETTER

There are some things I say repeatedly to my children, indeed have done so over the years, and cannot seem to stop myself, even though I can see them rolling their eyes as I open my mouth to let out the first few well-worn words. "When I was a child, we only got presents at birthdays and Christmas" is one of the most-used phrases to roll off the mother-tongue; another is "You weren't allowed to talk back to your mother like that in my day." And as I write, I am rather embarrassed by the petulance I'm somehow unable to hear in my voice when I say these words out loud.

You may have some sympathy for my children, I realize, as it occurs to me that I probably have never written a book in which I don't at some stage, confess that "although I am extravagant, I am never wasteful." Reader, roll your eyes as you will, here comes that moment again. I don't wish to be a repetitive bore (and fear, perhaps with reason, turning into my paternal grandmother who seemed to have stories and anecdotes on a perpetual loop) but this mantra, if you like, is at the core of my cooking practice.

Of course it's a debatable point. There are people who would say that throwing away a stale loaf is less wasteful than adding milk, cream, chocolate chips, and so luxuriously on, before burning fuel to bake it into a pudding in the oven. While there is a case to be made – if a puritanical one – for cutting your losses in the kitchen, I am just not genetically programmed to throw food away. Have tried. Can't do it. But, anyway, this form of recycling, which is to say, turning the remnants of last week's shopping into this week's treat, seems to me to be at the very heart of what being a cook – as opposed to a chef – is all about.

Of course, I'm not saying that I'd expect to find time to make a banoffee cheesecake rise out of the sad ashes of a blackening bunch of bananas all that often, but when I do, the sense of glorious satisfaction that comes with it, the glow of simple, straightforward pleasure at just using something up, is quite as delicious as the cheesecake itself. This isn't smugness, though I admit it could be confused with it. It's an innocent joy, and one that brings calm and content, qualities not notably present in much of our daily lives.

And all this is by the by compared with the purely practical benefits. Why go shopping and spend money unnecessarily when a quick forage in the refrigerator can conjure up a comforting minestrone or casual-dinner-party-suitable South Indian Vegetable Curry? Banish the rationing legacy that lingers dourly around the notion of kitchen husbandry. This is modern make-do-and-mend cooking, which means Strawberry and Almond Crumble, Pear Pandowdy, and the exuberant flavors of Panzanella, that tomato-and-basil-kissed bread salad from Tuscany. I mean, really: it would be a waste not to…

Apple and cinnamon muffins

I know this sounds unnecessarily contentious, or just plain muddle-headed, but I feel that the enormous popularity of the muffin has done it a great disfavor. It's simply this: many people's notion of a muffin is the store or café-bought kind. Now, I would rather eat compacted sawdust than most of the muffins I see bulging menacingly from coffee-shop shelves. But I see muffins being bought and eaten, and presume they are passable: that's not quite my beef – to mix my foodstuff metaphors for a moment. The muffins that come from muffin-making factories are not the same as muffins that emanate from domestic ovens: the former are too tender-crumbed and too cartoonishly aerated. Thus, everyone who bakes muffins at home feels a failure for presenting something with a modestly domed (or even flatter) top.

That's not failure – that's a muffin, man. Nor should a muffin be merely an un-iced cupcake. I know sugar sells, but for food to be worthy of my consideration at breakfast, its sweetness must be tempered. This apple and cinnamon baby is a case in point. It's filling and fruity, and feels like something that ought to be a contradiction in terms: a wholesome treat. Spelt flour here provides a certain rough-hewn nuttiness – rather than the hessian weave of whole wheat – but if you can't find spelt flour or can't be bothered to look for it, know that regular all-purpose flour can be used in its stead. You'll simply end up with a lighter-crumbed creation.

You could make these any time you wish, but for me the prompt comes when I see a pair of apples wilting in my fruit bowl. A withered-skinned apple is distasteful on so many counts, least of which is that the only apples I like to eat are those so sharp and crunchy they almost hurt when you bite into them; the worst is that the vision of the fruit, with its sad, wrinkled skin, if not quite a memento mori, is certainly a pitiless reminder of time's ravages. Some people see eternity in a grain of sand; I see the fragility of a finite life in a fruit bowl – it's not good. But pah! What do I care, when there's food to be eaten? And apples long past their prime make for magnificent muffins. What's more, unlike your usual muffin, these taste good cold and old (well, a day or two) as well.

Makes 12

2 apples
1¾ cups spelt flour (or use all-
  purpose flour)
2 teaspoons baking powder
2 teaspoons ground cinnamon
⅔ cup (packed) light brown sugar,
  plus 4 teaspoons for sprinkling
½ cup honey

¼ cup plain yogurt
½ cup flavorless vegetable oil
2 eggs
½ cup raw (unblanched) almonds

1 x 12-cup muffin pan

♥ Preheat the oven to 400°F and line your muffin pan with paper muffin cups.

♥ Peel and core the apples, then chop into small dice (about ¼ inch, but please don't measure) and put them to one side.

♥ Measure the flour, baking powder, and 1 teaspoon of the ground cinnamon into a bowl.

♥ Whisk together the ⅔ cup brown sugar, the honey, yogurt, vegetable oil, and eggs in another bowl or pitcher.

♥ Chop the almonds roughly and add half of them to the flour mixture, and put the other half into a small bowl with the second teaspoon of ground cinnamon and the 4 extra teaspoons brown sugar. This will make the topping for the muffins.

♥ Now fold the wet ingredients into the dry. Add the chopped apple, and stir to combine but don't over mix. To remind you: a lumpy batter makes for a lighter muffin.

♥ Spoon this bumpy batter into the paper cups, then sprinkle the rubbly topping mixture over them.

♥ Pop the pan into the preheated oven, and bake for about 20 minutes, by which time they will have risen and become golden.

♥ Take the pan out of the oven and let it stand for about 5 minutes before gingerly taking out the muffins and placing them on a wire cooling rack.

MAKE AHEAD NOTE
The night before, you can measure out dry ingredients into a bowl, and mix liquid ingredients, and leave them covered in the refrigerator overnight. In the morning, prepare and dice apples, chop almonds and proceed with fifth step and recipe as above. Best eaten on day of making but muffins can be baked up to 1 day ahead and stored in airtight container, layered with parchment paper. Reheat in warm oven for 5–8 minutes before serving. Will keep for 2–3 days.

FREEZE NOTE
The muffins can be frozen in airtight container, layered with baking parchment, for up to 2 months. Thaw for 3–4 hours on wire rack at room temperature and reheat as above.

Strawberry and almond crumble

If I'd had to choose one thing that cooking could not make better, I'd have put good money on its being a bad (as in unripe and tasteless) strawberry. I'd be embarrassed even to own up to trying to improve it, were it not for the fact that I read an article by Simon Hopkinson, a revered British chef, in which he advised using said strawberries in a pie. So I did. Well, that's not quite true: I am lazier than he is, so I made a crumble. I don't know what, how, or why it happened, but this is a crumble of dreams. The oven doesn't, as you'd think, turn the berries into a red-tinted mush of slime, but into berry-intense bursts of tender juiciness. This is nothing short of alchemy: you take the vilest, crunchiest supermarket strawberries, top them with an almondy, buttery rubble, bake, and turn them on a cold day into the taste of English summer. Naturally, serve with lashings of cream: I regard this is as obligatory, not optional.

Serves 6

1 pound strawberries, hulled
¼ cup sugar
¼ cup almond meal/flour
4 teaspoons vanilla extract

for the topping:
heaping ⅔ cup all-purpose flour
1 teaspoon baking powder

5 tablespoons cold butter, diced
1¼ cups sliced almonds
scant ½ cup turbinado sugar
heavy cream, to serve

1 x ovenproof pie dish approx.
 8 inches diameter x 2 inches deep
 (approx. 1¼ quarts capacity)

❤ Preheat the oven to 400°F. Put the hulled strawberries into your pie dish (I use a round one) and sprinkle over them the sugar, almond meal, and vanilla extract. Give the dish a good shake or two to mix the ingredients.

❤ Now for the crumble topping: put the flour and baking powder in a mixing bowl and rub in the cold, diced butter between thumb and fingers (or in a freestanding mixer). When you've finished, it should resemble rough, pale oatmeal. Stir in the sliced almonds and turbinado sugar with a fork.

❤ Tip this over the strawberry mixture, covering the strawberries in an even layer and giving a bit of a press in at the edges of the dish. Set the dish on a cookie sheet and bake in the oven for 30 minutes, by which time the crumble topping will have darkened to a pale gold and some pink-red juices will be seeping and bubbling out at the edges.

♥ Let stand for 10 minutes before serving, and be sure to put a pitcher of chilled heavy cream on the table alongside.

MAKE AHEAD NOTE
The crumble can be assembled 1 day ahead. Cover with plastic wrap and store in the refrigerator until needed. Bake as directed in recipe, but allowing extra 5–10 minutes' cooking time, and check crumble is piping hot in the center.

FREEZE NOTE
Crumble topping can be made and frozen in resealable plastic bags, for up to 3 months. Sprinkle topping direct from freezer over fruit, breaking up large lumps with your hands. The assembled but unbaked crumble can be frozen, wrapped in a double layer of plastic wrap and a layer of aluminum foil, for up to 3 months. Thaw for 24 hours in the refrigerator and bake as above.

132

Banoffee cheesecake

I could write a whole book of banana recipes, so often do I end up with a black claw of softening fruit beckoning from the corner of the kitchen. Toss them away? Never. I can't cope with the waste, even if what I tend to do is throw expensive ingredients at them to come up with ever more lavish ways not to discard them. Some of those recipes are dotted throughout my other books, but I have managed to restrain myself here, and I like that challenge: using up food isn't dreary and merely thrifty; it can feel like the most liberating, inspiring way of cooking. And I love the way a handful of mournfully overripe, positively unprepossessing bananas have given rise to this vulgarly triumphant cha-cha-cha of a cheesecake. Well, it is a cheesecake, but the texture is not the usual smooth – sometimes cloying or even palate-cleaving – cream; rather, it is aerated and moussy and as light as its perfume is, contrariwise, compellingly heady.

You can make the caramel (to us Brits, toffee) sauce while the cheesecake is cooking or cooling. Either way, you want the sauce completely cold, but it shouldn't go into the refrigerator; it will come to no harm sitting out, covered, overnight, or for a couple of days in a cool place. The cheesecake is a different matter: it needs the overnight stay in the refrigerator, and longer won't hurt it.

When you make this, do ensure that the cream cheese is at room temperature before you start whisking or processing it. If it starts off cold, it will never – whisk it or blitz it as wildly as you will – cook to the requisite lusciousness.

Serves 10

for the base:
18 sheets graham crackers (2½ cups crumbs)
6 tablespoons soft unsalted butter

for the cheesecake:
4 overripe medium-sized bananas
¼ cup lemon juice
3 x 8-ounce bars cream cheese, at room temperature
6 eggs

¾ cup (packed) plus 1 tablespoon light brown sugar

for the caramel sauce:
7 tablespoons soft unsalted butter
½ cup golden syrup (such as Lyle's)
⅓ cup light brown sugar

1 x 9-inch springform cake pan
1 x roasting pan, for water bath

♥ Preheat the oven to 325°F and put a full kettle on to boil. Wrap the outside (underneath and sides) of your springform pan with a double layer of plastic wrap, then cover that thoroughly with a double layer of aluminum foil. The idea is to give a good waterproof casing to protect the cheesecake as it bakes in its water-bath later.

♥ Process the graham crackers with the butter until you have a sandy rubble that is beginning to clump, and press into the bottom of the prepared pan. Set this in the refrigerator and clean out the processor, making sure you have no crumbage left whatsoever.

♥ Mash the bananas well with a fork, add the lemon juice, and set aside for a moment.

♥ Process the cream cheese until smooth, then add the eggs and sugar. Last of all, add the mashed bananas and lemon juice, processing until you have a smooth mixture.

♥ Take out of the refrigerator the well-wrapped, cracker-lined springform pan, sit it in the center of a roasting pan, and pour the cheesecake filling into your springform.

♥ Now put the roasting pan and springform into the oven and pour the recently boiled water into the roasting pan so that it comes halfway up the springform. Cook for 1 hour and 10 minutes, checking after 1 hour. The very center of the cheesecake should still have a hint of a wobble, but should seem set on top.

♥ Remove from the oven and, still wearing your oven mitts, take the springform out of the water bath and place on a cooling rack. Gently and carefully peel away the outside layers of plastic wrap and foil, and let the cheesecake continue cooling on the rack.

♥ Put the cheesecake into the refrigerator but don't cover it till it's fully chilled, then leave overnight – and remember to remove it from the refrigerator about ½ hour before you want to eat it.

♥ To make the sauce, melt the butter with the golden syrup and sugar in a saucepan over a gentle heat until everything comes to a bubble, then let it bubble, keeping an eye on it, for 1–2 minutes. It will be a foamy, amber mixture like liquid honeycomb. Then let it cool slightly before pouring into a small pitcher and leaving to cool further; it will thicken as it cools.

♥ To help unmold the cheesecake, work a thin, flexible spatula around the top edge, before unspringing from the pan, then put it on a serving plate, preferably one with a lip. Whisk the caramel sauce in the pitcher and drizzle some over the cheesecake, leaving the rest for people to add greedily as they eat.

MAKE AHEAD NOTE
Make the cheesecake up to 2 days ahead and cool as directed. Cover when completely cold, with a plate or plastic wrap, making sure that covering does not touch surface of cheesecake. Unmold and serve as directed in recipe. The sauce can be made 2–3 days ahead and kept in an airtight container in cool place. It can also be covered and kept in the refrigerator for up to 1 month.

Coconut and cherry banana bread

The title of this cake conjures up something much gaudier than is actually the case. The cherries – which could indeed have been candied – are dried, and the banana bakes to make for a slightly drab, manila-tinted sponge. To look at, I'll grant you, this is not a joyous creation, but its damp and luscious taste is all the more heightened for being unforeseen. I like that. Those who look at life rather than taking a bite out of it are not deserving of the pleasures they deny themselves.

Cuts into 10–12 slices

1 stick plus 1 tablespoon (9
  tablespoons) soft unsalted butter,
  plus some for greasing
4 small–medium bananas (approx.
  1 pound with skin on)
¾ cup superfine sugar
2 eggs
1 cup plus 2 tablespoons all-
  purpose flour

2 teaspoons baking powder
½ teaspoon baking soda
⅔ cup dried cherries
1⅓ cups unsweetened shredded
  coconut

1 x 2-pound loaf pan

♥ Preheat the oven to 325°F. Put a paper loaf liner into your pan, or line the bottom of the pan with parchment paper and grease the sides.

♥ Melt the butter in a saucepan, and take it off the heat. Peel and mash the bananas in another bowl.

♥ Beat the sugar into the cooled, melted butter, then beat in the mashed bananas and the eggs. Fold in the flour, baking powder, and baking soda. Finally, add the dried cherries and shredded coconut.

♥ Fold well so that everything is incorporated, then pour and scrape into the lined loaf pan and smooth the top.

♥ Bake for about 50 minutes, but start checking after 45. When ready, the bread will be coming away from the sides of the pan and feel quite heartily bouncy on top.

♥ Once out of the oven, leave it in the pan for 10 minutes. Then carefully slip the cake out of the pan (still in the liner) onto a wire rack to cool.

MAKE AHEAD NOTE
The loaf can be made 2 days ahead. Wrap in parchment paper and store in airtight container. Will keep for 3–4 days in cool place.

FREEZE NOTE
The loaf can be frozen, tightly wrapped in double layer of plastic wrap and a layer of aluminum foil, for up to 3 months. Thaw overnight at room temperature.

NOTE
Unsweetened shredded coconut can often be found in health food stores.

Chocolate banana muffins

I think of muffins as a treaty weekend breakfast, but these look so darkly elegant, especially in their matching dark-brown, tulip-skirted party frocks, that they positively beg to be brought out with coffee after dinner.

Certainly, while most muffins are at their best pretty well straight out of the oven, the bananas in the mixture make sure these beauties keep their moist, eat-me texture long after those less favored have staled and lost their allure.

Makes 12

3 very ripe or overripe bananas
½ cup vegetable oil
2 eggs
½ cup (packed) light brown sugar
1½ cups all-purpose flour

3 tablespoons best-quality
  unsweetened cocoa powder, sifted
1 teaspoon baking soda

1 x 12-cup muffin pan

♥ Preheat the oven to 400°F and line a muffin pan with paper muffin cups. Don't worry about getting special ones: regular paper muffin cups will do the job. Mash the bananas by hand or with a freestanding mixer.

♥ Still beating and mashing, add the oil followed by the eggs and sugar.

♥ Mix the flour, cocoa powder, and baking soda together and add this mixture, beating gently, to the banana mixture, then spoon it into the prepared papers.

♥ Bake in the preheated oven for 15–20 minutes, by which time the muffins should be dark, rounded, and peeking proudly out of their paper cups. Let cool slightly in their pan before removing to a wire rack.

MAKE AHEAD NOTE
Make the muffins up to 1 day ahead. Store in airtight container, layered with baking parchment. Reheat in warm oven for 5–8 minutes. Will keep for 2–3 days in airtight container in cool place.

FREEZE NOTE
The muffins can be frozen in airtight container, layered with baking parchment, for up to 2 months. Thaw for 3–4 hours on wire rack at room temperature and reheat as above.

Cinnamon plums with French toast

This is a doubly gratifying recipe for the waste-averse: this French toast (a slightly fancier take on the simple breakfast dish of my childhood) is made with the remains of a loaf otherwise too stale to eat and the cranberry-sharp, cinnamon-scented compote uses up plums that were bought more in the spirit of optimism than good sense. If the weight of plums seems a lot for what is a using-up recipe, it is because the plums I first used for this were as big and shiny as billiard balls, and about as hard (if this is the kind of animal you're dealing with, too, then quarter rather than halve the fruits to poach them); and if you're lucky enough to have a plum tree, this would gratifyingly use up a glut.

While I love the scarlet-fleshed plums, which the cranberry juice glowingly enhances, any plum will do, and you could go for apple juice were you wanting a less sherbetty-sharp edge to the poached fruit's juices.

Similarly, do not think you should consider this compote only to go with the French toast: eat with Greek yogurt or granola at breakfast, with crème anglaise for a weekend-lunch dessert, with the Guinness Gingerbread (**p.305**) or, frankly, any time.

Serves 4, *with compote to spare*

for the plums:
1 cup sweetened cranberry juice
½ cup sugar

1 cinnamon stick
1 pound plums

♥ Put the cranberry juice and sugar into a wide saucepan and stir to help start dissolving the sugar. Then put the saucepan over a low heat until the sugar dissolves entirely.

♥ Halve the plums and remove the pits, then halve them again if they are big brutes.

♥ Once the sugar's dissolved into the red liquid, add the cinnamon stick, then turn the heat up, bring to a boil and let the pan bubble away for a couple of minutes until the mixture is on the way to becoming syrupy.

♥ Now turn the syrup down to a simmer and add the plum halves or quarters and cook them gently for about 10 minutes, although note that this is based on starting off with viciously unripe fruits, so you might need less time.

♥ Once the plums are tender but not disintegrating, remove the pan from the heat, cover, and leave to keep warm. You can make the plums in advance and either serve them at room temperature with the French toast, or warm them up again.

for the French toast:
2 eggs
¼ cup whole milk
½ teaspoon ground cinnamon
1 tablespoon sugar
4 large slices stale white bread
2 tablespoons soft unsalted butter

♥ Whisk together the eggs, milk, ground cinnamon, and sugar in a pie dish.

♥ Sit 2 pieces of bread in the eggy mixture, turning after each side has soaked up enough to color the bread yellow, so that it absorbs the liquid but doesn't fall to pieces.

♥ Melt half the butter in a frying pan and cook the 2 soaked pieces of bread for a couple of minutes each side. Transfer the yellow, eggy bread, scorched golden in parts, to warm waiting plates. Meanwhile, soak the next 2 slices.

♥ Melt the remaining butter to cook the last 2 slices in the same way.

♥ Serve alongside the beautiful scarlet plum compote.

MAKE AHEAD NOTE
The compote can be made 1 day ahead. Transfer to bowl to cool, then cover and refrigerate. Warm the compote gently in saucepan before serving.

FREEZE NOTE
Cooled compote can be frozen in airtight container for up to 3 months. Thaw overnight in the refrigerator and reheat as above.

Chocolate chip bread pudding

There are no versions of bread pudding I don't like, though the British variants – the one that uses stale bread as a bolstering filler in a squishy fruit loaf and the other, a milky-custard baked pile-up of buttery sandwiches – have obvious nostalgic appeal. This is my American-inspired take on it, one in which the staled bread is simply cubed before being drenched in an egg custard then softly baked. Well, that's the basic dish: this is fancier but not fussily so – still, the addition of chocolate chips, rum, and heavy cream do make quite a triumph of turning stale bread into a dinner party treat. Think of it as the food equivalent of wearing a party dress that is actually comfortable: a rare but precious pleasure.

Note: I tend to freeze stale bread in bags of crumbs or cubes and save them to use as needed.

Serves 4–6

9 ounces stale bread, cut into 1 inch cubes (approx. 5½ cups cubes)
½ cup bittersweet chocolate chips
3 eggs
3 tablespoons light brown sugar
2 tablespoons dark rum
½ cup heavy cream

2 cups whole milk
4 teaspoons turbinado sugar

1 x ovenproof dish approx. 9 inches diameter x 2½ inches deep (approx. 1½ quarts capacity)

♥ Preheat the oven to 325°F. Grease a round pie dish lightly with butter. Tip in the stale bread cubes; if your bread isn't stale, then leave slices to dry first, for a while, on a wire rack before cubing and using.

♥ Toss in the chocolate chips to spread evenly among the bread cubes.

♥ Whisk together the eggs, light brown sugar, rum, heavy cream, and milk. Pour this mixture over the bread and press the cubes down to coat them in the liquid.

♥ Leave all this to soak for 20 minutes, then sprinkle with the turbinado sugar and put straight into the oven for 40–50 minutes. If your oven browns unevenly, turn the dish around halfway through cooking.

♥ Let the dish stand for a while before serving – if you can. The smell as it bakes is almost overwhelming, and it can be hard to wait once it is out of the oven.

Assemble bread pudding 1 day ahead, but don't sprinkle with the turbinado sugar. Cover and keep in the refrigerator. Remove from the refrigerator and leave at room temperature for 15 minutes, then sprinkle with the turbinado sugar and bake as directed in recipe.

143

Pear pandowdy

A pandowdy is one of those wonderful American down-home terms for a kind of pie that is ramshackle and homespun, and this is something I am always happy to live down to. It is, I'm afraid, all too easy to find that one's bought pears are never at the right point to be pleasurably eaten, and this made-in-the-pan pie, with its loose draping of unfancy dough, is better than they deserve. I bolster these fortune-favored pears with a couple of apples – cooking is the only good use for a Golden Delicious in the grown-up world, anyway – but a plain apple pandowdy, which dispenses with the pears and doubles the apples, is a fine thing, too. Indeed, many a fruit can profitably be considered here, though keep to the appley base if you're thinking of including any berries or fruit that could get too mushy or watery when heat hits them.

Serves 6

4 Bartlett pears
2 Golden Delicious apples
3 tablespoons soft unsalted butter
¼ cup sugar, plus ½ teaspoon for
  sprinkling
finely grated zest 1 lemon

for the pastry:
1½ cups all-purpose flour, plus
  extra for dusting

pinch salt
5 tablespoons very cold butter, cut
  into ½-inch cubes
2 tablespoons cold vegetable
  shortening
½ cup cold whole milk
heavy cream, to serve (optional)

1 x cast iron skillet or ovenproof
  frying pan, 9 or 10 inches
  diameter

♥ Preheat the oven to 400°F.

♥ Peel the pears and apples, then quarter them, slice out the cores, and cut the pears into ¾ inch pieces and the apples into ½ inch pieces, dropping them into a bowl as you go.

♥ Using a skillet or frying pan that can go into the oven later, melt the 3 tablespoons soft butter over a medium heat, then add the diced fruit, sugar, and lemon zest, and cook over a lowish heat, stirring occasionally, for 10 minutes, by which time some of the fruit will have begun to caramelize gently. Take off the heat while you get on with the pastry.

♥ Put the flour and salt into the bowl of a **freestanding mixer** fitted with the flat paddle, add the very cold cubed butter and, using a teaspoon, drop in little lumps of cold shortening, then slowly mix to cut the fat into the flour; or just do this **by hand**.

♥ Still with the motor running, and the paddle turning slowly, add the milk a little at a time, just so that the dough binds, then remove from the bowl, squish it together with your hands, and drop it onto a lightly floured surface ready to roll out.

♥ Bring the pan of cooked fruit nearby (but not so near as to warm the dough), and roll out the dough until you have a rough circle about the diameter of the skillet. Drop the dough circle on top of the fruit, tucking in the edges a bit, and remember that the ramshackle look of this is the whole point. Make 3 slashes with the tip of a sharp knife, sprinkle with ½ teaspoon of sugar, and put in the oven for 25 minutes, by which time the white dough will have turned into a pale golden crust.

♥ Remember that the handle will be searingly hot, so transfer carefully to the table, and preferably cover the handle. Serve with heavy cream.

MAKE AHEAD NOTE
The pie can be assembled up to 2 days in advance. Make sure fruit and skillet have fully cooled before adding dough topping. Cover with plastic wrap and refrigerate. Bake as directed in recipe, allowing an extra 10–15 minutes' cooking time. Check filling is piping hot before removing from oven (stick a metal skewer or tip of small knife into the pie through one of the steam vents – it should feel hot to touch).

FREEZE NOTE
The filling and pastry can be made 1 month ahead. Freeze filling in an airtight container, and wrap pastry in a double layer of plastic wrap and then in a resealable bag. Thaw overnight in the refrigerator. Take dough out of the refrigerator about 30 minutes before rolling. Assemble pie and bake as in recipe, allowing extra 10 minutes' cooking time.

145

Panzanella

Panzanella, which sounds as though it should be the name of the beautiful heroine in a ballet or a fairy tale, is the word for a damp and tomatoey bread salad from Italy, which I first came across when I lived in Tuscany; and very useful it was too for finding a happy end to the brief life of that strangely unsalted, blink-and-it's-stale bread. But then, as anyone who has ever made their own bread (even once) knows, the fact that store-bought bread doesn't stale quickly is just plain spooky.

I have come across versions of this in which we, the hapless cooks, are instructed to cut off the crusts of the bread before using. I ignore such affectations (or imbecility, however you like to construe the request), as the whole point of the recipe is to use up bread – why would you throw half of it away before even starting? Still, I know that, as with many peasant dishes, this has become an upmarket restaurant favorite, so I do understand where the fiddliness might come in. And I don't want to sound too lofty: it's not so much that I find it intrinsically wrong to remove the crusts from the bread, I am just far, far too lazy.

My son Bruno loves this so much that I have been known to buy bread especially to make it at the beginning of a weekend. This is not quite as pathetic as it sounds (I hope) as even a mega-bowlful, made with an entire new Pugliese loaf (cut and made to stale perversely on purpose) doesn't last long in a house with teenage boys. But, truly, it is most satisfying to make when using up bread actually to hand. To be sure, you still have to go out and get a kingdom of fresh basil, but I feel better about the fact that the recipe is not just a good way of using bread past its bouncy best, but also a jubilant end for a handful of tomatoes so old they're moving beyond ripeness and towards skin-splitting, fuzzy-fleshed maturity.

Serves about 4, *as an accompaniment*

9 ounces staled Italian-style bread, cut into ¾ inch cubes or torn and crumbled into pieces (approx. 5½ cups cubes)
1 small red onion, cut into thin half-moons or finely chopped
¼ cup red wine vinegar
1 pound good ripe tomatoes
½ clove garlic
2 teaspoons kosher salt or 1 teaspoon table salt
pinch superfine sugar
½ cup extra-virgin olive oil
large bunch basil

♥ Sit the cubed bread on a wire cooling rack to keep dry.

♥ Put the half-mooned or chopped onion into a large bowl, big enough to take all the remaining ingredients later, pour the red wine vinegar over it, and leave to steep for at least 10 minutes.

♥ While the onion's steeping, put the tomatoes in a large bowl and pour boiling water over from a kettle to cover them, leaving for 5 minutes.

♥ Grate or mince some garlic over the vinegar and onions. I tend to use 1 clove, but stop when I'm about halfway through.

♥ Drain the tomatoes, then peel, remove the seeds and chop up the flesh, scraping it into the vinegar and onion bowl as you go. (There are times I don't bother with blanching and peeling the tomatoes, but I always get rid of the seeds.)

♥ Add the salt and a pinch of sugar, then tear or crumb the bread into the bowl. Pour the oil over it and add half the basil leaves. Using your hands (wearing a pair of disposable vinyl gloves if your skin is sensitive), toss and mix everything to combine.

♥ Ideally, you should leave this overnight to steep and mellow. If so, leave the remaining basil leaves and stalks on top, then cover with plastic wrap; if serving straightaway, add the remaining basil leaves and check for seasoning.

MAKE AHEAD NOTE
Make the salad up to 1 day ahead, cover, and refrigerate. Remove from the refrigerator about an hour before serving, to let come to room temperature. Toss in reserved basil leaves just before serving.

150

Minestrone

This is a wonderful Monday night supper, easily made after some foraging in the refrigerator. Any vegetable soup is a great way of transforming the odd leek or zucchini a little past its prime along with any other bits and pieces that are not plentiful enough to be of use alone, but this Italianate version is my favorite. It is worth noting here, too, that should you have a random collection of pasta, each sort not quite enough to yield a serving, then you can bung them all in a resealable bag and beat them briefly but brutally with a rolling pin, so that you have a home-made *pastina mista* to throw in soup when you need it. And whenever you come to the end of a piece of Parmesan, put the rind in a freezer bag, freeze it, and leave it (up to 3 months) until you're making soup, in which case you can add it, unthawed, to the pot to imbue the minestrone as it cooks with its savory intensity too.

I find that the fresh vegetable and pasta are filling enough, but if you need to bulk the soup up, do add a drained can of pulses or some frozen vegetables, as you need or have. Obviously, I don't expect you to have exactly the same vegetables left over at the end of the weekend, or whenever, so please use the amounts and varieties below as guidance only.

Serves 4

2 tablespoons basil flavored oil or regular olive oil
1 leek, cleaned, halved lengthwise then thinly sliced
1 zucchini, peeled, quartered lengthwise then chopped
approx. 8 ounces white, green or savoy cabbage, shredded
2–3 ounces green beans, trimmed and halved

1 quart vegetable broth (from can, carton or cube), preferably organic
4 ounces soup pasta, such as ditalini
1 tablespoon dry white vermouth or white wine (optional)
salt and pepper, to taste
grated Parmesan cheese, to serve

♥ Warm the oil in a heavy-based saucepan, then add the small pieces of leek and zucchini and cook on a medium heat for about 5 minutes, stirring and pushing bits about with your wooden spoon every now and again.

♥ Add the shredded cabbage and small lengths of green beans and let cook for another 5 minutes, stirring occasionally.

♥ Heat the broth until almost boiling, then pour the hot broth into the pan (and add any

152

rinds of Parmesan you may have), bring to a bubble, turn down to low, clamp on a lid, and let simmer, covered, for 20 minutes, then fish out the rinds, if you feel so inclined.

♥ Uncover, bring to a bubble again, and throw in the pasta, letting it cook for about 10 minutes, or following the instructions on the pasta box. Unlike regular pasta, though, soup pasta should never, in my book, be al dente.

♥ Once the pasta is cooked, add the vermouth or white wine (Federico Fellini used to splash up his minestrone with whisky), let it bubble into the soup for a few seconds, then take the pan off the heat, season to taste, and let cool for at least 10 minutes and up to 40, so that when you eat the minestrone, topped with some grated Parmesan, it is comfortingly warm rather than searingly hot. I rather love it left for maximum time, when it is a solid pasta pottage at almost room temperature. Heaven. Or *paradiso*.

MAKE AHEAD NOTE
The soup can be made 1–2 days ahead. Transfer the soup to non-metallic bowl to cool, then cover and refrigerate. Reheat gently in a saucepan, stirring occasionally, until piping hot, then cool slightly before serving.

FREEZE NOTE
The cooled soup can be frozen in airtight container for up to 3 months. Thaw overnight in the refrigerator and reheat as above.

South Indian vegetable curry

This is another way of making sure the odd handful of beans or other vegetable fragments can be eaten up when none of them individually can offer a meal in themselves. You can vary the vegetables according to what you have.

Serves 4

2 tablespoons garlic flavored oil
1 onion, peeled, halved and cut into half-
  moons
pinch kosher salt
1 green chile, seeded and finely chopped
¾ inch chunk fresh gingerroot, peeled
  and cut into thin strips
¼ teaspoon crushed red pepper flakes
1 teaspoon turmeric
1 teaspoon ground cumin
1 teaspoon ground coriander
1 teaspoon ground ginger
1 x 14-ounce can coconut milk

1 quart vegetable broth
1 teaspoon sugar
1 tablespoon tamarind paste
12 ounces cauliflower, broken into florets
  (approx. 3½ cups)
12 ounces broccoli, broken into florets
  (approx. 3½ cups)
2 ounces green beans, trimmed and halved
  (large handful)
4 ounces fresh baby corn or snow peas,
  halved (approx. 1½ cups)
6 ounces sugar snap peas (approx. 2 cups)
2 tablespoons chopped dill or cilantro, or
  mixture

♥ Heat the oil in a thick-bottomed Dutch oven or large saucepan and fry the sliced onion sprinkled with some salt until it begins to soften, then add the chopped fresh chile and ginger strips and stir every now and again while cooking for a minute.

♥ Now add the crushed red pepper flakes, the turmeric, and ground cumin, coriander, and ginger. Stir well and cook for another minute or so before pouring in the coconut milk, broth, sugar, and tamarind paste. Stir to combine.

♥ Bring to a boil, add the cauliflower florets first, then the broccoli. Cook for 10 minutes, then add the green beans and baby corn (or snow peas). Check the vegetables after about 5 minutes or so to see if they are almost done, letting them cook for longer if they need it.

♥ Once the vegetables are tender, add the sugar snap peas and season to taste, then when the sugar snaps are hot, serve, generously sprinkled with the herbs of your choice, in a bowl on top of some plain rice, or with some warmed Indian flatbread on the side for dunking.

MAKE AHEAD NOTE
The curry sauce can be made 1 day ahead. Transfer to non-metallic bowl to cool, then cover and refrigerate. Transfer to a Dutch oven or large saucepan and reheat gently until boiling, then add vegetables as recipe instructs.

FREEZE NOTE
The cooled sauce can be frozen in an airtight container for up to 1 month. Thaw overnight in the refrigerator and use as above.

Making leftovers right

Although it may sound odd to suggest further uses for a recipe in itself made up of last-chance-saloon bits and pieces, if you do have a smallish amount of this curry left over, you should know it makes for a wonderful sauce – just heat it up in a saucepan until piping hot over a fillet or two of flounder, briefly steamed in a mixture of water and sake.

SAUCE FOR
FLOUNDER

MY SWEET SOLUTION

No one needs to make a dessert. Let me make that quite clear. I suppose you could say that no one needs to eat one, either. But – to misquote the familiar lovers' phrase – the stomach wants what the stomach wants. Different organ, same urgency. Anyway, by saying it's not necessary to make a dessert (the French and Italians, both peoples pre-eminently bound up in their respective country's cooking traditions, routinely buy in from the patisserie or gelateria) doesn't mean it isn't desirable. And I'm not talking from the point of view of the eater, either.

You know that I'm not of the cook-to-impress school. Anxiously producing food with an eye on the clapometer is surely the most direct route to joylessness in the kitchen I can possibly think of. The picture of the attention-seeking, craven cook is not an attractive one. (I hope my discomfort here is not evidence of repressed recognition.) And yet it would be disingenuous to claim that the pleasure of our guests is immaterial. Nor should it be. When we invite friends over for a meal, that invitation, that meal, means something. Of course, I'm happy to sit around my kitchen table with a loaf of bread, a wedge of cheese and some friends. I wouldn't consider them friends if I felt otherwise. And I'm not above phoning for a pizza, either. But there are times when grand plans for something more approaching a serious soirée have been made, but life has intervened, and there's scarcely time to cook; or maybe the evening being orchestrated is what management consultants call a Distant Elephant. It's a simple analogy: an elephant in the distant horizon looks teeny-tiny, inconsequential, unthreatening. When you get close up, you realize, all too late, your mistake: forget teeny-tiny, this is a great big elephant and it's ready to trample you underfoot. Now apply this concept to the dates you blithely marked – like dots in the distance – far ahead in your diary.

Even if you're looking forward to your guests with unstinting enthusiasm, you may suddenly find that you're unable to rustle up a dinner in time. You may have thought a chapter devoted to dessert was only going to complicate your life; but no, it's here precisely to make it easier. I mean, you don't even have to cook and you've magicked into being a Chocolate Key Lime Pie, a Frangelico Tiramisu, a fruit tart that looks as if it came from a French cake shop, No-churn Piña Colada Ice Cream, and other lusciously rewarding desserts. With the exception of the Brownie Bowls, which take around 20 minutes from start to finish, everything is made in advance, your work done and panic over. And, frankly, you could serve bread and water beforehand and by the end of dinner everyone at the table would be marvelling, thrilled by the effort you'd made.

Chocolate key lime pie

It's extraordinary how potent cheap confectionery is. Proust may have had his madeleines, but my taste memories are shamelessly low-rent; I am forever, it seems, trying to recreate the so-long-ago-savored delights of the candy jar. This is yet another evocation of the chocolate-lime candies of my childhood. Luckily, it tastes how I impossibly remember them, not as they would really be, were I to eat one now.

My version of this classic American pie doesn't have the traditional meringue topping, nor, of course, does it require Florida key limes – limey limes do it for me.

Serves 6–8

21 sheets graham crackers (3 cups crumbs)
1 tablespoon unsweetened cocoa powder
4 tablespoons soft unsalted butter
¼ cup bittersweet chocolate chips
1 x 14-ounce can sweetened condensed milk, preferably chilled

4 limes, to give approx. 2 tablespoons finely grated zest and ¾ cup juice
1¼ cups heavy cream
1 square best-quality bittersweet chocolate

1 x loose-bottomed 9-inch fluted tart pan, 2 inches deep

♥ Put the crackers, cocoa powder, butter, and chocolate chips into a food processor and process to a dark, damp, sandy consistency. Tip into a fluted tart pan, and press onto the base and up the sides. Place in the refrigerator to chill while you make the filling.

♥ Pour the condensed milk into a bowl. Zest the limes into another bowl and reserve for decoration later. Add the juice of the limes to the condensed milk, whisking to mix.

♥ Pour in the heavy cream and whisk together – in a freestanding electric mixer or with a hand-held one – until thick, then spoon the mixture into the chilled cracker crust and use the back of the spoon to finish off the top in a swirly fashion, leaving the soft filling encircled by dark crust.

♥ Chill the pie in the refrigerator for 4 hours (if the condensed milk was chilled), until firm, or, ideally, covered overnight. When you are ready to serve, unmold the pie from the tart pan, but leave it on the base.

♥ Grate the chocolate to give a light dusting to the top of the pie and then sprinkle with the lime zest. This is important because without food coloring the pie will seem too pallid to conjure up the limes that flavor it. Serve immediately, as it will become soft if kept out of the refrigerator for too long.

MAKE AHEAD NOTE
The pie can be made 1 day in advance. When chilled and firm, tent with aluminum foil (try not to touch surface of pie with foil as it will leave marks) and store in the refrigerator. Store the zest in a bowl, tightly covered with plastic wrap. Decorate with zest just before serving. The pie will keep for a total of 2–3 days in the refrigerator.

FREEZE NOTE
The pie *can* be frozen for up to 3 months, but be warned it may "weep" on thawing, so it is not ideal for freezing. Open-freeze the undecorated pie just until solid, then wrap the pie (still in its tart pan) in double layer of plastic wrap and layer of aluminum foil. To thaw, unwrap the pie and tent with foil (try not to touch surface of pie with foil as it will leave marks), then thaw overnight in refrigerator. Decorate with fresh zest.

Chocolate brownie bowls

While I appreciate that making something which requires a specific mold may not seem very public-spirited, I promise that you will find the 6-cavity dessert shell pan, as it is properly named, quite as useful as the loaf pan you are regularly called on in these pages to use. What this particular pan gives you is beautiful little cakes which, when turned out, have an indentation in them; thus they become edible bowls for ice cream, whipped cream, or whatever topping you choose. If you can't get this pan, then there are some delightful cakelet pans in pretty shapes which can be used for this type of dessert.

And there's no reason why you couldn't make an edible bowl out of whichever cake you wanted: but for me, the best bowl is a brownie bowl. The brownie mixture here isn't designed to make quite the gooey ones I usually go for, as I want to be able to turn them out of the pan without fear of sticking, and they need to be slightly more cake-like to hold up to the filling.

These are a dream ending to any dinner, but knowing that they are easy-peasy to make (a one-pan job) and that they take just over 10 minutes to bake is even dreamier. You could do these in advance, store and then serve them reheated and warm, or just as they are; but whenever possible I like to make them, bake them, and leave them to cool a little, while we're eating our entree, then add scoops of ice cream after. I love the way the ice cream begins to drip into the warmth of the malted chocolate brownie bowls beneath.

You can fill or top them however you so please. In the meantime, let me suggest:
Squirty whipped cream, strawberries, and strawberry sauce
Chocolate mint ice cream and chocolate sauce
Vanilla ice cream and chocolate sauce
Strawberry ice cream and pink sprinkles
Coffee ice cream, maple syrup, and pecans
Dulce de leche ice cream and caramel sauce

Serves 6

1 stick plus 1 tablespoon (9 tablespoons) soft unsalted butter plus extra for greasing
½ cup plus 2 tablespoons superfine sugar
2 tablespoons malted milk powder (such as Ovaltine)
2 tablespoons best-quality unsweetened cocoa powder
½ cup boiling water, from a kettle
½ cup buttermilk

1 egg
1 teaspoon vanilla extract
1 cup all-purpose flour
½ teaspoon baking soda

to serve:
whipped cream, sprinkles, fruit, ice cream, sauces, nuts, all to choice

1 x 6-cavity dessert shell pan

♥ Preheat the oven to 400°F and lightly butter, or spray with baking spray, the indentations in the pan.

♥ Melt the butter in a thick-bottomed saucepan over a low heat and add the sugar, stirring with a wooden spoon to help it dissolve into the butter. Turn off the heat.

♥ Put the malted milk powder and cocoa into a mug or measuring cup and whisk in the boiling water until smooth. Add this liquid to the warm pan of butter and sugar, stirring to combine with a wooden spoon.

♥ To the emptied-out mug or measuring cup (no need to wash out) add the buttermilk, egg, and vanilla and whisk together before stirring this mixture into the pan, too.

♥ Finally, whisk in the flour, baking soda, and – using a small ladle for ease – fill the 6 bowl indentations. You will have enough mixture to fill them three-quarters of the way up, which is what you want.

♥ Place in the preheated oven for about 12 minutes. When they're cooked – they will feel gently bouncy if you press on the surface – set the pan on a wire rack for 5 minutes before turning out the little brownie bowls. Fill while still just warm or when cooled, as desired.

MAKE AHEAD NOTE
The bowls can be baked up to 1 day ahead and stored in airtight container, layered with parchment paper. Reheat in warm oven for 5–8 minutes before serving.

FREEZE NOTE
The bowls can be frozen in airtight container, layered with parchment paper, for up to 2 months. Thaw for 3–4 hours on wire rack at room temperature and reheat as above.

OPPOSITE:
top left: Dulce de leche ice cream and caramel sauce; *top right:* Vanilla ice cream and chocolate sauce; *center left:* Coffee ice cream, maple syrup, and pecans; *center right:* Chocolate mint ice cream and chocolate sauce; *bottom left:* Strawberry ice cream and pink sprinkles; *bottom right:* Squirty whipped cream, strawberries, and strawberry sauce

Frangelico tiramisu

It makes me blush now when I remember my once snooty disdain for tiramisu. Still, I feel that my slight against the dish has been repaid in full, and then some. This version had been hovering at the back of my mind for quite some time before I first made it. Now try and stop me. Frangelico is one of my favorite sticky liqueurs: I love the bottle, which comes looking as though it's dressed in a cassock; I love the taste and smell, the nuttiest of all hazelnuts. There's almost a buttery richness, but – and this is what heads off the sweetness – a dark smokiness beyond, much darker than its appropriately hazelnut hue would lead you to expect.

In bars in Italy, especially in the northwest, you can get a *caffè corretto* with Frangelico, in other words a shot of espresso fortified (literally "corrected") with a hit of this. Of course, you can have your coffee "corrected" with a choice of many liqueurs, but this is my favorite (I'm also very keen on a snifter of espresso liqueur to which a drop or two of Frangelico has been added), and that exact co-mingling of flavors is what I'm aiming for here.

The recipe that follows is for an amply proportioned tiramisu, enough to fill a 9-inch square dish and feed a good 12 people. I went completely over the top during the photo shoot, and doubled quantities to make enough to fill the huge heart you see opposite. Before then, I never really believed you could have too much of a good thing. Mind you, it didn't put me off for long: I'm always up for a bowl of this boozy, creamy lusciousness, and I think you'll find that others are, too.

Note: As this dish contains raw egg, it is not suitable for people with compromised or weak immune systems, such as younger children, the elderly, or pregnant women.

Serves 12, *though doesn't have to*

1 cup espresso coffee, or 8 teaspoons espresso powder dissolved in 1 cup boiling water
1 cup Frangelico hazelnut liqueur, plus more for the filling (below)

for the filling:
2 eggs, separated
⅓ cup superfine sugar

¼ cup Frangelico hazelnut liqueur
1 pound (2 cups) mascarpone
30 savoiardi cookies (ladyfingers), approx. 14 ounces
¾ cup chopped roasted hazelnuts
3 teaspoons unsweetened cocoa powder

1 x 8-inch square dish

♥ Combine the coffee and 1 cup Frangelico in a pitcher, and allow to cool if the coffee is hot.

♥ Whisk the egg whites till frothy. In a separate bowl, beat the yolks and sugar with the ¼ cup Frangelico for the filling.

♥ Add the mascarpone to the yolks and sugar mixture, beating it in well to mix. Gently fold in the foamy egg whites, and mix again.

♥ Pour half of the coffee and Frangelico mixture into a wide shallow bowl and dunk enough savoiardi cookies for a layer, about 4 at a time, into the liquid, coating both sides.

♥ Line your tiramisu dish with a layer of soaked savoiardi cookies: they should be damp, but not falling to pieces (though it wouldn't matter if they did). Pour any leftover liquid from the dipping process over the layer you have made.

♥ Put half the mascarpone mixture on top of the soaked cookies and spread to make an even layer.

♥ Pour the remaining coffee and Frangelico mixture from the pitcher into the shallow bowl and make another, final layer of savoiardi, dipping as before and layering on top of the mascarpone in the dish.

♥ Pour any leftover liquid over the savoiardi layer, and cover with the final layer of mascarpone. Cover the dish with plastic wrap and leave overnight, or for at least 6 hours, in the refrigerator.

♥ When you are ready to serve, take the tiramisu out of the refrigerator and remove the plastic wrap. Mix the chopped roasted hazelnuts with 2 teaspoons of the cocoa powder and sprinkle this over the top layer of mascarpone. Then dust with the final teaspoon of cocoa powder, pushing it through a strainer for lighter coverage, over the nut-rubbly tiramisu.

MAKE AHEAD NOTE
The tiramisu can be made 1–2 days ahead and stored in the refrigerator. It will keep for up to 4 days in total and leftovers should be refrigerated immediately.

FREEZE NOTE
The tiramisu can be frozen for up to 3 months. Wrap the tiramisu (without hazelnut and cocoa topping) in double layer of plastic wrap and layer of aluminum foil. Thaw overnight in the refrigerator and top with nuts and cocoa, as directed in recipe.

Lemon meringue fool

I'm a fool for a fool: that classic but oh-so-easy British dessert. This version is not merely a speedy simple one, but rather a lemon meringue pie without the chewing. It slips down with celestial lightness and a rush of lemon. Think of it as Eton Mess, Amalfi style.

Makes enough to fill 4 small martini glasses, or 2 goblets for greedy people

⅔ cup good-quality store-bought lemon curd, plus a little to decorate

1–2 teaspoons limoncello (lemon liqueur) or lemon juice

1 cup heavy cream

4 small meringue cookies (store-bought is fine)

lemon zest, to serve

♥ Put the lemon curd into a bowl and stir in the limoncello (or lemon juice), adding more if it seems too thick to fold into some whipped cream in a moment.

♥ Pour the heavy cream into another bowl and whisk until just thick. It should hold its shape, but not be so thickly whipped that it looks dry: it will thicken more as you fold in the lemon curd.

♥ Drizzle half the lemon curd mixture over the cream and fold in with a rubber spatula, then do the same with the remaining half. You don't want it all folded in completely: whipped cream rippled with lemon is what you're aiming for.

♥ Crumble the meringue cookies with your fingers into the fool, and gently fold most of this in to mix. Spoon it into 4 small martini glasses (or fill 2 larger goblets) and decorate with some lemon zest curls and a drizzle of lemon curd, scraped out of the bottom of the bowl it was mixed in, or spooned out of a jar. If you have any thin, crisp cookies – think along the lines of langues de chat (cat's tongue cookies) – for eating alongside, put them on the table on serving.

MAKE AHEAD NOTE
The fool can be made 2–3 hours ahead. Spoon into glasses, then cover and refrigerate. Decorate as directed in recipe.

FREEZE NOTE
The fool can be frozen for up to 3 months, though the meringue cookies will go soft. Spoon into freezer-proof glasses and wrap each in a double layer of plastic wrap. Thaw overnight in the refrigerator and decorate as directed in recipe.

Orange and blackberry trifle

I know that I could simply have put this in the Making Leftovers Right entry for the Marmalade Pudding Cake on **p.269**, but having made it once with that, I saw – as experience happily now testifies – that the trifle (and it *is* a mere trifle to make) in all its gorgeous 1920s flapper colors of jet and coral, is easily made from new. I'd say from scratch, but I mean you can start with a store-bought orange pound cake – in other words, you don't need to be using leftovers – and proceed as below. Or you can take any plain pound cake, then sandwich slices of it with marmalade and use these as the trifle base. A bit of extra marmalade wouldn't go amiss on any store-bought replacement, as the home-made version is heavy with its fragrantly bitter scent.

    I love this just as it is, lying grandly on a stand or platter, but it also would look beautiful piled in, and peeking through, glasses or goblets. The latter would give this more of a conventional trifle appearance, but ever since I made my first, then-called plate trifle in my second book, I have been drawn to this casual but indulgent pile-up approach. In any event, this is a very freestyle kind of a dessert: do with it what you will.

Serves 4–6

12 ounces Marmalade Pudding cake
  (p.269) (about ⅓ of the cake)
⅓ cup Cointreau or other orange liqueur
zest and juice 1 orange or 2 clementines
  (scant ½ cup)

1 cup heavy cream
10 ounces blackberries (about
  2 cups, or blueberries if
  blackberries can't be found)

♥ Cut the cake into slices and arrange on a plate or wide, shallow dish. Drizzle with the orange liqueur.

♥ Zest the orange or clementines into a bowl and leave the zest to one side. Then squeeze the juice from the orange or clementines, pouring this over the liqueur-soaked cake.

♥ Whip the cream until thick but softly so, and spoon unfancily over the top of the saturated, not to say gloriously sodden, cake.

♥ Arrange the blackberries over the top of the whipped cream, then scatter with the reserved zest.

MAKE AHEAD NOTE
The base can be prepared a couple of hours ahead, then finish with whipped cream, fruit, and zest as directed in recipe.

Old-fashioned cheesecake

I've made many a cheesecake, and as I go I seem to get farther and farther away from its – and my – Eastern European origins. But you know, the play is part of the pleasure. There's no less joy to be had, though, from returning to the start of it all, and this is really what cheesecake was – a great solid block of it – when it first came over here. You can still find this, occasionally, in delis, but it's rare. I love its denseness and lemoniness, and the way it reminds me of tea with my granny, with her austere china and indulgent love.

Makes 16 rectangular slabs

Ingredients should be at room temperature before you start

for the base:
1½ cups all-purpose flour
1 teaspoon baking powder
¼ cup superfine sugar
2 tablespoons soft unsalted butter
1 egg
3 tablespoons whole milk

for the filling:
1 pound 10 ounces (3½ x 7.5-ounce packages) farmer cheese, preferably with no added salt

¾ cup superfine sugar
4 eggs, separated
½ cup cornstarch (or potato flour)
3 tablespoons lemon juice
1 teaspoon vanilla extract
½ teaspoon salt (omit if farmer cheese has salt added)
1 cup heavy cream, softly whipped

2 x aluminum foil pans or 1 foil-lined baking pan approx. 13 x 9 x 2 inches

♥ Preheat the oven to 325°F, and if you're using the disposable foil pans, put one inside the other – to help with any wibbly-wobbling as you transfer your uncooked cheesecake to the oven later – and put a cookie sheet in the oven for them to sit on.

♥ For the base, put the flour and baking powder in the bowl of **a food processor** along with the ¼ cup superfine sugar, 2 tablespoons soft butter, and 1 egg. Process and then, with the motor running, add the milk and when the mixture begins to clump together, stop. **Or, if doing this by hand**, rub the butter into the flour in a bowl and then beat in the other ingredients with a wooden spoon.

♥ Tip the mixture out into a foil pan or foil-lined baking pan. Using your hands or the back of a spoon, press this in to make as even a layer as possible. Bake in the oven for 10 minutes. Let it cool a little before pouring in the cheese mixture.

173

♥ Put the farmer cheese in a bowl and beat in the sugar followed by the egg yolks. Beat in the cornstarch (or potato flour, which is the more old-fashioned and authentic choice, but there's nothing in it really, tastewise) followed by the lemon juice, vanilla extract, and salt (if using), and then fold in the softly whipped cream.

♥ In another bowl, whisk the egg whites until soft peaks form and then add a ladleful to the cheese mixture and stir in vigorously. Fold the rest of the whites in more gently in 3–4 batches.

♥ Pour and scrape the filling into the dough-lined foil pan, then carefully transfer to the oven and leave to bake for 1 hour, by which time it will be set on top and, although it won't feel cooked completely underneath, the surface should be slightly scorched in places. I love that.

♥ Remove to a wire rack to cool, still in its pan, and be prepared for the fact that it will probably crack a bit as it cools. Regard this as the stamp of authenticity. Chill the cheesecake, covered, overnight in the refrigerator, before serving.

MAKE AHEAD NOTE
Make the cheesecake up to 2 days ahead and cool and chill as directed. Do not cover until completely cold, then cover with plastic wrap, making sure that the covering does not touch the surface. The cheesecake will keep in the refrigerator for up to 4 days total.

FREEZE NOTE
The cheesecake can be frozen for up to 1 month. Make sure it is thoroughly chilled then wrap it, still in its pan, in double layer of plastic wrap and layer of aluminum foil, ensuring that wrapping doesn't touch the top surface. Thaw overnight in the refrigerator and eat within 2 days. Some condensation may appear on surface on thawing, but it is fine to eat.

174

Chocolate peanut butter cheesecake

Since I've established my bona fides with the previous recipe, I feel a bit less apologetic for the overindulgent vulgarity that is this cheesecake here. But, really, why should I be sorry? You won't be once you've eaten it; though perhaps I should warn that it's not for the faint-hearted. Unashamed indulgence, wallowingly so, is what this recipe is all about: think Reese's Peanut Butter Cup in cheesecake form. For that reason, I don't bake this in a water bath as I do the Banoffee Cheesecake on **p.133**. The water-bath is excellent if you want a silky texture, but for me, the peanut butter constituent demands a certain amount of pleasurable, palate-cleaving clagginess. And baked like this, too, the top gets a slight crust when it's cooked, making it all the easier to spread the chocolate topping.

Serves 10–12

Ingredients should be at room temperature before you start

for the base:
½ x 14-ounce box graham crackers (2 cups crumbs)
½ cup salted peanuts
½ cup bittersweet chocolate chips
4 tablespoons soft unsalted butter

for the filling:
2 x 8-ounce bars cream cheese
3 eggs

3 egg yolks (freeze the whites to make the meringues on **p.262**)
1 cup superfine sugar
½ cup sour cream
1 cup creamy peanut butter

for the topping:
1 cup sour cream
1 cup milk chocolate chips
2 tablespoons light brown sugar

1 x 9-inch springform pan

♥ Preheat the oven to 325°F, then process the crackers, peanuts, bittersweet chocolate chips, and butter for the base in a food processor. Once it comes together in a clump, turn it out into a springform pan and press into the bottom and up the sides to make the crunchy crust. Put in the refrigerator while you make the filling.

♥ Process the filling in the cleaned or wiped-out processor bowl, putting in the cream cheese, eggs and egg yolks, sugar, sour cream, and peanut butter and whizzing to a smooth mixture.

♥ Pour and scrape the filling into the base in the chilled springform pan and cook for 1 hour, though start checking after 45 minutes. The top – only – should feel set and dry.

175

♥ Take the cheesecake out of the oven while you make the topping. Warm the sour cream and milk chocolate with the brown sugar gently in a small saucepan over a low heat, whisking to blend in the chocolate as it melts, and then take off the heat.

♥ Spoon and spread the topping very gently over the top of the cheesecake, being as careful as you can in case you break the surface of the cheesecake. (Not that anything bad will happen; you'll just have chocolate marbling the cake a bit.) Put it back in the oven for a final 10 minutes.

♥ Once out of the oven, let the cheesecake cool in its pan and then cover and put into the refrigerator overnight. When you are ready to eat the cheesecake, take it out of the refrigerator, just to take the chill off: this will make it easier to spring from the pan. Don't let it get too warm, though, as it will become a bit gooey and be hard to slice.

MAKE AHEAD NOTE
Make the cheesecake up to 2 days ahead. Cool and chill as directed. Do not cover until completely cold, then cover with plate or plastic wrap, making sure that covering does not touch surface. Unmold and serve as directed in recipe. This will keep in the refrigerator for up to 4 days total.

FREEZE NOTE
The cheesecake can be frozen for 1 month. Make sure is is thoroughly chilled then wrap, still in its pan, in a double layer of plastic wrap and a layer of aluminum foil. Thaw overnight in the refrigerator and eat within 2 days. A small amount of condensation may appear on surface of the cheesecake after thawing, but it is still fine to eat.

No-fuss fruit tart

This is perhaps one of the most useful desserts you can have in your repertoire. Not that it is the job of a dessert to be useful: a dessert exists merely to delight. Still, dinner does need to be made, even when there's precious little time for it, and that should be a delight, too. So here's the deal: there is pitifully little work to be done to make this berry-dazzler of a tart, and enormous pleasure to be derived from its consumption.

All you do is bash a few graham crackers a day or so in advance and make the base – getting one course out of the way early is my way of managing – then stir lemon curd and cream cheese together, and use this cream to line the crumb-covered tart pan. I use store-bought lemon curd here, but even if it comes out of the jar, it must be of good quality. And when it is whipped into the cream cheese, that cream cheese must be at room temperature, as should the lemon curd in its jar. The combination produces a layer of what tastes like cheesecake cream: light, lemony, luscious.

I used to put the berries on top of the cream pretty much last-minute, but then I found that a leftover wedge, after the party, looked inviting after being in the refrigerator overnight, and so I now finish assembling the tart ahead of time. But if you prefer to add the fruit nearer to serving, I completely understand.

Don't feel you must obey the fruit orders too literally: any mixture of berries (or indeed other fruit) would do, and you could well use a smaller amount and top the tart less extravagantly.

Serves 8–10

27 sheets graham crackers (3¾ cups crumbs)
6 tablespoons soft unsalted butter
2 x 8-ounce bars cream cheese, at room temperature
1 cup lemon curd, at room temperature
4 ounces blueberries (1 cup)
4 ounces blackberries (1 cup)

4 ounces raspberries (1 cup)
4 ounces redcurrants or pomegranate seeds (⅔ cup)
4 ounces small strawberries (1 to 1½ cups)

1 x loose-bottomed 10-inch fluted tart pan, 2 inches deep

♥ Process the crackers and the butter to a sandy rubble and press into the sides and bottom of a deep-sided fluted tart pan. Place in the freezer (or refrigerator if that is not possible) for about 10–15 minutes.

♥ In a clean **processor bowl**, process the cream cheese and lemon curd (or just mix **by hand**) and spread into the bottom of the chilled tart pan, covering the base evenly.

♥ Arrange the fruit gently (so it doesn't sink in too much) on top of the lemony cream cheese in a decorative manner (see right), leaving some of the strawberries unhulled, with their picturesque stalks attached.

♥ Place the tart in the refrigerator, preferably overnight, though for at least 4 hours. It does need to get properly cold in order to set enough for the tart to be unmolded and sliced easily.

178

MAKE AHEAD NOTE
The tart can be made 1 day ahead. Cover loosely with plastic wrap or aluminum foil, being careful not to press on the filling, and refrigerate. Will keep for around 4 days.

FREEZE NOTE
The tart, without fruit topping, can be frozen for up to 3 months if made with regular cream cheese, but be warned it may "weep" on thawing, so is not ideal for freezing. Open-freeze tart until firm, then wrap (still in its pan) in double layer of plastic wrap and layer of aluminum foil. To thaw, unwrap and cover loosely with plastic wrap then thaw overnight in the refrigerator. Decorate and serve as directed in recipe.

No-churn piña colada ice cream

Flushed with the success of an earlier creation, the no-churn margarita ice cream, I bring you the no-churn piña colada ice cream. Rich coconut, sharp pineapple, smooth cream: we are in business! You don't have to share my weakness for a kitsch tipple to enjoy this. Certainly, it helps – but the benefit is psychological, not gastronomical.

I assure you the toasted shredded coconut for scattering over is not mere garnish: you need it to bring the sharpness into focus. Eaten plain, the sweet coconuttiness of the ice cream is overwhelming. It doesn't entirely make sense, but it is the case. As an alternative to the sweetened shredded coconut, you could search out some of the fresh coconut that is already out of its hairy shell and chunked up for you at the supermarket. You should be able to push this through a coarse grater or slicer onto the ice cream.

Serves 6–8

½ cup pineapple juice, from a carton
⅓ cup Malibu (white coconut rum)
generous few drops coconut flavoring

2 teaspoons lime juice
1 cup confectioner's sugar
2 cups heavy cream
⅔ cup sweetened shredded coconut, to serve

♥ Pour the pineapple juice and Malibu into a large bowl, and add the coconut flavoring and lime juice.

♥ Add the confectioner's sugar and whisk to dissolve.

♥ Whisk the cream in a separate bowl until soft peaks form. Whisk in the pineapple juice mixture in a thin stream, until combined.

♥ Taste to see if you need more coconut flavoring or a squeeze more lime juice (and remember it won't be as strong when frozen), then spoon and smooth the ice cream into an airtight container and freeze.

♥ On serving – and, oh, how this cries out for hollowed-out coconut shells as serving vessels – toast the shredded coconut in a hot, dry pan until just turning golden and remove to a bowl. Sprinkle a little over each person's portion and leave the rest for people to add as they eat.

FREEZE NOTE
The ice cream *can* keep for up to 3 months in freezer, but will become icy, so it's better up to 1 month only and at its best within 1 week of making.

Grasshopper pie

I was watching an episode of *Glee* on TV and one of the characters ate her way through about 4 slices of Grasshopper Pie. Any food scenes on film and television make me miss important plot lines, so involved am I in what's being cooked or eaten, but I entirely overreacted to this one. I knew I had to cook such a pie, even before I had any idea what was in it. And – let's be frank – if you still carry on with the proceedings once you *do* know, there is no excuse. Not that I am trying to put you off. Far from it: I consider this (for all that I always call it Ghostbuster Pie by mistake) an instance of miraculous luck. If I'd read about it, I'd have made a horrified little twist of the mouth and flicked quickly on – and I never would have found out how inexplicably heavenly this is, and maybe nor would you. I am grateful – indeed gleeful – for my good fortune and bad habits: if I hadn't been prone in front of the TV, I would remain unilluminated.

I have used marshmallows in cooking before, and see no real reason to prepare an apologia for them. But I will tell you that what they bring to the creation is a particular consistency, which is aerated and unbelievably light; on the tongue this feels like ice cream that isn't frozen but is still set.

As improbable as all the ingredients are separately, let alone in conjunction, I must tell you that I keep them all to hand for the many occasions I need to burst out a Ghostbuster. I think this is one of my most popular desserts – and, for my part, it is wonderfully versatile. It's almost as if it seems to go with nothing, so goes with everything. Having said that, it is especially good and sweetly refreshing after anything spicy.

A final note: for the full effect, you must make sure your crème de menthe is green and your crème de cacao white.

Serves 8–10

for the base:
28 chocolate creme filled sandwich
   cookies (such as Oreos or
   Newman-Os)
2 ounces good-quality bittersweet
   chocolate, chopped (or ¼ cup chips)
3 tablespoons soft unsalted butter

for the filling:
3 cups mini-marshmallows

½ cup whole milk
¼ cup crème de menthe
¼ cup crème de cacao blanc
1½ cups heavy cream
few spots or drops green food coloring
   (optional)

1 x loose-bottomed 10-inch fluted tart
   pan, 2 inches deep

♥ Take out and set aside 1 cookie. Process the rest of the cookies and the chocolate in
a food processor until they form a crumb mixture, then add the butter and carry on
processing until it all starts to clump together.

♥ Press into a high-sided fluted tart pan, making a smooth base and sides with your hands
or the back of a spoon. Put into the refrigerator to chill and harden.

♥ Melt the marshmallows in a saucepan with the milk over a gentle heat and, once the
milk starts to foam (not boil), take off the heat and keep stirring until the marshmallows
blend into the milk to make a smooth mixture.

♥ Pour the mixture out of the saucepan into a heatproof bowl, then whisk in the crème de
menthe and crème de cacao. Leave until cool.

♥ Whisk the cream until it starts to hold soft peaks then, still whisking, add the cooled
marshmallow mix. This filling should be thick but still soft, not stiff or dry, so that it will
eventually drop easily out of the bowl into the chilled pie crust.

♥ When the marshmallow mixture and cream are combined, add a few drops of food
coloring (unless you prefer not to) and whisk it in.

♥ Spread the filling into the chilled base, swirling it about with an icing spatula or silicone
spatula to fill evenly, then put the pie back in the refrigerator, covered, to chill overnight or
for a minimum of 4 hours until firm.

♥ Crush the remaining cookie and sprinkle over the top of the pie before serving.

MAKE AHEAD NOTE
The pie can be made 1–2 days ahead. When chilled and firm, tent with aluminum foil (try not to
touch surface with foil as it will leave marks) and store in the refrigerator. Decorate just before
serving. The pie will keep 3–4 days total.

FREEZE NOTE
The pie can be frozen for up to 3 months. Open-freeze undecorated pie just until solid, then wrap
pie (still in its tart pan) in double layer of plastic wrap and layer of foil. To thaw, unwrap pie and
tent with foil (try not to touch surface with foil as it will leave marks), then thaw overnight in the
refrigerator. Decorate before serving.

OFF THE CUFF

Whether you really want to be listening to me on the subject of what to keep in your cupboards, refrigerator, and freezer is a moot point. While not exactly a hoarder, I come as near as dammit. When shopping, I cannot bear to put any item into my basket without chucking in an extra one for luck. Perhaps it is to do with some atavistic refugee mentality (I have forbears who rowed their way from Holland to the UK), but no kitchen I could ever own would come near to being understocked.

Don't worry: I won't send you on some compulsive shopping spree or make you, like me, end up with a freezer so tightly packed, you risk frostbite unloading everything just to unearth a bag of frozen peas. Wisdom, we're told, lies in learning from other people's mistakes, and you would certainly be wise to heed mine. And since even the greediest of stockpiling doesn't mean you have all eventualities covered – and I should know – it does make sense to put a system into play whereby you can feel confident that what you're stocking up on will actually provide a meal some day.

I'm not saying you should count on these ingredients necessarily providing a meal in its entirety (though there are recipes here which do just that), but you can make your cooking life very much simpler by ensuring you keep a stash of less everyday ingredients, so that when you're doing a quick dash round the local store to acquire supper, you're not searching in vain for some recondite paste or flavoring. But on top of that, you really can prepare yourself comfortably for those days when impromptu guests show up or you are simply in no position to shop.

I need to know that not only do I have some pasta on hand (and what used to be the pasta cupboard has now morphed into a huge basket known as The Harvest Festival) but also the wherewithal to make some sauces for it. And while my Slut's Spaghetti is chief among those, there are other contenders, too. A read-through of any of the following recipes will give you an indication of the various ingredients needed.

As for the freezer, frozen shrimp and squid (the latter I buy in 1-pound bags from the fish seller) can be real life-savers. In the refrigerator, I make sure I have chorizo (the Spanish sausages for cooking), packages of feta and halloumi, as well as pancetta cubes. These are all chilled foodstuffs with a long life that lend themselves to meals at a moment's notice, and I relish the luxury of being able to rely on them.

I'm not sure it would be helpful to list everything I keep in the kitchen (not least because it would be too shaming an exercise for me) but I did want to outline just a few, above – if only to show that the ability to throw together supper with little or no notice isn't a skill or a talent, but a question of canny shopping. Go to it!

Slut's spaghetti

Well, how could I resist this translation of *pasta alla puttanesca*, whore's pasta as it usually is described in English? The general consensus seems to be that this is the sort of dish cooked by slatterns who don't go to market to get their ingredients fresh, but are happy to use stuff out of jars and cans. I hold my hands up to that. Or maybe one should just attribute the name gamely to the fiery tang and robust saltiness of the dish? But, anyhow, what better recipe to start off this section devoted to the fruits of the larder.

Please fire up the sauce if you want, but do know that even though the first mouthful might seem not quite hot enough, the heat builds as you eat. I sometimes go a little cross-cultural in my chili-case and use hot pickled jalapeños from a jar found on the Tex-Mex shelves of the supermarket. And while you're there, do look out for the tiny French nonpareil (or *nonpareilles*) capers: they may be smaller, but they pack more of a pungent punch than the larger capers.

Serves 4–6

3 tablespoons olive oil
8 anchovy fillets, drained and finely
  chopped
2 garlic cloves, peeled and thinly
  sliced, crushed or grated
½ teaspoon crushed red pepper
  flakes, or 1–2 tablespoons jarred
  or canned jalapeño peppers
  (preferably red), drained, sliced,
  and diced, or to taste

1 pound spaghetti
1 x 14-ounce can diced tomatoes
1¼ cups drained pitted black
  olives, chopped a bit
2 tablespoons small capers, well
  rinsed and drained
2–3 tablespoons chopped fresh
  parsley, to serve (optional)
salt and pepper, to taste

♥ Put water for pasta on to boil, though you don't need to get started on the sauce until it is pretty well boiling.

♥ Pour the oil into a wide, shallowish frying pan, Dutch oven, or wok, and put on a medium heat.

♥ Add the finely chopped anchovies and cook for about 3 minutes, pressing and pushing with a wooden spoon, until the anchovies have almost "melted," then add the garlic and red pepper flakes (or sliced, then diced jalapeños) and cook, stirring, for another minute.

♥ This is probably the stage at which you will want to be salting the boiling pasta water and adding the spaghetti to cook, following the package instructions.

188

♥ Going back to the sauce, add the tomatoes, olives, and capers and cook for about 10 minutes, stirring every now and again, by which time it will have thickened slightly. Taste for seasoning.

♥ Just before the pasta is ready, remove about an espresso cupful of cooking water, and reserve it. When the pasta is cooked as desired, drain and add the spaghetti to the sauce in your wok or pan, adding a little reserved pasta water, if needed, to help amalgamate the sauce. Scatter with chopped parsley, if there's some to hand, and serve in slatternly style, preferably with an unfiltered cigarette clamped between crimson-painted lips.

MAKE AHEAD NOTE
The sauce can be made 2 days ahead. Transfer to non-metallic bowl to cool, then cover and refrigerate as soon as possible. Reheat gently in large saucepan, frying pan, or wok, stirring occasionally, until piping hot.

FREEZE NOTE
The cooled sauce can be frozen in resealable container for up to 3 months. Thaw overnight in the refrigerator and reheat as above.

Japanese shrimp

I call these Japanese shrimp out of respect for the sake and wasabi I cook them in, but I am not claiming they are part of the culinary repertoire of Japan. Whatever its emanation, I must tell you this is probably the dish I cook for myself the most often. It's pretty well instant, it is definitely fabulous and it makes me feel smug and holy. Having said that, I should own up that I don't halve this recipe when I'm eating alone.

In keeping with virtuous mode, but also because it's easier, I eat this over salad, letting the savory liquid dress and drench the leaves. It is good, too, and more robust, with brown basmati (a quick microwave-able package of already steamed rice can be the lazy answer) or soba noodles. Of course, it would be at its very peak of perfection if made with the raw organic shrimp I like to keep in my refrigerator, but I can't count on having them, whereas the frozen ones are always the clunk of a freezer door away. (If possible, thaw frozen seafood gradually.) Sometimes, I am in such a hurry, I pour some garlic flavored oil in the wok and fling in ready-chopped gingerroot and chiles from the freezer (bought like that, not the result of efficient planning) or from a jar, followed by the shrimp, then splosh with wasabi-fortified sake, lime juice, and water, and cook as below. Dinner in comfortably under 5 minutes equals weekday salvation.

Serves 2

2 tablespoons water
2 tablespoons sake
½ teaspoon kosher salt or ¼ teaspoon table salt, or to taste
1 tablespoon lime juice
½ teaspoon wasabi powder (or 1 teaspoon paste)

2 teaspoons garlic flavored oil
2 scallions, thinly sliced
8 ounces frozen shell-off large shrimp
salad leaves, rice, or noodles, to serve
2–3 tablespoons chopped fresh cilantro, to serve (optional)

♥ In a pitcher, cup, or bowl, mix together the water, sake, salt, lime juice, and wasabi.

♥ Heat a wok, skillet, or deep, heavy-based frying pan and, when warm, add the garlic flavored oil and scallions and stir-fry for a minute or so, then tip in the frozen shrimp and cook for about 3 minutes or until they start to turn pinkish and lose their frozen glaze.

♥ Add the liquid mixture to the pan, bring to a bubble, and cook for another 2 minutes, stirring the shrimp about a bit in the sauce.

♥ When the shrimp are completely cooked through, serve over salad, rice, or noodles, sprinkling with fresh cilantro, should you have some.

Speedy seafood supper

This is another instance of how your freezer can be your friend in forgetful times. If you haven't remembered to go shopping or haven't got time, energy, or inclination, this is for you. Obviously, you need to have a stock of the mixed seafood in your freezer; I keep bags of shrimp, scallops, and squid in mine. If possible, thaw frozen seafood gradually. If I have a couple of tomatoes in the house that need eating up, I seed and finely chop those rather than open a can of tomatoes.

My favorite way to eat this is with nothing more than some crusty bread to dip into the juices. If you've got only stale bread in the house, splash it with cold water and put it in an oven preheated to 400°F for 10 minutes. If you're canny, of course, you'd keep some frozen semi-baked loaves or rolls in the house.

Serves 2–4, *with bread, and could stretch to 6 if tossed through some pasta*

pinch saffron threads
1 cup freshly boiled water
4 teaspoons garlic flavored oil
6 scallions, thinly sliced
½ teaspoon dried tarragon
½ cup dry vermouth or dry white wine

½ x 14-ounce can diced tomatoes
1 teaspoon kosher salt or ½ teaspoon table salt, or to taste
1 pound frozen mixed seafood
pepper, to taste
fresh herbs, to serve (optional)

♥ Put the saffron threads in a bowl and add 1 cup freshly boiled water.

♥ Warm the garlic flavored oil in a wide, shallow, heavy-based pan over a medium heat, and fry the scallions and dried tarragon for a minute or so.

♥ Add the vermouth (or wine) and let bubble for a minute, then add the saffron in its yellow water, followed by the tomatoes, and let it all come back to a boil. Add half the amount of salt specified above.

♥ Turn up the heat to high, add the frozen seafood, and bring the pan back to a boil, then turn down the heat to medium and cook at a robust simmer till the seafood is hot and cooked through, which should be 3 or 4 minutes (or following the package instructions).

♥ Season with pepper to taste, and add the rest of the salt if required, sprinkle with any available herbs, if you feel like it, and serve, for pleasurable mopping, with some crusty bread.

Pasta with pancetta, parsley, and peppers

I always have a stash of pancetta cubes in the refrigerator to spruce up whatever else I may have on hand, but here they rather take center stage. If you want to use lardons instead, then do. They should be the same – the *cubetti di pancetta*, Italian, and the *lardons*, French.

This may be an off-the-cuff standby, but it really sings for our supper. The salt of the bacon, whichever way you cut it, is balanced fruitily by the sweet softness of the charred bell peppers. Against the fire of the red pepper flakes, there is the bright freshness of the lemon, though if you wanted to you could substitute some vinegary capers.

For me this is perfect post-hangover food, better even than the hotter Slut's Spaghetti on **p.188**; alcohol leaves me wanting not just chiles and carbs, but the bolstering comfort of a bit of fat, too.

I feel the pasta's storecupboard status doesn't rule out the inclusion of fresh parsley, since my kitchen is never without it. But know that this is altogether do-able without. I should admit, too, that when you cook it, the pasta will probably look slightly better sauced than it does opposite; during the shoot, I quite dopily – waiting for the pasta to cook – chucked the panful of sauce into the colander by mistake, when my timer went off. Still, I salvaged most of it, and these things happen to us all.

Serves 2, *heartily*

1 teaspoon garlic flavored oil
1 x 5-ounce container (⅓ cup) pancetta cubes or diced pancetta (or approx. 10 slices smoked bacon, snipped)
½ teaspoon crushed red pepper flakes

zest and juice 1 lemon
2 tablespoons cold water
1 x 12-ounce jar flame-roasted peppers
1 cup parsley leaves, chopped
8 ounces spaghetti
salt and pepper, to taste

♥ Put a big pot of water on to boil for the pasta.

♥ Heat the oil in a medium-sized, heavy-based pan (one you can toss the cooked pasta into later). Fry the pancetta cubes (or bacon) until they start to crisp, then add the red pepper flakes, grated lemon zest and juice, and 2 tablespoons water.

♥ Let this mixture bubble for a minute. Scissor the drained peppers (still in the colander) into bite-sized pieces, then add these to the pan with half the chopped parsley.

♥ Salt the pasta water once it is boiling and cook the pasta following the package instructions. Fish out a cupful of pasta water just before you drain it. When the pasta is cooked, drain loosely and tip into the waiting pan of sauce.

♥ Toss everything together well, and add some pasta water if you need it, then season and sprinkle with the remaining parsley.

195

Pantry paella

For a pantry standby, this is a bit of a showstopper. Of course, I include my freezer here, not least because the freezer is probably the most useful pantry of them all. That is where my supplies not only of frozen shrimp and squid are filed, but also where I stash bits and bobs of leftover roast meats (bagged and frozen immediately after cooling, for up to 3 months; if possible, thaw seafood slowly), most of which could find their way into this, as much as into the pilaf on **p.198**. Any pork leftovers, though, will always end up, and honorably, in this paella. And if there is no pork, I'd either add chicken or (more authentically) some diced chorizo sausages, of which I keep a stock in the refrigerator.

I'm sure a card-carrying Iberophile could find this deficient in numerous ways – not least the fact that I pronounce it in the English style, sounding the "l"s – but I defy you to eat it and not want second helpings.

Serves 4 hungry *personas*

pinch saffron threads
¼ cup oloroso sherry
2 tablespoons regular olive oil
3 scallions, thinly sliced
1 clove garlic, peeled and thinly
  sliced
1¼ cups Bomba (or other) paella
  rice, or arborio rice
8 ounces raw frozen shrimp, thawed
3 tubes (1 cup) frozen baby squid,
  thawed and sliced

1½ cups diced cooked pork
1¼ cups frozen peas
2 cups chicken broth (ready-made,
  concentrate, or cube), preferably
  organic
salt, to taste
1 lemon, cut into wedges (to serve)
small bunch chopped fresh
  cilantro, to serve

♥ Put the saffron threads into a small pan over medium heat with the sherry and warm them, not letting the pan come to a boil. Leave to cool. Heat the oil in a wide, heavy-based pan. Cook the scallions for a few minutes.

♥ Add the sliced garlic to the pan and cook for a minute or so more. Add the rice, slicking it in the oil, and then the shrimp, sliced baby squid, pork, and peas, and turn everything in the oil.

♥ Heat the chicken broth, or make up the concentrate/cube with boiling water, and add the hot stock to the pan, followed by the warmed sherry and saffron. Stir to mix and bring back to a bubble, then turn down to the gentlest simmer, but leave uncovered.

♥ Cook *without stirring* for 15–20 minutes, by which time the rice should have absorbed the liquid and be tender.

♥ Now you can fork the rice through to separate the grains, and check the seasoning, adding salt to taste.

♥ Serve the paella edged with lemon wedges and sprinkled with cilantro.

197

Mixed meat pilaf

This is enormously gratifying, especially when you know it is made from the leavings from other meals and a quick trawl through the kitchen. True, the fresh cilantro, parsley, and pomegranate seeds that I mark optional for serving elevate the pilaf from a dish you savor while eating to a dish you savor before eating too, but it is a recipe that allows for any amount of additions and omissions. Just ransack your refrigerator and pantry and proceed accordingly.

Serves 2–3

1 tablespoon vegetable oil
1 onion, finely chopped
½ teaspoon cumin seeds
½ teaspoon coriander seeds
½ teaspoon dried thyme
scant 1¼ cups basmati rice, or a mixture of brown basmati, red Camargue, and wild rice
2 cups chicken broth (can, carton, or cube), preferably organic
approx. 2 cups shredded cold meat

salt and pepper, to taste
2–3 tablespoons toasted pine nuts or sliced almonds, or a mixture
2 tablespoons chopped fresh parsley, to serve (optional)
2 tablespoons chopped fresh cilantro, to serve (optional)
2–3 tablespoons pomegranate seeds, to serve (optional)

♥ Warm the oil in a heavy-based saucepan which comes with a lid, then add the chopped onion and cook for 5 minutes over a lowish heat, stirring frequently, before adding the cumin and coriander seeds and thyme, and cooking, as before, until the onion is soft; this should be about another 5 minutes, giving 10 minutes cooking time in total.

♥ Add the rice and push it about in the oily, spiced onion with a wooden spoon or rigid spatula until it is slicked and glossy. Heat the broth until almost boiling, then pour the hot broth into the pan and bring to a boil. Cover the pan firmly with a lid and cook over the lowest heat possible for 15 minutes for regular basmati rice, or up to 40 minutes for the 3-way rice mix.

♥ Add the shredded meat and fork it all through, then replace the lid and leave it all to cook for another 5 minutes to let the meat heat through and the rice finish cooking.

♥ Check that the meat is piping hot and the rice is tender, season to taste, then take off the heat and fork through most of the pine nuts, herbs, and pomegranate seeds, if using (or tip into a dish before doing this), and decorate each bowl of pilaf with the remaining bits.

Small pasta with salami

Although this started off as a last-minute children's dinner (when I was faced unexpectedly with having to provide mid-evening sustenance to hungrily marauding teenagers), it has turned into a bit of a house special. I always have beans, tomatoes, and pasta in the cupboard and my refrigerator is piled high with packages of salami, bought for filling toasted sandwiches and general grazing. If you want to use a proper *salame* (by which I mean the sausage, not pre-sliced) and cut it into chunks yourself, by all means do, but you will need to double, at the very least, the weight below. For speed and simplicity (and, pointedly, this is child's play), the pre-sliced salami does the trick, and I rather love the way the strips, when cooked, look like a lapdog's tongue.

I dare say you could use regular short pasta, not the midget size I stipulate here, but I never have. Whenever I'm asked for this dish, I am made to understand fully that deviation would not be tolerated.

Serves 3–4

2⅔ cups (11 ounces) ditalini or
   mezzi tubetti pasta
3 ounces (about 15 slices) Milano
   salami, scissored into strips
1 x 14-ounce can diced tomatoes,
   plus ½ can water

2 tablespoons butter
1 bouquet garni (mixed herb
   sachet or bag – optional)
1 x 15-ounce can cannellini beans,
   drained and rinsed

♥ Bring some water for the pasta to a boil and salt generously – or to taste – then put in the ditalini or mezzi tubetti, which will probably need around 10 minutes (though check the package), and get on with the sauce while it cooks.

♥ Warm a fairly wide, heavy-based saucepan – you can see the one I use on the right – and toss in the salami strips, not worrying if they clump together. Stir with a wooden spoon over a medium heat for a minute or two.

♥ Tip in the tomatoes and rinse about ½ can water around in the empty can and then add that, too.

♥ Drop in 1 tablespoon butter and stir well with your wooden spoon, then add the bouquet garni, if using, and the drained beans, stir and leave it to bubble away – firmly but gently – while the pasta finishes cooking.

♥ Just before draining the pasta, lower in a measuring cup and take out a little of the cooking water.

♥ Stir the drained pasta into the sauce, remove from the heat, and now stir in the remaining butter. If you think the sauce needs it, splash in some of the pasta cooking water, and stir again with your wooden spoon. Leave to stand for 2 minutes before serving, removing the bouquet garni (if used) as you do so.

201

Chorizo and chickpea stew

If ever there were justification for cupboard love, this would be it: a full-on feast thrown together to enormous effect, simply with ingredients that you can more or less keep on permanent standby. And, like so many of these recipes, it's pretty well instant. After all, if you haven't got time to shop, it's hardly likely you'll be able to spend many hours at the stove.

I am, anyway, a huge fan of bulgur wheat – think couscous, only more robust – but cooked like this, with some strands of pasta tossed in hot oil first, it really has something extra. I was taught to do this, just chatting stoveside, by an Egyptian friend when I was in my twenties, and I've never seen any reason to change the drill. He, actually, didn't use torn-up spaghettini but, rather, lokshen, which are the short lengths of vermicelli customarily found in *echt* chicken soup.

This is a tradition about as far away from the chorizo-cooking culture as you could get, but the chickpea-studded, tomatoey and paprika-hot stew goes extremely well with the nubbly grain. I keep a stock of cherry tomatoes in sauce in the cupboard, but regular canned tomatoes could be substituted easily enough.

Serves 4

2 tablespoons regular olive oil
2 ounces spaghettini or vermicelli,
  torn into 1-inch lengths
2¾ cups bulgur wheat
1 teaspoon cinnamon
2 teaspoons kosher salt or 1
  teaspoon table salt
1 quart water
2 bay leaves
12 ounces chorizo, cut into coins
  and then halved

¼ cup amontillado sherry
½ cup (about 16) soft dried
  apricots, snipped into pieces with
  scissors (optional)
2 x 15-ounce cans chickpeas
  (garbanzo beans) or mixed beans,
  rinsed and drained in a colander
2 x 14-ounce cans cherry
  tomatoes, plus 1½ cans water
salt and pepper, to taste
fresh cilantro, to serve (optional)

♥ Warm the olive oil in a thick-bottomed saucepan on a medium heat.

♥ Fry the pasta bits in the oil for a minute, stirring, until they look like slightly scorched straws.

♥ Then add the bulgur wheat and stir for another minute or two.

♥ Stir in the cinnamon and the salt, and then pour the water into the pan. Add the bay

leaves, and bring to a boil, then turn down to the lowest heat, add a lid, and leave for 15 minutes, until all the water has been absorbed.

♥ Put another thick-bottomed saucepan on a medium heat, add the chorizo pieces, and fry until the orange oil runs out. Then add the sherry and let it bubble away. Add the apricots (if using), along with the chickpeas (or beans) and canned tomatoes, and ¾ fill each empty tomato can with water and swish it out into the pan. Put on a high heat to bubble for about 5 minutes. Add salt and pepper to taste.

♥ Serve with the bulgur wheat and, if there's any on hand, some chopped cilantro.

MAKE AHEAD NOTE
The stew can be made up to 2 days ahead. Transfer to non-metallic bowl to cool, then cover and refrigerate as soon as possible. Reheat gently in large saucepan, stirring occasionally, until piping hot.

FREEZE NOTE
The cooled stew can be frozen in airtight container for up to 3 months. Thaw overnight in the refrigerator and reheat as above.

I'd be surprised if you had any chorizo and chickpea stew left over, but expect some bulgur wheat.
I make a lot as I feel happier knowing I'm in the running for some tabbouleh. Yes, I know that the tabbouleh, with its reliance on fresh herbs (and they should be present, at about double the volume at least of bulgur wheat, in any self-respecting tabbouleh) is absolutely not a storecupboard recipe. But just because you didn't have time to go to the stores today, doesn't mean you won't have time tomorrow. Besides, it seemed wrong to separate satellite recipe from mother ship.

To make this you really only need to adhere to roughly double the volume of herbs to bulgur. To be frank, the best way to do this is neither by weight nor volume, but taste.

Serves 2–4

1½ cups leftover cooked bulgur wheat

2 cups chopped mint

2 cups chopped flat-leaf parsley

¼ cup chopped dill (optional)

2–3 medium-sized (1 cup chopped) tomatoes, seeded

3 scallions, finely chopped

zest 1 lemon and juice ½, plus more to taste

2 tablespoons garlic flavored oil (or 2 tablespoons regular olive oil plus 1 clove garlic, minced)

splash fruity extra-virgin olive oil

1 teaspoon kosher salt or ½ teaspoon table salt, or to taste

pomegranate seeds (optional)

♥ Put the cold cooked bulgur wheat, the chopped herbs, tomatoes, and sliced scallions into a bowl. Zest in the lemon and mix.

205

♥ Now pour in the juice of ½ lemon, along with the garlic flavored oil (or regular olive oil with some minced garlic), the splash of extra-virgin olive oil, and the salt, and mix with a fork. Taste to see if you want any more lemon juice or salt. And if there are any pomegranate seeds on hand, sprinkle some over on serving; lovely alongside pretty much anything, but do consider a block of halloumi, sliced and fried in a hot, dry pan.

Indian roasted potatoes

I know there are a lot of spices here to keep in the cupboard, but these potatoes are a fantastic brunch dish with a Bloody Maria (see **p.441**) and some fried eggs; moreover, I can't tell you how useful this is to bring out when you're roasting a chicken – again – and want to give supper a less quotidian feel. Look – you'll never find me complaining about a plain roast chicken ever, ever, ever, but that doesn't make me any the less appreciative of a recipe that will add a bit of an exotic party feel to a comfy favorite. It's not a sin to want to spice things up occasionally.

This doesn't have to involve any swinging from the chandeliers, culinarily speaking: in fact, it is a shamelessly lazified version of an altogether more hands-on Indian original.

Serves 6

2 pounds (4 or 5 large) potatoes, unpeeled
2 tablespoons peppery cold-pressed canola oil (see Kitchen Confidential **p.16**) or regular olive oil
2 teaspoons ground turmeric
1 teaspoon fennel seeds
1 teaspoon cumin seeds
1 teaspoon nigella seeds
1 teaspoon black mustard seeds
½ teaspoon hot chili powder
1 head garlic
½ red onion, finely diced
juice 1 lime
salt to taste

♥ Preheat the oven to 400°F. Scrub and then dice the unpeeled potatoes into 1–1½ inch cubes.

♥ Put the potato cubes into a resealable bag with the oil and spices, seal it, then shake everything about in the bag to coat the cubes.

♥ Tip them onto a wide, shallow lipped baking sheet – high sides stop the potatoes from crisping up. Break up the head of garlic and scatter the unpeeled cloves around the potato cubes.

♥ Cook in the oven for 1 hour without turning. Meanwhile, put the diced onion into a bowl, cover with the lime juice and toss, then leave to macerate while the potatoes cook.

♥ When the potatoes come out of the oven, transfer them to a warmed serving dish and sprinkle with some salt. Lift the onion dice out of the lime juice and scatter these over the potatoes.

MAKE AHEAD NOTE
The potatoes can be cut 1 day ahead. Submerge in cold water until needed, then drain and pat dry. Leftovers should be refrigerated when cool and can be kept for 2 days. Reheat in a 400°F oven for about 15 minutes, until piping hot.

Making leftovers right

Any stray, cold potatoes can be added to the Quesadillas on **p.433** *along with the sliced avocado to great effect. In which case, you might want to dispense with the jalapeños in that recipe.*

Curly pasta with feta, spinach, and pine nuts

This can be a life saver when you suddenly find you have a tableful of people unexpectedly for supper, and all the more valuable should any of them be vegetarian. But it doesn't have to be regarded as for emergencies only: it's far too good to be kept behind closed doors simply in stealthy readiness. Anyhow, I like to know that I always have the wherewithal to cook something at a moment's notice.

A salty brick of wrapped feta, like halloumi, can live unopened for ages in the refrigerator, and my spinach is frozen. As we were always told in childhood, spinach is very good for you, giving you all the minerals it absorbs through the soil. Unfortunately, it will absorb the less healthy stuff too, which is why it is worth buying organic spinach even when frozen: this is what I stock up on and recommend you do, too.

The curly pasta I favor here are called cavatappi (literally, corkscrews) – and, should this be of help, are no. 87 in the De Cecco catalogue – but fusilli are probably easier to find and fit the bill, equally.

Serves 6, *as a main course*

⅓ cup pine nuts
2 tablespoons garlic flavored oil
1 onion, peeled and sliced
salt and pepper, to taste
1 pound cavatappi, fusilli, or other
  short pasta

¼ teaspoon allspice
1 pound frozen leaf spinach,
  preferably organic
8 ounces feta cheese, crumbled
3–4 tablespoons grated Parmesan
  cheese

♥ Put abundant amounts of water on to boil for the pasta.

♥ Toast the pine nuts by tossing them about in a hot, dry, heavy-based frying pan (for ease use one that will take the sauce later) until they become golden, then remove to a cold plate.

♥ Heat the garlic flavored oil in the pan, and add the onion slices. Keep them on a lowish heat, stirring, for about 8–10 minutes, until soft. If they look like they're getting too brown, sprinkle with a little salt (to help draw out the juices and slow down browning).

♥ When the water comes to a boil, add salt and then the pasta.

♥ When the onion is ready, add the allspice. Then add the frozen spinach: you need to keep stirring this, to help the frozen spinach melt consistently.

♥ Just before you drain the pasta, scoop out about an espresso cupful of cooking water, and add to the spinach sauce mix.

♥ Crumble the feta into the spinach sauce, stirring as the billiard baize of spinach becomes creamy with the cheese melting into it. Stir in 3 tablespoons of the Parmesan, before tasting to see if you want to add any more.

♥ Drain the pasta and toss into the feta spinach sauce to mix, then season to taste. Decant into a, preferably warmed, serving bowl, then add the toasted pine nuts and toss through before serving.

Making leftovers right

PASTA SALAD *I do not consider myself a pasta salad person, rather the contrary, but I promise you that this pasta, albeit leftover, still has something to give. Cover and refrigerate it (for up to 2 days) straight after its first outing. To make a salad, fork it about a bit to break it up, then add some lemon juice and olive oil, a sprinkling of salt and a grinding of pepper, all to taste; box it up and take it to work with you for your lunch.*

210

Standby starch

This is exactly what it says: an almost instant solution to the problem of having a meal to bulk up without time to cook potatoes or rice. True, I often use a package of gnocchi on such an occasion, but they are less versatile. This goes with pretty well everything: a stew, roasted chicken, some grilled fish or meat; furthermore, it can turn a paltry amount of cold meat into a substantial supper, especially if you add a drained, de-glooped can of chickpeas to the couscous before it gets soaked.

And about the soaking, I should be open. I know this is not the correct, the authentic way to cook couscous. You should actually soak it in cold water before steaming it over a simmering pan. But I find this works, and – as with the sprightly Arugula and Lemon Couscous on **p.90**, which is cooked differently, but still not traditionally – it improves the quality of my cooking and eating life (is there any other?) immensely.

Serves 4–6, *as part of a meal*

1⅓ cups couscous
¼ teaspoon dried thyme
½ teaspoon ground cumin

1⅔ cups chicken (or vegetable) broth (carton, can or cube), preferably organic
salt and pepper, to taste

♥ Put the couscous in a bowl with the thyme and cumin.

♥ Heat the broth until almost boiling, then stir the hot broth into the couscous, cover the bowl with plastic wrap (or with a large plate), and leave for 10–15 minutes.

♥ Remove the plastic wrap; all the liquid should have been absorbed. Fluff up the couscous with a fork and season well with salt and pepper. If you have a roasted chicken or other meats you are eating with this, then do add any pan juices to the finished couscous at the last minute to add extra flavor.

Halloumi with beets and lime

It's almost shameful how good dinner can be when it's just a case of opening a couple of packages. I wouldn't have guessed it myself, had it not been for the fact that I had some people over for dinner and had to rustle up a vegetarian option at the last minute. Halloumi, otherwise known in my house as "squeaky cheese," is a fantastic standby: I think of it as vegetarian bacon, though not exclusively; I am a committed carnivore but couldn't envisage life without a package or three in my refrigerator at all times. Beets I am more wary about, but I happened to have a vacuum-sealed package of small peeled and steamed beets, left as is and not poisoned with vinegar, and suddenly felt compelled to mix the intense saltiness of the former with the sometimes overwhelming sweetness of the latter.

It didn't just work: it *really* worked. True, I blended the beets with some lime juice and olive oil, but if you haven't got a blender, just chop up the beets and tumble them over the hot halloumi before spritzing with a bit of lime. And when I say "lime," know that I am here, as often, referring to plastic squeezy lime: think lime-shaped bottle in vivid green plastic to depict its contents, the juiced fruit always available (and see **p.17**).

Any salad you have in the house will be good with this halloumi and beet mix, though I would be particularly grateful had I any of the darker, more peppery leaves to sit the halloumi on, with some warm pita, or any bread, on the side. Alternatively, you could stretch to a side salad, making a dressing out of lime juice, ground cumin, and olive oil and adding some peppery tortilla chips as you toss leaves and dressing together.

I know the slices of halloumi with their splodge of deep pink look a bit cheffy on their plates, but try and ignore that. One bite will let you know that this is a dish for the glutton, not the tiresomely fastidious gourmet.

Serves 2

8 ounces halloumi cheese	2 teaspoons lime juice, or to taste
6 ounces cold cooked beets (1 large or 2 small beets, or approx. ¾ of an 8-ounce vacuum-sealed package)	2 tablespoons regular olive oil

♥ Cut open the package of halloumi over the sink, to lose all the briny juices, then transfer to a board and slice. I get 8 slices out of 1 block, but I know if I stopped rushing or had more dexterity (or any knife skills) I could easily get 10.

♥ Put on some disposable vinyl gloves (to avoid that touch of the Lady Macbeths, and see **p.17**) and get out 2 little beets, or 1 large, from the package, and chop roughly before

212

blitzing with a handheld stick blender (or in a standard blender), adding the lime juice and oil as you go.

♥ Warm a large, dry, non-stick frying pan over high heat and, when hot, add the slices of halloumi. Keep the heat high and after a minute or so the halloumi should have scorch marks on the underside, then flip the slices over (I find a pair of cook's tongs most suitable for the task) and cook likewise, before transferring to a pair of salad-lined plates.

♥ Divide the beet and lime purée between the 2 plates, dolloping it alongside the halloumi strips, and serve with some warm bread.

MAKE AHEAD NOTE
The beet purée can be made 1 day ahead. Cover and refrigerate until needed and whisk before using.

213

Pepper, anchovy, and egg salad

This is yet another recipe which comes via Anna Del Conte; it's also one that, by comfort-inducing coincidence, my mother used to make, too. Neither of them would approve, I'm sure, of my lazy shortcut in the form of the ready fire roasted and skinned sweet peppers that I buy in jars from the supermarket or a Spanish deli: Anna, I imagine, would tut at the lowering of standards and my mother would have tutted even more loudly at the extravagance. There is a positive concerto of disapproval going on inside my head. Luckily, it is instantly dispelled on eating. I cook to please others, certainly, but above all to please myself, and this pleases me very much.

Serves 4–6, *depending on what goes alongside*

4 eggs

2 x 12-ounce jars flame-roasted peppers, drained

1 garlic clove, peeled

salt and pepper, to taste

¼ cup regular olive oil

2 tablespoons chopped fresh parsley, plus more for sprinkling (optional but preferable)

1 tablespoon drained capers (preferably tiny nonpareils), from a jar

about 12 anchovies, from a jar

♥ To make a tender-yolked, not-quite-hard-boiled egg, bring room-temperature eggs to boil in a pan of water. Turn off the heat and leave them for 10 minutes. Refresh the eggs with cold water and then peel them. For seriously hard-boiled (advisable for those with a compromised or weak immune system, such as the old and frail, the very young, and the pregnant), keep the heat under the pan for the 10 minutes. Once peeled, the eggs won't take long to cool down, although I prefer to eat them before they are outright chilly.

♥ Cut the drained, roasted peppers into strips and arrange them on a serving plate.

♥ Cover the peeled garlic clove with some salt in a bowl, and then crush the garlic to make a paste. Add a good grinding of pepper and the oil, sprinkle in the 2 tablespoons parsley (if using), and stir to mix.

♥ Quarter the eggs and arrange with the roasted peppers, then scatter with the drained capers and add the anchovy fillets.

♥ Spoon the garlic (and parsley) sauce over the salad, then decorate with a little more parsley and serve with some good French bread.

MAKE AHEAD NOTE

The hard-boiled eggs can be made up to 4 days ahead. Cool but leave shells on, then store in airtight container in the refrigerator, and remove shells just before serving.

215

Everyday brownies

It's not as if I were short of a brownie recipe or two: I have over the years made them on easy autopilot; but I am no less grateful for this everyday, no-notice version. They are less extravagant – I use cocoa powder in place of the good-quality chocolate, and stud the mixture with a newsstand's or convenience store's bar or two of milk chocolate – although to taste them, you would never, never guess. They ooze with such dark elegance and deep, deep chocolatiness.

This is the recipe you turn to when a child or colleague informs you last thing that you're expected to make something for a bake sale tomorrow. You can just smile serenely and head for the cupboard. If you're working from a more restrained array, so are clean out of light brown sugar, and there's no chance to nip to a convenience store for the chocolate, then just use 1½ cups regular white sugar and up the butter to 1½ sticks and the cocoa to a heady 1 cup.

A final note or, rather, nag: when I say cocoa powder, I do mean unsweetened cocoa; do not under any circumstance ever substitute drinking chocolate.

216

Makes 16

1¼ sticks (10 tablespoons) unsalted butter
1¾ cups (packed) light brown sugar
¾ cup unsweetened cocoa powder, sifted
1 cup all-purpose flour
1 teaspoon baking soda
pinch salt
4 eggs

1 teaspoon vanilla extract
approx. 6 ounces milk chocolate, chopped into small nuggety chunks (or 1 cup chips)
confectioner's sugar, to dust (optional)

1 x aluminum foil–lined baking pan or foil pan, approx. 13 x 9 x 2 inches

♥ Preheat the oven to 375°F. Melt the butter over a gentle heat in a medium-sized saucepan.

♥ When it's melted, add the sugar, stirring with a wooden spoon (still over a low heat) to help it blend with the melted butter.

♥ Whisk together the cocoa powder, flour, baking soda, and pinch of salt, and then stir into the pan; when mixed (this will be a very dry mixture, and not wholly blended at this stage), remove from the heat.

♥ In a bowl or pitcher, whisk the eggs with the vanilla extract and then mix into the brownie mixture in the pan.

♥ Stir in the chopped chocolate and quickly pour and scrape into a foil–lined baking pan or disposable foil pan, spreading the mixture with a spatula, and cook in the preheated oven for approx. 20–25 minutes. It will look set, dark and dry on top, but when you feel the surface, you will sense it is still wibbly underneath and a cake tester will come out gungy. This is desirable.

♥ Transfer the pan to a rack to cool a little before cutting into 16 pieces and dusting with confectioner's sugar. I love these gorgeously warm. But then again, I love them cold, too. Actually, when cold they are properly speaking more brownie-like: gooily tender within and chewy on top.

MAKE AHEAD NOTE
The brownies can be made up to 3 days ahead and stored in airtight container. Will keep for total of 5 days.

FREEZE NOTE
The brownies can be frozen for up to 3 months in airtight container, layered with baking parchment. Thaw overnight in cool place.

Part II

KITCHEN COMFORTS

CHICKEN AND ITS PLACE IN MY KITCHEN

I have written before of my mother's roast chicken, our Saturday lunch ritual, the way she always cooked two chickens at the same time (one to eat, as she'd say, and the other for picking at from the refrigerator) and the lemony and rich, yet calming, savory scent that filled the air as they cooked. And for me, a chicken remains the basic unit of home. I don't really feel a kitchen is mine until I've cooked a chicken there.

Even if I don't always follow my mother's practice of dedicating an entire bird for casual consumption, a refrigerator feels all wrong to me unless there is some cold chicken in it, either to pick at or, with minimal tweaking, to be turned into another meal. My methods of roasting a chicken have changed a little over time; it's less often now that I smear the pale breast thickly with butter before putting it in the oven, finding these days that a golden trickle of flavorsome oil does the trick just as well. I can never, though, quite stop myself from popping either a squeezed-out or still plump and juicy lemon half inside the cavity.

I have, though, become increasingly fussy about the type of chicken I'm cooking. My mother would have been enormously skeptical about the contemporary emphasis on the free-range and organic, seeing it as little more than a scam to make people spend more money than they need to. If I disagree, it may in part be because we know a lot more about the obscene practices of factory farming than she ever did; but I concede, too, that she came out of a wartime childhood, and regarded any form of profligacy as poor form. I justify my extravagance (as she'd have seen it), not in a particularly lofty way: a generally uncharacteristic squeamishness comes upon me at the thought of eating the spooky stuff. Besides, the flavor I get from a superior bird is a juicy enough reward. As a quite terrible gravy maker, I relish the fact that an organic chicken seems to make its own: the rich, amber liquid that collects at the bottom of the pan needs no more than a spritz of vermouth or lemon, or just some water from the kettle to help scrape up the flavor-rich nuggets that stick there. Plus, this flavor really does go bone-deep, and a single carcass left over from an organic bird makes the basis for a soup later in the week. But I realize that I am lucky to be able to make the choice, and feel grateful rather than crusading on the issue.

Wherever your chicken has come from, count on giving it 20 minutes per pound at 400°F plus 20 minutes overall, although I sometimes leave out the 20 minutes overall part and roast the chicken in a hotter oven at 425°F. There are two things I should add: the chicken will take longer to cook if it is refrigerator cold, and you should check when it comes out of the oven that it is properly cooked through, by cutting into the flesh between the body and the thigh. The liquid that runs out should be clear once the chicken's cooked; it's worth remembering, though, that the dark meat of an organic bird is actually darker, and redder, than the dark meat of a factory-farmed one. The leg and thigh meat will keep a slightly pink tinge. But if you have any doubts, know that the more luscious meat of the organic bird means that cooking it for longer shouldn't dry it out.

PLAIN ROAST
CHICKEN

My daughter prefers her roasted chicken with a side-order of "Pie Insides" (which is to say, the Leeks in Bechamel Sauce from **p.370**) and proper, old-fashioned roasted potatoes. Since I felt my recipe for these didn't need an outing in its own right elsewhere on these pages, it seemed only fair – to make life easier in the kitchen now – to give a rapid reprise here. I work on the principle of 1 big potato per person and 1 extra for luck per 4 people. Peel each potato, and cut a central triangle-shaped piece out of the middle, which gives you 1 piece with 2 slanted edges, and 2 pieces each with 1 slanted edge. Put all your cut up potatoes in a saucepan filled abundantly with cold, salted water, bring to a boil, and then let them bubble away rambunctiously for 4 minutes. Meanwhile, heat a large roasting pan in the oven (425°F if you have a single oven and your chicken's cooking in it, but if you've got a double oven, let the potato oven burn hotter, at 450°F) with about 1 pound goose fat or 1 quart corn oil in it. Drain the potatoes, let them dry off a little, then put them back into their still hot saucepan, sprinkle over some semolina, using about 1 teaspoon per pound of potatoes. Clamp the lid on and shake the pan about briefly, just to make the par-boiled potatoes a little fuzzy around the edges and then transfer them carefully to the hot fat and cook for 20–30 minutes per side, or until gloriously golden outside and fluffily tender inside.

And if you want the taste of a roasted chicken dinner without quite as much fandango, then I suggest my Oz-inspired roast chook with leeks and butternut squash. Put your chicken in a large pan, halve and seed a butternut squash (but do not bother to peel), cut it into roughly 2 inch chunks and tumble it into the pan along with 2 or 3 fatly sliced leeks (or 1 leek and a couple of chunked-up, but unpeeled, potatoes) and an unwaxed lemon cut into 8, before drizzling with garlic-infused oil, adding a sprig or two of rosemary or thyme, and roasting in a 425°F oven in the traditional manner.

A roasted chicken, cooked in either of the above ways, will always find a place in my home, and repeatedly, but nothing can ever feel as important to me as my Mother's Praised Chicken (opposite), which is not merely a recipe, but my family's culinary fingerprint. It's not quite poached, not quite braised, and so I've settled on "praised" – which feels exactly right, as for me both cooking and eating it feel like a devotional act.

My mother's praised chicken

This may well be – indeed is – the smell, the taste, the dish that says "family" to me and my siblings, and brings our long-absent mother back to the kitchen and the table with us. But the fact that I've cooked it more often and over more years than I've cooked anything else doesn't make writing a recipe for it any easier. If anything, it makes it harder, much harder.

Relax: obviously, it's not the reliability from a practical perspective that's in question; rather, I cook this so often I know that one written-down version of it can't take into account or begin to convey all its possible permutations. For example, you could toss in some cubed pancetta before you add the chicken and maybe use hard cider as your flavor-giving alcoholic beverage of choice; or you could add some gingerroot, freshly grated or sliced, along with the oil and use Chinese cooking wine or sake in place of the white wine or vermouth and put cilantro stalks in, along with the parsley or instead, and add fresh, seeded red chile, cut into fine almost-rings, as well as chopped cilantro, at the end. At all times, you can play with the vegetables: fennel, if you're a fennelphile, brings a beautiful aniseed fragrance, which, if you cared to, you could boost by adding a splosh of pastis in place of the wine; you can similarly think of adding parsnips and some chunks of squash or pumpkin, though these would probably be better added halfway, or even later in the cooking process. And very often, when all is heaped into the pan at the beginning, just before it is left to cook itself into aromatic succulence, I grate in the zest of 1 lemon, then squeeze in the juice and maybe add a sprinkling of dried mint, too. I could go on and on.

By its very nature, this symbolizes the very free-style form of cooking that a recipe seems to argue against. So, let me reassure you that really all you need to know is that you simply brown the chicken before adding vegetables and just enough liquid to cover, and cook them slowly before eating

on top of rice. I like brown basmati here, and work on ⅓–½ cup per head before cooking, depending on the ages and appetites of the eaters. On the whole, I tend to go for the higher rather than lower measure – no huge surprise, I'm sure – not because I think it's all needed, but because one of my favorite uses of leftover meat is a variation of a salad I make with leftover turkey at Christmas: chunks or shreds of cold chicken stirred into cold brown basmati rice, with pomegranate seeds, sunflower seeds or any mixture of similar seeds, fresh dill, lemon juice, salt, and 1–2 drops of gorgeously flavored oil (a rich, mustardy yellow cold-pressed canola – see Kitchen Confidential, **p.16** – being my favorite).

But we'll get to leftovers later and, obviously if you want, you can ditch the rice and think of serving steamed potatoes, instead. And if you can steam them above the chicken, so much the better. But rice it has to be in our house. Since I have a rice cooker, this also happens to be the easy option for me; though, most pressingly, it is part of the ritual for us. And, as I am presenting this in its role as a family favorite, my kitchen perennial, in fact, I feel I can allow myself to be bossier than normal, even telling you how you should eat it: by this I mean the Lawsonian familial practice of adding fresh fronds of dill and some English mustard – just a pinprick or great, sinus-clearing teaspoonfuls – as we greedily, gratefully eat.

Serves 4–8 *(cooked this way it seems to go much further than roasted chicken, so you can feed more the first time, or have plenty for the rest of the week)*

1 large chicken, preferably organic
2 teaspoons garlic flavored oil
scant ½ cup white wine or dry white vermouth
2–3 leeks, cleaned, trimmed, and cut into approx. 2 inch logs
2–3 carrots, peeled and cut into sticks
1–2 celery stalks, sliced
approx. 2 quarts cold water
1 bouquet garni (mixed herb sachet or bag) or 1 teaspoon dried herbs

fresh parsley stalks or few sprigs, tied or banded together
2 teaspoons kosher salt or 1 teaspoon table salt
2 teaspoons red peppercorns, or good grinding pepper

to serve:
chopped leaves, from parsley stalks above
chopped fresh dill
English mustard

♥ Get out a large, flame-safe cooking pot (with a lid) in which the chicken can fit snugly: mine is about 11 inches wide x 4 inches deep.

♥ On a washable board, un-truss the chicken, put it breast-side down, and press down until you hear the breastbone crack. (As you may imagine, I like this.) Then press down again, so that the chicken is flattened slightly. Now cut off the ankle joints below the drumstick (but keep them); I find kitchen scissors up to the task.

♥ Put the oil in the pan to heat, then brown the chicken for a few minutes breast-side down, and turn up the heat and turn over the chicken, tossing in the feet as you do so. Still over a vigorous heat add the wine or vermouth to the pan and let it bubble down a little before adding the leeks, carrots, and celery.

♥ Pour in enough cold water to cover the chicken, though the very top of it may poke out, then pop in the bouquet garni or your herbs of choice, and the parsley stalks (if I have a bunch, I cut the stalks off to use here, but leave them tied in the rubber band) or parsley sprigs along with the salt and red peppercorns (I just love these beautiful red berries) or a good grinding of regular pepper.

♥ The chicken should be almost completely submerged by now and if not, do add some more cold water. You want it just about covered.

♥ Bring to a bubble, clamp on the lid, turn the heat to very low, and let cook for 1½–2 hours. I tend to give it 1½ hours, or 1 hour 40 minutes, then leave it to stand with the heat off, but the lid still on, for the remaining 20–30 minutes.

♥ Serve the chicken and accompanying vegetables with brown basmati rice, adding a ladleful or two of liquid over each shallow bowl, as you go, and putting fresh dill and mustard on the table for the eaters to add as they wish.

FREEZE NOTE
The cooked meat can be frozen, as soon as it is cool, in resealable bags or airtight containers for up to 2 months.

Making leftovers right

For my first leftovers outing, I tend to heat up what liquid is left (remembering to use it within 1–2 days), along with some of the shredded cold chicken, squeeze in lemon or lime juice and stir in some English mustard, and eat it just as it is or over noodles or rice, either way garnished with fresh dill and maybe some parsley or cilantro, too. There's certainly the salad mooted in the introduction to the recipe to consider, and then there are the meals I make if there have been only 4 of us at the table for the original poached chicken and I thus have enough for a meal later. It's not only, you see, that chicken cooked this way goes further: it makes it all so luscious and succulent that you never have cold, dry chicken syndrome to worry about. So much so, that I'd say that if you are ever thinking of making a chicken salad, cook it like this first. (Please remember to take the chicken off the bone and refrigerate it as soon as possible, tightly wrapped in aluminum foil – and use it up within 3–4 days.)

CHICKEN,
BACON, AND
AVOCADO
SALAD

This is one of my favorite combinations, and though I know that, with some good bread to eat alongside, this could stretch to 4, I could much too easily fork it all down myself. The combination of succulent cold chicken, the soft clay of the avocado, the crunch of the lettuce, and the salty shards of bacon make for addictive eating. Give me a BLC over a BLT any day!

I love a faintly sweet vinegar here, and plump for a moscatel, but I know it's not easily come by. I do think it's worth tracking one down (it is so often my vinegar of choice) but otherwise a seasoned rice vinegar is generally stocked by supermarkets these days and makes for a fine substitute. Unless you like a really sweet vinaigrette, I wouldn't go the balsamic route.

Serves 2–3 *(2 very generously, but could serve 4 as a modest lunch with a baguette or a pile of soft wraps)*

1 teaspoon garlic flavored oil
4 slices smoked bacon
½ iceberg lettuce, torn into fork- or bite-sized pieces
3 cups shredded cooked chicken
2 smallish avocados
2 teaspoons Dijon mustard

1 tablespoon (sweetish) vinegar, such as moscatel or seasoned rice vinegar
pepper, to taste
splash olive oil or canola oil (optional)
1 tablespoon chopped chives, to serve

♥ Heat the oil in a frying pan and fry the bacon until crisp. Remove to a piece of aluminum foil or paper towel, but don't wash out the pan.

♥ Put the lettuce into a large salad bowl and add the shredded cold chicken.

♥ Halve the avocados, removing the pits, and scoop out spoonfuls of the pale green flesh onto the lettuce and chicken.

♥ Add the mustard to the oily bacon juices in the pan, whisking to combine. Then whisk in the vinegar, grind in pepper to taste, pour over the salad and swiftly and deftly toss to mix, adding a splash of olive or canola oil, if more oil is needed.

♥ Break the bacon up into pieces, crumbling most of it into the salad, and toss again.

♥ Finally, sprinkle with the remaining bacon and the chives.

CHINATOWN
CHICKEN
SALAD

There are many versions of this salad, but I've majored on one that provides the most crunch factor, not least because I sometimes leave out that essential ingredient, the wonton wrapper. When I'm in an Asian store, I buy a package or two, but the truth is they only come frozen and you don't need a whole package for the salad. (Still, they are delicious as a Chinese version of the Italian fried and sweetened pastry strips: just fry as below and dust with confectioners' sugar: good with coffee.) I love the name of this salad so much, I won't consider changing it even if, in place of wontons, I throw in a similarly crunchy handful of tortilla chips.

228

Serves 6, *as a main meal*

2 ounces (about 12) wonton
   wrappers (or handful tortilla
   chips)
vegetable oil (for frying wontons)

for the dressing:
1 red or green chile, seeded and
   finely chopped
2 teaspoons chopped fresh
   gingerroot
4 teaspoons lime juice or rice
   vinegar
3 tablespoons soy sauce
splash Asian sesame oil
½ teaspoon sugar

for the salad:
½ cup salted peanuts, chopped into
   pieces or whole, if desired
1 iceberg lettuce, shredded
1½ cups (6 ounces) bean sprouts
4 scallions, cut into thirds and
   julienned
1 red bell pepper, seeded and cut
   into fine strips
4 cups shredded cooked, cooled
   chicken
handful fresh chopped cilantro, to
   serve

♥ If you are using the wonton wrappers, begin by heating about ½ inch oil in a frying pan.

♥ Once the oil is hot, peel off the papery wrappers from the pack and add them, in batches of 3–4 at a time, to the pan. Be careful, they need just a few seconds a side to turn golden, and will continue to darken as you remove them to a cookie sheet lined with some paper towels.

♥ Continue cooking the wonton wrappers in batches until you have a baking sheet full of crisp golden squares. Let cool a little, while you get on with the salad they are to adorn.

♥ Mix the dressing ingredients in a jug or a screw top jar, stirring together or shaking, to mix.

♥ In a large bowl, toss together the peanuts, lettuce, bean sprouts, scallions, red bell pepper, and shredded cold chicken.

♥ Add half the cooled wonton wrappers or tortilla chips (if using), breaking them into pieces into the bowl, then dress the salad, tossing again to mix before adding the other half of the crispy wonton wrappers (or the tortilla chips) and the chopped cilantro, sprinkling both on top. Serve at once.

MAKE AHEAD NOTE
The wontons can be fried 2–3 hours ahead. Leave on some paper towels at room temperature until needed.

229

This is another example of the rewards of culinary recycling. Of course, frying up croutons doesn't take very long, but my tortilla-chip version feels stresslessly instant. I think of it as a quick-time variant, mainly because I otherwise make my Caesar with croutons of roasted, cubed, garlicky potatoes – and very well that goes down, too. If you prefer, you could, fattoush-style, replace the tortilla chips with pita bread which you split, toast, then break into shards.

People can be awfully tiresome about anchovies (not that the rusty strips of something salty left to die on pizzas are what anchovies should truly taste of) and, in any case, they are not part of the original Caesar, so I haven't listed them below. However, in the interests of transparency I should tell you that I do add them to my own quick Caesar when ransacking the kitchen to assemble this. I either mush one or two pinky-brown fillets up in the dressing or, if I have some of those silvery marinated anchovies, like slim sardines, I just toss them in with the chicken.

Note: Because there's a raw egg in this, you should not give it to anyone who might have a weak or compromised immune system, such as pregnant women, young children, or the elderly.

Serves 2

1 egg
2 tablespoons extra-virgin olive oil
1 teaspoon garlic flavored oil
3 tablespoons grated Parmesan
 cheese
juice ½ lemon
½ teaspoon kosher salt or ¼
 teaspoon table salt (use none if
 you add anchovies)

generous handful (approx. 2
 ounces) plain tortilla chips
1 romaine lettuce, or 2 hearts
2 cups cold shredded chicken
pepper, to taste

♥ Crack the egg into a bowl and whisk well, as you add the oils, Parmesan, and lemon juice. If you're not going to add an anchovy or two, whisk in the salt.

♥ Break the crisp lettuce into bite-sized pieces and put into a salad bowl. Drop in the shredded cold chicken and mix to combine, and season with pepper, to taste.

♥ Toast the tortilla chips for a couple of minutes in an oil-less frying pan over medium heat.

♥ Give the dressing another whisk, pour it over the salad, and toss to mix. Add the tortilla chips (and some anchovies, if you like) and toss again before wolfing down.

Even if you don't have much chicken left over, you should still make this. A few shreds will be plenty. (And this recipe is worth bearing in mind even when your starting point is not leftover chicken: if you were to throw in some frozen shrimp at the end, making sure you cook them through [and if possible, frozen seafood should be thawed gradually], this would make for a fabulous off-the-cuff supper.) This is a very laissez-faire recipe all round, actually: when I cooked it for the photo shoot I forgot to put the vegetables in and it was still heavenly. I did try to make up for my absent-mindedness by giving the tender-shoot stir-fry a beauty-shot of its own, so you can see the mixture of baby bok choy, spindly asparagus, Chinese kale, peanut shoots, and Chinese chives. But I happily use some leafy greens and a julienned or sliced scallion along with a handful of bean sprouts instead. Similarly, if you can't get the ravishing cellophane packages of almost equally cellophane noodles (or glass noodles), don't be put off making this; udon, soba, rice noodles, spaghetti, or linguine could be substituted.

Serves 2–3 *as a main course, 4–6 as a starter*

1 quart chicken broth
6 ounces thin rice noodles or glass
  or cellophane noodles (made from
  mung beans)
scant 1 cup coconut milk
1 x 1–1½ inch piece fresh
  gingerroot, peeled and sliced
  thinly, then cut into skinny strips
2 tablespoons fish sauce
1 fresh red or green chile, seeded
  and cut into strips

1 teaspoon turmeric
1 teaspoon tamarind paste
1 teaspoon light brown sugar
2 tablespoons lime juice
2 cups cooked shredded chicken
8 ounces tender-shoot, stir-fry, or
  other assorted vegetables
2–3 tablespoons chopped fresh
  cilantro, to serve

232

♥ Put the chicken broth in a good-sized saucepan to heat up.

♥ Put the noodles in a bowl and pour boiling water over or cook following the instructions on the package.

♥ Add the remaining ingredients, except the vegetables, to the pan and bring to a boil.

♥ When the chicken is piping hot, add the vegetables and when they are tender – a minute or two should be plenty if you're using the tender shoots – add the drained noodles. Or simply divide the noodles between bowls and pour the soup over them.

♥ Serve sprinkled with chopped fresh cilantro.

Poached chicken with lardons and lentils

I know I tend towards negativity if caught in the wrong mood or when hungry, but I feel that it is asking for trouble to wait for other people to give you comfort in this world. Perhaps this is a melodramatic way of introducing my poached chicken with lardons and lentils, but that's how strongly I feel about it. For some reason, a lot of people are surprised that anyone would bother to cook a proper meal when eating alone, but I'm a firm believer that it's a Good Thing: the succour that comes from the self can be very sustaining and, moreover, I find that cooking for myself stops me, paradoxically, from eating too much. If I go without dinner, I am practically welded to the refrigerator all night.

Besides, sometimes I just need the sort of food that comforts and bolsters and makes the world feel a safe place. This is that food. In fact, it is what many would call their "go-to" recipe in times of stress; no food can dispel unhappiness, but cooked properly, wholesomely, and lovingly, it can make one feel stronger. This also makes a perfect comfort supper for 2, in which case just double the chicken and add only 1 cup extra water.

Don't get me wrong: you don't have to be unhappy to want to eat this; in fact it can be the perfect supper when merry. If I'm going to a party and fear that I will be filled with sour wine or just come back starving, I cook this in advance then totter into the kitchen once I'm back, for a quick bit of reheating. I spoon in more English mustard (I have a weakness for the strong stuff) when I eat, but that's all I need to add. Although, if there is some of the Jumbo Chili Sauce (see **p.121**) in the refrigerator, it certainly gets drizzled on.

If you want to lose the lardons, do, but for me everything's better with bacon. Still, I can see that those after goodness and purity might want to lose that luscious salty fat. Not me, though . . .

Serves 1

2 tablespoons garlic flavored oil
4 ounces smoked lardons, or cubed
  pancetta (or 8 slices smoked
  bacon, snipped)
1 carrot, peeled and halved
  lengthwise, roughly chopped
1 leek, cleaned, trimmed and
  halved lengthwise, roughly
  chopped
3 tablespoons chopped fresh parsley

½ teaspoon dried mint
grated zest 1 lemon
¾ cup puy lentils
1 teaspoon English mustard
1 chicken supreme (i.e., a skinned
  breast with peg bone in),
  preferably organic
2 cups water
salt and pepper, to taste

♥ Fry the lardons (or bacon), carrot, leek, parsley, mint, and lemon zest in the oil for about 7 minutes, stirring frequently, in a smallish, heavy-based saucepan (big enough to lay 1 chicken breast in) that has a lid.

♥ Stir in the lentils and cook for another minute, before adding the yellow gloop of mustard and stir that in, too.

♥ Set the chicken on top of everything in the pan, and add the water. Bring to a boil, put on a lid, and simmer very, very gently for 45 minutes, until the chicken is cooked through and the lentils are tender. Season with salt and pepper, to taste.

♥ You can eat now, but everything is at its most tender best made in advance and reheated. I let it cool in the pan with the lid off, but for no longer than 1 hour, then put the lid back on and stash the pan in the refrigerator. Later, I warm it in the pan with the lid on, until everything's piping hot again. Why add to the washing up?

MAKE AHEAD NOTE
Let it cool and refrigerate as soon as possible (within 1 hour), then reheat, within 1–2 days, as directed in recipe and until piping hot right through.

A DREAM OF HEARTH
AND HOME

By some coincidence (although, as Freud says, there probably isn't such a thing), as I sit down to write an introduction to a batch of recipes that have given succour to me, no less than to those I've cooked them for, it is exactly a decade since I was finishing *How to Be a Domestic Goddess* – a book whose title may have been wilfully misunderstood, but whose message (I like to think) has been taken unapologetically to heart.

Not that any apologia is needed, by those of us who warm our souls by the stove. Besides, to replay the arguments in defense of baking – what could be thought of as trotting out the post-modern manifesto I mooted ten long years ago – might seem an act of jumpy defensiveness. I do want to say one thing, though: a domestic goddess I ain't. But that was not the point in the first place: the title – that title – was never intended as some self-styled appellation. The American critic and satirist H.L. Mencken said that there should be some special typeface – like italics, only slanted backwards – called "ironics," and perhaps that was the font I should have chosen. But it's not just that irony is difficult to get across in print; it's not the whole story. The vision of the gingham-aproned Madonna of the Muffins, yes, that part was intended to be gently ironic, knowingly ridiculous, but my belief in the comfort to be gained from some stoveside pottering, and the sense of warm accomplishment that baking can confer – that I was giving to you straight.

I still feel that it is in some way the transformational element of baking that speaks so directly to us; it is, after all, a belief in the possibility of transformation, of perfectability, that both Eastern and Western cultures share. It may sound absurd to link our basic, hopeful sense of human purpose to the "menial" act of whipping up a cake, but I know, I feel, that the link is there. Moreover, why disparage the menial in the first place?

And that leads to me to one last point in what is in danger of becoming an Apologia Pro Vita Mea: what always stunned me about the broad-brush claim that to celebrate cooking is to be the enemy of womankind was that it seemed so essentially anti-feminist to denigrate an activity just because it had always been traditionally female.

The subtitle of *Domestic Goddess* was "Baking and the Art of Comfort Cooking," and comfort cooking is what this chapter is also about. I regard the kitchen as my place of comfort – whether I'm boiling an egg, making a cup of tea or mixing up a batch of cupcakes – but there is something about baking that marks out for me a special, less frenetic time, when I can allow myself to cook for the sheer pleasure of it. I know it doesn't always seem this way, but a cake is not actually one of the basic necessities of life. Even to make one is a kind of luxury. And I, appropriately, luxuriate in it.

I am aware that many of you shudder at the very idea. So let me tell you a couple of things. For years I thought that there were cooks and there were bakers, and I was definitely in the first camp. But it's not so. Whereas cooking is looser, less rigorously rule-bound – while you can decide you want three carrots in your stew one day, and two another, you can't say, "I feel like putting three eggs in my cake today," if the recipe calls

236

for two – it is, in a sense, the constraints of baking that free one up. You don't need to think too much; you just *do*.

It's the certainties of baking that offer such sweet solace, along with the fragrance that wafts from the oven, scenting the house with soothing smells. The grind of daily life can be so fraught that, when my head is buzzing after an overcharged week, it's at the oven I can begin to decompress. A little stirring, some rhythmic mixing: don't knock it till you've tried it.

And, like everything else, the more you do, the easier it becomes. Although it would be nearer the truth to say that none of this is very difficult in the first place. That's to say, if you can read and follow instructions, you can bake. It is that simple.

- When baking, all ingredients should be at room temperature, unless otherwise specified.
- For freezing or keeping, cakes and cookies should be cooled first. Where no freezing or make-ahead tip is given alongside a recipe, neither is recommended.
- Recommended keeping time is for best quality, though cakes and cookies may well keep for a couple of days longer.

Maple pecan bundt cake

As I get older, I realize how stamped one is, ineluctably, by character and temperament; and that only by accepting this can one begin to curb or change patterns of thinking or behavior. You may think I am straying from my field here, but, as I've said before, anything that is true out of the kitchen is as true in it, and of it. However, although I've no doubt that the way one cooks is a function of said character and temperament, sometimes I believe that cooking can actually help us to escape our natures.

To wit, I had always thought there was nothing about me that is temperamentally suited to baking: I am impatient, clumsy, bad at authority. But you know what? I've made do. My creations are always going to look a little ramshackle, and there are times when I take a cake to someone and feel the need to lie, telling them my children frosted it, but baking gives me pleasure and I can follow a recipe for long enough to mix up a batter. And to accommodate my lack of finesse, I've found a way of choosing a pan that makes me look good. I'll explain: making a cake mixture is always simple, but pour it into a fancy bundt mold and you'll bake a cake that looks like a work of art. You have to splash out on a bundt pan that is heavy (so the cake doesn't burn) and non-stick (so it comes out like the picture on the box), but from then on it's plain sailing, or happy baking.

Perhaps the notion of escaping one's nature is sadly flawed from the get-go. But I do find that in cooking, I can sometimes express those sides of my character I wouldn't really want to air in any other way. I think of myself as the sort of person who hates fussiness and daintiness, and yet give me a bundt pan that could turn out a cake looking like Chartres cathedral – OK, cut me some slack here – and I'm lit up with delight.

So long as the quality of the bundt pan is good, it doesn't matter (to me) what shape it's in. Choose whichever mold you like best; luckily they all come in roughly the same size, 10 inches across at the widest point, and with a 10–12 cup capacity. Stasher and hoarder that I am, I'm afraid, I have far too many shapes to choose from in my cupboard, from mother-of-the-bride hat, through turreted castle, to the fleur-de-lys embellished beauty here (**pp.241 and 242**). The reason I chose this particular shape for this cake, was that it seemed to show its nutty, gooey stuffing off to maximum effect once sliced. Some bundt cakes are at their most beautiful when showily whole; this one cuts into prettily shaped and pleasing slices.

And this is the cake that emblematically scratches that Domestic Goddess itch: it's feel-good food (for cook and eater) by way of some simple stirring. The nutty, syrupy filling is simply forked into being; you could make the cake batter with no more equipment than a bowl and a wooden spoon. But I'm afraid even my alter ego, the Domestic Goddess, is lazy, so I use an electric mixer. But beware the processor here: it's easy to overmix as you blitz, and while a dense sponge is good, a rubbery one – clearly – is not.

239

Not only do I love making this cake, but I get a rare feeling of calm contentment just seeing it on its stand on the kitchen surface. Then there's the eating of it, a greedy slice alongside a mid-afternoon mug of coffee, which produces nothing less than a surge of body-and-soul-bolstering joy. Now, this is what a weekend is for . . .

Cuts easily into 12 slices

for the maple pecan filling:
½ cup all-purpose flour
2 tablespoons soft unsalted butter
1 teaspoon ground cinnamon
1¼ cups pecans (or walnuts),
  roughly chopped
½ cup maple syrup

for the cake:
2 cups all-purpose flour
1 teaspoon baking powder

1 teaspoon baking soda
1 stick plus 1 tablespoon (9
  tablespoons) soft unsalted butter
¾ cup superfine sugar
2 eggs
1 cup sour cream
1–2 teaspoons confectioner's sugar,
  for decoration
flavorless oil, for greasing

1 x 10-inch (10 cup) bundt pan

♥ Preheat the oven to 350°F. Using flavorless oil (or a squirt of baking spray) grease your bundt pan, and leave upside down on newspaper for the excess oil to drain out.

♥ Make the filling for the cake by mixing together the ½ cup flour and 2 tablespoons butter with a fork, till you end up with the sort of mixture you'd expect when making crumble topping. Then, still using the fork, mix in the cinnamon, chopped pecans (or walnuts), and maple syrup, to form a sticky, bumpy paste. Set aside for a moment.

♥ For the cake, measure the 2 cups flour, the baking powder, and baking soda into a bowl.

♥ Now, cream the butter and sugar (i.e. beat well together until light in texture and pale in color), then beat in 1 tablespoon of the flour mixture, then 1 egg, then another tablespoonful of flour mixture, followed by the second egg.

♥ Add the rest of the flour mixture, beating as you go, and then finally the sour cream. You should expect to end up with a fairly firm cake batter.

♥ Spoon just more than half the cake batter into the oiled bundt pan. Spread the mixture up the sides a little and around the funnel of the pan to create a rim. You don't want the sticky filling to leak out to the sides of the pan.

♥ Dollop the maple filling carefully into the dent in the cake batter, then cover the filling with the remaining batter. Smooth the top and put the pan into the oven for 40 minutes, though it's best to check with a cake tester after 30 minutes.

♥ Once cooked, and the cake tester comes out clean where it hits the sponge (obviously, any gooey filling will stick to the tester), let the cake cool on a wire rack for 15 minutes in

240

its pan, then loosen the edges with a small spatula, including around the middle funnel bit, and turn the cake out onto the rack.

♥ When the cake is cold, dust with confectioner's sugar by pushing a teaspoonful or so through a small strainer.

MAKE AHEAD NOTE
Can be baked up to 2 days ahead. Wrap tightly in plastic wrap and store in airtight container. Dust with confectioner's sugar just before serving.

FREEZE NOTE
The cake can be frozen, tightly wrapped in a double layer of plastic wrap and a layer of aluminum foil, for up to 3 months. Thaw overnight at room temperature and dust with confectioner's sugar just before serving.

Blueberry cornmeal muffins

Mixing up a batch of muffins during the week, while in theory perfectly do-able, ain't never gonna happen. It's not a time issue (you just stir the batter into being, and perfunctorily at that), and the 20 minutes they take to cook could be easily accommodated during the time it takes to plead with one child to get up, while finding another's missing sneaker. It's rather that too much bad temper would ooze its way into the batter along with the blueberries. Weekday mornings are undeniably fraught, even if kitchen activity is the least of it, and the only thing that makes them manageable, if only just, is routine. To deviate one bit from that would blow the system.

True, the weekends more often find me in pancake-making mode, but a muffin can be (not even snarlingly) accommodated too. My friend and agent, Ed Victor (provider of the meatloaf on **p.458**, and much sustenance in general) says that he likes to exercise first thing in the morning, as it enables him to get on with his day feeling superior and smug. That may be going too far: I'd rather get there by making a muffin. It might count as upper body exercise.

I always feel that little bit more downhome diva when I use cornmeal, though I suspect this is my weakness for kitchen-kitsch Americana speaking. But I take my pleasures where I can, and advise you to do so too. Those of us who feel happy just looking at a quaint farmstead-wholesome container of cornmeal, or at the sight of a scoopful of that almost-sparkling, pale-yellow grain, are to be envied, not ridiculed. (Or a bit of both.) But it isn't just a kind of city-child sentimentality about the great rural spaces that makes me go for cornmeal here. I love its subtly sweet graininess – both wholesome and comforting at the same time, a rare combination – into which the blueberries pop jammily, their juices oozing into the golden gritty crumb.

I beat my drum quite loudly enough on **p.128** to feel I shouldn't need to raise the matter again here, but nevertheless, a reminder: a home-baked muffin is not a dome-headed muffin. And the extra heft given by the cornmeal ensures a decidedly flat-topped muffin, but also makes that crusty top rather deliciously chewy above the loose-textured, berry-studded sponge.

As with most muffins, you get the best of them if you eat them while still warm.

Makes 12

1 cup all-purpose flour
¾ cup cornmeal
2 teaspoons baking powder
½ teaspoon baking soda
¾ cup superfine sugar
½ cup vegetable oil or other
    flavorless oil

½ cup buttermilk
1 egg
¾ cup blueberries

1 x 12-cup muffin pan

♥ Preheat the oven to 400°F and line a muffin pan with paper muffin cups.

♥ In a large bowl, mix the flour, cornmeal, baking powder, baking soda and sugar.

♥ In a measuring cup or bowl, pour in the oil and buttermilk, and whisk or fork in the egg.

♥ Stir the oil mixture into the bowl of dry ingredients – remembering that lumpiness is a good thing when making muffins – and fold half the blueberries into your thick golden batter.

♥ Divide this batter between each muffin cup (they will be about two-thirds full) and drop the remaining blueberries on top; you should have about 3 for the top of each muffin.

♥ Bake in the oven for 15–20 minutes, till a cake tester comes out cleanish (obviously it will be stained if it hits a berry). Leave the muffins in the pan on a wire rack for 5 minutes, then remove the muffins, in their cases, to the wire rack and let cool a little (not too much) before you serve or eat them.

MAKE AHEAD NOTE
Best eaten on day of making but muffins can be baked up to 1 day ahead and stored in airtight container, layered with parchment paper. Reheat in warm oven for 5–8 minutes before serving. Will keep for 2 days in a cool place.

FREEZE NOTE
Can be frozen in airtight container, layered with parchment paper, for up to 2 months. Thaw for 3–4 hours on a wire rack at room temperature and reheat as above.

Red velvet cupcakes

I first made these cupcakes at the request of my stepdaughter Phoebe, a good few years ago, but such was their popularity *chez moi* (not that French should be spoken around them) that I have been at it ever since. There isn't space to go into their history here, but whatever the origins of this cake, making a batter that includes such an amount of food coloring takes an act of faith. I don't feel there's any way I could talk you into it were you not ready, but I suppose you could always use some grated beets as a natural substitute, if you insist.

Some recipes specify ⅓ cup of red food coloring, but one's got to draw the line somewhere, and I prefer food coloring pastes, not least because you always need less for the same intensity of color. But I should warn you that the heaping tablespoonful of red food coloring paste specified below is more or less the entire contents of one of the little containers. I make these so often (and Christmas-red, whatever the season, is my red of choice) that I've now managed to get my hands on a catering size jumbo-container, and have also learned to keep a pair of disposable vinyl gloves at hand (see **p.17**).

If you want to make this as one big cake (though I won't go so far as to suggest you make it in the shape of an armadillo, as per the groom's cake in the film *Steel Magnolias*) as I did for my daughter Mimi's sixteenth birthday (yes, I gulp as I say that; only yesterday, it seems, I was writing about making the Barbie cake for her fourth), then know that the amounts below make enough batter for 2 x 10-inch cake pans filled not too deep, and enough frosting to squish them together and decorate the top.

Talking of the frosting, when I make these for Mimi, I am under strict instructions to do without the cream cheese, making just a butter cream; the buttery cream-cheese frosting I make for Phoebe is not, however, authentic either. The frosting traditionally used to top these vibrant little numbers is called a cooked flour frosting. Well, yes . . . and now are you glad I didn't go into detail about their *fons et origo*?

246

Makes 24

for the cupcakes:
1⅔ cup all-purpose flour
2 tablespoons unsweetened cocoa
   powder, sifted
2 teaspoons baking powder
½ teaspoon baking soda
7 tablespoons soft unsalted butter
1 cup superfine sugar
1 heaping tablespoon Christmas-
   red paste food coloring

2 teaspoons vanilla extract
2 eggs
¾ cup buttermilk
1 teaspoon cider vinegar or other
   vinegar

2 x 12-cup muffin pans

♥ Preheat the oven to 325°F and line the muffin pans with paper muffin cups.

♥ Combine the flour, cocoa, baking powder, and baking soda in a bowl.

♥ In another bowl, cream the butter and sugar, beating well, and when you have a soft, pale mixture, beat in the food coloring – yes, all of it – and the vanilla.

♥ Into this vividly colored mixture, still beating, add 1 spoonful of the dry ingredients, then 1 egg, followed by some more dry ingredients, then the other egg, followed by the rest of the dry ingredients.

♥ Finally, beat in the buttermilk and vinegar and divide this extraordinary batter between the 24 cups in the prepared pans. Bake in the oven for about 20 minutes, by which time the red currant-sorbet-colored batter will have morphed into a more sombre, but still juicily tinted, sponge – more maroon acrylic than red velvet, to be honest.

♥ Leave them to cool on a wire rack and do not ice with the frosting opposite till absolutely cold.

248

Buttery cream-cheese frosting

As I've said earlier, you can use all butter rather than half butter and half cream cheese for this frosting. Equally, decorate as pleases you, too. I like to use red sugar (sometimes called red sanding sugar) to hint at their deeply toned interiors, and some bittersweet chocolate in a vain attempt at something a little more elegant. For the children (whose taste I am anyway pandering to here) I advise, instead, a shake of some chocolate-flavored sprinkles from a jar.

for the icing:
1 x 1-pound box confectioner's sugar (no need to sift if using a processor)
½ x 8-ounce bar cream cheese
1 stick (½ cup) soft unsalted butter

1 teaspoon cider vinegar or lemon juice
chocolate sprinkles and red sugar, for decoration (optional)

♥ Put the confectioner's sugar into a processor and whizz to remove lumps.

♥ Add the cream cheese and butter and process to mix. Pour in the cider vinegar (or lemon juice) and process again to make a smooth frosting.

♥ Frost each cupcake, using a teaspoon or small frosting spatula.

♥ Decorate with chocolate sprinkles and red sugar, or as desired.

MAKE AHEAD NOTE
The cupcakes can be baked 2 days ahead and stored, un-iced, layered with parchment paper in airtight containers. The frosting can be made 1 day ahead: cover with plastic wrap and refrigerate; remove from the refrigerator 1–2 hours before needed to let them come to room temperature then beat briefly before using. Best frosted and eaten on same day but frosted cupcakes can be kept in the refrigerator in airtight container for up to 1 day. Bring to room temperature before serving.

FREEZE NOTE
Un-frosted cupcakes can be frozen, layered with parchment paper, in airtight containers for up to 2 months. Thaw for 3–4 hours on a wire rack at room temperature. Frosting can be frozen separately in airtight container for up to 3 months; thaw overnight in the refrigerator then bring to room temperature and beat briefly before use.

250

Gooseberry and elderflower crumble

I am never more serene than when I have a crumble baking in the oven. True, all things are relative and serenity is not one of my virtues, but the slow, rhythmic, repetitive activity of rubbing butter into flour – pressing the pads of index and middle fingers flutteringly against the more hardworking pad of the thumb – is in itself calming. More reassuring still is that old-fashioned, Grandma's-house smell, with its sweet promise of dessert to come. In my book, there is no such thing as a bad crumble, but some are better than others. What I'm after is the juicy contrast between slightly tart fruit and the melting butteriness of the rubble on top of, and sinking just a little into, it. For me, this means rhubarb – and we've been there in the past – or gooseberry. Both can justifiably lay claim to the crown, but gooseberry is perhaps the true queen of crumbles.

Admittedly, the gooseberry, most frequently found in farmers markets and farm stands, has a real blink-and-you'll-miss-it season, but that is what underscores my compulsion to cook with it when the fruit is readily available. Of course, you could always freeze them – first loose, on a tray, then stashed in tightly closed resealable bags – and make this crumble at will throughout the year, but it's not quite the same. (Though I say that as someone who has been known to buy imported strawberries in February.)

So, by all means, use the recipe that follows as a blueprint, taking whatever fruit you may use in the gooseberry's stead up to a 2½ pounds if there is much trimming and peeling to be done. The tarter the substitute fruit the better, and do reduce the sugar if good sense indicates it. Elderflower cordial is a non-alcoholic syrup with a delicate, slightly floral flavor from elderflowers. It is popular in England, mixed with water, as a refreshing drink. The elderflower cordial here is to perfume the gooseberries – it is, after all, a traditional English pairing – and for other fruit I would add a small slosh of vanilla extract instead.

One final note: please do not feel that if you don't make the crumble topping by hand, you are unworthy of creating it. On days when time or mood just do not allow for even 5 minutes with my hands in a bowl, I routinely use my freestanding mixer to do the work.

Serves 8

2 pounds gooseberries	2 teaspoons baking powder
¼ cup superfine sugar	1¼ sticks (10 tablespoons) cold unsalted
1 tablespoon unsalted butter	butter, diced
1 tablespoon elderflower cordial	heaping ½ cup turbinado sugar, plus 1
	tablespoon for sprinkling
for the crumble topping:	
1⅓ cups all-purpose flour	1 x pie dish approx. 9 inches diameter x
	2½ inches deep

♥ Preheat the oven to 375°F and slip in a cookie sheet or lipped baking sheet.

♥ Hull the gooseberries and put them in a wide saucepan over a gentle heat with the superfine sugar, tablespoon of butter, and elderflower cordial for about 5 minutes, shaking the pan every now and again, until the butter has melted and the gooseberries are slicked with glossy, fragrant jade juices.

♥ Decant these to your pie dish and put to one side while you make the topping.

♥ If you're **making this topping by hand**, put the flour and baking powder in a large bowl, shake or fork to mix, then add the cold, cubed butter and rub it in, lightly, between the pads of your fingers. Or just mix in using the flat paddle of a **freestanding mixer**. Stop when you have a soft, sandy mixture with the odd larger, almost fava-bean-shaped, lump.

♥ Add the heaping ½ cup turbinado sugar and use a fork to mix in gently – a spoon or mixer or even your fingers might make the butter start to clump.

♥ Top the waiting fruit in its pie dish with the crumble mixture, making sure it is evenly dispersed right up to the inner edges of the dish. Some bubbling up of fruity juices is inevitable – and, indeed, desirable – but it's good to guard against overflowing.

♥ Scatter the remaining tablespoonful of turbinado sugar over the top, then pop the crumble in the oven on the heated-up cookie sheet, and bake for 35–45 minutes until the top is lightly browned. This is best served when it has been left to stand for 10 minutes, and eaten with cold pouring cream.

MAKE AHEAD NOTE
The crumble can be assembled 1 day ahead. Cover with plastic wrap and store in the refrigerator until needed. Bake as directed, but allowing an extra 5–10 minutes' cooking time, and check it is piping hot in the center.

FREEZE NOTE
Crumble topping can be made and frozen in resealable plastic bags, for up to 3 months. Sprinkle topping direct from freezer over the fruit, breaking up large lumps with your hands. The assembled but unbaked crumble can be frozen, wrapped in a double layer of plastic wrap and a layer of aluminum foil, for up to 3 months. Thaw for 24 hours in the refrigerator and bake as above.

NOTE
Elderflower cordial can be purchased on-line.

Devil's food cake

Forget the name, this cake is heavenly. The crumb is tender, the filling and frosting luscious. When I made it one Friday, I expected my children, resident food critics much in the mold of The Grim Eater, to find it too dark, too rich, not sweet enough: you get the gist. Instead, I came down on Saturday morning to find nothing but an empty, chocolate-smeared cake stand and a trail of crumbs.

You may prefer to prepare this the other way round from me, and get the frosting underway before you make the cakes. Either way, read the recipe through before you start cooking (I shouldn't have to remind) to get the shape of things in your head, not least because the frosting is softer and stickier than you may be used to. While you're making it, don't panic. The mixture will seem very runny for ages once the chocolate has melted and you will think you have a liquid gleaming glaze, beautiful but unfit for purpose; leave it for about an hour, as stipulated, though, and it will be perfect and spreadable. It never quite dries to the touch, but this is, in part, what makes the cake so darkly luscious. Goo here is good.

Serves 10–12

for the cake:
½ cup best-quality unsweetened
  cocoa powder, sifted
½ cup (packed) dark brown sugar
1 cup boiling water
1 stick plus 1 tablespoon
  (9 tablespoons) soft unsalted
  butter, plus some for greasing
¾ cup superfine sugar
1½ cups all-purpose flour
½ teaspoon baking powder
½ teaspoon baking soda

2 teaspoons vanilla extract
2 eggs

for the frosting:
½ cup water
2 tablespoons dark brown sugar
1½ sticks (¾ cup) unsalted butter, cubed
11 ounces best-quality bittersweet
  chocolate, finely chopped (or 2 cups
  chips)

2 x 8-inch round cake pans

♥ Preheat the oven to 350°F. Line the bottoms of both cake pans with parchment paper and butter the sides.

♥ Put the cocoa and ½ cup dark brown sugar into a bowl with a bit of space to spare, and pour in the boiling water. Whisk to mix, then set aside.

♥ Cream the butter and superfine sugar together, beating well until pale and fluffy; I find this easiest with a freestanding mixer, but by hand wouldn't kill you.

♥ While this is going on – or as soon as you stop if you're mixing by hand – whisk the flour, baking powder, and baking soda together in another bowl, and set aside for a moment.

♥ Dribble the vanilla extract into the creamed butter and sugar – mixing all the while – then drop in 1 egg, quickly followed by a scoopful of flour mixture, then the second egg.

♥ Keep mixing and incorporate the rest of the dried ingredients for the cake, then finally mix and fold in the cocoa mixture, scraping its bowl well with a spatula.

♥ Divide this fabulously chocolatey batter between the 2 prepared pans and put in the oven for about 30 minutes, or until a cake tester comes out clean. Take the pans out and put them on a wire rack for 5–10 minutes, before turning the cakes out to cool.

♥ But as soon as the cakes are in the oven, get started on your frosting: put the water, 2 tablespoons dark brown sugar, and 1½ sticks butter in a pan over a low heat to melt.

♥ When this mixture begins to bubble, take the pan off the heat and add the chopped chocolate, swirling the pan so that all the chocolate is hit with heat, then leave for a minute to melt before whisking till smooth and glossy.

♥ Let stand for about 1 hour, whisking now and again – when you're passing the pan – by which time the cakes will be cooled, and ready for the frosting.

♥ Set one of the cooled cakes, with its top side down, on a cake stand or plate, and spread with about a third of the frosting, then top that with the second cake, regular way up, and spread the remaining frosting over the top and sides, swirling away with your spatula. You can go for a smooth look, but I never do and probably couldn't.

MAKE AHEAD NOTE
The cake layers can be baked 1 day ahead and assembled before serving: wrap tightly in plastic wrap and store in airtight container. Frosted cake will keep for 2–3 days in airtight container in a cool place.

FREEZE NOTE
Un-frosted cake layers can be frozen on day of baking, each wrapped in a double layer of plastic wrap and a layer of aluminum foil, for up to 3 months. Thaw for 3–4 hours on wire rack at room temperature.

Chocolate chip cookies

It seems strange that I've managed to write seven books (I don't count this one, since at time of writing I feel to include it might jinx it) without one plain chocolate chip cookie (by which I mean a plain cookie with chocolate chips in it). It's true that the Totally Chocolate Chocolate Chip Cookie made an appearance once, and it's only because I've been buoyed up by its success that I've felt confident enough to create this one. For here's the thing: you'd think a plain cookie with a few chocolate chips folded into the mixture would be a simple matter. It's not. It's never difficult to make, just difficult to get right. I may be picky, but to my mind, or my mouth, a cookie that's too crisp feels dry and disappointing, and a cookie that's too chewy tastes like dough. I want a bit of tender, fudgy chewiness, but an edge of crisp bite, too.

      I've tried. I can't tell you how often I've tried. Many cookies have been baked, and many have been eaten. What do they say? Dirty work, but someone's got to do it. And the cookie recipe that follows is happy evidence that my hard work has not been for naught.

Makes approx. 14

1¼ sticks (10 tablespoons) soft
  unsalted butter
⅔ cup (packed) light brown sugar
½ cup superfine sugar
2 teaspoons vanilla extract
1 egg, refrigerator-cold
1 egg yolk, refrigerator-cold

2 cups all-purpose flour
½ teaspoon baking soda
1 x 11.5-ounce bag milk chocolate
  morsels or chips

1 x large cookie sheet

♥ Preheat the oven to 325°F. Line a cookie sheet with parchment paper.

♥ Melt the butter and let it cool a bit. Put the brown and white sugars into a bowl, pour the slightly cooled, melted butter over them, and beat together.

♥ Beat in the vanilla, the cold egg, and cold egg yolk, until your mixture is light and creamy.

♥ Slowly mix in the flour and baking soda until just blended, then fold in the chocolate chips.

♥ Scoop the cookie dough into a quarter-cup measure or a ¼ cup round ice-cream scoop and drop onto the prepared cookie sheet, plopping the cookies down about 3 inches apart. You will need to make these in 2–3 batches, keeping the bowl of cookie dough in the refrigerator between batches.

♥ Bake for 15–17 minutes in the preheated oven, or until the edges are lightly toasted. Let cool on the cookie sheet for 5 minutes before transferring to wire racks to cool completely.

MAKE AHEAD NOTE
The cookies can be made up to 3 days ahead and stored in an airtight container. Will keep for a total of 5 days.

FREEZE NOTE
The baked cookies can be frozen in airtight container or resealable bags for up to 3 months. Thaw for 2–3 hours at room temperature. Unbaked cookie dough can be scooped onto parchment-lined cookie sheets and frozen until solid. Transfer frozen dough to resealable bags and freeze for up to 3 months. Bake direct from frozen, as directed in recipe but adding extra 2–3 minutes to baking time.

    And you could always freeze the spare egg white (bag it, label it and freeze for up to 3 months) for meringues (see **p.262**) at a later date. Use within 24 hours of thawing.

257

Baked egg custard

There are some smells that make me almost weepy with gratitude. This custard, as it bakes tenderly in the oven, filling the house with the scent of nutmeg and vanilla and nursery-sweet egginess, is one, bringing, as it does, instant, airborne comfort.

Food that tastes like this – like an ideal childhood, smooth and sustaining – should be simple to make, and this is. There are two steps that might give you pause, not because either of them is difficult but because they could be thought – erroneously – to be dispensable. I'm referring to the straining of the egg, sugar, and milk mixture into the dish, and the placing of the dish in a water bath. Don't even think about giving either a miss, for these two steps are what give the custard its melt-in-the-mouth softness.

I think this is at its best cooked in a relatively small dish (about 7 inches diameter) but I realize this is not a standard pie dish size. You can use one, but in a wider dish (the regulation issue is 9 inches diameter) the custard is shallower and will need to bake for 30 minutes less than stipulated below. I can't promise the less deep version will be as good, but it's still worth the effort, for cook and eater alike.

Serves 4, *or 2 greedy people eating it warm once and cold later*

butter, for greasing
2½ cups whole milk
4 eggs
¼ cup superfine sugar
2 teaspoons vanilla extract

fresh nutmeg

1 x round ovenproof dish approx. 7 x 2½ inches

♥ Preheat the oven to 275°F and butter a round ovenproof dish. Pour the milk into a saucepan and heat until hot but not actually boiling. Or, if you like, you can pour it into a pyrex jug and zap it in the microwave.

♥ In a bowl that's large enough to take the milk as well, whisk the eggs, sugar, and vanilla. Then, still whisking, pour in the hot milk.

♥ Sit the buttered dish in a roasting pan to make a *bain marie* – your water bath (see next step). Strain the custard mixture through a strainer into the buttered dish, then grate some nutmeg generously over the top.

♥ Now pour freshly boiled water into the pan, to come about halfway up the baking dish, and gingerly (you don't want slopping and spillage) put it into the oven and cook for 1½ hours. You want the custard set, but only just. Take the pan out of the oven, and the dish out of the pan, and let the custard cool a little before eating. I find a baked custard at its seductive best when it's warm rather than hot. The egg custard should not be allowed to stand at room temperature for more than two hours.

Coffee caramel meringues

It's hard to believe that out of nothing more than egg whites and sugar comes a creation quite as spectacular as a meringue. It seems miraculous, but then I am no specialist in the chemistry of cooking. Eating is my thing, and I am simply happy to wallow in the texture-sensation that is the contrast between crisp outer shell and a center that has still a bit of squish to it. Left plain, and served with some tart berries and a dollop of softly whipped cream, a meringue is hard to beat. But that's not to say we shouldn't try.

The coffee-caramel route almost drove itself: both the sound of the words and the taste of the combination give me pleasure, and had to be fused for me, in meringue form. I add a little brown sugar to the meringue mixture, both for mellowness and to deepen the manila tint, and the caramel sauce is rich in it, too. Go sparingly with the sauce: you want the merest dribble, really. Still, although the meringues are obviously sweet, the coffee taste keeps the sugar in check and allows for the absurd addition of a caramel sauce in the first place.

You don't have to add the liqueur to the sauce or top the buff-colored meringues with a sprinkling of chopped hazelnuts, but it works for me.

Makes 8–10

for the meringues:
1 cup superfine sugar
⅓ cup (packed) light brown sugar
2 teaspoons instant espresso
  powder
pinch cream of tartar
4 egg whites
¾ cup toasted chopped hazelnuts,
  for topping (optional)

for the caramel sauce:
1 tablespoon butter
¼ cup golden syrup (such as Lyle's)
2 tablespoons light brown sugar
¼ cup heavy cream
2 teaspoons Frangelico hazelnut
  liqueur (optional)

for the filling:
2½ cups heavy cream

1 x large lipped baking sheet or
  half sheet pan

♥ To make the meringues: preheat the oven to 275°F and combine the 1 cup superfine sugar and ⅓ cup light brown sugar, the espresso powder, and cream of tartar in a bowl, and set aside.

♥ Whisk the egg whites in a grease-free bowl (the purists' choice is copper, but I am happy with stainless steel) until they are beyond foamy and soft peaks have started to form.

♥ Begin to add your sugar mix 1 tablespoonful at a time, whisking all the while, until you have a glossy thick meringue the color of oyster silk lingerie.

♥ Line a lipped baking sheet with parchment paper and spoon out dollops of meringue (about 2 big soup spoonfuls) to give roughly 2 inch-diameter circles of meringue. Spike or fluff the tops as you go to give texture; you should get 8–10 meringues.

♥ Sprinkle the top of each meringue with ½ teaspoon chopped hazelnuts or so, saving the rest for later.

♥ Put in the preheated oven for about 45 minutes, by which time the meringues should be dry on the outside, but still gooey in the middle, and a little fragile to the touch. Take out of the oven, but do not remove them from the baking sheet.

♥ To make the sauce: melt the butter, golden syrup, and light brown sugar in a saucepan over a low heat, swirling gently (but not stirring) occasionally, then bring to a boil and let it bubble for 2 minutes.

♥ Take the pan off the heat and whisk in the ¼ cup cream and the liqueur (if using). Pour into a small heatproof pitcher – you won't have more than about ⅔ cup here – to get cold.

♥ When you are ready to assemble the meringues, whip the 2½ cups heavy cream until firm but not stiff. Crush a dent – don't worry about making a splintering mess – into the top of each meringue, then split it a little and fill from above with a dollop of whipped cream. Drizzle on some of the sauce and sprinkle with some more chopped hazelnuts.

MAKE AHEAD NOTE
The meringues can be made 1 day ahead and stored in airtight container. Sauce can be made 1 day ahead: store in the refrigerator in a bowl or pitcher covered with plastic wrap. Remove from the refrigerator 1–2 hours before it's needed to let come to room temperature.

263

Swedish summer cake

My greed doesn't confine itself to eating food. I love reading about it, too. My collection of cookery books is now nearing 4,000, which gives you some indication of my mania, but doesn't tell the whole story. In addition to the books I buy compulsively – once you have a collection, there is no good argument, ever, for *not* adding to it – there are the pages I tear out of magazines and the scribbled notes I take when I eat at friends' houses. And my most treasured are the recipes people give me that have been passed down through their family. When I say "give," I should be a little more honest: I hector and badger, especially if I think someone may be able to hand over a recipe with particular significance for me.

Just as living in Italy in my late teens started me on a lifetime's love of Italian cooking, so summering in Scandinavia between the ages of eight and twelve has left me with a profound nostalgia for Scandinavian food. When I mentioned this once (and even dared try a little long-forgotten Swedish) to Anna Engbrink, who was working at Scott's, a restaurant in London I seemed to visit rather too often (my husband being a chain-smoker and this being one of the few eateries with outside space in which to smoke), she told me about her grandmother's cooking. I pressed her, week in, week out, for her grandmother's recipe for a cake they seem to make all over Scandinavia to celebrate Midsummer's Day, and after an awful lot of begging, she produced this. Or rather, a version of the recipe that follows. Anna's grandmother, unsurprisingly, was Swedish; but those long-ago big-skied summers of mine were spent mostly in Norway, and so I instinctively changed the recipe slightly to give it a taste of the Norwegian Midsummer *bløtkake* I remember. *Bløtkake* simply means "wet cake," and my custard filling is a lot runnier than Anna's grandmother, or any other Swedish (or Danish for all I know) cook, would make it. Not only do I prefer this, but it's a lot quicker and simpler.

Not that any of this recipe is actually complicated, but I don't deny that its assembly can be fiddly, or that it reads a lot harder than it cooks. This is always the way with recipes that are process-heavy, even if the individual processes are not in themselves demanding. I've given each part – cake, custard, assembly – its own ingredients list, because it's easier to cook that way; but to make shopping more straightforward, I'd advise you to read through all three parts first and jot down what you need.

When I read the original recipe given me by Anna, I was touched most by the appended note that said "my grandmother used to make us pick the strawberries fresh out of her garden while she made the bases." All very Elvira Madigan, I know, but more than that, it reminded me of going into the woods behind the house where we used to stay in Norway, to pick blueberries for breakfast.

Rest assured, that if you, like me, have no strawberries growing in the garden, indeed no garden, this cake will bring the sweet scent of a Scandinavian summer straight to your kitchen.

The cake cuts into 8–10 generous slices

for the vanilla custard filling

VANILLA
CUSTARD

I make this up first, indeed a day before I get on with the cake, because splitting the processes lightens the overall burden, and you need this properly cold before you use it. Since it takes under 5 minutes to make, whenever you do it – providing you leave time for it to cool, about 3 hours – it won't be a major hassle.

   If you hate waste as much as I do, then freeze the egg whites (for up to 3 months), marking the bag that there are 2 whites inside (or you may forget how many), then thaw in the refrigerator and use them within 24 hours of thawing, to make meringues at a later date. (You could knock up half a batch, i.e. 4 or 5, of the Coffee Caramel Meringues on **p.262**, whenever the mood takes you or the occasion lends itself.)

2 egg yolks

2 tablespoons superfine sugar

2 teaspoons cornstarch or potato
  flour

1 cup whole milk

½ vanilla bean or 1 teaspoon
  vanilla extract

♥ If using the vanilla bean, put everything in a saucepan over a low to medium heat, stirring non-stop, until it starts to thicken. *Do not let it boil.* If using the vanilla extract, as I tend to, put everything in except the extract and proceed as above.

♥ When it starts to thicken – just over 3 minutes at medium heat, but just under 5 if you keep the flame cautiously low – take it off the heat. Remove the vanilla bean, if using.

♥ Transfer to a cold bowl, mix in the vanilla extract, if using, and continue stirring until it is a little cooler, then cover with plastic wrap – touching the surface of the custard – to stop the custard from forming a skin when it's cold. Or wet a piece of parchment paper and place that right on top of the custard.

CAKE *for the cake*

This is much easier when made with the assistance of gadgetry, be it a hand-held electric mixer or freestanding mixer; but since the existence of the cake pre-dates the invention of either, it can obviously be made with a wire whisk and elbow grease.

266

3 eggs

1¼ cups superfine sugar

⅓ cup hot water from a recently
  boiled kettle

1½ teaspoons baking powder

1 cup all-purpose flour

butter, for greasing

9-inch springform pan

♥ Preheat the oven to 350°F and line the bottom of the springform pan with parchment paper, and butter the sides.

♥ Whisk the eggs and sugar together briskly until pale and moussy and more than doubled in volume, then, still whisking but slightly more gently, add the hot water.

♥ Mix the baking powder and flour in a separate bowl and gradually whisk these in, making sure there are no lumps. You may need to stop once or twice to scrape down the sides of the bowl.

♥ Pour and scrape the mixture into the prepared pan and bake in the preheated oven for approximately 30 minutes, or until it is golden, well-risen, and a cake tester comes out clean.

♥ Let the cake stand in the pan on a wire rack for 5–10 minutes before – carefully – unmolding and leaving it to cool on the rack.

to assemble the cake

If, like me, you are clumsy, this is the hardest bit. On the other hand, any clumsiness is either easily concealed or adds to the homespun charm of it all. It pays to be positive here. What I mean is that, if you do not have excellent knife skills or a steady hand, you may find it hard to cut this cake horizontally into 3 equal layers. Don't worry. I broke one of the layers while cutting the cake you see on the previous page, but once it's sandwiched with berries and custard cream, this doesn't really show. Perhaps it leans a little in one direction, so that the custard filling drips more from one side than another, but I love that look. I don't want this cake neat, which is just as well.

1¾ pounds good strawberries
2–3 teaspoons superfine sugar,
  depending on sweetness of berries

2 cups heavy cream
2 teaspoons vanilla extract

♥ Put 8 ounces strawberries to one side, and start preparing the rest. Hull these, halve the smaller berries and quarter the larger ones, dropping them into a bowl. Sprinkle with sugar – how much depends on how tart or sweet the berries, shake, and leave until they glisten: 10 minutes will be just fine, though 1 hour would make them juicier and glossier.

♥ Whip the heavy cream until it holds its peaked shape when the beaters are lifted out.

♥ Fold a third of the whipped cream into the fully cooled vanilla custard you made earlier (see previous page).

♥ When the cake, too, is thoroughly cool, take out a serrated bread knife and, courageously, slice the cake horizontally into 3 layers. It wouldn't be the end of the world, I suppose, if you simply cut it into 2 layers.

♥ Put one cake layer on its serving platter or stand, and top with half the vanilla-custard-cream, then arrange half the macerating strawberries on top, concentrating more on the outer edges of the cake than the center. Top with the second layer of cake and repeat as before with the rest of the custard-cream and cut berries.

♥ Now set the third cake layer on top and cover with the waiting whipped cream, arranging the 1 cup reserved strawberries as desired: I hull most of them, and cut some, but like to have a few whole, unhulled berries lying plumply and decoratively here and there.

MAKE AHEAD NOTE
The custard can be made 1 day ahead, and cooled and refrigerated immediately. The strawberries can be cut 1 day ahead and stored in a covered bowl in the refrigerator; remove from refrigerator and sprinkle with sugar 1 hour before serving.

FREEZE NOTE
The unadorned cake layers can be frozen on day of baking, for up to 1 month. Slice cake and re-assemble with a circle of parchment paper between each layer of cake. Wrap cake in a double layer of plastic wrap and a layer of aluminum foil. Thaw for 3–4 hours on a wire rack at room temperature and use the same day.

Marmalade pudding cake

Now, this *is* a beauty. I don't mean flash or fancy – rather the opposite; there is something austerely handsome about its appearance, and yet gorgeously warming about its taste. But then, this laid-back Sunday-lunch pudding is what kitchen food is all about. I'm happy to leave the picture-perfect plate-decoration dessert to the professional chef and patissier. When I want to eat one, I'll go to a restaurant. That way, everyone's happy.

I don't want to be too prescriptive about this marmalade pudding cake – which has the surprisingly light texture of a steamed sponge – as it doesn't seem in the spirit of things. I love the bitter edge of a thick-shred, dark marmalade and so tend to go for a proper, glamorously auburn, tawny one here; if this is too full-on for you, choose a fine-shred marmalade, instead.

Serves 6–8

2 sticks plus 1 tablespoon (1 cup plus 1 tablespoon) soft unsalted butter, plus extra for greasing
⅓ cup superfine sugar
⅓ cup (packed) light brown sugar
⅔ cup marmalade, plus ⅓ cup for the glaze
1½ cups all-purpose flour

½ teaspoon baking soda
1 teaspoon baking powder
4 eggs
zest and juice 1 orange (reserve juice ½ orange for the glaze)

1 x 8-inch square Pyrex or other ovenproof dish

♥ Preheat the oven to 350°F, and butter the ovenproof dish.

♥ Put the ⅓ cup marmalade and juice of ½ orange into a small saucepan and set aside to make a glaze later.

♥ Put all the other ingredients for the cake batter into a food processor, process them, and then pour and scrape the batter into the buttered dish, smoothing the top. **If you're not using a processor**, cream the butter and both sugars by hand or in a freestanding mixer, beat in the marmalade followed by the dry ingredients, then the eggs, and finally the orange zest and juice.

♥ Put in the oven and bake for about 40 minutes – though give a first check after 30 minutes – by which time the cake mixture will have risen and a cake tester will come out cleanish. Remove from the oven and leave in the dish.

♥ Warm the glaze mixture in the saucepan until melted together, then paint the top of the

cake, letting the chunks or slivers of peel be your sole, unglinting decoration on top of the mutely gleaming pudding-cake. Know that this cake will keep its orange-scented warmth for quite a while once out of the oven, so you could make it before you sit down for the main course.

♥ Use a large spoon or cake slice (or both) to serve, and put a pitcher of cream or crème anglaise on the table to eat with.

Making leftovers right

*I urge you to try to keep some of this cake back and, once it's cold, wrap it well and keep it in the freezer (in an airtight container for up to 1 month) until you need something effortless for a casual dinner party. All you need do (and see **p.171** for exact measurements and step-by-simple-step guide) is to thaw for 3–4 hours at room temperature, arrange some slices on a plate, douse with orange juice and liqueur, and top with blackberries strewn with orange zest.*

  But I admit it's hard to override the temptation to keep (for up to 2 days in the refrigerator, covered with plastic wrap) whatever pudding-cake may be left from its first outing and heat up the odd bowlful, or just eat it cold straight from the dish.

ORANGE AND
BLACKBERRY
TRIFLE

Lemon polenta cake

This cake is a sort of Anglo-Italian amalgam. The flat, plain disc is reminiscent of the confections that sit geometrically arranged in patisserie windows in Italy; the sharp, syrupy sogginess borrows from the classic English teatime favorite, the lemon drizzle cake. It is a good marriage: I love Italian cooking in all respects save one – I find their cakes both too dry and too sweet. Here, though, the flavorsome grittiness of the polenta and tender rubble of almond meal provide so much better a foil for the wholly desirable dampness than does the usual flour.

But there is more to it than that. By some alchemical process, the lemon highlights the eggy butteriness of the cake, making it rich and sharp at the same time. If you were to try to imagine what lemon curd would taste like in cake form, this would be it.

Although I am greedily happy to slice and cram messily straight into my mouth, letting damp clumps fall where they will, this cake is best eaten – in company at least – with spoon and fork. Either way, consider it a contender for coffee-time comfort and casual dinner-party celebration alike.

Cuts into 16 slices *(though I wouldn't presume people will eat just 1 each . . .)*

for the cake:
1¾ sticks (14 tablespoons) soft unsalted butter, plus extra for greasing
1 cup superfine sugar
2 cups almond meal/flour
¾ cup fine polenta/cornmeal
1½ teaspoons baking powder (gluten-free if required)

3 eggs
zest 2 lemons (save the juice for the syrup)

for the syrup:
juice 2 lemons (see above)
heaping 1 cup confectioner's sugar

1 x 9-inch springform pan

272

♥ Line the base of your springform pan with parchment paper and grease its sides lightly with butter. Preheat the oven to 350°F.

♥ Beat the butter and sugar till pale and whipped, either by hand in a bowl with a wooden spoon, or using a freestanding mixer.

♥ Mix together the almond meal, polenta, and baking powder, and beat some of this into the butter-sugar mixture, followed by 1 egg, then alternate dry ingredients and eggs, beating all the while.

♥ Finally, beat in the lemon zest and pour, spoon, or scrape the mixture into your prepared pan and bake in the oven for about 40 minutes. It may seem wibbly but, if the cake is cooked, a cake tester should come out cleanish and, most significantly, the edges of the cake will have begun to shrink away from the sides of the pan. Remove from the oven to a wire cooling rack, but leave in its pan.

♥ Make the syrup by boiling together the lemon juice and confectioner's sugar in a smallish saucepan. Once the confectioner's sugar has dissolved into the juice, you're done. Prick the top of the cake all over with a cake tester (a skewer would be too destructive), pour the warm syrup over the cake, and let cool completely before taking it out of its pan.

MAKE AHEAD NOTE
The cake can be baked up to 3 days ahead and stored in an airtight container in a cool place. Will keep for a total of 5–6 days.

274

FREEZE NOTE
The cake can be frozen on its lining paper as soon as cooled, wrapped in a double layer of plastic wrap and a layer of aluminum foil, for up to 1 month. Thaw for 3–4 hours at room temperature.

Coffee and walnut layer cake

Neither of my grandmothers, nor indeed my mother, was a baker but this cake is nonetheless *the* cake of my childhood. When I was little, I used to make it for my younger sister's birthday every year, beating away vigorously with my bowl and wooden spoon. This, however, is a simplified version: everything just goes into the processor.

The cake I made and ate when young was more milky coffee than espresso, but here I've bolstered it without consideration of my children. If that's your constituency or concern here, or if you yourself have a nostalgic longing for muted sweet comfort, replace the 4 teaspoons of instant espresso powder with 2 teaspoons of instant coffee granules dissolved in a tablespoonful of boiling water.

Cuts into 8 generous slices

for the sponge:
½ cup walnut pieces
1 cup plus 2 tablespoons superfine sugar
2 sticks (1 cup) soft unsalted butter, plus some for greasing
1⅓ cups all-purpose flour
4 teaspoons instant espresso powder
2½ teaspoons baking powder
½ teaspoon baking soda
4 eggs
1–2 tablespoons milk

for the buttercream frosting:
3¼ cups confectioner's sugar
1½ sticks (¾ cup) soft unsalted butter
2½ teaspoons instant espresso powder, dissolved in 1 tablespoon boiling water
approx. 10 walnut halves, to decorate

2 x 8-inch round cake pans

♥ Preheat the oven to 350°F. Butter the 2 cake pans and line the base of each with parchment paper.

❤ Put the walnut pieces and sugar into a **food processor** and blitz to a fine nutty powder. Add the 2 sticks butter, flour, 4 teaspoons espresso powder, baking powder, baking soda, and eggs, and process to a smooth batter. Add the milk, pouring it down the funnel with the motor still running, or just pulsing, to loosen the cake mixture: it should be a soft, dropping consistency, so add more milk if you need to. (**If you are making this by hand**, bash the nuts to a rubbly powder with a rolling pin and mix with the dry ingredients; then cream the butter and sugar together, and beat in some dry ingredients and eggs alternately and, finally, the milk.)

❤ Divide the mixture between the 2 prepared cake pans and bake in the oven for 25 minutes, or until the cake has risen and feels springy to the touch.

❤ Cool the cakes in their pans on a wire rack for about 10 minutes, before turning them out onto the rack and peeling off the parchment paper.

❤ When the cakes are cool, you can make the buttercream. Pulse the confectioner's sugar in the **food processor** until it is lump-free, then add the butter and process to make a smooth frosting.

❤ Dissolve the instant espresso powder in 1 tablespoon boiling water and add it while still hot to the processor, pulsing to blend into the buttercream.

❤ If you are doing this **by hand**, sift the confectioner's sugar and beat it into the butter with a wooden spoon. Then beat in the hot coffee liquid.

❤ Place 1 cake layer upside down on your cake stand or serving plate. Spread with about half the buttercream; then place on it the second cake layer, right side up (i.e. so the 2 flat sides of the cake layers meet in the middle) and cover the top with the remaining buttercream in a ramshackle swirly pattern. This cake is all about old-fashioned, rustic charm, so don't worry unduly: however the frosting goes on is fine. Similarly, don't fret about some buttercream oozing out around the middle: that's what makes it look so inviting.

❤ Gently press the walnut halves into the top of the frosting all around the edge of the circle, about ½ inch apart.

MAKE AHEAD NOTE
The cake can be baked 1 day ahead and assembled before serving. Wrap cake layers tightly in plastic wrap and store in airtight container. The buttercream can be made 1 day ahead: cover with plastic wrap and re-frigerate; remove from the refrigerator 1–2 hours before needed to allow to come to room temperature, then beat briefly before use. The frosted cake will keep for 2–3 days in airtight container in a cool place.

FREEZE NOTE
The un-frosted cake layers can be frozen on day of baking, each wrapped in double layer of plastic wrap and a layer of aluminum foil, for up to 3 months. Thaw for 3–4 hours on wire rack at room temperature. Frosting can be frozen separately in airtight container for up to 3 months. Thaw overnight in the refrigerator, then bring to room temperature and beat briefly before use.

Venetian carrot cake

I long thought that carrot cake was an American invention, until I found out that an early version was made by Venetian Jews in the original ghetto.

This modest disc is very different from the gargantuan US model with its rich sweet cream-cheese filling and topping, and although – apart from a glorious goldenness – it's not much to look at, it is divine to eat. It has the added virtue of being attractive to those with dairy and gluten allergies: it came to me dairy free, and I decided to use almond meal in place of regular flour to keep the gluten-averse brigade happy, and more particularly because it tastes perfect to me like this.

Only those with less austere eating habits will care to dollop alongside each damp, crumbling wedge of cake my Italianate nod to the American cream-cheese frosting – a soft, rum-flavored mascarpone cream.

Serves 8–10

for the carrot cake:
3 tablespoons toasted pine nuts
2 medium carrots (approx. 2 cups grated)
½ cup golden raisins
¼ cup rum
¾ cup superfine sugar
½ cup regular olive oil, plus some for greasing
1 teaspoon vanilla extract
3 eggs
2½ cup cups almond meal/flour

½ teaspoon nutmeg
finely grated zest and juice ½ lemon

for the mascarpone cream (optional):
1 cup mascarpone
2 teaspoons confectioner's sugar
2 tablespoons rum

1 x 9-inch springform pan

♥ Preheat the oven to 350°F. Line the base of your cake pan with re-usable non-stick silicone liner (see **p.14**) or parchment paper, and grease the sides with olive oil. Toast the pine nuts for 3–4 minutes in a fatless frying pan, watching carefully; the oven alone is not enough to scorch out the paleness.

♥ Grate the carrots in a processor (for ease) or with a coarse grater, then sit them on a double layer of paper towels and wrap them, to soak up excess liquid.

♥ Put the golden raisins in a small saucepan with the rum, bring to a boil, turn down, and simmer for 3 minutes.

♥ Whisk the sugar and oil – I use my freestanding mixer, but it wouldn't be much of a fuss by hand – until creamily and airily mixed.

♥ Whisk in the vanilla extract and eggs and when well whisked, fold in the almond meal, nutmeg, grated carrots, golden raisins (with any rum that clings to them), and, finally, the lemon zest and juice.

♥ Scrape the mixture into the prepared springform pan and smooth the surface with a rubber spatula. The batter will be very shallow in the pan.

♥ Sprinkle the toasted pine nuts over the cake and put it into the oven for 30–40 minutes, or until the top is risen and golden and a cake tester comes out sticky but more or less clean.

♥ Remove from the oven and let the cake sit in its pan on a wire rack for 10 minutes before unspringing and leaving it on the rack to cool.

♥ Remove the cake to a plate to serve; mix the mascarpone with the confectioner's sugar and rum, and put in a bowl to spoon alongside, for those who want.

MAKE AHEAD NOTE
The cake can be baked up to 3 days ahead. Wrap carefully in plastic wrap and store in airtight container in a cool place. Will keep for total of 5–6 days.

FREEZE NOTE
The cake can be frozen (still on base of the pan, if easier), carefully wrapped in a double layer of plastic wrap and a layer of aluminum foil, for up to 3 months. Thaw overnight at room temperature.

Flourless chocolate lime cake
with margarita cream gluten free

There is something about a flourless chocolate cake that makes it so damn easy to eat. This is one of my go-to favorites for dessert when I have friends over for dinner.

Serves 8–10

6 ounces bittersweet chocolate, chopped (¾ cup chips)
1¼ sticks (10 tablespoons) soft unsalted butter, plus some for greasing
6 eggs
1¼ cups superfine sugar
1 cup almond meal/flour

4 teaspoons best-quality unsweetened cocoa powder, sifted
zest and juice 1 lime
confectioner's sugar, to dust (optional)

1 x 9-inch springform pan

♥ Preheat the oven to 350°F, line the base of your springform pan with parchment paper, and butter the sides.

♥ Melt the chocolate and butter together either in a heatproof bowl suspended over a saucepan of simmering water, or in a microwave (following manufacturer's instructions), then set aside to cool slightly.

♥ Beat the eggs and sugar together until about tripled in volume, pale and mousse-like. I do this **using a freestanding mixer**, but **a hand-held electric model** would be just fine too; obviously, **by hand** is possible but would demand tenacity and muscle.

♥ Mix the almond meal with the cocoa powder and fold this gently into the egg and sugar mixture, followed by the slightly cooled chocolate and butter. Finally, fold in the zest and juice of your lime.

♥ Pour and scrape this mixture into the prepared pan and bake in the preheated oven for 40–45 minutes (though start to check at 35); the cake will be just firm on top, but still have a bit of wobble underneath.

♥ Remove from the oven and set the cake in its pan on a wire rack to cool. Once the first heat has left it, drape a clean kitchen towel over the cake to stop it getting too crusty, though a cracked and cratered surface is to be expected; it's crunch I'm avoiding here.

❤ When cold, unmold, dust with confectioner's sugar if you wish, and serve with the jaunty Margarita Cream that follows.

MAKE AHEAD NOTE
The cake can be baked up to 3 days ahead. Store in airtight container in a cool place and dust with confectioner's sugar just before serving.

FREEZE NOTE
The cake can be frozen (still on base of pan if easier), wrapped carefully in a double layer of plastic wrap and a layer of aluminum foil, for up to 1 month. Thaw overnight at cool room temperature and dust with confectioner's sugar just before serving.

Margarita cream

I love the biting lime notes of this cream. Although its taste plays on the hint of lime in the cake, it also acts as a foil: sharp and light against the rich bittersweet chocolate.

¼ cup lime juice (2–3 limes),
  or from a bottle (Kitchen
  Confidential p.17)
1 tablespoon tequila

1 tablespoon triple sec or Cointreau
¾ cup confectioner's sugar
1 cup heavy cream

❤ Stir the lime juice, tequila, and orange liqueur together in a good-sized bowl, then whisk or fork in the confectioner's sugar and let it dissolve in the sour, strong liquid.

❤ Whip the cream in a separate bowl until it just hold its shape, then whisk in the margarita mixture and keep whisking until you have a light, floaty, aerated mixture, then serve immediately with the Chocolate Lime Cake above. (Though there's nothing to stop you presenting this in small glasses, on some other occasion, to be eaten like syllabub.)

282

Buttermilk scones

Last summer, I gave up on going abroad and took a staycation in Cornwall. Apart from one gorgeous, glinting day, it rained and blustered and blew, and I loved it. There I was, with a fire burning inside, the mackerel-colored sea swirling outside, living off the fat – that's to say, the rich, thick, clotted cream – of the land.

    If you can't find clotted cream (sometimes called Devonshire cream) then feel free to lavishly spoon softly whipped heavy cream onto the scones instead. The buttermilk in these scones not only gives them a slight tang, all the better to enjoy the jam and cream on top, but is also what yields such a melting, tender crumb.

    These scones do look as though they are suffering from cellulite (I dare say we all might, if we ate too many of them), but proper scones should not have the smooth-sided denseness of the store-bought variety. And they are so worth making. Until you have made a batch of scones, you won't have any idea how easy they are to throw together. Frankly, it shouldn't take longer than 20 minutes to make and bake them, from start to finish. Even though the process is hardly lengthy enough to warrant cooking them in advance, I like to make up quite a big batch – and this recipe will give you about 18 scones – and freeze some (they thaw incredibly quickly) to produce a near-instant cream tea at some future date.

Makes 17–18

3⅓ cups all-purpose flour	1¼ cups buttermilk
2 teaspoons baking soda	1 egg, beaten, for an egg-wash (optional)
2 teaspoons cream of tartar	
2 teaspoons superfine sugar	1 x large lipped baking sheet or half sheet
4 tablespoons (¼ cup) unsalted butter	pan
2 tablespoons soft vegetable shortening	1 x 2-inch biscuit cutter, preferably fluted

♥ Preheat the oven to 425°F and line a large lipped baking sheet with parchment paper. Put the flour into a bowl with the baking soda, cream of tartar, and sugar.

♥ Chop the butter and the vegetable shortening into pieces and drop them into the flour.

♥ Rub the fats into the flour – or just mix any old how – and then pour in the buttermilk, working everything together to form a dough.

♥ Lightly flour your work surface. Pat the dough down into a round-edged oblong about 1¾ inches thick, then cut out 2-inch scones with a biscuit cutter. (Mine are never a uniform height, as I pat the dough into its shape without worrying whether it's irregular or not.)

♥ Arrange the scones fairly close together on your lined baking sheet, and brush with beaten egg (to give golden tops) or not, as you wish. Bake for 12 minutes, by which time the scones will be dry on the bottom and have a relatively light feel. Remove them to a wire rack to cool, and serve with clotted or whipped cream and Jumbleberry Jam (see opposite).

MAKE AHEAD NOTE
Scones are best on day they are made but day-old scones can be revived by warming in oven preheated to 300°F for 5–10 minutes.

FREEZE NOTE
Baked scones can be frozen in airtight containers or resealable bags for up to 1 month. Thaw for 1 hour at room temperature and warm as above. Unbaked scones can be put on parchment-lined trays and frozen until solid. Transfer to resealable bags and freeze for up to 3 months. Bake direct from frozen, as directed in recipe, but allowing extra 2–3 minutes' baking time.

284

Jumbleberry jam

As the name suggests, this jam does not rely on a do-or-die ratio of berry ingredients. Although there is one ratio that *does* matter, which is the equal weight of berries and sugar. When I rooted the recipe out of one of my kitchen notebooks, what I found was a not very helpful scribble that I hope I can illuminate here. In my defense, the whole point of Jumbleberry Jam is that you use up what you've got. It doesn't matter if you don't use all the fruits I've specified below, or if you use them in different proportions. Essentially a recipe is only an honest account of how something was made at a given time. If it helps you feel safer, by all means emulate more closely what I made, and for this I suggest 7 ounces of red currants, 6 ounces each of black currants and blackberries, 3 ounces each of raspberries, strawberries, and blueberries.

If this jam-making is a mopping-up operation (and I did give serious consideration to placing this recipe in the Cook It Better section), then I would probably make half the amount, and not bother with the blueberries, since they tend to cost more and have less taste than other berries in season; but if I have some blueberries knocking around (and I do have a weakness for them in muffins or mixed with pomegranate seeds in yogurt), I'm happy to pluck them from the refrigerator and toss them in the pan, too.

If you have a good proportion of red currants (which are naturally pectin-rich), then you may prefer to leave out the added pectin. I use extra pectin because I am impatient – I know it makes the jam set faster, and that means I don't need to fret that it won't set.

Makes enough for approx. 6 x 1-cup jars

1¾ pounds mixed berries, such as red and black currants, raspberries, strawberries and blueberries (5½ cups prepared fruit)
4 cups sugar

1 x 1.75-ounce envelope powdered fruit pectin (such as Balls original fruit pectin)
6 x 1-cup sealable jars

♥ Sterilize your jars (see **p.285**). Put a few small plates into the freezer to help you later to tell, without a thermometer, when the jam has reached setting point.

♥ Quarter the strawberries (unless they are very small, in which case halve them), and put these with all the berries into a large, wide saucepan; bear in mind that the fruit and sugar will froth up hugely as they cook. Add the sugar and powdered pectin, and give a good stir.

♥ Stop stirring and put the pan on a low heat.

♥ Give the pan a gentle shake now and then, to encourage the sugar to melt into the fruits, but *resist* the temptation to stir. When the sugar has dissolved, you may turn up the heat.

♥ Bring to a boil, then turn down to a medium heat so that you have a consistent, vigorous simmer, i.e. a contained boil that is not threatening to boil over! Keep an eye on your pan but *do not stir.*

♥ After about 12–15 minutes, take a plate from the freezer, remove the pan from the heat and, carefully, take a teaspoonful of jam and smear it on the plate. Set the plate down for a couple of minutes and then push the surface of the jam with a teaspoon or finger; if it is beginning to wrinkle, the jam has set. If it doesn't set, return the pan to the heat and repeat the process after a few minutes. If you prefer to use a candy/sugar thermometer, you will see when it hits 220°F, which is the jelling point for jam.

♥ When you judge the jam to be ready, take it off the heat. Put a jam funnel into the neck of a sterilized jam jar and carefully fill with jam, sealing each jar when you've finished, and then let cool completely.

MAKE AHEAD NOTE
Can be stored in a cool, dark place for up to 1 year. Once opened, store in the refrigerator and use within 1 month.

Gooseberry chutney

I'm a pushover for a chutney: not only because I like eating it, but because I derive so much pleasure from making it. I almost feel that I should be ashamed of how easy it is. Not that I've ever pretended it's hard work, but somehow putting a jar of home-made chutney on the table just *seems* so smug.

There is only one problem with chutney, which is that those of us who are drawn to make it, deriving a sense of calm and security from filling cupboards with good things, tend to be hoarders by nature. I can keep chutney hidden away for too long, much in the way that I leave new clothes (far too special to be worn, of course) hanging in the wardrobe.

In a funny way, I find if I make less, I'm better at using up what I have. Perhaps that's because making small batches – like the 3 little jars here – is altogether less of an operation. You don't start to feel like you're opening a cannery; rather that you're making the most of the beautiful gooseberry's short season. And you are. Though, please, check out the crumble on **p.251**, too.

Anyway, enjoy the 3 jars here: give one to a friend, maybe, but savor the rest with cold ham, a loaf of bread and slab of cheese, dollopped alongside the Roasted Duck Legs on **p.388** or, in an Anglo reworking of the classic French *maquereaux aux groseilles*, served as a suitably zingy relish with some plain grilled mackerel.

Makes enough for 3 x 1-cup jars

1¼ pounds gooseberries, washed and de-bearded

1 onion, peeled and finely chopped

2 teaspoons finely chopped, seeded red chile

2 teaspoons finely chopped fresh ginger root

1 teaspoon ground turmeric

½ teaspoon ground cloves

1 teaspoon ground cilantro

1 teaspoon ground cumin

1 tablespoon kosher salt or 1½ teaspoons table salt

1⅓ cups turbinado sugar

1½ cups apple cider vinegar

3 x 1-cup sealable jars (or 1 x 3-cup) with vinegar-proof lids

♥ Sterilize your jars (see **p.285**).

♥ Put the gooseberries, chopped onion, chile, ginger, turmeric, cloves, cilantro, cumin, and salt into a pan.

♥ Tip in the sugar, pour in the vinegar, and give everything a good stir. Bring to a boil and cook over a medium heat, at a brisk simmer, for 30–40 minutes, until the mixture thickens and some of the berries have oozily popped.

♥ Ladle into your sterilized jars, sealing with their lids, and let cool completely.

MAKE AHEAD NOTE
Make the chutney 2 months before use to allow it to mature. Store in a cool, dark place for up to 1 year. Once opened, store in the refrigerator and use within 1 month.

NOTE
Look for gooseberries at farmers' markets and farm stands.

289

Spiced pumpkin chutney

Like the gooseberry chutney above, this is notionally a season-celebrating recipe, too. I suppose you could make this chutney equally well with butternut squash, which seems almost perpetually available these days, but the bulging bright hugeness of a pumpkin is fabulously compelling. Just taking one home from the store feels as if you're celebrating the harvest festival in a significant way.

If it is a whole pumpkin you've lugged home, then you might be wise to check the index for any mention of butternut or squash and modify the recipe to accommodate your autumnal glut. If you buy your fruit and veg from a grocery store or farmers' market rather than in a supermarket, you should be able to buy pumpkin by the half or quarter or, if you're in luck, to the desired weight.

Makes enough for 6 x 1-cup jars or 1¼ quarts

2¾ pounds pumpkin, to yield approx. 7 cups once peeled, seeded, and diced

2 medium onions

1 Granny Smith apple, cored

⅔ cup golden raisins

2 red or green chiles, seeded and chopped

1½ cups light brown sugar

1 teaspoon ground cinnamon

1 teaspoon ground ginger

1 teaspoon ground cloves

2 teaspoons kosher salt or 1 teaspoon table salt

2 heaped tablespoons minced fresh gingerroot

2⅔ cups white wine vinegar

6 x 1-cup sealable jars (or 1 x 1¼-quart) with vinegar-proof lids

♥ Sterilize your jars (see **p.285**).

♥ Peel and seed the pumpkin, then cut it into very small dice. Peel and finely chop the onions and apple.

♥ Put all the ingredients into a large, wide saucepan and bring to a boil, stirring to dissolve the sugar.

♥ Simmer over a medium heat for about 1 hour, by which time the chutney will have thickened and the pumpkin become tender. The timing for this process can vary according to the pumpkin, so watch the pan after 45 minutes and cover loosely if the chutney is thickened but the pumpkin still not soft.

♥ Spoon into sterilized jars, put the lids on, and let cool completely.

MAKE AHEAD NOTE

Make the chutney 2 months before use to allow it to mature. Store in a cool, dark place for up to 1 year. Once opened, store in the refrigerator and use within 1 month.

Blackberry vodka

Bottling my own liqueur makes me feel homespun and happy, as if at any minute I might be paying a visit to some invalid neighbor bearing homemade calf's foot jelly. It's completely nonsensical, of course, but in the scheme of things there are greater nonsenses than pottering about with a preserving jar.

Perhaps it's the very unnecessariness that makes work like this so comforting. Most of the time we cook because a meal needs to be put on the table, and gratifying though feeding people is, the task can feel relentless, too. I can see why some might find this recipe a time-wasting exercise and not to be countenanced; I on the other hand, feel grateful if there is ever any time to be wasted, and celebrate it – like this.

Makes enough to fill a 3-cup (750ml) bottle plus scant 1 cup

3 cups vodka (1 x 750ml bottle)
1¼ pounds blackberries
1 cup sugar

1 x 1½-quart wide-necked bottle or
sealable jar (such as a hermetic
seal jar), for steeping
1 x 3-cup (750ml) vodka bottle or 1
quart sealable bottle for keeping
(optional)

♥ Sterilize (see **p.285**) your wide-necked bottle or jar, and pour in the vodka. Keep the original vodka bottle for decanting into later (you can soak it to get rid of the label), or consign it for recycling if you have another, prettier, bottle to use instead.

♥ Tip the blackberries and sugar into the jar, and then seal with the lid.

♥ Shake the jar patiently until the sugar dissolves – it will eventually, just keep shaking the contents from side to side.

♥ Put the jar in a cool, dark place, not too inaccessible as you will need to shake it daily for a couple of weeks, then once a week after that for about a month.

♥ After about 6–8 weeks – a few weeks more won't hurt, though – sterilize the vodka bottle or other bottle of your choice, strain the vodka of its berries (reserving the fruit if you want to make the Drunken Fool that follows), then decant the liqueur into the bottle. And if you don't intend to bottle this, but just to lower a ladle in and tip straight into shot glasses, then don't bother to strain.

♥ You will have scant 1 cup blackberry vodka left over if you re-use your original vodka bottle, as the addition of the berries and sugar will have given you more liquid. Pour this into a 1-cup hip flask, or use to make the Drunken Fool that follows, along with a shot of the stuff for each person eating it.

MAKE AHEAD NOTE
The strained blackberry vodka can be kept in a cool, dark place for 1 year.

It feels criminal to throw the berries away, once they've given their life's blood to your vodka. By themselves, they'd be a poor excuse for a treat, but folded into softly whipped cream with some crumbled store-bought meringue cookies they seem to get their second wind, and earn your double delight by providing a most gratifyingly named dessert.

Makes enough to fill 6 small martini glasses

1¼ cups heavy cream
1 tablespoon confectioner's sugar
the blackberries retrieved from
  their vodka

8 small store-bought meringue
  cookies
few dashes of the freshly made
  blackberry vodka

♥ Softly whip the cream with the confectioner's sugar. Be careful not to overwhip, as stirring in the soaked blackberries makes it thicken up quite a bit.

♥ Fold in the blackberries, and crumble in the meringue cookies.

♥ Dribble in a little blackberry vodka and ripple through gently by folding, briefly, again.

♥ Fill 6 small martini glasses with the fool, top each with a dash of blackberry vodka, then serve with wafers or cookies of your choice, and a shot of blackberry vodka for those who want.

295

CUT AND COME AGAIN

In the old days, the sort of cakes that could be made, brought out, and sliced when guests called, then rewrapped and put back in the crock until next needed, were called "cut and come again"; these were good, plain cakes that kept well, and were serviceable, welcoming, and spoke of the quiet comforts of home.

Well, I'm not sure the term "quiet comforts" has much meaning, other than symbolic or indeed ironic, in my home, but I love the feeling that I've got something on the kitchen counter to offer any one passing, with a cup of tea or coffee. Not even the man mending the boiler leaves without an aluminum foil–wrapped package.

Because the whole point of the cakes or bars that follow is that they don't need a special occasion to be made or eaten, and because it dispenses with any sticking issues (as well as with washing up), I confess to using disposable aluminum-foil pans for many of them. And I have settled on a utility-size pan (12¾ x 9 x 1^{27}/$_{32}$ inches but labeled as "for 13 x 9 x 2 inch recipes") which is easily found in stores and supermarkets.

Seed-cake

I think of seed-cake as quintessentially English: elegant and plain and wholesome without being indelicately heavy. Of course, that is not "English" in any real, living sense. My own memories of it are from childhood, sometime in the last century, let's be frank, and even then seed-cake was anachronistic, bespeaking an Edwardian age of Madeira m'dear, or some earlier fusty Victorian time when caraway was thought to be beneficial to the digestion.

Actually, the recipe pre-dates even the fussy Victorians. It is the cake eaten by poor Jane Eyre on one of the few happy days of her childhood, when she savors some snatched time with her beloved schoolfriend, Helen, and their teacher, Miss Temple, who "got up, unlocked a drawer, and taking from it a parcel wrapped in paper, disclosed presently to our eyes a good-sized seed-cake."

I remember being uplifted by the thought of seed-cake, if not the taste, when I was young. I recall, too, seeing a recipe for it in my mother's yellow-paged, obviously unillustrated *Mrs. Beeton's Book of Household Management*; to me both Brontë and Beeton incarnations were hushed evocations of the ultimate comforting seed-cake.

Nevertheless, I have played fast and loose with both versions: Miss Temple's cake would not have been made using chemical rising agents and Mrs. Beeton's was a great deal more sensible and less rich than mine. Still, I make no apologies: I put this buttery, marzipanny version here because I love it, and hope you will, too. Besides, the addition of almond meal makes the cake keep longer without drying out, the better to come again and cut it.

I want your guests to feel with Jane that "we feasted that evening as on nectar and ambrosia; and not the least delight of the entertainment was the smile of gratification with which our hostess regarded us, as we satisfied our famished appetites on the delicate fare." Reader, that smile of gratification – the sometime domestic goddess's badge of honor – is yours: with scant work, but miraculous effect, you've earned it.

Cuts into a good 16 slices

1½ sticks (¾ cup) soft unsalted butter, plus
  extra for greasing
¾ cup plus 2 tablespoons superfine sugar, plus
  1 extra tablespoon for sprinkling
1 cup all-purpose flour
2 teaspoons baking powder

¾ cup almond meal/flour
4 teaspoons caraway seeds
3 eggs

1 x 2-pound loaf pan

♥ Preheat the oven to 350°F. Line the 2-pound loaf pan with a paper loaf-pan liner or line the bottom with parchment paper, and butter the sides.

♥ Cream the butter and ¾ cup plus 2 tablespoons sugar together, beating until light and fluffy.

♥ Combine the flour, baking powder, almond meal, and caraway seeds in a bowl and add 1 tablespoonful to the creamed butter-sugar mixture, then, beating steadily, add 1 egg at a time, with a spoonful of dry ingredients between each egg.

♥ When all your ingredients are combined, spoon into the lined loaf pan, and smooth the top before sprinkling with the remaining tablespoon of sugar. Bake for about 45 minutes, though check at 35 and be prepared to go on for 50 minutes. It will smell heavily aromatic when cooked, and the top and edges will be starting to turn crisply golden.

♥ Cool in the pan on a wire rack, and when no longer hot to the touch, slip the cake in its liner out of the pan onto the rack. The center of the cake will sink a little as the cake cools, but this is the way of the loaf (as you can see more clearly in the picture of the Chocolate Orange Loaf Cake on **p.309**); it's not that you or your oven have done anything wrong.

MAKE AHEAD NOTE
This cake can be baked up to 2 days ahead. Wrap tightly in plastic wrap and store in airtight container in a cool place. Keeps for up to 7 days in total.

FREEZE NOTE
The cake can be frozen, wrapped in a double layer of plastic wrap and a layer of aluminum foil, for up to 3 months. Thaw overnight at room temperature.

Raspberry almond bars

Strictly speaking, this doesn't really fit into the "cut and come again" category as the fresh fruit, those raspberries seeping tartly into the soft frangipane that blankets them, makes this something you can't have hanging around for long. But here's the thing: it goes fast. And it's true to say that anyone who cuts themselves a piece most certainly does come to cut again, the second slice following swiftly on the first.

Only the rare few consider pastry-baking a casually undertaken activity; and yet this pie in a pan is the work of moments. An aluminum foil pan helps (and helps the dough cook to a crisp buttery finish fast, too) but the real lifesaver is this press-in, no-roll dough – my everyday answer to the pastry problem, real or imagined.

Makes 16 bars

for the base:
1½ cups all-purpose flour
½ cup confectioner's sugar
pinch salt
2 sticks (1 cup) soft unsalted butter,
  plus some for greasing

1 x rectangular aluminum foil or
  cake pan, approx. 13 x 9 x 2 inches

for the filling:
1¼ sticks (10 tablespoons) soft unsalted
  butter, plus extra for greasing
4 eggs
¾ cup superfine sugar
1½ cups almond meal/flour
1 cup seedless raspberry jam
8 ounces (1½ cups) fresh raspberries
½ cup sliced almonds

♥ Preheat your oven to 350°F. Line the cake pan with aluminum foil and grease it, or grease your foil pan.

♥ Mix the flour, confectioner's sugar, salt, and 2 sticks butter in a food processor until you have a cohesive dough. Press into the bottom of your pan. Be patient – I promise you have enough to fill the bottom – just work the dough with the back of a spoon or your hands (preferably your knuckles), to get an evenish surface.

♥ Bake the base for 20 minutes, then let cool in the pan for about 5 minutes.

♥ While the base is in the oven, melt the 1¼ sticks butter for the filling in a small saucepan, then take off the heat to cool a little, say the 5 minutes while the base is cooling.

♥ Put the eggs, superfine sugar, and almond meal into a food processor and blitz to a paste. With the motor running, pour the slightly cooled melted butter down the funnel and stop when all is combined, though you may want to scrape down the contents then pulse to finish.

♥ Whisk the jam in a bowl to make it a little more spreadable, and duly spread it over the base, then tumble the raspberries over the jam. Scrape the almond filling out of the processor, and spread over the raspberry layer.

♥ Sprinkle with the sliced almonds, and bake for about 45 minutes, testing after 35: it is ready when it's risen with gentle puffiness and has become tinted gold from the heat.

♥ Cool – or not if you can't wait (but be wary of the hot jam layer) – before slicing.

MAKE AHEAD NOTE
Crust and filling can be prepared 1 day ahead of baking. Press crust into pan, wrap with plastic wrap, and refrigerate. Put filling in a bowl and cover with plastic wrap, then refrigerate. Remove from the refrigerator 1–2 hours before use to allow to come to room temperature and beat briefly before spreading over the base.

FURTHER NOTE
Leftovers can be kept in the refrigerator, covered with plastic wrap, for 1–2 days. If possible bring to room temperature before serving.

Treacle tart bars

On paper, I admit that the notion of a dough, plain to the point of dourness and draped with syrup thickened with breadcrumbs, sounds unappetizing. How is it then that it is the most desirable delicacy, and one of my favorite desserts in the world? And oh my, oh my – am I *really* pleased to have found a way of making a treacle tart without tears? For this is not a temptation anyone in their right mind (not that I would presume) could resist. Perhaps it's better not to ask, but simply eat in gratitude.

The breadcrumbs do need to be fresh, itself a bit of a misnomer, as the bread will be stale before being processed (or grated) to a crumb. I always keep a stash of these in my freezer, and don't even bother to thaw them before using. If you can find a source of proper breadcrumbs outside the home, that's fine, but don't even think of using that orangey powder which comes in boxes and calls itself breadcrumbs.

Yes, the recipe calls for quite a lot of breadcrumbs, but once the crumbs have soaked up the buttery, lemony syrup, what you have is a gorgeous chewiness, more fluffy than heavy. The plain base makes complete sense: you need elegant balance for the near temple-aching sweetness of the ginger-colored topping.

Which brings us to Devonshire clotted cream or alternatively, whipped cream, my accompaniment of choice here: mad though it sounds to think of a substance that is over 50 percent fat as having a tamping-down effect, its lusciousness seems to temper the sweetness with cool efficiency. Still, those who'd prefer to eat this not as a cream-topped slice, but swathed with crème anglaise and spooned out of a bowl, will not find any argument from me.

Makes about 16 bars

for the base:
1⅓ cups all-purpose flour
4 tablespoons (¼ cup) soft unsalted
  butter, plus some for greasing
4 tablespoons (¼ cup) vegetable
  shortening
1 tablespoon lemon juice (reserve
  zest for the topping)
2 tablespoons ice-cold water

for the topping:
1 x 1-pound container (1½ cups)
  golden syrup (such as Lyle's)
2 tablespoons soft unsalted butter
2⅓ cups fresh breadcrumbs
zest lemon (see ingredients for the
  base)
1 egg, beaten

1 x rectangular aluminum foil pan or
  cake pan, approx. 13 x 9 x 2 inches

♥ Preheat the oven to 350°F. Line your cake pan with aluminum foil and grease it, or grease your foil pan.

♥ Put the flour, 4 tablespoons butter, and vegetable shortening for the base into a food processor and blitz until you have a crumbly rubble.

♥ Combine the lemon juice and ice-cold water and pour down the funnel with the engine running until the mixture clumps together, making a pale, damp dough.

♥ Press this dough into the bottom of your foil/cake pan, using the back of a metal spoon or your hands to make a relatively thin, smooth, even base. Bake in the oven for 20 minutes.

♥ Meanwhile, melt the golden syrup and 2 tablespoons butter in a heavy-based saucepan on a low heat. Stir in the breadcrumbs, not worrying that you appear to have a thick, sawdusty, sticky mixture.

♥ Take the pan off the heat, let cool a little, then add the lemon zest and beat in the egg. Pour the mixture over the cooked pastry base and put back into the oven for 20 minutes.

♥ When it's ready, the filling should have risen slightly and look as if it is just about set: dry at the edges, but with the promise of stickiness at the center.

♥ Take out of the oven and let cool only a little: this must be sliced, and is best eaten while still fragrantly warm.

MAKE AHEAD NOTE
The bars can be made up to 1 day ahead. Cool in pan and cover with plastic wrap then refrigerate. Reheat in oven preheated to 350°F for 20 minutes, or until warmed through.
Leftovers can be kept in the refrigerator, covered in plastic wrap, for 2–3 days.

FREEZE NOTE
The bars can be frozen in the pan, wrapped tightly in a double layer of plastic wrap and a layer of aluminum foil, for up to 1 month. Thaw overnight in the refrigerator and reheat as above.

302

Guinness gingerbread

I adore the deceptive plainness of gingerbread. It is definitively unfancy, and yet the flavor is so rich, and its deep-toned tang so subtle. Here the tang is a little more emphatic, as sour cream and licorice-evocative Guinness give heady lift, but still this is – for all the treacly sugar and pungent spices – gentle and cozy-making, though almost alarmingly addictive.

So although this started life in my kitchen as a spot-hitting accompaniment for a hot drink, I find that a small square with some diced mango makes for a fantastic end to a simple kitchen supper and, eaten still warm with some of the sour and scarlet plums on **p.140**, is a perfect easy weekend dessert.

Makes 24 small, squat squares or 16 generous rectangular slabs

1¼ sticks (10 tablespoons) butter, plus some for greasing
1 cup golden syrup (such as Lyle's)
1 cup (packed) plus 2 tablespoons dark brown sugar
1 cup Guinness
2 teaspoons ground ginger
2 teaspoons ground cinnamon
¼ teaspoon ground cloves

2 cups all-purpose flour
2 teaspoons baking soda
1¼ cups sour cream
2 eggs

1 x rectangular aluminum foil pan or cake pan, approx. 13 x 9 x 2 inches

♥ Preheat your oven to 325°F. Line your cake pan with aluminum foil and grease it, or grease your foil pan.

♥ Put the butter, syrup, dark brown sugar, Guinness, ginger, cinnamon, and ground cloves into a saucepan and melt gently over a low heat.

♥ Take off the heat and whisk in the flour and baking soda. You will need to be patient and whisk thoroughly to get rid of any lumps.

♥ Whisk the sour cream and eggs together in a measuring cup and then beat into the gingerbread mixture, whisking again to get a smooth batter.

♥ Pour this into your cake/foil pan, and bake for about 45 minutes; when it's ready it will be gleamingly risen at the center, and coming away from the pan at the sides.

♥ Let the gingerbread cool before cutting into bars or squares.

305

The gingerbread can be baked up to 1 week ahead. Wrap in parchment paper followed by layer of plastic wrap and store in airtight container in a cool place. Keeps for a total of 2 weeks.

The gingerbread can be frozen, wrapped in layer of parchment paper and double layer of aluminum foil, for up to 3 months. Thaw on wire rack at room temperature for 3–4 hours and cut into squares.

306

Chocolate orange loaf cake

A loaf cake is just the thing to have about your kitchen: it promises sustenance without showiness; and the rich and scented sombreness of this one confers more gravitas than the flighty words "chocolate cake" would seem to convey.

But then this is no decadent fancy, rather a slice-able slab of cocoa-rich serenity. The chocolate is intoxicatingly present, deep and dark in taste, but the texture of its crumb is light. When I was a child, there was a chocolate bar that was advertised as "the sweet you can eat between meals without ruining your appetite." Hard to believe now, isn't it? However, the thing about this cake – which has a citrus tang so mellow it comes through as warm spice – is that you feel you can snaffle a slice mid-morning or mid-afternoon without feeling the slightest bit weighed down, digestively or psychologically.

Cuts into 10–12 slices

1¼ sticks (10 tablespoons) soft unsalted butter, plus extra for greasing
dab flavorless vegetable oil, for greasing syrup spoon
2 tablespoons golden syrup (such as Lyle's), or dark corn syrup
1 cup (packed) dark brown sugar
1 cup all-purpose flour

½ teaspoon baking soda
3 tablespoons best-quality unsweetened cocoa powder, sifted
2 eggs
zest 2 regular oranges and juice of 1

1 x 2-pound loaf pan

♥ Preheat the oven to 325°F and line your loaf pan with parchment paper and grease the sides, or line with a paper loaf-pan liner.

♥ Beat the already soft butter with the syrup – if you dab a little oil on your tablespoon measure with a sheet of paper towel, the syrup shouldn't stick to the spoon – and the sugar until you have a fairly smooth caffè Americano cream, though the sugar will have a bit of grit about it.

♥ Mix the flour, baking soda, and cocoa powder together, and beat into the syrup mixture 1 tablespoonful of these dry ingredients before beating in 1 egg. Then add another couple of spoonfuls of the dry ingredients before beating in the second egg.

♥ Carry on beating in the remaining dry ingredients and then add, still beating, the orange zest and finally, gradually, the juice. At this stage, the batter may suddenly look dimpled, as if slightly curdled. No need to panic!

♥ Pour and scrape into the prepared pan and bake for 45 minutes, though check 5 minutes before and be prepared to keep it in the oven 5 minutes longer if need be. A cake tester won't come out entirely clean, as the point of this cake, light though it may be, is to have just a hint of inner stickiness. Let cool a little in its pan on a wire rack, then turn out with care and leave on the rack to cool.

MAKE AHEAD NOTE
The cake can be baked up to 3 days ahead. Wrap tightly in plastic wrap and store in airtight container. Will keep for 5 days total.

FREEZE NOTE
The cake can be frozen, tightly wrapped in a double layer of plastic wrap and a layer of aluminum foil, for up to 3 months. Thaw overnight at room temperature.

Sweet and salty crunch nut bars

Be still, my beating heart! On second thoughts, perhaps this is not the best thing to say here, given the likelihood of this lusciously over-the-top piece of chocolate excess inducing just such an outcome. I wouldn't want to make this very often, so impossible is it to walk away from with conviction. I fear it is the kitchen equivalent to crack cocaine.

    Still, as the French might well say, "Everything in moderation, even moderation." This is gloriously intemperate, riotously vulgar. I love it.

    The key is in the blaring balance between sweet and salty: it's like several klaxons going off in your head as you eat. And it's strange that while I would normally eschew an all-milk chocolate offering, I prefer it here to the bittersweet-and-milk mixed version. Not that either is bad, and since the jury is matched on this, I feel it is only right to alert you to the options. For what it's worth, I like the darker version in a round pan and cut into panforte-type skinny wedges, and my preferred milk chocolate version set in a rectangular pan and cut into chunky, squat slabs (rather as I feel and look after eating too many of them).

The round springform pan cuts into approx. 24 slender(ish) slices; the aluminum foil pan yields 18 large or 36 small pieces

7 ounces bittersweet chocolate (or 1 heaping cup chips) *and*
4 ounces milk chocolate (or ½ cup chips) (*or* 11 ounces milk chocolate instead)
1 stick plus 1 tablespoon (9 tablespoons) unsalted butter
3 tablespoons golden syrup (such as Lyle's)

2¼ cups salted peanuts
6 ounces honeycomb candy or 4 x 1.4-ounce Crunchie bars

1 x 10-inch springform pan or 1 x rectangular aluminum foil pan approx. 13 x 9 x 2 inches

♥ Line your springform pan with aluminum foil or use a foil pan.

♥ Break up or chop the chocolate into pieces, and drop into a heavy-based saucepan. Add the butter and syrup, put on a low heat, and melt gently together.

♥ Tip the peanuts into a bowl, and crush the honeycomb or Crunchie bars with your hands, letting the golden-glinting rubble fall into the nuts.

♥ Take the melted chocolate mixture off the heat and stir in the peanuts and crushed honeycomb candy, then tip straight into the springform pan or foil pan. Smooth the top of the mixture as much as you can, pressing down with a silicone spatula or vinyl-disposable-gloved hand.

♥ Put into the refrigerator for about 4 hours and, once set, cut into slices as desired.

MAKE AHEAD NOTE
The bars can be made 1 day ahead. Transfer slices to airtight container, layered with parchment paper, and store in the refrigerator. Keeps for 3–4 days.

NOTE: Crunchie bars can be bought on-line.

Rice Krispie brownies

While this undeniably lacks the dignity of, say, the Chocolate Orange Loaf Cake, I don't feel it needs to apologize for itself, or I for it. There's a time and a place for everything, even a raucous piece of confectionery made from melting butter, chocolate and syrup and using this rich goo to stick little drop-pearls of puffed rice together.

True, there's nothing subtle about these, and, what's more, they contain milk chocolate, bittersweet chocolate, *and* extra chocolate chips, but as Mae West famously did say: "Too much of a good thing can be wonderful." The other day, inspired yet further by excess, I threw in some white chocolate chips as well.

The 8-inch pan cuts into 16 squares; the rectangular pan gives 24 slices. *(Even smaller pieces make excellent if counter-intuitive dinner-party accompaniments to a post-prandial espresso.)*

7 tablespoons unsalted butter
5 tablespoons golden syrup (such as Lyle's)
6 ounces good-quality milk chocolate, chopped (or ¾ cup chips)
2 ounces good-quality bittersweet chocolate, chopped (or ¼ cup chips)
5½ cups Rice Krispies

¾ cup milk chocolate morsels or chips (or use half dark and half white chocolate chips)

1 x 8-inch square cake pan or 1 rectangular aluminum foil pan approx. 13 x 9 x 2 inches

♥ Line your cake pan with aluminum foil or get out one of your trusty foil pans.

♥ Put butter, golden syrup, and chopped chocolates (not the morsels) in a heavy-based and fairly wide saucepan and melt over a low heat.

♥ Stir to mix the glossy goo, take it off the heat, then quickly pour and stir in the Rice Krispies.

♥ Still off the heat, quickly stir in the chocolate morsels, and spoon and scrape the mixture into your pan of choice. I find it easier, once the gunk is in the tin, to smooth the top with hands covered in a pair of disposable vinyl gloves.

♥ Put in the refrigerator to set for about 4 hours before cutting.

MAKE AHEAD NOTE
The brownies can be made up to 2 days ahead. Wrap pan tightly with plastic wrap and store in a cool place. In warm or humid weather, store in the refrigerator. Cut into squares before serving. Keeps for 3–4 days.

Blondies

These began life, in one of my many ink-splodged and grease-stained notebooks, as Chocolate Chip Oatmeal Squares, morphed into Chewy Chocolate Chip Squares, and have now earned a place in my kitchen, enduringly, as Blondies. The oatmeal in the earliest title had to go: the ingredient remains, hidden – as this was intended as a bit of a kiddie-pleaser, and the smaller people won't even consider anything that promises oatmeal. I felt that offering up the promise of chewiness along with chocolate chips would do the trick, which it did. And once – having produced a batch just a few days after making brownies – I said that these were, in a way, blondies. The name stuck. It has been known to suggest some sort of intended disparagement, but none at all is implied here. On the contrary, I have an almost fanatical fervor for these squishy-bellied beauties.

Indeed, I made so many versions, I began to wonder if my compulsion to get them right was altogether healthy; I feared it might be to do with the condensed milk. There's something about cooking with ingredients that should make me blush which in fact draws me obsessively towards them. Mostly, I have quite a rigid "three strikes and you're out" rule. But I couldn't give up with these, and it wasn't until my fourth (or was it fifth?) go, that I felt truly happy – even ecstatic – with what I'd made. My first attempt produced something that was impossibly sweet and, although gorgeously gungy within, took so long to cook that the crust became too crunchy, and I knew I had to re-jig. I then made a version that tasted more like an oat bar and, although grown ups liked it, I felt sure I could do better. At this point, my daughter said rather strictly, "Mum, you've gone from one extreme to the other. Find some middle ground," and I knew she was right. But as it turned out, there was no miraculous Third Way. I suspected I was beginning to lose the plot when I cooked a different version three days running. But that was a plot worth losing, as it turned out I found the answer.

The chocolate chips ought really to be white to live up to the pale promise of the title, but the condensed milk gives enough of that vanilla-richness as it is. Besides, we all know that (outside Scandinavia) there is no such thing as a natural blonde over twenty-four; so you could just say that, with the dark splodges of chocolate dotted about, the Blondies are just showing their roots.

313

Makes 16 pieces

2 cups quick-cook oats, not instant
⅔ cup all-purpose flour
½ teaspoon baking soda
1¼ sticks (10 tablespoons) soft
 unsalted butter
½ cup (packed) light brown sugar
1 x 14-ounce can condensed milk

1 egg
½ x 12-ounce bag bittersweet or
 semi-sweet chocolate morsels or
 chocolate chips (1 cup chips)

1 rectangular aluminum foil pan
 or cake pan approx. 13 x 9 x 2
 inches

♥ Preheat the oven to 350°F and line your cake pan with aluminum foil – this makes it easier to get the Blondies out once they're cooked – or use a foil pan.

♥ Combine the oats, flour, and baking soda in a bowl.

♥ In another bowl, mix or beat the soft butter with the sugar until pale and airily creamy, then beat in the condensed milk followed by the oats, flour, and baking soda mixture.

♥ When these are well mixed, beat in the egg, and into this relatively thick mixture fold the chocolate chips.

♥ Dollop this thick, bumpy batter into the prepared pan, and smooth it down with a spatula, then cook in the preheated oven for about 35 minutes. When ready, it will be quite a pronounced dark gold around the edges and coming away from the pan. It will look and feel cooked on top, though just beneath it will still seem frighteningly squishy, not to say, wibbly. But it firms up as it cools in the pan, so to end up with the requisite chewiness you have to take it out of the oven while it feels a tad undercooked.

MAKE AHEAD NOTE
The blondies can be baked up to 3 days ahead and stored in airtight container. Will keep for 5 days total.

FREEZE NOTE
The blondies can be frozen for up to 3 months in airtight container, layered with parchment paper. Thaw overnight in a cool place.

314

AT MY TABLE

Earlier in this book, I discussed the sort of food I most often cook for friends when an unforgiving schedule or just general midweek pandemonium rules out any more expansive stoveside pottering. These recipes, here, I think of rather as my weekend collection, the Coldwater Creek of the kitchen. Of course, in true life (as my children used to call reality, when they were little) the actual day of the week is not the deciding factor. But the food that follows certainly smacks of Saturday supper to me, if only in spirit.

I use the word supper pointedly: I feel I can never emphasize enough that whatever else I'm inviting people to, it's certainly not a formal dinner party. For me, the distinction is pre-eminently one of tone, and maybe this in turn is a case of managing my and my guests' expectations. In the old days, people used to issue invitations by announcing that they were "at home"; the only place I want to receive people is in my kitchen, indeed "at my table." I want the food to be welcoming and expansive, but I don't feel the need to demonstrate my bona fides with a show of formality.

As always, I prefer not to rely on a succession of courses. I have no objection to providing a little something for people to pick at over cocktails (see **p.410**, or rely unapologetically on the traditional bar snacks of nuts or olives), and I neither resent cooking nor recommend austerity. But having to jump up throughout a meal, clearing and resetting the table, doesn't sound like a very agreeable way to spend an evening.

One of the things I love about having friends over to eat is being able to relax into it. As someone whose greed can make choosing from a menu anxiety-laden, I revel in the simplicity of the home kitchen, for all that you have to cook the food rather than order it. Plus, you don't have to add fancy flourishes to justify a mark-up (you're not charging, after all) any more than you have to seduce anyone with novelty or impress with technical wizardry. A richly brown vat of beef braised in beer may not have the picture-perfect prettiness to earn it a place on a restaurant menu, but I regard this gorgeous stew as one of the most welcoming dishes to come out of a home kitchen. The comforts of the carbonnade are not to be underestimated. Sometimes, having people over for supper gives license for delicious extravagance – I wouldn't roast a pan of lemony, roasted potato-studded seafood every day, any more than I would summon forth a bubbling pan of San Francisco fish stew – whereas, at other times, a tableful of friends demands a celebration of the down-home and unluxurious, such as jerk chicken with rice and peas. There's no one right thing to cook for supper any more than there is any one right way to live your life.

And if I skip an appetizer, you'll never hear me ruling out something special to end with. Grapes, cheese – and no more than that – may do on some days; on others, there is the panoply of desserts elsewhere in these pages.

Roasted seafood

This recipe is, for me, the perfect having-friends-for-supper food: it has just the right element of quiet, easy prep before people arrive and simple last-minute action as they're sitting at the table.

Of course, it's entirely right that roasted seafood feels like a treat: after all, it doesn't come cheap. But when it's fresh, tender-fleshed, and cooked *à point*, it is surprisingly filling and on just the right side of rich; the sharpness of the lemon and blanketing starch of the potato keep it all in check. Oven-cooking seems to intensify all the flavors, but in a way that underscores rather than overwhelms: this is, above all, a chic and simple feast.

You can embellish, but it's not necessary: all I'd suggest is a green salad with and perhaps the No-Fuss Fruit Tart (see **p.177**) after. But if the season's not right for that, or you're catering for people who go gooey at the sight of chocolate, then bring out the Flourless Chocolate Lime Cake on **p.281**.

318

Serves 6

1½ pounds white-skinned potatoes (about 3 baking potatoes)
8 cloves garlic, unpeeled
2 small red onions
1 unwaxed lemon
¼ cup regular olive oil
12 ounces small clams in their shells
6–8 baby squid

1¼ pounds or 16 unpeeled raw colossal-size shrimp with their heads on
3 tablespoons dry white vermouth or white wine
salt and pepper
2–3 tablespoons roughly chopped parsley, to serve

♥ Preheat the oven to 425°F. Cut the potatoes, without peeling, into thick slices and each slice into quarters. Put them into a large roasting pan with the whole cloves of garlic.

♥ Quarter the onions, peel them (I find it easier to do it this way around), then halve each quarter horizontally. Quarter the lemon and cut each quarter into ½-inch pieces. Add the onion and lemon to the pan with the potatoes and garlic.

♥ Drizzle over 2 tablespoons of the oil and cook in the oven for 1 hour.

♥ Meanwhile, soak the clams in a bowl of water – if any are smashed or don't close after they've soaked, throw them away. Slice the squid into rings.

♥ After 1 hour, take the pan out of the oven and place on a low heat on the stove top so that the pan doesn't cool while you add the seafood.

♥ Arrange the drained closed clams, baby squid rings, and whole raw shrimp over the potatoes, garlic, lemon pieces, and onions.

♥ Splash the seafood with the remaining 2 tablespoons of oil and the vermouth, then season with salt and pepper.

♥ Put the roasting pan back in the oven for 15 minutes, by which time the clams should have opened and the shrimp pinked up. Discard any clams that have not opened.

♥ Scatter with freshly but not too finely chopped parsley and serve straight from the pan: it couldn't look more beautiful.

MAKE AHEAD NOTE
Potatoes can be prepared 1 day ahead. Submerge in a bowl of water and store in the refrigerator. Drain and pat dry before using. Onions and lemons can be cut 1 day ahead and stored in bowls tightly covered with plastic wrap in the refrigerator.

Date steak

All steak is a treat, but this juicy strip steak with its sweet and sharp barbecue sauce is something special: perfect for a little dinner *à deux* on a Saturday night or any other evening when the occasion calls for it.

It may sound a little too hearty, if we're talking romantic suppers, to be suggesting a baked potato with sour cream on the side, but you and I both know that would be too right to avoid. You could always consider just the one potato, half each. I think, too, some crisp green beans alongside for crunch and general liveliness, but I take a laissez-faire attitude here and know that you won't go far wrong whatever you choose to serve with this.

Serves 2

2 tablespoons dark brown sugar
2 tablespoons red wine vinegar
1 tablespoon Dijon mustard
1 tablespoon soy sauce
1 tablespoon red currant jelly

2 teaspoons chopped fresh gingerroot
1 tablespoon tomato paste
1 tablespoon garlic flavored oil
2 boneless strip steaks (top loin),
  approx. 10 ounces each

♥ Put the sugar, vinegar, mustard, soy sauce, red currant jelly, ginger, and tomato paste into a small saucepan and whisk together over a gentle heat.

♥ Bring to a boil, then turn down the heat and let simmer for about 5 minutes until the sauce has thickened slightly; now take it off the heat and leave to one side while you cook the steaks.

♥ Either fry or grill the steaks: if you are frying, heat the garlic flavored oil in a heavy-based skillet or frying pan first; if you are grilling, paint the meat with the oil before placing it on a very hot grill pan.

♥ Cook the steaks for about 3 minutes a side, for warmed through but still rare meat – how long you need to cook them depends on the thickness of the meat and, of course, how you like your steaks.

♥ Take the steaks off the heat and double-wrap in aluminum foil; let them rest for about 5 minutes out of a draft.

♥ Open the foil and put any juices that have collected there into the saucepan of barbecue sauce, whisking to mix.

♥ Put the steaks on 2 warmed plates and pour or drizzle the sauce over them, to taste.

MAKE AHEAD NOTE
The sauce can be made 1 day ahead. Transfer to a non-metallic bowl, cover with plastic wrap, and refrigerate. Warm gently and add meat juices before serving.

NOTE
If you can only buy 1-pound steaks, then cook the steak for a couple of minutes extra per side, or until done to your liking. You may prefer to share one steak between two people, thinly sliced and slathered in the sauce.

Spatchcocked Cornish hen
with baby leaf salad and sourdough croutons

It's not often that I'd suggest 1 Cornish hen for 2 people, but spatchcocking, by splitting it down the back and opening it out, then halving and sitting it on the richly fruited, nut-studded salad makes this more of a meal. I'm not stopping you from having a bird apiece, but I don't believe you need to; this feels like a feast. By all means serve with some delicious wine, but for an unextravagantly treaty and altogether romantic weekend supper for 2, I don't think you can do better.

Serves 2

1 Cornish hen
2 tablespoons regular olive oil
½ teaspoon of paprika
3–4 sprigs fresh thyme, plus more
   for decoration
4 garlic cloves, unpeeled
1 tablespoon golden raisins
2 tablespoons dry white vermouth
   or white wine
1 tablespoon pine nuts

1–2 thick slices sourdough bread
6 ounces (about 6 cups) watercress, spinach,
   and arugula salad or other feisty leaves
½ teaspoon Dijon mustard
½ teaspoon kosher salt
1 tablespoon moscatel vinegar
3 tablespoons cold-pressed
   canola oil (see Kitchen Confidential
   p.16) or good extra-virgin olive oil

♥ Preheat the oven to 400°F and leave the bread slices out on a wire rack to dry a little. To spatchcock the Cornish hen, get some strong, sharp scissors (or poultry shears) and cut down either side of the spine, take out the spine, then press down on the breast of the Cornish hen to open it out flat. Cut the Cornish hen in half. Put it into a small roasting pan; you can toss in the spine to give extra flavor for the dressing later.

♥ Drizzle over 1 tablespoon of the olive oil, sprinkle over the paprika and thyme sprigs, and throw in the unpeeled garlic cloves. Roast for 30–40 minutes or until the Cornish hen is reddish-gold on top, and cooked through.

♥ Meanwhile, put the golden raisins into a small saucepan with the vermouth (or white wine). Bring to a bubble on the stove top, take off the heat, and leave for about 10 minutes – or, better still, leave to cool while the Cornish hen is roasting.

♥ Toast the pine nuts in a hot, dry frying pan until golden and put to one side. Slice the crusts from the bread and cut into croutons. Heat the remaining tablespoon of olive oil in the frying pan and fry the croutons until golden and crisp. Remove to a plate.

♥ Once the bird is cooked, take the pan out of the oven and let stand for 5–10 minutes. Discard the spine and burnt thyme. While you're waiting, you can arrange the salad leaves on a couple of plates.

♥ Whisk together the Dijon mustard, salt, vinegar, and 3 tablespoons of the cold-pressed canola or extra-virgin olive oil in a bowl, then remove the Cornish hen and garlic cloves to a board, add the juices from the roasting pan to the dressing, and whisk again. If you want to get every last bit of pan-flavor out, add a little hot water from a recently boiled kettle and swirl it around the pan before adding this, too, to the dressing, then whisk in the soused golden raisins.

♥ Set each half of Cornish hen on top of the salad on the plates and add 2 garlic cloves (provided they don't look too burned, though scorched and caramelly is good). Give the dressing one final whisk and pour it over, then strew with the toasted pine nuts, croutons, and a few fresh sprigs of thyme.

MAKE AHEAD NOTE
Cornish hen can be spatchcocked 1 day ahead. Put in roasting pan and cover tightly with plastic wrap. Store in the refrigerator.

Chicken with 40 cloves of garlic

When I was young, this old French classic was still – though in a quiet way – very much in vogue. I dare say it was because the novelty of using so many garlic cloves had not worn off; it seemed somehow dangerously excessive. Even today, most people wouldn't think it quite unremarkable to put 40 cloves of garlic in a casserole. Certainly, if you peeled and chopped – let alone minced – the garlic, it would be inedible, but garlic cloves cooked encased in their skins grow sweet and caramelly as they cook, like savory bonbons in their sticky wrappers, rather than breathing out acrid heat. This is a cozy dinner, not a caustic one.

This dish entered my canon under someone else's auspices. A few years ago, for the fortieth birthday of a then-colleague and friend of mine, Nick Thorogood, his partner asked everyone to contribute something written expressly for purpose to be compiled in a fat tribute of a book. Since most of Nick's and my conversation dwells, with almost fetid passion, on food, it seemed only proper to write a recipe for him. And given that it was his fortieth birthday, this seemed the right recipe.

It is not quite the classic version (not that there is only one: food is as variable as the people who cook it) but it sticks to the basic principles. Maybe because the white meat on chicken tends towards the utterly tasteless these days, I prefer to use not a whole chicken, but thigh portions only. Naturally, this wouldn't make sense if you were raising your own chickens, then slaughtering them for the pot, as was the custom when this recipe came into being (and very good it would have been, too, for adding oomph to an old bird) but if you're following the contemporary shopping model, it works very well. For some reason, I veer towards recipes that can easily be cooked in one of my wide and shallow cast-iron Dutch ovens (and see the entry on Braisers in Kitchen Caboodle **p.3**), and this fits the bill perfectly.

By all means, add some steamed or boiled potatoes alongside if you wish, but I'd prefer, by far, a baguette or two to be torn up and dunked into the flavorsome juices; though don't rule out the option of sourdough toast, which is the perfect vehicle for spreading the sweet-cooked garlic onto. Otherwise, some green beans or baby peas or a plain green salad is all you need for a sure-fire salivation-inducing supper.

Serves 4–6

2 tablespoons regular olive oil
8 chicken thighs (with skin on and
  bone in), preferably organic
1 bunch or 6 scallions
8–10 sprigs fresh thyme
40 cloves garlic (approx. 3–4 heads),
  unpeeled

2 tablespoons dry white
  vermouth or white wine
1½ teaspoons kosher salt or ¾
  teaspoon table salt
good grinding pepper

♥ Preheat the oven to 350°F. Heat the oil on the stove top in a wide, shallow ovenproof and flameproof Dutch oven (that will ultimately fit all the chicken in one layer, and that has a lid), and sear the chicken over a high heat, skin-side down. This may take 2 batches, so transfer the browned pieces to a bowl as you go.

♥ Once the chicken pieces are seared, transfer them all to the bowl. Finely slice the scallions, put them into the Dutch oven, and quickly stir-fry them with the leaves torn from a few sprigs of thyme.

♥ Put 20 of the unpeeled cloves of garlic (papery excess removed) into the pan, top with the chicken pieces skin-side up, then cover with the remaining 20 cloves of garlic.

♥ Add the vermouth (or white wine) to any oily, chickeny juices left in the bowl. Swish it around and pour this into the pan too.

♥ Sprinkle with the salt, grind over the pepper, and add a few more sprigs of thyme. Put on the lid and cook in the oven for 1½ hours.

MAKE AHEAD NOTE
Chicken can be browned and casserole assembled 1 day ahead. Cover tightly and store in the refrigerator. Season with salt and pepper and warm the pan gently on the stove top for 5 minutes before baking as directed in recipe.

Making leftovers right

If I do have any chicken left over – and I don't think I've ever had more than 1 thigh portion – I take out the bone then and there and put the chicken in the refrigerator. Later (within a day or two), I make a garlicky soup, by removing the chicken, adding some chicken broth or water to the cold, jelled juices, placing it over a high heat and, when that's hot, shredding the chicken into it and heating it through thoroughly, till everything is piping hot. You can obviously add rice or pasta. Otherwise, mash any leftover garlic into the concentrated liquid (which will be solid when cold), chop up some leftover chicken, and put it all into a saucepan with some cream. Reheat gently until everything is piping hot, and use as a pasta sauce or serve with rice.

GARLICKY
SOUP

329

GARLICKY
CHICKEN
SAUCE

Carbonnade à la flamande
or Beer-braised beef casserole

There is something about cooking the classics that feels like coming home. In part, this is because I was brought up on them. But there's more to it than autobiographical lure; there is a reason why these old favorites endure. With every apology to all Belgians, real French food – as opposed to the frou-frou rosette-rapacious restaurant variety – is everything home cooking should be: comforting, transporting, with a reach that far extends the pettifogging, constraining vagaries of fad and fashion.

In truth, I do feel bad including this Belgian classic – *carbonnade* for the francophone contingent, *stoofvlees* for the Flemish – within the French culinary canon. I intend no disrespect to the land of Hercule Poirot, René Magritte, and Jacques Brel, but am referring here to a manner of cooking rather than a geographical entity. And, actually, although it's rare to find the French including any foreign dish in their own domestic repertoires, this beer-braised beef stew (along with its kitchen compatriot, *lapin aux pruneaux*) was long ago cheerfully assimilated into the kitchens of France.

This carbonnade surely earns a place in yours, as it has in mine. It's time it resurfaced over here, I feel. This is a simple enough recipe – I scarcely bother to sear the meat – that feeds a huge tableful of people cozily. And – always comforting music to my ears – it is at its best if cooked ahead, cooled, and then refrigerated before being reheated. True, it takes a long time to cook (not that you have to do a thing to it while it's in the oven) but you can pleasurably wallow in the rich, warm scent as it does. Obviously, embark on this only when time is no issue. Should you be a freeze-ahead kind of a person, know that a vat of this cooked over the weekend makes many near-instant weekday meals ahead, when time may be scarcer but the need for comfort greater.

In some parts of Belgium (as well in France and the Netherlands) a little vinegar is added; I find the bitterness of beer needs no accentuation. In fact, to counter that I add a little dark brown sugar (you could, though it's unorthodox, throw in some prunes instead) but it's not just the sweetness I'm after. Originally, gingerbread was sprinkled into the stew as it cooked, to season and thicken it: the combination of allspice and dark sugar here evoke that spiced richness; I let flour, more prosaically, thicken it.

The Belgians, Lor' love 'em, like to eat this with *frites*. I take a less complicated route and, as those in the Alsace region of France do with their coq au vin, I often eat my beer-braised beef with pappardelle or other wide egg noodles. I also recommend serving it with fluffy gnocchi to soak up the juices and, to that same end, a big bowl of steamed or mashed potatoes.

The beer itself should be an ale, good and dark, but there are so many fantastic Belgian ales and beers widely available now that the choice is yours, though an English dark ale could be substituted. And – *ça va sans dire* – have beer, not wine, on the table to drink alongside.

A final note: it is the beef shank that makes this stew so sweetly succulent; by all means substitute regular stew steak, if you must, but it will never cook to the melting softness of shank.

Serves 8

1 tablespoon duck or goose fat or oil of your choice

8 ounces (½ cup) smoked lardons, cubed pancetta, or 16 slices smoked bacon, snipped

4 onions, chopped

2 teaspoons dried allspice

2 teaspoons dried thyme

3¼ pounds boneless beef shank, in approx. 2 inch cubes

⅓ cup all-purpose flour

2⅔ cups beef broth (canned, carton or cube is fine), preferably organic

4 teaspoons grain mustard

3 tablespoons dark brown sugar

2⅔ cups dark Belgian ale, or English dark ale

4 bay leaves

1 teaspoon kosher salt or ½ teaspoon table salt

good grinding pepper

♥ Preheat the oven to 300°F.

♥ Get out a large, heavy-bottomed Dutch oven and, on the stove over a medium to high heat, melt 1 tablespoon fat, or warm 1 tablespoon oil. Add the lardons or bacon pieces and cook, stirring frequently, for 5–10 minutes, till they've crisped up a bit.

♥ Add the chopped onion, stirring well so that they're mixed into the bits of bacon, and turn down the heat to low and cook – stirring every now and again – for 10 minutes, by which time the onions will have softened.

♥ Stir in the allspice and thyme and then tumble in the cubed beef shank and, for ease, with a pair of spatulas or suchlike, toss and turn the meat in the pan.

♥ Shake in the flour and stir to mix as best you can.

♥ Pour the broth into a large pitcher and stir in the mustard and sugar and then add the ale (if it will fit) before pouring this over the stew in the pan.

♥ Stir to mix, then let come to a boil, add the bay leaves and salt and a good grinding of pepper, then clamp on the lid and stagger to the oven with the heavy pan.

♥ Cook gently for 3 hours, until the meat is fork tender, and – if you can bear it – let cool, uncovered, before covering and refrigerating, then leaving it to bring joy to another day. Still, it's fabulous enough the day it's cooked and patience is an overrated virtue.

MAKE AHEAD NOTE
The stew can be made up to 2 days ahead. Transfer to non-metallic bowl to cool. Cover and refrigerate as soon as possible. To reheat, put stew back in Dutch oven and reheat very gently on stove, until piping hot; or reheat in oven at 300°F for 1 hour, until piping hot.

FREEZE NOTE
The cooled stew can be frozen, in airtight container, for up to 3 months (and you can freeze in smaller portions for weekday suppers). Thaw overnight in the refrigerator and reheat as above.

Pappardelle with butternut and blue cheese

This is one of those welcoming, big-bowl suppers, perfect for feeding friends cozily rather than assaulting them with a panoply of courses. (Not that I'd say no to some Guinness Gingerbread after, though – see **p.305**.) Its comfiness, however, doesn't detract from its sumptuousness. This recipe – and let me attest to this unhesitatingly – makes no claims to Italianate authenticity: squash with sage and pine nuts, *si*, but blue cheese, too? *Beh . . .* as they say in Italy when they wish to signal that they are perplexed and yet world-wearily confirmed in their prejudices, their ironic acceptance of the way the world turns. And, yes, adding blue cheese to an otherwise fairly traditional sage-scented squash-sauced pasta can, in Italy, be legitimate cause for such a response.

But since this very dish has passed muster with the ultimate arbiter of *la cucina italiana*, Anna Del Conte (author of the *Gastronomy of Italy*, and many other learned, practical, inspiring, must-have manuals and proper, enjoyable reads), I'm not going to fuss and fret about a rogue ingredient. But it's not Anna Del Conte's approbation (reassuring though it was) that makes me happy both with its creation in my kitchen and its inclusion here: the point is, ultimately, it's my own palate I have to rely on. If I didn't trust that, I could neither cook food nor write about it.

I must say, bountiful though this dish is, I often greedily halve it for just two of us: once you start eating it, you never want to stop. I feel that all too often, I confess, but here it's the punchy play of tastes and textures contrasted with the gentle, comforting tangle of the thick pasta ribbons that I give myself up to so blissfully. Soft, oniony cubes of squash are answered by the salty, sharp, and pungent cheese; a little sage breathes its necessary but not overbearing bitterness, and the waxy, scorched pine nuts give quiet crunch, a hint of nubbliness, to this meltingly gorgeous concoction. I claim no credit, nor feel that wallowing in its deliciousness is any kind of boasting: it's just the ingredients at work – and boy, they really do.

Having said that, I am prepared to be lenient as regards omissions or substitutions: leave out the blue cheese if you want, or put some crumbled feta or goat's cheese (chèvre) in its place, or – if you can find it – some Italian ricotta salata. While this is indisputably at its best with pappardelle, those wide and hefty ribbons, which sometimes come with one ruffled edge, I think there is a good case to be made for rigatoni, the oversized corrugated tubes, or conchiglie, the toothsome, ridged, shell-shaped pasta, too. Just bear in mind, that with a sauce that is so richly resonant, the pasta must be robust.

333

Serves 4–6

1 large butternut squash, approx. 2¾–3¼ pounds, or 1¾ pounds ready-cubed	½ cup water
	salt, to taste
	⅔ cup pine nuts
1 medium–large onion	1 pound pappardelle or other robust pasta
2 tablespoons regular olive oil	
¾ teaspoon smoked paprika	6 fresh sage leaves
1 tablespoon unsalted butter	5 ounces soft blue cheese, such as Saint Agur
3 tablespoons marsala	

♥ Peel and seed the butternut squash, and cut into roughly 1-inch cubes.

♥ Peel and finely chop the onion and fry in the olive oil in a large heavy-based saucepan that can accommodate the pasta later. When the onion starts to become golden, add the paprika.

♥ Tumble in the cubes of butternut squash and then add the butter, turning everything together in the pan. Once the squash is slicked with the oniony oil and butter, add the marsala and water. Let the pan come to a bubble, then put the lid on, turn down the heat, and simmer for about 20 minutes or until tender.

♥ Meanwhile, put a large saucepan of water on for the pasta, adding salt only when it comes to a boil; and toast the pine nuts separately in a hot, dry frying pan on the stove top until scorched a dark gold, then tip them into a bowl or plate to cool.

♥ Lift the lid off the squash pan and check the butternut is tender; if not, then cook for a little longer without the lid on – the squash should hold its shape and not turn to a mush. Once it's ready, season to taste – go easy with the salt because the blue cheese will add extra saltiness later – and take off the heat and let it wait for its happy union with the pappardelle.

♥ Cook the pasta following the package instructions, though check a couple of minutes before the manufacturers declare it will be ready. While waiting for the pasta to cook – you should give the pan a loose stir or swirl every now and again – you can finely chop the sage leaves and crumble the cheese. Sprinkle most of the sage over the squash, keeping some back, and give a quick stir; but keep the cheese for now.

♥ Before you drain the pappardelle, lower a mug or cup into the pan and collect a little pasta-cooking water, then tip the drained pasta into the resting sage-sprinkled squash pan and slowly turn the pasta in the sauce to combine; or you can do this in a capacious warmed bowl. If you find the sauce too dry, or if it all needs a little help coming together, add some of the pasta-cooking water – the starch in it encourages the sauce to emulsify, the better to cling to the pasta.

♥ Drop in the crumbled cheese and about half of the pine nuts, then – much as though you were tossing a salad – gently combine, before sprinkling the other half of the pine nuts and the reserved chopped sage on top.

MAKE AHEAD NOTE
Squash sauce can be cooked 1 day ahead. Simmer until the squash is just tender, then transfer to non-metallic bowl to cool. Cover and refrigerate as soon as possible. Reheat gently in a saucepan before adding sage, and continuing as directed in recipe.

FREEZE NOTE
Squash sauce can be frozen, in airtight container, for up to 3 months. Thaw overnight in the refrigerator and reheat as above.

335

Venetian lasagne

I call this "Venetian" lasagne, not only because in place of the layers of pasta, there are slim slabs of polenta, which I always associate with Venice (although there the polenta would be white rather than made with the golden grains I use here, and I doubt a Venetian would own up to using instant polenta), but also because even the word Venetian has such dreamily evocative associations.

True, few people go to Venice to eat, but I am happy to feel transported there as I ease myself into this comforting pile-up of rich meat sauce and sweet, grainy, cheese-thickened polenta, dreaming of the mournful and inky winter evening light over the lagoon.

But back to the practicalities of the everyday kitchen: I use instant polenta (one of my faithful standbys), but I find that disregarding the package instructions to make it up with water and using chicken broth (again making the most of a storecupboard staple), rather than boiling up bones myself, as well as stirring in Parmesan, makes a big difference. I must backtrack, though, and draw attention to this tripling of my slatternly ways by admitting that I throw in grated Parmesan out of a container. This is a newish vice, but the truth is I have found, in the chilled section of my local supermarket and emanating from Italy, tubs of fresh, ready-grated Parmesan (organic to boot – as if that were a mitigating factor) that is still tender-crumbed and authentic, if mild, tasting, rather than that sawdust with the stink of a teenage boy's socks that used to pass itself off (and maybe still does) as Parmesan. If my heroine, the aforementioned Anna Del Conte, were to catch wind of this, she would, I'm sure, be disgusted. But I have to be honest, and I do keep containers of grated and shaved Parmesan in the refrigerator, and very useful they are, too. By all means, grate your own Parmesan, or use Cheddar (which is easier to grate, and all the Italians I know are mad for it).

The beauty of this recipe is that it is both a luscious treat and an easy fix. Both components – polenta and meat sauce – are made in advance, and then there is the simple matter of layering up and cooking it in the oven when you want to eat. Plus I have been known to use (both to mold the polenta and cook the finished article) disposable aluminum foil pans (and see Kitchen Confidential **p.19**), thus dispensing with pan washing into the bargain.

Serves 8–10

1 ounce (scant 1 cup) dried porcini
  mushrooms
½ cup marsala
½ cup water
2 tablespoons regular olive oil
1 onion, peeled
1 medium carrot, peeled
1 celery stalk
1 teaspoon dried thyme
2 teaspoons kosher salt or 1
  teaspoon table salt, or to taste
1 pound ground beef, preferably
  organic

3 tablespoons tomato paste
1 x 14-ounce can diced tomatoes
1 bay leaf
2½ cups instant polenta
1 chicken bouillon cube, or enough
  chicken broth to make up the
  polenta following the instructions
  on the package
1 tablespoon soft butter
1½ cups grated Parmesan cheese

3 x aluminum foil trays or ovenproof dishes/roasting pans approx. 13 x 9 x 2 inches

♥ Put the porcini mushrooms, marsala, and water into a small saucepan and bring to a boil, then take off the heat and scissor the softened mushrooms into smaller pieces.

♥ Warm the oil in a heavy-based saucepan with a lid, and finely chop the onion, carrot, and celery either by hand or in a processor and scrape them into the pan.

♥ Let the vegetables soften over a gentle heat for about 5 minutes or so, then stir in the thyme and salt.

♥ Add the ground beef, breaking it up with a fork, and let it brown a little. Then stir in the tomato paste, canned tomatoes, and bay leaf.

♥ Add the porcini mushrooms with their dark, gorgeously flavored liquid and bring the contents of the pan to a boil. Once the sauce is bubbling, put the lid on, turn the heat down to very low, and leave to simmer gently for about 45 minutes to 1 hour. If you're using a wide pan, the shorter time should be enough; if the sauce is piled up higher, you'll probably need the full hour.

♥ While the sauce is simmering, make the polenta layers. First dampen your chosen pans by letting some water from the cold tap splash them a bit.

♥ Make up the polenta in a saucepan following the package instructions, but first dissolve a chicken bouillon cube in the specified amount of water, or use chicken broth instead of water.

♥ Stir as instructed with your wooden spoon, and when the polenta has thickened, add, beating as you go, the tablespoon of butter and ¾ cup of Parmesan. Taste to see if you want any more seasoning. Once the polenta is thick and coming away from the sides of the saucepan, quickly divide it between the damp pans, spreading each one to an even as

337

possible layer using a silicone spatula you've passed under a cold tap. It will set almost instantly. You can put aside these polenta layers and your meat sauce for now.

♥ When you are ready to assemble the lasagne, preheat the oven to 400°F. Using 1 polenta-lined pan as your dish, spoon half of the meat sauce over the polenta.

♥ Deftly tip out (it's not hard) one of the other polenta layers and place this over the meat sauce in the pan you're working on and then add the last half of meat sauce.

♥ Top with the final layer of polenta from the third pan, then sprinkle the remaining ¾ cup of Parmesan cheese over the top.

♥ Bake for 1 hour if your meat sauce was cold, and about 45 minutes if it was still warm. The cheese should have melted and become slightly golden, and the lasagne must be piping hot right through.

MAKE AHEAD NOTE
The lasagne can be made and assembled 2 days ahead. Cover the pan tightly with plastic wrap or aluminum foil and refrigerate. Bake as directed in the recipe; however, the refrigerator-cold lasagne may need extra 10–20 minutes' cooking time, and check the lasagne is piping hot in the center.

FREEZE NOTE
The assembled lasagne can be frozen, wrapped in double layer of plastic wrap and a layer of foil, for up to 3 months. Thaw for 24 hours in the refrigerator then bake as above.

338

Sweet potato supper

This is one of those creations that came into being simply because, while trolling around the supermarket one evening, I was overwhelmed with desire for sweet potatoes and then lured by some asparagus tips, only to come home to find a packet of lardons, that French cubed bacon, winking at me from the refrigerator. It had to be. I've now made it quite a few times, on those evenings when I'm too tired to be paying an awful lot of attention – or busy with other duties – and yet not in any particular hurry to eat (as I so often am) five minutes ago.

Obviously, you can fiddle as you wish, but I am very, very happy with its beautiful and earthy intensity, as it is. Still, I like to add a little fire on eating, by having a bottle of mango chili sauce on the table alongside. Tabasco would be fine, too. And if you want to gussy it up a little, arrange the potatoes on 2 plates lined with fancy salad on serving.

Serves 2

2 sweet potatoes or yams (washed and dried but not peeled), each cut into quarters

8 ounces (½ cup) smoked lardons, cubed pancetta, or 16 slices smoked bacon, snipped

8 ounces asparagus tips

6 cloves garlic, unpeeled

a few sprigs fresh thyme or 1 teaspoon dried thyme

3 tablespoons cold-pressed canola oil (see Kitchen Confidential **p.16**)

salt to taste

salad leaves, to serve (optional)

chili sauce, to serve (optional)

1 x large round roasting pan approx. 10-inches diameter, or any regular roasting pan

♥ Preheat the oven to 425°F, and get out a roasting pan for all the ingredients – I use one like a giant tarte tatin pan, but a regular smaller pan would be fine, too.

♥ Arrange the sweet potato chunks in the pan and then drop in most of the lardons or bacon, followed by the asparagus tips and garlic cloves and, finally, the remaining lardons.

♥ Sprinkle with the thyme, pour the oil over, then bake in the oven for 30 minutes, before turning the sweet potatoes over and baking for a further 30 minutes.

♥ Let everything cool just a little – you'll only burn your tongue otherwise – before dividing between 2 plates, strewn (or not, to choice) with salad leaves, and sprinkling with some salt or chili sauce, or both, as mood dictates.

Homestyle jerk chicken
with rice and peas

I should start by saying that my home version of Jerk Chicken is different from the street-food, hot and crisp, that I've eaten in Jamaica straight out of what looks like a metal barrel on its side. Well, it would be different, wouldn't it? It's not that I haven't tried to replicate the recipe, using whole quarters of chicken, with the bone in and the skin on, but it hasn't felt right. A domestic oven just doesn't get hot enough, and although the spiced chili crust gets gratifyingly crisp, the skin doesn't – it can't – and flabby skin is not to be countenanced. Thus, although the vinegary, limey, rum, and spiced marinade makes the meat lusciously tender, you have to jettison its outer casing entirely. This seems too much of a waste to me.

Now, you will rarely find me suggesting breast meat, let alone a breast fillet, so you have to believe me when I say that the heat of the marinade, and the meat's edible carapace work best when offset by the meltingly tender white meat within. And, in turn, I must say that I have never managed to make, or find, white meat that turns out so luscious and succulent. It's a miracle all round. I'm stunned, but grateful. I have nothing to add, save the suggestion that you could consider working the same magic with some lean pork tenderloin, too.

Don't cook this, though, unless you like it hot. And I mean hot. There's no point choosing to make this and then trying to find a way to tame it, say by taking out the seeds from the chiles (though you could, if you must). Besides, although it packs a major punch, the sweet, creamy, coconutty rice that just has to be served with it, offers the perfect counterbalancing salve. In the same spirit, I suggest the No-Churn Piña Colada Ice Cream (see **p.180**) to follow.

Serves 6, *with the Rice and Peas that follow*

6 chicken breasts (without skin or
  bone) or chicken supreme joints
  with the wing bones still attached
2 teaspoons ground allspice
2 teaspoons dried thyme
2 teaspoons cayenne pepper
2 teaspoons ground ginger
2 teaspoons ground nutmeg
2 teaspoons ground cinnamon
2 cloves garlic, peeled

1 1¾ piece gingerroot, peeled and cut
  into chunks
2 tablespoons dark brown sugar
¼ cup dark rum
¼ cup lime juice
¼ cup soy sauce
½ cup cider vinegar
2 fresh red chiles, whole
1 onion, peeled and quartered

343

♥ Slash the chicken breasts, 3 slashes a breast, each cut about 1 inch deep on the diagonal. Put in a rectangular dish, slashed-side down.

♥ Put all the other ingredients in the processor and blitz to a dark, earthy paste, then pour and spread over the chicken pieces and leave to marinate out of the refrigerator for 2–4 hours or in the refrigerator (covered) overnight.

♥ Preheat the oven to 400°F. Double-line a shallow roasting pan with aluminum foil. Tip into it the chicken with its marinade, slashed-side up, and roast for 30 minutes.

♥ Take the pan out of the oven, to pour off excess watery juices. Use a pastry brush and spoon to put any paste back on the chicken, then return it to the oven and cook for a further 30 minutes, by which time it will be cooked through and tender with a thick fiery crust. You could get started on the Rice and Peas once the chicken's back in the oven for its final stint.

MAKE AHEAD NOTE
Jerk paste can be made 1 day ahead. Transfer to non-metallic bowl and press a piece of plastic wrap onto the surface. Cover bowl tightly with second layer of plastic wrap and refrigerate. The chicken can be marinated up to 24 hours in advance. Cover dish tightly with plastic wrap and store in the refrigerator.

FREEZE NOTE
The chicken in its marinade can be frozen, in a resealable bag, for up to 1 month. Thaw overnight in the refrigerator – put the bag in a bowl to catch any leaks.

344

Rice and peas

Although this Caribbean staple is called Rice and Peas it is, in fact, rice and beans. Traditionally gungo peas – also called gunga peas, Congo peas, no-eye peas or, most familiarly, pigeon peas – are used, but don't make it a sticking point. I've often used black-eyed peas and, once or twice, cranberry or kidney beans. The truth is, as the song almost has it, any bean will do.

Serves 6

1 x 15-ounce can gungo peas or
 black-eyed peas
1 tablespoon vegetable or
 peanut oil
1 onion, peeled and finely chopped
1 red chile, seeded and finely
 chopped

2 cloves garlic, peeled and finely chopped
2 cups long grain rice
1 x 14-ounce can coconut milk
2½ cups chicken or vegetable broth
1 teaspoon chopped fresh thyme
 leaves
salt, to taste

♥ Drain and rinse the gungo peas, and heat the oil in a heavy-based saucepan that has a lid.

♥ Fry the onion for about 5 minutes, stirring every now and again, letting it soften and brown a little. Then add the chopped chile and garlic, and give everything a good stir around.

♥ Now stir in the rice, making sure it is all slicked with oil, then pour in the coconut milk and chicken or vegetable broth, and stir in the drained gungo peas.

♥ Bring to a bubble, clamp on the lid, turn down the heat to very low, and let it cook gently for 15 minutes.

♥ Check the rice is cooked through and the liquid is all absorbed – give the rice another 5 minutes if need be. Sprinkle with the freshly chopped thyme, and season with salt if desired, forking it through.

♥ Pile up each dinner plate with coconutty rice and set a piece of hot-crusted chicken proudly on top.

Making leftovers right

Should you have leftovers – and don't count on it if you are 6 round the table – refrigerate as soon as cooled and within 1-2 days you can simply snip some chicken into the rice and reheat until piping hot. However, I love this in a new form: a thick, coconutty soup punctured by fiery bursts of tender meat. Add some coconut milk and chicken broth to the leftover rice, along with some freshly grated gingerroot and a spritz of lime juice, and heat up, adding the chicken, cut into strips or small chunks, once it starts bubbling. When the meat's piping hot, season to taste then pour your soup into a bowl (or bowls) and scatter with freshly chopped cilantro and slurp gratefully.

345

COCONUTTY
RICE SOUP

San Francisco fish stew

As a European, I find the flash and glint of the New World alluringly exotic, but the truth is this robust fish stew is, originally, a Continental concoction. Think of it as a bi-coastal offering, one that started in Genoa and has flourished in San Francisco. Its real name is *cioppino* – pronounced *chopeeno* – and this is rather a chop-chopeeno, since what I have produced is a slightly speeded-up version.

You can find this cooked with white wine or red, and I go for the latter, not least because it makes a change (as does the inclusion of tomatoes) from the way I'm used to cooking fish, but also because I love the rich gutsiness of the dish it produces. It makes sense to use a Californian red and, believe me, that is no hardship. At my last supper, I hope to have a glorious vintage of Ridge Geyserville to wash everything down.

For me, at home, whatever they do in restaurants, this is very much a main-course stew, not a first-course soup, and, as such, I sometimes put a bowl of steamed baby potatoes on the table, too, for people to spear and dip into the wine-dark seafood as they go. If you feel like it, you can make garlicky croutes to go alongside, instead: just get a baguette, cut it into long thin diagonals; put 3 tablespoons olive oil into a dish and mince or grate in a clove of garlic and then brush the thin slices of bread with this, before baking on a broiler pan in an oven preheated to 400°F for about 10 minutes. But, you know, just a couple of plain baguettes pulled apart at the table or – more in the San Franciscan vernacular – a loaf of sourdough cut into squat slices is accompaniment enough.

Its Genoese origins explain the final and customary addition of basil; I mention this below, but have forgone it myself. Sometimes, I add a leaf or two to each bowl at the end, but as often find that I am happy without that final flourish. If the basil on offer isn't fragrantly inviting, don't bother, but perhaps consider using some basil-infused oil to fry the onion in upfront.

Serves 4–6

1 tablespoon olive or basil- flavored
  oil
1 red onion, peeled and chopped
1 bulb fennel, quartered and sliced
  thinly across
1 long red chile, seeded and chopped
2 cloves garlic, peeled and chopped
3 tablespoons chopped fresh parsley
salt, to taste
2 cups good red wine
1 x 14-ounce can diced tomatoes
½ pint cherry tomatoes, halved

1 pound mussels
1 pound clams
8 colossal size shrimp (shell on),
  12 ounces total, thawed if frozen
  (when possible, thaw seafood
  gradually)
14 ounces red snapper fillet or
  monkfish, or any available hearty
  fish, cut into chunks
a few basil leaves (optional)

♥ Heat the oil in a heavy-based saucepan that comes with a lid, and cook the chopped onion and fennel for about 5 minutes. Then add the chile, garlic, chopped parsley and a sprinkling of salt, cooking for another 5 minutes.

♥ Add the red wine, canned tomatoes, and halved cherry or grape tomatoes. Bring to a boil and then simmer for 10 minutes with the lid on.

♥ In a sink filled with cold water, soak, clean and sort through the mussels and clams, pulling the beards off the mussels. You must discard any mussel or clam shells that are cracked or that remain open after soaking – tap any open shells on the side of the sink and, if they stay open, throw them away.

♥ Add the whole shrimp and the chunks of fish to the pan, then let it come back to a boil with the lid on and simmer for about another 5 minutes.

♥ Drain the mussels and clams and tip them into the stew, give it a quick stir, then clamp on the lid and let it cook on a medium to high heat for 5 minutes or until the mussels and clams have opened.

♥ Let stand for a moment, for any grit that might have been in the shellfish to sink to the bottom, then ladle the fish stew into warmed bowls and, if you feel like it, sprinkle a few basil leaves on top as you serve with garlicky croutes or sourdough slices alongside. Don't force open or eat any mussels or clams that have not opened during cooking or that have damaged shells – these should be discarded.

THE SOLACE OF STIRRING

It may not be a ground-breaking claim to say that risotto must, surely, be the ultimate comfort food, but perhaps lack of originality here serves only to make the case: the low murmur of universal agreement on the subject is entirely the appropriate response. We all know, too, just what makes it so comforting: the carb-kiss of all that starchy rice brings with it a dreamy kind of calm that all-too-often eludes us. On top of that, there is the fact that every mouthful you eat is exactly the same as the one that precedes it, and the one that follows. In some moods that crucial lack of challenge, as well as the soporific, baby-feeding repetition of taking spoon from dish to mouth and back again, unthinkingly, can be soothing in itself. You don't focus, you just feed: this is bowl food at its becalming best.

But what no one seems to say, or even to realize, is that the actual process of making risotto is the first essential de-stressing step. The best place, often, to soothe the savage breast is stove-side, but making risotto is, I've found, more than anything else a way to heal and help a busy head. In yoga, that frenzied buzzing and constant internal chatter is known as monkey-brain: if you've got it, you'll know it, and believe me, a spot of risotto-making is the nearest cure I'll ever get to simian cerebellum syndrome.

I find any simple form of cooking calming in itself, but risotto-making (like baking) relies on the ritual of unchallenging but repeated actions. Unlike baking, the rewards are all but instant. Twenty minutes after you've tipped the rice into your saucepan, you've decompressed and dinner's on the table. But the principle of mindless repetitive activity holds; more, it's intensified. When you cook risotto, it's not just that you are required to stir, but that you are required to do nothing but stir. You can't leave the pan and tend to anything else, you just have to stand there and stir, stir, stir. There's something so mesmeric, so absorbing about this constant stirring that I begin to understand the Buddhist notion of becoming one with what you're doing. After a while, I all but hypnotize myself, staring into the pan as I stir, watching as the rice absorbs the broth, adding more broth and watching that, too, being absorbed; after a while, I am not aware of anything other than the stirring. This is as near to meditation as I'll ever come.

Of course, I know that I make life easier for myself: were I to make my own broth for each risotto, I'd be having to fuss about for days before the actual event. I believe in emergency measures, underwritten by quality control. I buy cartons of organic broth from the supermarket, though I am never without the back-up of a bouillon cube. But then, I have nothing against making life easier; neither should you.

And that is, indeed, the very point: risotto isn't just comfort food but, most crucially, comfort cooking.

Saffron risotto

This is my version of a proper risotto alla Milanese, and it's not so very different from the way I learned to cook it when I was young and lived in Italy. I have dispensed, regretfully, with the luscious *midollo* to start it off with, but please, I implore you, if you wish to proceed with all due respect, beg a friendly butcher for some bone marrow and add it along with the butter at the beginning, though maybe reduce the butter a bit.

At the point at which the wine is thrown over the rice, the Milanese would, as a rule here, go for red wine; most often, I'd go for white wine or dry white vermouth in a risotto, but here my choice is for dry marsala. I love its throaty richness, and moreover, its oaky tinge seems more in keeping with the gold of the risotto.

Serves 2 *as a main course (with some left over) or 4 as an appetizer or side dish*

1 quart chicken or vegetable broth (canned, carton, or cube is fine), preferably organic

1 x ½-ounce envelope saffron threads (about 1 teaspoon)

3 tablespoons butter, plus 1 tablespoon extra

1 tablespoon regular olive oil

3 tablespoons finely chopped shallots, or ½ onion, finely chopped

1¼ cups risotto rice

½ cup dry marsala

¼ cup freshly grated Parmesan cheese, plus extra to serve

salt and pepper, to taste

♥ Heat the broth in a saucepan, add the saffron threads, and put over the lowest heat just to keep it warm.

♥ Melt the 3 tablespoons butter and 1 tablespoon oil in a wide, shallow, heavy-based saucepan over a low to medium heat, add the chopped shallots (or onion), and cook for a couple of minutes or so, stirring frequently with a wooden spoon, until softened.

♥ Add the risotto rice and keep stirring for a minute or so, then turn up the heat and add the marsala – which will bubble up excitedly – stirring until it is absorbed.

♥ Start ladling in the hot, golden, saffron-infused broth, letting each ladleful become absorbed as you stir before even thinking of adding the next.

♥ Stir and ladle until the rice is cooked but with still a slight bite to it – about 18 minutes, maybe a little before – by which time you will probably have finished all your broth.

However, if you find the rice is cooked to the texture you like before the broth has run out, do not finish it.

♥ Turn off the heat, stirring still, and beat in the remaining tablespoon butter and the Parmesan, then season to taste. Serve immediately, by straightaway spooning this soft, gloopy, gloom-banishing mixture into warmed shallow bowls or plates, with some grated Parmesan on the table.

Much as I love arancini, *which I think of as the Italian version of Scotch eggs, that's to say a ball of leftover risotto, stuffed with mozzarella or ham or both, or whatever the cook chooses, then covered in breadcrumbs and deep-fried, I would no more cook one than I would a Scotch egg. Well, there's part of me that is fascinated to have a go, but calm good sense intervenes before I can give in to the madness. The saffron patties with bacon that I make with leftover risotto are perhaps even more delicious – and certainly easier both to make and digest. But note that the cooked rice, to be kept, must be refrigerated as soon as cooled, or within 1 hour, and used within 2 days.*

SAFFRON
RICE CAKES
WITH BACON

I'm working on the premise that you might have about 1 cup of risotto left. Heat a heavy-based frying pan and cook 4 slices of bacon until crisp, and remove these to a piece of aluminum foil and make a package out of that to keep them warm. Now spoon into the pan little mounds of risotto to land in patty-shapes about 2½ inches in diameter (you should get 4 little cakes) and fry the patties in the bacon fat, giving them 2 minutes a side, until piping hot all the way through, before transferring to plates and topping each golden patty with a slice of bacon.

You know it makes sense.

354

Risotto Bolognese

There's no denying that this recipe involves a fair bit of fiddle-faddling, but so soothing is the process, so welcoming and enveloping the savory smells emanating from stove and oven as it cooks, so ambrosial the taste, so universally rewarding the experience, that the labor involved can be embraced gladly. If you don't appreciate this, then you don't deserve it.

This is really a meat sauce risotto, but that makes it sound too sloppy, too unspecial. This is no run-of-the-mill meat sauce, not least because it contains veal broth. I buy jars of good-quality veal broth to have on standby, as I know I'd make this much less often were I to have to go shopping especially. However, I'd make it even less if I had to make my own veal broth. And if it seems unorthodox to be cooking the meat sauce in the oven, I agree, it is. You can ignore me, and just cook everything on the stove top. But putting the pan in the oven and leaving it there to cook is hardly what British soccer team managers would call a Big Ask. Besides, the method is vastly superior: flavor is intensified, texture is more melting and tender. If I have the time, this is now my ragù route of choice.

The meat sauce here, that ragù which for us is always Bolognese, is runnier than you would make if this were dressing pasta, and pointedly so: it is all these meaty juices with which the rice will become so delectably swollen later.

A final note: I have marked the anchovies "optional," simply because I know that some people have a thing about them. As a general rule, I would advise you to pay no heed to such faddiness, not least because good anchovies just melt into the sauce, bringing their salty resonance with them. However, if you are feeding children with laser detectors in place of palates and who cannot cope with fish of any sort, give up now. As a point of fact, children just do have more taste buds than us, and to them food tastes so much more vehemently of itself; when they say they cannot, *just cannot*, eat broccoli (though thank goodness, it's about the one vegetable my children would eat), it's because that brassic tinny-ness we taste is magnified enormously in their uncorrupted little mouths. And when old people say that food doesn't taste as it used to, it is probably their taste buds which have deteriorated rather more than the food – although sometimes, it's undeniably both.

Serves 6–8

1 onion, peeled and quartered
1 carrot, peeled and halved
1 celery stalk, halved
1 small clove garlic, peeled
handful fresh parsley
6 slices bacon
4 anchovy fillets (optional)
3 tablespoons unsalted butter, plus
  1 tablespoon extra
½ teaspoon regular olive oil
8 ounces ground beef, preferably
  organic

⅓ cup marsala
1 x 14-ounce can diced tomatoes
1 tablespoon tomato paste
2 tablespoons whole milk
2 quarts veal broth (2 cups plus 6
  cups), preferably organic
2 bay leaves
2½ cups risotto rice
⅓ cup grated Parmesan cheese,
  plus extra to serve
salt and pepper, to taste

♥ Preheat the oven to 300°F. Put the onion, carrot, celery, garlic, parsley, bacon and anchovy into a processor and whiz to a fine mush.

♥ Heat the 3 tablespoons butter and ½ teaspoon oil in a deep Dutch oven with a tight-fitting lid. Tip in the contents of the processor and cook for about 5 minutes until softened.

♥ Add the meat and let it brown a little, breaking it up in the pan, then add the marsala. Process the tomatoes until smooth, and add to the meat.

♥ Stir the tomato paste into the milk and then add this mixture to the pan, along with 2 cups veal broth and the bay leaves.

♥ Bring to a boil on the stove, then clamp on the lid and transfer the pan to the oven for 1 hour.

♥ Once the meat sauce is out of the oven, fish out the bay leaves. Heat the remaining 6 cups veal broth in another saucepan and keep that warm over a very low heat, then put the meat sauce on a low heat next to it.

♥ Stir the rice into the meat sauce, and then add a ladleful of the hot broth. Stir until the rice and sauce become thick again and then add another hot ladleful of broth.

♥ Continue to add the broth as needed, though only a small ladleful at a time, stirring all the time as you go. Check to see if the rice is cooked after about 18 minutes – you may not need all the broth before this happens.

♥ When it's ready, turn off the heat and stir or beat in, with your wooden spoon, the cheese and the extra tablespoon of butter before seasoning to taste and doling out into shallow warmed bowls. Serve with extra Parmesan, if you like.

MAKE AHEAD NOTE

The meat sauce can be cooked up to 2 days ahead. Transfer to non-metallic bowl to cool then cover and refrigerate as soon as possible. Return to the Dutch oven and reheat gently, stirring occasionally, until piping hot, then add the rice and continue as directed in recipe.

FREEZE NOTE

The cooled meat sauce can be frozen in airtight container for up to 3 months. Thaw overnight in the refrigerator and reheat as above.

Making leftovers right

BOLOGNESE PATTIES

I could keep eating the risotto Bolognese forever – it's only incredible self-control that makes me stop, and so that I can make these gorgeous risotto burgers with the leftovers. (And note that rice leftovers should be refrigerated as soon as cooled or within 1 hour, and used within 2 days.) Really, these are patties topped with a slice of melting cheese, but risotto burgers are what my children called them the first time they had them, and now that they are teenagers, I cling to their sweet little ways of now-distant memory.

Working on the presumption that you have 1½ cups of leftover risotto, make into 3 patties about a handful-size each, measuring roughly, when formed, 3 inches in diameter. Put these in the refrigerator for 1 hour, then preheat the oven to 400°F.

When the patties have had their time in the refrigerator, get out an oven-proof cast iron skillet or frying pan, and put a little oil in it. Fry the patties for 5 minutes then, using 2 spatulas, flip them over to cook for 3 minutes on the other side. Don't worry if they break up a bit, as you can push them back into shape in the pan.

Transfer the pan of patties to the oven to cook for 10 minutes, topping them with thinly sliced cheese of choice after 5 minutes, and make sure they are piping hot right through before serving, perhaps with peas.

358

Squink risotto

I have said that I usually use white wine or dry white vermouth in a risotto, but I must concede that the recipes here don't appear to bear this out. I've got an excuse with this one, too: the whole point of this risotto is that it's black, tinted by the squid ink (the squink of my title), and I had no desire to lessen its impact with some pallid white wine. But it's not just a question of color: the squid ink is so richly, headily flavored that nothing less than a robust red would stand up to it.

As strange as it might sound for so exotic a dish, this may even pass muster as a storecupboard standby. The rice, the broth and the squid ink (it comes in sachets, from a good fishmonger, or Italian deli, or online source) can be kept easily. I have marked the squid-ring topping as optional, but even that can live in the freezer for a few months.

While I am more than happy to eat it plain black, I can't help feeling cheered by the jaunty *tricolore* adornment provided by the squid rings, red chile pepper, and parsley. Not that I'm sure being cheered is altogether the point of such a beautiful, sombre dish, the perfect date meal for Goths.

Serves 2 *as main course, or 4 as starter*

8 ounces (cleaned weight) baby
   squid (optional)
1 quart vegetable broth (can,
   carton, or cube is fine), preferably
   organic
2 tablespoons regular olive oil, plus
   2 teaspoons
6 scallions, thinly sliced
1 clove garlic, peeled

1¼ cups risotto rice
½ cup red wine
2 sachets squid ink
1 fresh red or green chile, seeded
   and finely chopped
small handful chopped fresh
   parsley (approx. 2 tablespoons)
pepper, to taste

♥ Cut the squid (if using) into thin rings and set aside while you get on with the risotto.

♥ Heat the broth until almost boiling, and keep the broth warm in a saucepan on the lowest heat.

♥ Warm the 2 tablespoons oil in a large, heavy-based saucepan and soften the sliced scallions for 2 minutes on a low heat. Keep stirring and don't let them burn.

♥ Grate in the garlic and turn up the heat. Toss in the rice and turn it in the oil so it is slicked and shiny.

♥ Pour in the red wine and let it bubble up over the rice.

♥ Wearing disposable vinyl gloves, snip in the squid ink and carefully dunk the squeezed-out sachets into the separate pan of hot broth to get out any remaining ink.

♥ Then add and keep adding ladlefuls of hot broth to the rice, letting one ladleful be absorbed before adding the next, stirring all the while.

♥ When the rice has had 15 minutes, you can be less assiduous on the stirring front and get on with the squid, if you're using this.

♥ In a frying pan, heat the remaining 2 teaspoons olive oil and the chile until sizzling, then add the squid rings and cook, stirring or shaking the pan a little, for 3 minutes. Season with ground pepper, to taste.

♥ By this time, the black risotto should be ready, so divide it between warmed shallow bowls or plates, top with chile and squid, if using, and scatter with parsley.

361

THE BONE COLLECTION

The nerer the boon the swetter is the flesshe, as John Trevisa's fourteenth-century translation of Bartholomew's *On the Properties of Things* has it or, less euphoniously (especially when you consider that Trevisa must have had a Cornish accent) and according to current versions of this age-old adage, the nearer the bone the sweeter the meat. There's something about the ecstatic appetite evoked, along with a certain sibilant, tongue-flickering menace of the earlier construction that particularly appeals to me, or perhaps that I read into it. By contrast, the contemporary version, with its jaunty assonance, seems to imply a brisk, look-on-the-bright-side cheerfulness in the face of rationing and insufficiency, whether imposed by war or want. But any which way, the saying holds deliciously true: ask any butcher or committed carnivore. The lean, boneless cuts may be more fashionably desirable (and expensive) but for sheer, exuberant flavor and meat that truly earns the cliché "melt-in-the-mouth," you need to sink your gnashers into one of the cheaper, fattier cuts on the bone.

Being a brutalist, I relish a trotter or a knuckle and the whole cartilaginous variety of supermarket-unfriendly cuts. I just love the particular sweet denseness of the meat that cleaves close to the bone, and the silkiness you get only from a fat-stippled cut. But there's more to it than that: it's also the repudiation of waste I appreciate. The Italians insist that they eat every part of the pig except the squeal. Ours, a more squeamish society, blanches at eating any cut of meat that resembles the part of the animal it once was. It's not a crime to be so disposed, though if you are, then much of this chapter is not for you. But don't turn away just yet. Even those (vegetarians aside, of course) who cannot contemplate chowing down on a knuckle or shin, or sucking out the gloopy essence from a marrow bone may yet take pleasure in a succulent shoulder or shank of lamb, deep-flavored duck legs perched upon the cubes of golden potatoes they're roasted with, a platter of sticky, sauce-shiny spareribs, and the magisterial cut of beef on the bone.

There are two decisive factors – quite apart from the food – in cooking: one is time, the other cost. What you save on one, you generally have to spend on the other. While it's not a failsafe rule, it's a very useful rule of thumb. To wit, many of the cuts below are gratifyingly cost-cutting but rely on the low and slow approach in the kitchen. If it seems as if these recipes sit at the opposite end of the culinary spectrum from the "express" approach, that's only partly true. When speed is of the essence, well, maybe a ham hock isn't the supper to choose, but for ease, it's hard to beat. Food that's a long time a-cookin' isn't necessarily a lot of fuss to fix. The recipes that follow are a kitchen-friendly case in point.

Patara lamb shanks

Lamb shanks have been a British gastro-pub and modish favorite for a while, and with reason. I've done my round of North African flavored braises and honey-sweetened stews, and even tried out a plain roasted version or two myself, but this, the Lamb Shank Panaeng I had at Patara, my local Thai restaurant, was a revelation. Now, it would be much more complicated if you were making the panang paste yourself, but the chef assured me that the option of using a bought paste was respectable, and recommended in particular the Mae Ploy brand. I was happy to comply, and now have a stash of their panang curry paste in the refrigerator at all times. (The spelling, in English, can vary from panang and panaeng to penang, I've found, but it is only ever going to be a transliteration, so variations are to be expected.) My change in name for the recipe is a mark of gratitude to the restaurant who provided it. I should state, though, that I have, with humility and respect (along with a deal of laziness and some housewifely concerns for wastage), made a modest change from their original.

As with Thai curries generally, the overall consistency of the sauce is relatively runny; all the better, then, to be mopped up with copious quantities of plain, steamed rice.

If you're lucky, you will be able to find the recommended brand of paste at the supermarket but, failing that, any Asian store should have it. And if you can't find the Thai basil (you will need a specialist grocery store for this), you can substitute fresh cilantro.

Serves 6

1 tablespoon vegetable oil
6 lamb shanks
salt and pepper
3 x 14-ounce cans coconut milk
1 quart water
¼ cup panang curry paste
3 tablespoons fish sauce

1½ tablespoons light brown sugar
spritz of lime juice, plus whole limes
  cut into wedges
small bunch Thai basil or fresh
  cilantro
rice, to serve

♥ Preheat the oven to 325°F. Heat the oil in a large wide Dutch oven or ovenproof saucepan, and season the lamb shanks with salt and pepper before browning them in the pan. You may need to do this in batches to get them properly colored, removing them, as you go, to a large bowl.

♥ Get rid of the oil in the pan carefully, then put the shanks back in with the coconut milk and 1 quart water, which should just about cover the lamb. Cover tightly with a lid or aluminum foil and cook in the preheated oven for 2–2 ½ hours, until exquisitely tender.

♥ Once out of the oven, remove the shanks to a roasting pan, along with 1 quart of the coconutty broth they have been cooking in. Cover with foil and put back in the oven, turning it down to 300°F. Leave the rest of the broth in your original Dutch oven.

♥ Add the panang paste, fish sauce, sugar, and spritz of lime to a bowl and whisk with a ladleful or so of the coconutty cooking liquid from your original Dutch oven, then whisk this mixture back into the Dutch oven. Take the roasting pan of shanks out of the oven, then add the shanks back to the Dutch oven. (You will just have to cope with throwing away the quart of coconut liquid from the roasting pan. You *could* always let it get cold, remove the lamb fat, freeze, and use the liquid for another curry, but I find I end up throwing it away at some future date.)

♥ Chop the Thai basil (or cilantro) and add most of that, keeping some back for a final sprinkling at the end. Put the Dutch oven over a medium heat and simmer the lamb for 5 minutes or so, making sure everything is heated through.

♥ Serve the lamb shanks in wide, shallow bowls with Thai scented rice or jasmine rice, giving each person a shank and a ladleful of sauce. Sprinkle some more Thai basil (or cilantro) over each bowl, and serve with lime wedges.

MAKE AHEAD NOTE
Cook the lamb for 1¾ hours. Transfer to non-metallic bowl to cool, then cover and refrigerate. Can be kept in the refrigerator for up to 2 days. When ready to use, put lamb and cooking liquid back into the Dutch oven, heat on the stove until just boiling, then cover and transfer to oven for 45 minutes to 1 hour, until the meat is piping hot. Continue with recipe as directed.

FREEZE NOTE
Cook and cool as above, then freeze for up to 3 months in airtight container. Thaw overnight in the refrigerator and reheat and finish as above.

Ham hocks in cider
with leeks in bechamel sauce

I've played around with all sorts of cooking liquids for ham – and stand by my Coca-Cola, cherry coke, ginger ale, and other fanciful yet foolproof versions – but my fallback choice for good, old-fashioned-tasting ham, the sort that emanated reassuringly from my mother's kitchen, is hard cider. The slightly sour, spiked apple juice sets off the saltiness of ham so well, and at the same time brings its tender sweetness to the fore. I prefer a good, dry hard cider; but I can see the argument for using sweet cider (or, indeed, apple juice) – my only reservation being that I find the broth yielded by these too sweet to be ideal for leftover usage, and it seems a pity to lose out on a good pot of Cidery Pea Soup later (see **p.374**). My stipulation of smoked ham, below, is simply an honest statement of my own preference: if you want to use "green" ham, please do; so much – so importantly – in cooking is just a matter of taste.

  I don't peel my carrots here, since I tend to use organic ones which aren't sprayed, but if you feel safer doing so, then you should. I can never see the point of peeling onions when they're just going into a stockpot, though.

  The partners to the ham have to be, for me, my mother's leeks in bechamel sauce and a bowl of plain boiled or steamed potatoes. In fact, what I really like to do is steam the potatoes above the pan of cider-bubbling ham for the last hour or 45 minutes (depending on their size) of its cooking.

367

Serves 6, *with the Leeks in Bechamel Sauce that follows*

2 smoked ham hocks (just over 3¾ pounds each)
1 quart hard cider, preferably dry
2 celery stalks, halved
2 carrots, each cut into 2 or 3 pieces
4 small onions, halved
stalks from fat bunch Italian parsley, or small bunch parsley

1 tablespoon black peppercorns
1 tablespoon fennel seeds
3 cloves
1 tablespoon dark brown sugar

♥ Soak the hocks overnight in cold water in a cool place, to de-salt them. Alternatively, just under an hour before you plan to cook them, put the hocks in a pan, cover with cold water, bring to a boil, drain, and then proceed normally with the next step.

♥ Drain and rinse the hocks, then put them into a pan with all the other ingredients. Add cold water to more or less cover the hocks, and bring to a boil.

♥ Simmer the hocks for about 2 hours, partially covered with a lid, by which time the meat should be tender and coming away from the bone. Take the hocks out of the broth and let them cool a little on a cutting board before you slice or chunk up the meat, discarding fat, skin, cartilage, and bones – although I admit I happily eat a bit of the detritus as I carve, no matter how much it spooks those around me. Let the broth cool in the pan while you eat.

♥ Strain the cooking liquid after you've eaten the ham – it's easier to do when it isn't piping hot – and set aside for future use (see **p.372**).

MAKE AHEAD NOTE
Ham hocks can be cooked 1 hour ahead of serving. Once cooked, transfer pan to a cool place and leave, covered, for up to 1 hour. To reheat, put the pan back on the stove and bring up to a simmer before transferring hocks to a cutting board.

FREEZE NOTE
Cooled broth should be transferred to airtight container and kept in the refrigerator for 1–2 days or frozen for up to 3 months.

FURTHER NOTES
If wished, hocks can instead be braised in their liquid, in a roasting pan tented with aluminum foil. Bring to a bubble on the stove top before putting into a 325°F oven for 2 hours.
Chunked or sliced ham leftovers can be stored in the refrigerator, tightly wrapped in aluminum foil, for up to 3 days.
Leftovers can also be frozen for up to 2 months.

Leeks in bechamel sauce

This is so much the taste of my childhood, that I've found it hard to turn it into a conventional recipe; I've always cooked it without weighing or measuring, and somehow feel inhibited about cooking it in any way other than on autopilot (as though by concentrating I can't remember). But, luckily, I have one Hettie Potter as Boswell to my kitchen-bound Johnson, and together we have made a necessarily reliable blueprint.

For all that, I do have a few little muttering footnotes to the ingredients and method, and they are as follows:

Sometimes, I slice the leeks into much longer logs, cutting each large leek into 3 or 4; more commonly, though, I slice them relatively thinly, which makes for something more approximating a vegetable-loaded sauce than a sauce-swathed vegetable. Either is good; but the latter is more comforting, and quicker to cook.

I often make this to accompany roast chicken, roast pork, or sausages, in which case I splosh vermouth or white wine into the leek-water; when I'm cooking it with the Ham Hocks, it seems foolish not to use some of the cidery ham-cooking liquid instead.

Although I have given proper instructions to melt the butter before adding the flour when making the roux, I confess I usually do as my mother impatiently did and put butter, flour, broth (and see below) into the pan at the same time and stir all together as they melt.

My mother always put half of a crumbled chicken bouillon cube in her bechamel sauce and I instinctively follow her lead. However, in times of forgetful housekeeping, when I've found myself with no bouillon cubes, I've discovered that a touch of English mustard can similarly spice up the sauce. The rule is taste as you go, and if you think you want more broth or more mustard or a little of both, then add . . .

Serves 6 *amply with the hocks*

4 trimmed leeks, cut into approx.
  1 inch chunks
¼ cup vermouth (or ¼ cup ham broth
  from Ham Hocks **p.367**)
2 teaspoons kosher salt or 1
  teaspoon table salt (half these
  quantities if using ham broth)

for the bechamel sauce:
5 tablespoons soft unsalted butter

½ cup all-purpose flour
¼ teaspoon English mustard powder
  or ½ teaspoon made English mustard
  or ½ chicken bouillon cube
1 cup whole milk
1 cup leek water, plus ¼ cup
generous splodge heavy cream
  (optional)
freshly ground white pepper, to taste

♥ Put the chunked leeks into a saucepan, add the vermouth (or ham broth), then enough water just to cover them. Add the salt (halve the amount if you're using ham broth rather than vermouth), bring to a boil, and let bubble for 10 minutes, uncovered.

♥ Meanwhile, melt the butter in a heavy-based saucepan, whisk in the flour and the mustard or crumbled bouillon cube, and cook this, your seasoned roux, for a couple of minutes, whisking all the while, until you have a bubbly, yellow paste.

♥ Drain the leeks over a measuring jug and reserve the liquid.

♥ Whisk the milk into the roux a little at a time, and keep whisking until the sauce looks as if it might come away from the sides of the pan. Now whisk in 1 cup of the leek water, then change to a wooden spoon and simmer the sauce for about 10 minutes, stirring patiently.

♥ Taste, and season the sauce with salt or a little more chicken bouillon cube if you prefer.

♥ Add the leeks to the sauce, stir gently with your wooden spoon, and add ¼ **cup**, give or take, of the leek water, as needed.

♥ Taste again, and add a tablespoon or so of cream, if you feel so inclined. Turn out into a warmed bowl and grind some white pepper over before serving.

MAKE AHEAD NOTE
The leeks can be made 2 days ahead. Transfer cooked leeks and sauce to a bowl. Press a piece of plastic wrap or parchment paper on to the surface to prevent a skin from forming, and cool. Cover and refrigerate. Reheat very gently in a saucepan, stirring frequently to prevent the sauce from burning. Add a splash of extra milk if the sauce is too thick. Not recommended to use reheated leeks in sauce for pies or pasties that follow.

CIDERY HAM
STOCK

*The first thing to do – shortly after cooking the Ham Hocks – is to taste the ham and cider liquid, or cidery ham broth (however you like to think of it), to see whether its life is worth preserving. Be strict with yourself: I have at times talked myself into re-using a ham broth that is either too salty or too sweet (even when diluted), only to waste time making soups no one wants to eat. But let us presume that the cider and ham broth you have, murky in color though it will be, is ready for recycling; if you've followed the recipe for Ham Hocks in Cider (see **p.367**), it certainly should be, though feel free to dilute with water to taste.*

*If you think you won't get round to using it up in the next day or so – and you may well not be in the mood to revisit the flavors of meals just gone by – be sure to freeze the broth (as soon as it's cooled), well strained and in batches of 1 cup. Otherwise, you will probably do as I do and keep it in large pitchers in the refrigerator only to have to throw it away, wastefully, after a couple of days. (As the child of parents who were themselves children in the Second World War, I'm still made to shudder at the thought of committing the crime of waste.) Anyway, with the broth in the freezer, you know you have flavorful liquid to hand to add to a **meat sauce** – even, yes, one made of ground beef – or to a **deeper-toned béchamel**. You can use it to **poach chicken**, or in place of water in pretty well any stew (though be mindful that those eating such chicken or beef stews must be pork eaters), or to add – however unItalian this may be – to certain **risotti** and to make fabulous **soup**. I often rejig the Chickpea and Pasta Soup from* How to Eat *by sloshing in some ham broth (though here saltiness is particularly to be guarded against, as you don't want the chickpeas to toughen as they cook, so I wouldn't use only ham broth to make up the liquid), and it makes a fantastic base for a sweet potato and squash soup.*

*But probably the soup I make most often is my Cidery Pea Soup (see **p.374**); indeed, any time I've had the ham one weekend, I know the soup will be my children's supper (and mine) early in the week that follows. And slurped with much appreciation – sometimes cruelly unfamiliar to a mother – it is. To bulk it up, on lazy days I add a plain, but nonetheless prized sandwich made with leftover ham, or a grilled cheese sandwich if the ham has all been eaten up.*

HAM AND
LEEK PIES

For a bit more of a treat, should there be ham as well as some leeks in bechamel sauce left, I make easy Ham and Leek Pies, as opposite. For these, I do no more than shred the ham, stir it into the leeks in bechamel sauce, and put it in bowls or ramekins (depending on how much, obviously, has been left over), then dampen the edges of my chosen receptacle with a little cold water, before topping with some cut-out circles from a sheet of puff pastry. It's not obligatory, but you could cut out a strip of puff pastry first to edge the rim of the bowl and help the lid stick. Either way, press down to crimp the edges and decorate as desired – you may want to be more tasteful than me and my lot – or not at all, before brushing with a little beaten egg. Then 15–20 minutes in a 425°F oven should be long enough to make sure the ham and leeks are safely bubbling away and the top is enticingly puffy and golden. If you're at all worried about whether the underneath will be cooked through, pierce the pastry with a sharp knife or cake tester, plunge it into the filling, then touch the cake tester (cautiously please) where it has touched the filling, and if it's piping hot, so will your pie be.

372

I concede it will be more effort (though still not difficult), but if you feel like making up some easily pickupable, greedily eaten pasties (hand pies) – and just the presence of the cider seems to invite it – then preheat your oven to 400°F, and make a dough by mixing together 1⅔ cups all-purpose flour, 1½ teaspoons baking powder, and ½ teaspoon of baking soda with 10 tablespoons cold vegetable shortening, before binding this with just enough ice-cold water (and a spritz of lemon juice) to make the mixture hold together.

With your dough made – and this is enough for 4 pasties, each of which in turn is enough to encase about 1 cup of leftover sauce-bound leeks and of shredded/chopped ham, mixed together – form it into 4 fat discs and then, on a lightly floured surface, roll out each disc into

a circle, roughly speaking. And I do mean roughly speaking: my circles bear no relation to a circle as understood by a geometrist; a circle as hastily rolled out by me at dinnertime has rather more resemblance to a map of Australia.

When you have your 4 circlish shapes in front of you, put a quarter of the ham and leek filling in one half of one circle, brush a little beaten egg around the edge, and fold over, so you have a bulging semi-circular hand pie in front of you. Curl the edge of the round side over, and crimp this rimmed edge, just by pinching together with your fingers, and proceed similarly with the remaining circles and filling. Put them on a lined cookie sheet, brush with beaten egg, bake in your preheated oven for 20 minutes, and eat as they are or alongside the Cidery Pea Soup (overleaf). You can't make up the pasties in advance, though you could certainly make up the dough ahead of time. Simply cover the 4 initial discs with plastic wrap and put them in the refrigerator, making sure you take them out in time to soften enough to be rolled out later.

Perhaps it was unfair to suggest the above merely as preambles to the soup: certainly the pies demand no further addition, though some cooked peas stirred into the ham and leek sauce just before pastry-topping and baking would certainly be delicious. Indeed, it is really only the pasties that I automatically bracket with the pea soup. But even then, you can always unbracket them, which gives you another meal.

373

*Whatever, the Cidery Pea Soup is easy
perfection. Bring 1½ quarts of your strained
leftover broth to a boil and add 7 cups of frozen
petits pois or peas along with the juice of 1 lime
(about 2 tablespoons), then bring back to a boil,
and cook the peas until they are tender enough
to be easily liquidized, about 7 minutes. It's
probably wise to let the cooked peas cool a little
bit before blending, in small batches, and then
taste to see whether you want to add the juice
of another lime or some seasoning. If you are
making this up ahead (whether to be left in the
refrigerator or freezer), you will probably need
to add more liquid, whether more ham broth
or water, on reheating. The above soup should
give you enough for 4 hearty eaters at a proper
mealtime, and would easily stretch to feed 6 as a
first course or lighter supper.*

Pies

MAKE AHEAD NOTE

The pies can be assembled 1 day ahead then tightly wrapped in plastic wrap and refrigerated.
Glaze with egg and bake as directed.

FREEZE NOTE

The assembled pies can be frozen, tightly wrapped in plastic wrap, for up to 1 month. Thaw overnight in the refrigerator and glaze and bake as directed. Do not refreeze if using previously frozen
puff pastry.

Pasties

MAKE AHEAD NOTE

The pastry can be made up to 2 days ahead. Wrap in plastic wrap and refrigerate.

FREEZE NOTE

The pastry can be made and frozen, tightly wrapped in plastic wrap, for up to 1 month. Thaw
overnight in the refrigerator before using.

Soup

MAKE AHEAD NOTE

The soup can be made and blended then transferred to resealable container to cool and refrigerated
as soon as possible. It will keep in the refrigerator for 1 day. Reheat gently in saucepan until piping
hot.

FREEZE NOTE

The cooled soup can be frozen for up to 2 months but only if the broth has not been previously
frozen. Thaw overnight in the refrigerator and reheat as above.

There are so many things to love about this salad: the contrast of the cat's-tongue pink of the ham against the greens of the beans and leaves. The peppery rasp of the leaves, the tenderness of the beans and that sweet-tinged saltiness of the shredded soft meat.

HAM
HOCK AND
EDAMAME
BEAN (OR
FAVA BEAN)
SALAD

"The restaurant chef starts with fresh ingredients, the home cook with leftovers," I was told when young, and it's not simply that this is an adage I've never forgotten, but more that it remains a truth I relearn daily. I have nothing against frequent or opportunistic food-shopping – on the contrary – but it's when I'm left to forage in the refrigerator, that I feel most giddy with excitement. That sounds like affectation or gush, but I mean it. What gives an edge to the feeling of liberated joy I get from cooking with whatever I can find is that slight prickle of anxiety that I won't come up with anything.

Not that this dish requires great creativity or culinary brilliance: parsleyed ham hock and fava bean salad is pretty much a French stalwart in general and was one of my mother's favorites in particular. But that's reassurance, not resignation, talking: novelty is nearly always to be avoided in the kitchen. If ingredients haven't been put together before, there's probably – this much time into human civilization – a pretty good reason for it.

The only fiddling I've done is not fad-driven, but rather a feature of my freezer contents at the time of cooking, and that's to add edamame beans – relatively newly available to me – in place of fava beans. If it's not long into fresh fava bean season, and you have access to them freshly picked, then these are the beans you should be using. If, like me, your supplies are coming from the freezer, then either bean is good, except that I find the edamame bean softer-skinned when cooked from frozen as instructed on the bag; with frozen fava beans, I prefer to let them thaw, then pop the green kidney-shaped beans out of their fibrous outer skins and merely blanch them instead. If you're looking for work, then by all means do as the Japanese do with their edamame, and remove the second skins to provide only the tender, bright green, inner beans.

You should know that one ham hock yields about 2½ cups of ham, once the flabby outer casing and other detritus have been removed from the picture. I never really see the point of cooking fewer than 2 ham hocks at the same time – they're cheap, and the meat sweetly delicious – so I would hope to have at least the wherewithal to make this salad, even if it's just in half quantities for my own greedy self. And it's so good that it's worth getting a ham hock or two to make this from scratch as a fantastic starter or part of a piece-meal, so to speak, for a busy kitchen-tableful any time.

Serves 2

1⅔ cup frozen shelled edamame beans (or fava beans, fresh or frozen)

4 ounces (about 1 cup) shredded cold ham

handful (or small bunch) mizuna or wild arugula

handful or small bunch parsley, finely chopped

½ teaspoon English mustard, from a jar

2 teaspoons white wine vinegar or muscat vinegar

2 tablespoons cold-pressed canola oil (see Kitchen Confidential p.16) or extra-virgin olive oil

pinch salt, or to taste

♥ Cook the edamame beans (or the frozen fava beans) in a pan of boiling, salted water following the package instructions. Or cook the fresh fava beans in salted water until tender. Drain and rinse with cold water to stop them continuing to cook, then leave them in a fresh bowl of cold water so they cool quickly.

♥ Put the shredded ham hock meat into a bowl with the cooked, cooled, and drained beans. Add the mizuna or arugula leaves to the beans and ham, and work through with your hands (or salad servers), then add half the finely chopped parsley and mix again.

♥ Whisk the mustard, vinegar, oil, and salt to blend, or just shake together in a small screw-top jar. (Or use an English mustard jar that has a tiny bit left in it, add the other ingredients, put the lid on, and shake.) Pour this dressing over the salad and then toss again, taste for seasoning, and pile mounds on a couple of plates, or keep in the same bowl if you prefer, before sprinkling with the remaining half of your chopped parsley.

MAKE AHEAD NOTE
The edamame beans can be prepared up to 1 day ahead. Drain well and transfer to non-metallic bowl. Cover with lightly dampened piece of paper towel, wrap bowl tightly with plastic wrap, and refrigerate.

377

Beer-braised pork knuckles with caraway, garlic, apples, and potatoes

I once appeared on a German TV chat show, filmed in Baden-Baden, I seem to remember, and with a set tricked out like a surreal Bierstube. I was thrilled to be there, for all sorts of reasons. Not that things got off to a good start. Did I not realize, my interviewer began with comic aplomb, that English cooking did not exactly have a fine reputation? Oh, how they all laughed, the members of the audience dotted around the George Grosz set. Oh, how I wish I had, too. Instead, I replied with some gracelessness that as far as the rest of the world was concerned, German cooking wasn't accorded much respect, either. The slight silence that followed didn't embarrass me quite as much at the time as it ought to have done. For this was unforgivable behavior, and not just because it ill-behove me as a guest to respond with such brutal, teen-snarky honesty. No, also because the underlying truth (more important than mere honesty) is that I have always felt the cooking of Northern Europe to be egregiously undervalued, and not least by all of us. I hope I went on to say that and, if I didn't, I hereby wish to make amends and full restitution.

For I have – and this is the point – a particular fondness for German food. Actually, I am more than fond: I adore it, every maligned bit of it. There is so much more to the cooking of Germany than wurst and sauerkraut, delicious though both are. You may – or may not, more likely – know of a cake by the name of *Bienenstich* (or "bee sting") that is quite simply confectionery of the gods. And, frankly, I'd go there any time for the bread alone. Then there are the potatoes . . . Now, I am ready to accept that there has been some small vogue over the years and the world for hot dogs and hamburgers, but in modish food circles this carb-heavy cuisine is never going to find much favor. Well, more fool them.

The following recipe is inspired by the *Schweinshaxe*, or pork knuckle, I ate when I was last in Germany, a couple of years ago. It's not just the knuckle I loved, but the whole

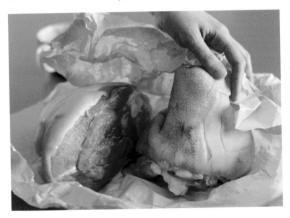

Germanic experience of it, and not least that language's word for it. For me, the joy of German – one of the most poetic, swishingly euphonious and liberating languages of the world – lies not just in the sound, but in its very formulation, most significantly the word structure that demands a mixture of independent, off-the-leash creativity and thunderous literal-mindedness, captivating in itself. I'm afraid my off-piste attitude towards, and sometimes clunky coinage of, compound-nouns along with my compulsive comma-usage, may be blamed on the many formative years spent immersed in German prose.

Rather evocatively, one of the traditional names for German pork knuckle is *Eisbein*, or "ice bone," which, it is said, refers to the fact that the knuckle or hock (different words for the same cut) used to be recycled, once all *Fleisch* had been eaten and the bone cleaned, as ice skates. You'll understand this more graphically if you wash the bone yourself and look at the shape it makes.

I hope that doesn't put you off, but then I have learned that eating the ankles of animals is not for the squeamish. The rest of us need not bother

ourselves with such fastidiousness. Talking of which, even I – shamelessly unrestrained at the table – was outfaced by my pork knuckle in Bavaria: there, a knuckle was one person's portion; here, as with the ham hock recipe on **p.367**, I presume one knuckle alone would feed three; and what with all the potatoes and apples alongside, and that glorious, fatty crisp rind on top, I wouldn't be surprised if the pair below could, without anyone going hungry, feed eight. You may as well go all-out first time round, and whatever is left over could be reheated.

What's important here is that the knuckle, with its pungent rub of garlic and caraway, is uncured or unpickled pig – in other words, pork, not ham – that you ask the butcher to score the rind for you, and that you do bother to braise-baste with beer. I happen to glory in the way that, when sliced and left to cook with the fat of the pork dripping on to them, the apples caramelize and the potatoes grow rich before they crisp up, but you could play it otherwise. Think, perhaps, of serving the knuckles with sauerkraut for tang (with or without some grated or chopped apple thrown in), or with roughly puréed peas for salving sweetness; both are traditional accompaniments, as would be a heaping bowl of plain boiled potatoes. One final must: whereas on all other eating occasions, I reach unquestioningly for English mustard, here I insist, for absolute gratification, on ordinary German mustard, not deli stuff but my *Tafelsenf* that comes so winningly in a dimpled mini beer mug.

Serves 6 *with healthy Teutonic appetites*

2 teaspoons kosher salt or 1
  teaspoon table salt
1 teaspoon caraway seeds
2 garlic cloves
2 pork knuckles, their rinds scored
2 onions
2 apples, cored and quartered

4 baking potatoes, or 2 pounds
  other large white-skinned
  potatoes, cut into quarters
  lengthwise
2 cups good amber or dark ale (not
  Guinness or stout)
2 cups boiling water

♥ Preheat the oven to 425°F. Put the salt and caraway seeds into a bowl, mince or grate in
the garlic, mix everything together, and rub the pork hocks with this mixture, getting well
into the slits in the scored rind.

♥ Peel the onions, slice into rounds, and make a bed or platform of them in a roasting
pan. Sit the hocks on this onion layer and cook them in the hot oven for 30 minutes.

♥ Take the pan out of the oven and quickly arrange the apples and potatoes around the
hocks, then carefully pour half the ale (1 cup) over, aiming for the hocks so they are basted
as the liquid pours into the pan. Put back in the oven, turning this down to 325°F, and
leave to cook at this lower temperature for 2 hours.

♥ Turn the oven up again to 425°F, baste the hocks with the rest of the ale, and leave to
cook at the higher temperature for another 30 minutes.

♥ Take the pan out of the oven and transfer the apples and potatoes to a warmed dish.
Lift the hocks onto a cutting board, leaving the onion and juices in the pan.

♥ Now put the pan on the stove top over a medium heat and add 2 cups boiling water,
stirring to de-glaze the pan to make a gravy.

♥ Take the crispy rind off the pork and break into pieces, pull apart or carve the meat, and
serve with the apples, potatoes, gravy, and some German mustard.

MAKE AHEAD NOTE
The pork and onions can be put in roasting pan up to 1 day ahead. Cover with plastic wrap and
refrigerate. Just before cooking, rub with the salt, caraway, and garlic and cook as directed.

Making leftovers right

*Leftover pork can be stored in the refrigerator, tightly wrapped in aluminum foil, for up to 3 days.
Eat it cold or reheat gently in a saucepan with leftover gravy, until piping hot. You should store
any leftover gravy in a separate airtight container in the refrigerator for 1–2 days. Leftover
pork can be frozen for up to 2 months, tightly wrapped in foil, then thawed overnight in the
refrigerator. Even if you have an amount too small to be useful by itself (a likely outcome), simply
bag and mark it up and freeze it for future use in the Pantry Paella (see **p.196**).*

Asian braised beef shank
with hot and sour shredded salad

The point of a stew, it should go without saying, is its flavor rather than its form. So, while the crunchy salad strips of carrot, scallion, and bell pepper do bring color and beauty to this otherwise brown study, at the same time their texture and Asian-flavored bite provide the perfect partner for the rich, aromatic spiciness of the soft-braised stew beneath.

Cooking the shin on the bone gives me a certain primitive pleasure, and the meat even more melting tenderness, but you can buy cubed beef shank off the bone (or other stew meat, if you must), in which case, you won't need as much in weight (see ingredients list).

Along with the stew and its crunchy, hot and sour topping, I serve gingery mashed parsnips and potatoes (see **p.386**), the ginger offering a muted echo of the South East Asian tones. While a plain bowl of rice would be a fine alternative, know that the aromatic mixture makes for fantastic, fiery potato patties (see **p.387**) the day or so after.

Serves 6

2 onions
1 x 2 inch piece fresh gingerroot
4 garlic cloves
2 teaspoons ground coriander
3 tablespoons vegetable oil
1 cup Chinese cooking wine, or dry
  sherry
¼ cup soy sauce
¼ cup, packed, dark brown sugar
2 quarts beef broth, preferably
  organic

2 tablespoons oyster sauce
¼ cup rice wine vinegar
2 cinnamon sticks
2 star anise
8 pounds beef shank on the bone,
  cut by the butcher into thick
  slices (or 2¼ pounds beef shank
  off the bone or other beef stew
  meat, cut into large cubes)

♥ Preheat the oven to 300°F. Quarter and peel the onions, peel and roughly slice the ginger, peel the garlic cloves, and put all these into the processor with the ground coriander.

♥ Blitz until finely chopped, then heat the oil in a large Dutch oven and fry this mixture gently, until soft and beginning to catch in the pan; this should take about 10 minutes, over a medium heat and with regular stirring.

♥ Pour in the Chinese wine (or sherry) and let it bubble up. Add the soy sauce, brown sugar, broth, oyster sauce, and vinegar. Bring to a boil, then drop in the cinnamon sticks and star anise.

♥ Add the pieces of beef shank and let everything come up to a bubble again, then clamp on a lid and put into the oven for 2 hours (regular stew meat may take longer).

♥ Take the Dutch oven carefully out of the oven and, using a perforated spoon, remove the beef to an ovenproof dish, cover with aluminum foil, and keep warm in the oven, while you vigorously boil the sauce in the Dutch oven on the stove, without a lid, until it has reduced by about half.

♥ Arrange the beef on a serving platter and pour the reduced sauce over the meat, then dress the top with the hot and sour shredded salad opposite. If you are using cubes of stew meat, rather than slices of shank, you'd probably do better to use a deeper dish.

MAKE AHEAD NOTE
Cook the beef for 1¾ hours then transfer to a bowl to cool. Cover, refrigerate, and store in the refrigerator for up to 2 days. When ready to use, return the beef to the Dutch oven and heat gently until sauce is just boiling. Cover and return to oven for 30 minutes, or until the beef is piping hot. Transfer meat to an ovenproof dish and finish sauce as directed.

FREEZE NOTE
Cook and cool as above then freeze for up to 3 months in airtight container. Thaw overnight in the refrigerator and reheat and finish as above.

Hot and sour shredded salad

Although I do pick at this salad straight from the refrigerator if I'm lucky enough to have any left over, I advise you to make it at the last minute, once the sauce for the Asian Braised Beef Shank above is reduced, and you're about to plate up. You could use half the salad to cover the serving dish of stew, and let people strew more on their plates as they eat.

Serves 6 *with the Asian Braised Shin of Beef*

3 carrots
4 scallions
1 long red chile
1 long green chile
small bunch cilantro

for the dressing:
juice of 1 lime
¼ cup Thai fish sauce
1 teaspoon superfine sugar

♥ Peel the carrots, cut into long slices, and then julienne them (i.e. cut into matchstick-like strips).

♥ Trim and halve the scallions and julienne as well.

♥ Seed the chiles and cut into juliennes, then finely chop the cilantro.

♥ Combine all the julienned vegetables and the chopped cilantro in a bowl. In another bowl mix the lime juice, fish sauce, and superfine sugar, and dress the vegetables with this, then top the Asian Braised Beef Shank with your salad.

385

Tangy mashed parsnips and potatoes

to go with the Asian Braised Beef Shank and to make hangover-friendly potato patties

I've already mentioned the ginger (see above), but the buttermilk, for all its connotations of homespun Americana, is essential here. For one, I find those connotations crucially comforting; for another, it provides necessary tartness, much to be savored against the sweet denseness of the ginger-heated mashed vegetables.

Serves 6–8

2¾ pounds potatoes
1½ pounds parsnips
1 x 4 inch long piece fresh
    gingerroot, cut in half lengthwise
4 teaspoons kosher salt or 2
    teaspoons table salt

2 teaspoons toasted Asian sesame
    oil
2 tablespoons olive oil
⅓ cup buttermilk

♥ Peel the vegetables, and chop the potatoes into 4 and the parsnips into 3 pieces. Remove the parsnip core if it is very fibrous. The parsnips should be cut bigger than the potatoes as they will cook more quickly.

♥ Put the potatoes into a saucepan with the parsnips on top of them, cover with cold water, and add the salt. Drop in the ginger pieces, bring to a boil, turn down to a robust simmer, and cook for about 20 minutes or until potatoes and parsnips are tender and cooked through. Then drain, and discard the ginger pieces.

♥ Put the potatoes and parsnips back in the warm pan and start mashing together, then add the sesame and olive oils and the buttermilk and give another good mash, before beating vigorously with a wooden spoon. Taste to check seasoning, adding more salt if needed.

MAKE AHEAD NOTE
The mashed vegetables can be made up to 1 hour ahead. Cover with a splash of milk to keep them from drying and clamp on a lid. Reheat gently, beating vigorously.

Making leftovers right

FIERY
POTATO
PATTIES
WITH FRIED
EGGS

My weakness is for generous portions. But although I call it a weakness, it is not something I am ashamed of; indeed, I feel out of sorts when I don't have food left over. In this particular case, generosity with portion size is a smart move. A mounding clump of aromatic vegetables left in the bowl (if you can manage not to eat it while clearing up) makes for utterly more-ish potato patties later. With their spiking of scallion, chile, and extra ginger, they are the perfect hungover breakfast, or a bolstering supper, eaten maybe with a fried egg on top.

The potato patties below are made with a fairly small quantity of mashed vegetables – about 2 cups.

Makes 6 or 7, *depending on size of patties*

approx. 2 cups leftover mashed
  parsnips and potatoes
1 egg, beaten
2 scallions, thinly sliced
1 red or green chile, seeded and
  chopped

1 teaspoon grated fresh gingerroot
1 tablespoon all-purpose flour, for
  dusting
1 teaspoon garlic flavored oil
1 egg per person, for frying

♥ Mix the vegetables with the beaten egg, thinly sliced scallions, chopped chile, and grated ginger.

♥ Once combined, wet a ¼-cup measure and scoop out individual amounts or just shape the mixture with wet hands into patties or flat rounds, and then dust lightly with flour.

♥ Heat the garlic flavored oil in a frying pan, and fry the potato cakes for 3–4 minutes a side. Top with fried egg or dollop with a spicy sauce, as needed.

387

Roasted duck legs and potatoes

Like the lamb chop recipe which follows, this is one of those leave 'em and love 'em meals. For all the ease of express-style food, there is a lot to be said for simply stashing something in the oven for an hour or two when stuck in too-tired-to-cook mode. True, one needs a little patience, which might make this more of a lazy weekend dinner than the answer to your everyday exhaustion issues. You don't need much alongside, perhaps a fennel salad dressed with a spritz or two of orange juice and a squeeze of lime, or some bitter green salad leaves.

When you're in a hurry, a duck breast can seem like the solution, but the leg, cheaper yet richer, is more of a treat for those who like to eat. Of course, it's fattier than the appropriately named and leaner *magret*: that's what makes the leg taste better. And, please – enough with the supposed health concerns. I mean, it's not as though the obesity epidemic was caused by overconsumption of duck legs. Besides, as the late great James Beard sniffily wrote: "A gourmet" – and that's him, not me, I'm just greedy – "who looks at calories is like a tart who looks at her watch."

Serves 2

2 duck legs
2 baking potatoes or 1 pound other
  large white-skinned potatoes

few sprigs fresh thyme
salt and pepper

♥ Preheat the oven to 400°F. On the stove, heat a small roasting pan (I use one like a slightly oversized tarte tatin pan) and sear the duck legs, skin-side down, over medium heat until the skin turns golden and gives out some oil.

♥ Turn the legs over, and take the pan off the heat while you cut the potatoes into 1-inch slices across, then cut each slice into 4. Arrange these potato pieces around the duck legs, then let a few sprigs of thyme fall over the duck and potatoes, and season with salt and pepper, before putting into the preheated oven.

♥ Cook for 2 hours, occasionally turning the potatoes, for optimal outcome, which is tender duck legs and crispy potatoes, though both will be ready to eat after 1½ hours.

Making leftovers right

*If you have even a small amount of meat left, you could bag and mark it up and store it in the freezer for up to 2 months for future use in a Mixed Meat Pilaf (see **p.198**). Thaw it overnight in the refrigerator.*

Greek lamb chops with lemon and potatoes

Fish or fowl, meat and veggies, there is very little that isn't made glorious when sprinkled with dried mint, crushed red pepper, lemon juice, and oil, and baked in a low oven. The particular joy of the lamb chops and potato wedges here is that the lamb fat adds depth and an almost caramelly crispness, while the lemon juice gives that requisite sharp edge.

I love the sort of lunch that needs no more than one pan and takes care of itself as it cooks. I used to make this dish routinely with ordinary lamb chops, but more recently have taken to using some rather fantastically square-cut shoulder chops I found at my local supermarket. I cook either for so much longer than you'd think necessary. If you have a very fierce electric oven, you may want to spear a potato after only 1 hour's cooking to check it (and it may be wise to slide a baking sheet on to a lower shelf to shield any base element from roasting pan splashes) but you would do better just to cook this in a cooler oven from the get-go. It's the long cooking that makes lamb, lemon, potato, cool mint, and hot pepper flakes, come together. And the juice that so slowly drips off everything, leaving a sticky brown salty syrup in its wake, is best savored by cleaning your plate – or giving the pan a stolen wipe – with a cracked-open piece of baguette, thickly-cut sourdough, or, frankly, any other bread going.

Serves 6–8

12 chunkily cut lamb shoulder
   chops (about 2½–3 pounds total)
   or 12 lamb loin chops or cutlets
3 baking potatoes or 1½ pounds
   other large white-skinned potatoes
3 tablespoons garlic flavored oil
2 teaspoons dried mint

1 teaspoon crushed red pepper
   flakes
2 teaspoons kosher salt or 1
   teaspoon table salt
2 lemons
small handful chopped parsley or
   generous sprinkling dill fronds, or
   mixture (optional)

♥ Preheat the oven to 400°F. Put the lamb chops or cutlets into a shallow roasting pan or half sheet pan.

♥ Wash but do not peel the potatoes, then cut them into 1 inch dice and tumble them about the lamb.

♥ Drizzle the oil over the lamb and potatoes, and sprinkle with the dried mint, red pepper flakes, and salt.

♥ Zest 1 lemon over the roasting pan, then juice both lemons and pour in the juice.

♥ Cook in the oven for 1 hour, not bothering to turn anything over, and feel free to leave in for 1½ hours, if the chops look as though they can take it.

♥ Serve sprinkled with chopped parsley or dill – for (optional) extra Greekish effect – and with a green or tomato salad alongside, should you feel like it, but consider, if you please, bread obligatory.

MAKE AHEAD NOTE
Potatoes can be cut up to 1 day ahead. Submerge in a bowl of cold water and store in the refrigerator. Drain and pat dry before using.

Conker-shiny spare ribs with pineapple and molasses

I'm sure my dentist would prefer it otherwise, but I am a sucker for a plate of ribs. The thing is, I am not happy merely to use my gnashers to tug meat and gristle from the bones – I eat dem bones, too. One of my party tricks in Chinese restaurants is to order a plate of ribs and then to send the plate back empty; I can do the same with a plate of grilled sardines. But to brag about this is as inelegant as the activity itself and, in any case, the bones beneath the sticky, succulent morsels of flesh in this recipe aren't cooked quite long enough to be palatable. Besides, some Health & Safety Officer would be on my case pronto were I to advise you other than to content yourself with chewing, gnawing, and sucking as you will, so long as you don't eat the bones.

Serves 4–6, *depending on greed of guests and what else is on the table*

16 (about 3¼ pounds) St. Louis-style pork spareribs, cut into invividual ribs

for the marinade:

juice and zest 1 lime
3 tablespoons soy sauce
3 red chiles, seeded and roughly
  chopped
1 x 2 inch piece fresh gingerroot,
  peeled and cut into thin slices
2 tablespoons peanut oil
2 tablespoons molasses, plus
  2 tablespoons for the sauce

2 star anise
1 cinnamon stick, broken into
  barky shards, or 1 teaspoon
  ground cinnamon
1 onion, peeled and cut into
  eighths
½ cup pineapple juice, from a can or
  carton

♥ Put the ribs into a large resealable bag; then stir the marinade ingredients together in a pitcher or measuring jug, and pour them into the bag.

♥ Tie a knot in the bag and squish everything around well before leaving in the refrigerator overnight, or for at least a couple of hours in a cool place in the kitchen.

♥ Preheat the oven to 400°F. Let the marinated ribs come to room temperature, then pour the whole contents of the bag into a roasting pan and put in the oven for 1 hour, turning the ribs over about halfway through the cooking time.

♥ Take the pan of ribs out of the oven and carefully pour the liquid contents of the pan into a medium-sized saucepan, then put the pan of dryish ribs back in the oven.

♥ Add the remaining 2 tablespoons of molasses to the saucepan, whisk to combine, then bring to a boil. Keep at a simmer for about 8–10 minutes, until it becomes foamy then syrupy, watching all the while.

♥ Take the ribs out of the oven and pour the dark sticky sauce over, turning the ribs to give them all a thick coating. Turn out on to a large flat plate – or just leave in the darkly slicked pan – and dig in.

MAKE AHEAD NOTE
Ribs can be put into the marinade a day ahead and refrigerated.

FREEZE NOTE
Uncooked ribs can be frozen in the marinade for up to 1 month. Thaw overnight in the refrigerator in a bowl or on a plate to catch drips, and cook as directed.

393

Shoulder of lamb
with garlic, thyme, black olives, and rosé wine

When I was a child, shoulder of lamb was a monthly staple of my paternal grandparents' Sunday lunches. These were the days before lamb was routinely served rare – though my mother's garlicky gigot definitely had a bohemian pinkish tinge – and the now unfashionably fatty joint was cooked for long enough for the fat to melt into the meat, imbuing it with a richness that belied the drab and mournful hue.

I cook a shoulder regularly still and am no less happy than my grandmother – indeed either of my grandmothers – to add a meagre amount of garlic to the meat when it goes into the oven, and serve red currant and mint sauces when it gets to the table. And, following my mother's habit, more often than not there's an onion sauce, as well. Perhaps I want to make up now for how little I appreciated the food of my childhood when I was young. Or maybe it's just that it tastes so good, the comfort and reassurance it offers are merely secondary. Certainly, much as I feel warmed by the thought – or rather, the re-enacted memory, which my cooking so often is – of a traditional English roast, I also purr at the prospect of borrowing the inherited rituals of others. I love a shoulder of lamb just as dearly when it is cooked not exactly according to the cuisine of my *grandmère*. I am more than ready to cook *à la française* and slowly roast a shoulder over some thinly sliced potatoes or jade green haricot beans.

The lamb here is, I like to think, a springtime or early summer take on the wintry-rich beef with red wine and anchovies in *How to Eat*. The scent of thyme and garlic while the lamb cooks, along with the upbeat petal-fresh pink of the wine, are for me, Provence without the clichés.

Raw in its pan, the lamb glows with an almost Martian-skied red; like my grandmother's, however, once cooked, it loses much of its rosy charm. But that's only when you're looking at it. This is food that convinces, compels, where it truly matters, when you eat it.

Depending on the weather, time of day, my mood or what I might be eating after, I serve either a lemony-dressed, almost retro frisée salad and a baguette or two, or a warm bowl of buttery green beans, cut in sliver-thin diagonals, and plain, steamed baby potatoes.

Serves 4–6

1 x approx. 4½-pounds shoulder of lamb, bone in
salt and pepper
1 head garlic in cloves

14 anchovy fillets
1 x 4-ounce jar pitted dry black olives (⅔ cup)
2 cups good rosé wine, preferably French
small bunch fresh thyme

❤ Preheat the oven to 300°F. Heat a roasting pan on the stove and seal the lamb, skin-side down, seasoning the exposed meat with a little salt and a generous amount of freshly ground pepper. Turn the shoulder over and cook for another minute just to seal the underside, seasoning the just-browned top as you wait.

❤ Take out the lamb and leave on a board, while you tumble your garlic cloves into the hot pan and strew with the anchovies and olives. Give everything a good stir.

❤ Pour the wine into the pan and tear over nearly half the thyme, then bring the juices to a boil. Put the lamb back in the pan, skin-side up, pour any meat juices that may have collected on the board into the pan; and, once it's boiling again, add most of the remaining sprigs of thyme (leaving some to adorn your serving plate). Turn off the heat and cover with aluminum foil.

❤ Put in the oven and cook for 2½ hours. When the lamb is ready, take it out of the pan onto a cutting board, and as you carve the meat, put the slices back into the pan with all the winey juices.

398

If you're lucky enough to have any leftover fragrant juices in which to reheat the cold meat, proceed gently but accordingly. In the more likely event that every last drop of juice will have been mopped up, reheat the lamb over a low heat in a saucepan into which you have poured a little wine, diluted in equal parts with water, and tumbled in a few capers. Heat the meat through till piping hot, then remove the cooked lamb from the liquid, stir in a small spoonful of Dijon mustard, and pour a small amount of this juice over the lamb on your plate. With any luck, you might have some reheated baby potatoes to eat alongside. My best advice though, is to eat up everything at the lamb's first, blessed outing. (Leftover lamb can be stored in the refrigerator, tightly wrapped in aluminum foil, for up to 3 days. Store leftover gravy in a separate airtight container in the refrigerator for 1–2 days. Leftover lamb can also be frozen for up to 2 months, tightly wrapped in foil.)

399

Minetta marrowbones

I've spoken elsewhere of my capacity for insistent, non-stop nagging when it comes to getting my hands on a recipe I want. It's not often that such a recipe emanates from a restaurant kitchen, but for this one I give grateful, greedy thanks to Keith McNally at whose Minetta Tavern I first ate these marrow bones, and to one of his chefs, Riad Nasr, who emailed me the recipe.

Now, it sounds odd to speak of my first having marrowbones at a New York restaurant, and that's not quite what I meant; but what they do at Minetta, and is so obvious I don't know why everyone doesn't, is to serve the shin bone – the shaft, it's called in the butchery trade – cut lengthways rather than across. It's just so much easier to eat this way.

But here's where I part company with my benefactors. For the chefs at the Minetta Tavern suggest soaking the bones in salted water for 36 hours, with a change of water (and salt, of course) every 8 hours. You know, there's only so far one can go . . . To be fair I did try this, and while I can see that the white, bleached-out look is better and more *refined* for restaurants, at home I prefer the full-throated flavor, and don't care about the look of the unsoaked, unbleached bone.

My idea of a heavenly dinner would be a tableful of greedy friends, a plateful of bones, and sourdough toast. We'd need, surely, nothing else. The Minetta Tavern suggests 2 marrowbones (that's to say 1, split) per person, and though I could easily double this, I should point out that at the Minetta they're offered as an appetizer.

So, consider what follows as instructions for feeding 2 people who will be going on to something else, or just you when you want nothing more than a solo feast – a kind of Bone Alone.

Serves 1–2, *as the occasion demands*

2 veal marrowbones cut by the butcher into troughs rather than pipes, thus exposing the marrow, and giving you 4 bones in total
fleur de sel or other salt flakes
freshly ground pepper
2 generous slices sourdough bread

1 clove garlic, peeled and cut in half lengthwise
2 tablespoons finely chopped fresh parsley
2 tablespoons finely chopped thyme leaves

♥ Preheat the oven to 425°F, then place the bones, cut-side up, in a shallow roasting pan and sprinkle generously with salt and pepper.

♥ Cook for 15–20 minutes, or until the marrow has puffed up slightly and is hot and cooked through.

♥ Slice the bread and either toast it or grill it on a grill pan. Rub one side of the toast with the cut sides of the garlic clove.

♥ Take the marrowbones out of the oven, transfer to a plate or plates, sprinkle with more salt flakes, as well as the chopped parsley and thyme, and put on the table with the garlicky toast. Spoon out the marrow onto your garlic-rubbed toast as you wolf this down.

Beef rib roast
with wild mushrooms and Cheddar mashed potatoes

I tried to stop myself from including a roast rib of beef here, and not simply because I gave this kingly cut, complete with Port and Stilton Gravy, its due in my Christmas book. I felt that, bone notwithstanding, the extravagance of the cut was at odds with the old-school thriftiness of the less showy cuts included elsewhere in this chapter. But we are allowed to feast on occasion. When celebration is due, I'd rather relish my luck or the opportunity and not persecute myself in a frenzy of right-minded, wrongful piety.

Now about this bone: it matters. Without it, you'll never get the sweet and tender flavor this dish just oozes. To make carving easier, however, ask the butcher to cut between bone and meat and to sit the meat back on the bone and tie it securely.

My 2-hour cooking stipulation ensures that beef is cooked the way I like it – quiveringly underdone – but you must add more time if you want it less rare. However you like it cooked, the beef must be at room temperature before it goes in the oven, and after an initial 15 minutes for all tastes, work on the principle of giving a joint 15 minutes per pound for rare, 20 minutes per pound for medium, and 30 minutes per pound for well done. Although, as ovens vary so much, you might be wise to invest (no major outlay incurred) in an instant read thermometer: that way, you can be sure the meat is cooked to your taste. As a rule of thumb, when the thermometer – plunged into the fleshy center – reads 140°F, your beef is rare, when it's 160°F, it's medium, and at 180°F, well, you've pretty much – in my book – got shoe leather. But if that's what floats your beefy boat, enjoy – and hope your guests do, too. (If you're leaving the beef to "rest" for 20–30 minutes after cooking – you might want to take 10–15°F off these temperatures because the meat will carry on cooking as it sits.)

The woodsy smell of the truffle oil, a fittingly luxurious anointment for the beef, is in turn a smart partner for the autumnal collection of mushrooms that accompany it, making gravy superfluous here. (If you want to, though, you could forgo the truffle oil and increase the garlic flavored oil and rub with porcini powder, if it can be found.) When you get the mushrooms, you'll see which ones must have their fibrous stalks removed, but don't throw these away: just add them to the beef's roasting pan before you stick it in the oven.

The Cheddar mashed potatoes are a family favorite – that's to say, this is the cheese to which my children are addicted – and you should feel entirely free to substitute any cheese of your choice. Cheesy mash may not be chic (thank goodness) but I love this element: it brings back to the beef the feel of a cozy Sunday lunch, despite the recondite fungi collection. Perhaps, with certain sorts of men and children present, you might, I rather fear, have to consider replacing the mushrooms with peas and gravy (see **p.454**). For the rest of us, the beef with mash 'n' mush will do beautifully, thank you.

Serves 8–10

1 x 4-rib standing rib roast, approx.
  8½ pounds total
3 teaspoons English mustard
  powder
1 teaspoon kosher salt or ½
  teaspoon table salt

1 teaspoon truffle flavored oil
1 teaspoon garlic flavored oil
1 leek
4 teaspoons marsala

♥ Take your beef out of the refrigerator in time for it to come to room temperature, which might – given the size of this beautiful beast – take up to 1 hour, and take off any wrapping. Preheat your oven to 425°F.

♥ Put the English mustard powder, salt, and truffle and garlic flavored oils in a small cup or bowl and make a paste, then massage this over the beef.

♥ Cut the leek in half lengthwise, then across, and drop the green strips into the center of a large roasting pan, pour over the marsala, and sit the beef on top. Toss any discarded mushroom stalks you may have (see facing page) into the roasting pan, too.

♥ Put the beef in its roasting pan into the oven and let cook for 2 hours for rare meat or more, according to choice (see **p.402** for more precise instructions). When the meat's had the heat-treatment it deserves, take the pan out of the oven and remove the beef to a cutting board, tent it with aluminum foil, and leave it to sit out of any draught for about 30 minutes.

♥ Let the pan stand for a while, as you'll want the juices (so long as there are no vegetarians coming) to pour into the mushrooms (see opposite) before serving. The juices that collect from the beef as it stands will be similarly needed.

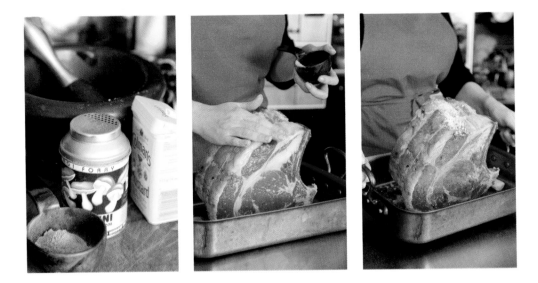

Wild mushrooms with leek and marsala

Serves 8–10, *as sauce for the beef*

2¼ pounds wild mushrooms
  (including porcini, chanterelles,
  oyster mushrooms, whatever the
  fields yield)
1 leek, washed and trimmed
7 tablespoons soft unsalted butter
2 teaspoons garlic flavored oil

2 teaspoons dried thyme
salt and pepper
1 cup marsala
few drops white truffle oil
  (optional)
small handful freshly chopped
  parsley, to serve

♥ Prepare your mushrooms. Don't wash them. (Mushrooms should never be washed.) Wipe off any earth or dust with a sheet of paper towel and remove woody or too fibrous stalks but do not throw them away: keep them to throw in the roasting pan as the beef cooks (see facing page). Don't cut the mushrooms: simply leave small ones as they are and tear larger ones into pieces.

♥ Quarter the leek lengthwise, then slice it thinly into beautiful, variegated green confetti.

♥ Put about a third of the butter, along with the garlic flavored oil, into a large heavy-based saucepan over a low heat and, when it's melted, turn up the heat to a bold medium and cook the leek pieces, stirring frequently. But be patient, you want the leek to cook properly and it could need a good 10 minutes, maybe 15, before it softens.

♥ Add the rest of the butter and the dried thyme and stir to help it all melt, then toss in the prepared mushrooms and stir gently but – again – patiently, so all mushrooms, give or take, come into contact with the heat. Put a lid on and let cook for 5 minutes.

♥ Remove the lid and give the mushrooms a good stir before replacing the lid and giving them another 5 minutes.

♥ Remove the lid again, add salt and pepper and half the marsala. Cook, stirring, for 30 seconds then put the lid back on and cook for 5 minutes more.

♥ Remove the lid yet again, add the remaining marsala, and cook with the lid off, stirring occasionally, for a few minutes or until the mushrooms are hot and most of the liquid is absorbed. This is when you could add the juices from the roasting pan and cutting board. Season to taste, adding a dribble of truffle oil if it feels like the right thing to do, decant to a warmed serving dish, sprinkle with chopped parsley, and serve with the beef.

MAKE AHEAD NOTE
The mushrooms can be cooked 1 day ahead up to the end of the 6th step above. Cool and transfer to airtight container and store in refrigerator. Reheat gently in saucepan, then finish cooking as directed.

Cheddar mashed potatoes

Serves 8–10, *with the beef*

4½ pounds Yukon Gold potatoes
1 cup whole milk

2½ cups grated mild Cheddar cheese
(or Colby, or Red Leicester, if your
grocery store sells either of them)
salt and pepper, to taste

♥ Peel the potatoes (unless you have a ricer to mash them, as I do), cut them in half, and drop them in a large saucepan of cold water.

♥ Lumber comically over to the stove with your giant pan, put the potatoes on a high heat, and when the water comes to a boil, salt them and turn down the heat to keep things at a resolute simmer for approx. 40 minutes, until the potatoes are tender and feel ready to be mashed when pierced with a fork.

♥ Carefully now, drain the potatoes, pour the milk into the emptied-out but still hot pan, and let the milk warm up, putting the pan over a low heat if need be.

♥ Turn off the heat and mash the potatoes with a potato ricer over the pan and into the milk – every now and again you will have to use the point of a sharp knife to help you remove the potato skins from the ricer. (Or you can just put the peeled and cooked potatoes with the milk in the pan, and mash by hand.)

♥ When all the potatoes have been mashed, put the pan over a low to medium heat and beat well with a wooden spoon until hot again.

♥ Add the grated cheese in 2 batches, beating well with your wooden spoon in between each addition.

♥ Season to taste, and serve piping hot.

MAKE AHEAD NOTE
The mashed potatoes can be made up to 1 hour ahead. Cover with a splash of milk to keep them from drying and clamp on a lid. Reheat gently, beating vigorously.

407

My children don't want me to do anything with the mashed potatoes except reheat them, which I do with a little milk, stirring, in a saucepan, or they do in a non-metallic bowl in the microwave.

The mushrooms (not that I can count on leftovers) I'm content to reheat gently with a little marsala, but the beef ... The beef deserves star treatment. That's to say, do nothing. Eat it cold, sliced in sandwiches, or with a hot baked potato and some mustard and pickles to make a meal. Horseradish comes into the equation now, too, though I don't feel it goes with the beef when it's hot and accompanied by the mush 'n' mash.

But there is another way of serving up cold, rare roast beef (or roast beeth as my late sister, Thomasina, used to say when she was little), and that's with the Thai Tomato Salad that follows. It lends the beef a divine and utterly different taste, which is exciting, but also useful given the size of the rib – and I just love it. What allows me to feel that this has all not been too hideously extravagant is that from the first feast come so many others. (Leftover sliced cooked beef can be stored in the refrigerator, tightly wrapped in aluminum foil, for up to 3 days and can be frozen for up to 2 months, tightly wrapped in foil.)

THAI
TOMATO
SALAD

I used to have the good fortune to live near a Thai restaurant that did an excellent takeaway. Along with whatever else I ordered, I always, always had the som tam, that hot, sour salad-cum-relish of shredded green pawpaw and halved cherry tomatoes. Now, green pawpaw is hard to come by, but cherry tomatoes? So this is my non-authentic adaptation, in the sense that it's a pawpaw salad without the pawpaw. The idea is the same, in that the fantastically spicy heat is still provided by chile, garlic, lime, and fish sauce; crushed unsalted peanuts, as per the original,

408

give that sourness-countering earthy rubble; and I cannot resist adding those beautiful, tiny dried shrimp. It's true they are no easier to come by than the green pawpaw, but they keep. Whenever I stock up on unfamiliarly alluring produce from the Far East, I get a bag of these teeny-tiny buff-striped coral creatures. Don't feel for one instant that you have to use them here, though: I know that some people are put off by these strange, almost other-worldly dried fish. When I last bought my shrimp, I had to buy a packet of watchful-eyed, silver streaks of dried anchovy, too, so beautiful did I find them, but everyone else in my house screams when they see them in the refrigerator.

Since I make this up as a quickly assembled salad, I don't put in anything I have to cook, but if you were to make more of a big deal of the salad, some trimmed, long green beans – just-cooked, drained, refreshed and drained again, so neither their crunch nor vivid greenness is lost – would be just fine and dandy added along with the scallions. And talking of which, if you have more of a taste for the rasp of raw onion, do replace those milder green shreds with some finely chopped shallots or half-mooned red onion.

Serves 4

scant 2 pints cherry or grape
tomatoes
3 tablespoons roasted unsalted
peanuts
1 x green chile, seeded and finely
chopped
2 tablespoons dried shrimp
(optional)

1 clove garlic, minced
¼ cup lime juice (2–3 limes)
1 tablespoon light brown or palm
sugar
3 tablespoons Thai fish sauce
3 scallions
3 tablespoons chopped cilantro

❤ Halve the tomatoes and put them into a serving bowl.

❤ Put the peanuts into a resealable bag and bash with a rolling pin to crush them into small rubble.

❤ In another (smaller) bowl, combine the crushed peanuts with the chopped chile and dried miniature shrimp (if using) and the minced garlic. Add the lime juice, sugar, and fish sauce. Whisk this mixture together.

❤ Pour this dressing over the halved tomatoes and toss them about to mix.

❤ Cut the scallions into 3 across, and then snip each third – carefully, so as not to cut yourself – into thin strips and toss these micro-matchsticks over the dressed tomatoes. Finally, sprinkle the chopped cilantro over and serve with the cold beef or, indeed, whatever takes your fancy.

MAKE AHEAD NOTE
The dressing, minus the peanuts, can be made 1 day ahead. Store in a screw-top jar in the refrigerator. Add peanuts and shake well before using.

KITCHEN PICKINGS

Much as I enjoy cooking, when I have friends over I don't always want to make a meal of it. I'm not looking to cut corners, but the opposite: I want everyone to laze expansively – a freeform fiesta – greedily grazing from bits and bites covering the kitchen table.

I enjoy indoor-picnicking, and sometimes the most relaxing way to have company is in a kick-your-heels-back kind of way. Just leave it all out there for people to enjoy, along with some attentively poured wine or a tinkling, glass-chinking cocktail or three.

Now what may seem like easy pickings at the table doesn't always guarantee a low-effort enterprise for the cook. But relax: nothing here is canapé-complicated. I prefer to leave it to professional caterers to puff and stuff a hundred choux buns, or fashion twiddly miniatures which seem to draw as much on crocheting techniques and origami as on time-consuming, if not superhuman, kitchen skills. No, the truth is a home cook need produce nothing more than a tray of plumply gleaming cocktail sausages to keep hospitality honor intact. Still, just because you don't need to do any more doesn't mean you won't want to. I take huge pleasure – real, heartswelling joy – from a table loaded with foodstuffs, so one of my motivations whenever I cook for others is my own blissful gratification. I have to try to keep everything in proportion: I remember my son answering me reprovingly, although he can't have been much more than three, when, after taking in the pleasing panorama of a plate-covered table before any guests arrived, I asked, "Is there anything more lovely than a tableful of food?" "Yes," he replied, "a tableful of people."

This is something we would all do well to remember when entertaining – even with a resolutely small "e" – as too many frenzied offerings pushed pleadingly under people's noses can create an atmosphere not of welcoming abundance but of fussing desperation. And that doesn't get the party started.

Now, it doesn't much matter whether the recipes that follow comprise a mezze-style mix-and-match meal, or whether they are produced singly or in modest pairs to accompany pre-meal cocktails and keep everyone occupied while you do some last-minute stirring, or, indeed, whether they are, in whatever combination, the edible elements of a cocktail party. The important thing is that they won't take so much out of you that you're exhausted before your guests show up.

Most times, I am more than happy to be rustling up these recipes as people are arriving – no trouble – but there are other occasions when I just know that answering the doorbell, taking orders for drinks and producing food at the same time might leave me, even among close friends, feeling a little flustered. With that in mind, I have added, to appropriate recipes, short pointers as to how best to prepare these ahead of time, even if only a little ahead.

Mood trumps food every time, and I say that as a greedy person. But here there's no conflict, and every reason, in the words of that British Eighties' pop classic "why you'll always find me in the kitchen at parties."

Home-made pork scratchings
with apple and mustard sauce

I love pork rinds; I love pork cracklins, even in their junk-food-packaged over-salted incarnation, too: this, here, is perhaps the best of both worlds. In fact, these make me so suffused with greedy pleasure that I do grasp why, for some, gluttony is considered a sin. For me, though, it is a blessing. Occasions of joy in life should be greeted with gratitude, not with guilt. A degree of caution is warranted, but only for practical – rather than spiritual – reasons. I'm assuming you won't be eating these, anyway, if you have concerns about fat or salt; but also, as it says on the packets of pork cracklins I buy, these are "only recommended for people with strong, healthy teeth." Ever since I came a cropper on a caramel candy last Christmas, I have become a little more responsible about indulging in potentially dangerous eating opportunities. Nothing as yet has happened to mar my blissful enjoyment of these, but since I regularly crunch the cartilage off chicken bones, and (as I've confessed earlier) leave nothing on my plate after ordering a plate of spare ribs or sardines in a restaurant, my teeth are kept as sharp as a dog's.

You need to go to a butcher to get the pork skin, so you may as well ask for it to be scored at the same time, to help it crisp up nicely in the oven. Your only responsibility where the skin is concerned, is to store it well. Plastic wrap of any sort will make it soggy, so either put it on the bottom shelf of the refrigerator still in the butcher's "peach" paper, or wrapped loosely in parchment paper, or just leave it open, in a roasting pan, on the bottom shelf of the refrigerator and away from other foods.

While these are gorgeous to crunch on with nothing more alongside than a cold beer or glass of wine, I can see no convincing argument for dispensing with the Apple and Mustard Sauce on **p.414**. And if you are like-minded, turn now to the sauce following as this needs to be cooked and cooled before you address yourself to the rinds.

Makes 25 *pieces*

1 pound pork skin (with some fat attached), in 2 scored slabs	salt, to taste

♥ Preheat the oven to 425°F. Cut the pork skin into 25 pieces (each approx. 1 x 1½ inches) with a sharp pair of kitchen scissors.

♥ Put the pieces of skin on a low-lipped baking sheet or slotted top of a broiler pan, skin-side up. Slide this onto a rack at the top of the hot oven for 25 minutes, and then turn the pieces over for a final 5 minutes.

♥ Once out of the oven, sprinkle generously with sea salt, and remove carefully to a plate lined with a sheet of paper towel for a moment to drain and cool a little, before serving on a few plates, alongside the mustardy applesauce or just by themselves if you wish.

MAKE AHEAD NOTE
The skin can be cut up 1 day ahead. Store as directed on previous page. The rinds can be cooked up to 1 hour ahead of serving, and should be eaten within 2 hours of cooking. Leave to stand in cool, dry place and pop back into hot oven for 5 minutes to reheat before serving.

Apple and mustard sauce

I love the contrast between warm pork rinds and cold, grainy sauce. If you want a simple no-cook option – not that making applesauce can be described as complicated – you could simply get out a jar of horseradish. But for me, it's the sharp apple that helps make these rinds such compulsive eating. I just dip one shard at a time into the sauce – warning: no double-dipping! – and crunch down.

The mustard not only gives piquancy to the applesauce, but also infuses it with a gorgeously golden hue. And do bear this sauce in mind to accompany any roasted pork or even just some plain broiled sausages.

3 large Granny Smith apples,
approx. 1 pound total
4 teaspoons English mustard
powder, plus more to taste
¼ cup maple syrup

½ teaspoon kosher salt or ¼
teaspoon table salt
juice ½ lemon
1 scallion, trimmed and left whole

♥ Peel and core the apples, and roughly chop them into pieces.

♥ Put the apples into a saucepan with the mustard, maple syrup, salt, lemon juice, and scallion (left whole just to give flavor).

♥ Put the lid on the pan and bring to a bubbling boil, then turn the heat down to a simmer and cook for 10–15 minutes, until the apples are soft, stirring once or twice.

♥ Remove the scallion and discard, then mash the sauce a little with the back of a spoon if necessary.

♥ Taste the sauce; if you fancy it a little hotter, add some more mustard, though it may be wiser to leave final seasoning till you've tasted the sauce cold.

♥ Serve, cold, though not refrigerator-cold, with the pork rinds, above.

MAKE AHEAD NOTE
The sauce can be made up to 2 days ahead. Transfer to non-metallic bowl to cool, then cover and refrigerate as soon as possible. Remove from the refrigerator about 30 minutes to 1 hour before serving, to serve cold but not chilled.

FREEZE NOTE
The cooled sauce can be frozen in airtight container for up to 3 months. Thaw overnight in the refrigerator and serve as above.

414

Dragon chicken

Every time I write a recipe for chicken wings it gets a little hotter, and this one – as its name suggests – positively breathes fire. If you want to reduce the heat, simply use fewer chiles, but I can promise you, while this, as written, certainly has zing and fiery flavor, that you don't need to be someone who always orders the hottest curry on the menu at an Indian restaurant to be able to eat it.

I like this quite as much the next day, to help get over the cocktails, as I do on the evening itself to munch while drinking.

Makes 20 chicken wings, serves 8–10

5 long red chiles, seeded and halved

1 red bell pepper, seeded and core removed

2 x 3-inch pieces fresh gingerroot, peeled and cut into small chunks

2 tablespoons kosher salt or 1 tablespoon table salt

2 teaspoons rice vinegar

⅓ cup garlic flavored oil

⅓ cup vegetable oil

20 chicken wings (left whole)

approx. 3 tablespoons chopped fresh cilantro, for serving

♥ Preheat the oven to 425°F. Process the chiles, bell pepper, ginger, salt, vinegar, and the 2 oils in a food processor and whiz until smooth.

♥ You can at this point leave your chicken wings to marinate in a freezer bag coated in the sauce for up to 24 hours if you want – or for 2 days if you omit the salt and add this later. Otherwise tip out the sauce over the chicken wings onto a shallow-sided aluminum foil-lined roasting pan or lipped baking sheet – don't use a high-sided pan, or the wings will braise rather than roast.

♥ Make sure all the wings are coated in the chile-flecked sauce, and then roast for 40 minutes.

♥ Transfer the wings to a serving platter and sprinkle with some cilantro.

MAKE AHEAD NOTE
Marinate wings in a bag in the refrigerator for up to 1 day – put bag in bowl or on plate in case of leakage. (You can marinate 2 days ahead if you omit the salt from the marinade, and sprinkle with salt before roasting.) Cook as directed in recipe.

FREEZE NOTE
The wings can be frozen in the bag of marinade, omitting the salt, for up to 3 months. Thaw overnight in the refrigerator – put bag in bowl or on plate in case of leakage. Sprinkle with salt before roasting. Cook as directed in recipe.

Wholegrain mustard and ginger cocktail sausages

I can never resist a cocktail sausage as an appetizer and, as I know I have told you before, couldn't quite contemplate a party without them. I also have a bit of a thing about ginger jam or preserve, and adore its rich, almost pungent heat, which wraps itself, along with the sharper hit of the grain mustard, like an aromatic blanket around the little sausages.

Please believe me when I say that the sausages and some toothpicks to pick them up with are quite enough as they are. I find it hard to explain what got into me as these little beauties were having their photograph taken, but I found myself compelled to fashion a storage vessel out of a loaf of bread and place the sausages inside. It's so not me, and yet I was unable to resist the lure: it was as if I were suddenly possessed by the spirit of a 1980s' European ski-chalet girl. Still, no reason to fight it, as I cannot tell you how deeply glorious the emptied-out sausage-sodden bread bowl is to rip into once your guests have left. (And you can freeze the scooped-out bread as breadcrumbs for future use.)

If you can't find ginger preserve, you can substitute thin-cut marmalade with 1 teaspoon ground ginger and 2 teaspoons fresh grated gingerroot stirred into it.

Makes 50

scant ½ cup ginger conserve
scant ½ cup wholegrain mustard
1 tablespoon garlic flavored oil
1 tablespoon soy sauce

50 skinny breakfast sausage links
1 round (approx. 9 inch diameter)
  thick-crust sourdough or rye
  bread loaf, for serving (optional)

♥ Preheat the oven to 350°F. In a bowl, whisk together the ginger conserve, mustard, garlic flavored oil, and soy sauce.

♥ Turn the sausages in the mustardy mix and then arrange them on either a large, shallow-sided pan or 2 smaller pans. The height of the pan's sides will determine how quickly the sausages color and cook.

♥ If you are using high-sided pans, they will need about 45 minutes in the oven; cooked in a shallower pan, 30 minutes should be fine. And do line with aluminum foil or use disposable foil pans, or cleanup will be a nightmare.

♥ To serve the sausages in their bread bowl, cut a circle around the top of the bread to take off a "lid." Put this lid on one side for a moment, and tear and pull out the doughy filling with your hands, leaving the crust intact so that you have a hollow bowl.

♥ Fill this emptied-out loaf with as many sausages as you can – you may have to top up with a few as you go – and then you can balance the lid at a jaunty angle for maximum effect and your guests' amusement. Serve with a small pot of toothpicks to spear the sausages, but if you're skipping the bread bowl option, let the hot sausages cool slightly before handing them out.

MAKE AHEAD NOTE
Put coating mixture in a resealable bag, add sausages, and refrigerate for up to 2 days – put bag in bowl or on plate in case of leakage. Cook as directed in recipe.

FREEZE NOTE
The sausages can be frozen in bag with coating for up to 3 months. Thaw overnight in the refrigerator – put bag in bowl or on plate in case of leakage. Cook as directed in recipe.

Spicy sausage patties with lettuce wraps

When I was therapeutically rolling the little patties into shape for my Toad in the Hole (see **p.453**) one Sunday evening, it occurred to me how good they could be, spiced and spruced up, as little picky things to go alongside a drink. And that they are. There is nothing to stop you just popping each plumptious patty into your mouth just as it is, but I like to wrap mine in a piece of lettuce, like a juicily edible parcel. This also turns them into a fantastic appetizer for a supper or dinner party, as it happens. And if you wanted to make more of a meal out of them, you could use tortillas or the thinner, more pliable lavash-style bread to wrap them; the Peanut Butter Hummus on **p.434** would serve as delectable glue, and I would – having lined my wrap with this – then place a piece of lettuce on the hummus before tucking in the patty and bundling it all up. Consider going the peking-duck-inspired route, too, by adding to the bulging package some strips of scallion and cucumber.

Makes 16 patties

1 pound good-quality sausages or
  sausage meat
1 teaspoon grated fresh gingerroot
1 green chile, seeded and chopped
1 red chile, seeded and chopped
2 teaspoons English mustard
1 garlic clove, peeled and grated
zest 1 lemon, finely grated
2 thin or 1 fat scallion, thinly
  chopped

2 teaspoons chopped fresh cilantro
1 tablespoon vegetable oil

to serve:
leaves from 1 escarole or iceberg
  lettuce, to wrap the sausage
  patties
pita breads or flat breads, warmed
2–3 limes, cut into wedges

421

♥ Cut a nick in the sausage skins and gently squeeze the sausage meat out of the casings into a bowl, or simply put the sausage meat in a bowl, then add the ginger, chiles, mustard, garlic, lemon zest, scallion, and cilantro.

♥ Mix everything together thoroughly, and then make patties by using a tablespoon measure for each one or just go by eye and feel, as you pull out roughly a walnut-sized amount (or a tiny bit less) at a time and shape it into a fat, little disc.

♥ Heat the oil in a frying pan and cook the patties over a medium heat for about 3 minutes a side. Watch they don't catch too much; you want them to look temptingly scorched on the outside, but not until you know they're properly cooked through.

KITCHEN PICKINGS | KITCHEN COMFORTS

♥ Transfer to a serving platter and arrange the lettuce leaves and breads to wrap the patties in on another plate. Put some of the lime wedges alongside, too, and anything else you want to eat with them.

MAKE AHEAD NOTE
The uncooked patties can be prepared 1 day ahead. Cover and refrigerate until needed, then cook as directed in recipe.

FREEZE NOTE
The uncooked patties can be frozen for up to 3 months. Put patties on cookie sheet lined with plastic wrap or parchment paper, cover with layer of plastic wrap and freeze until solid, then transfer to resealable bag. To thaw, transfer patties to cookie sheet lined with plastic wrap, cover with plastic wrap, and thaw overnight in the refrigerator. Cook as directed in recipe, dusting with a little all-purpose flour before cooking if the surface of the patties is slightly moist.

Pigs in blankets
with mustard dipping sauce

I am afraid I disgraced myself – or would have if I had any shame – when I came across these at a 4th of July party in the Hamptons given by my friend and agent, Ed Victor, and his wife Carol Ryan. I all but held the waiter hostage, frankly. I ate them throughout the party, and once everyone else had gone home, I settled down on a sofa to finish those that were left.

And then, back home, what pangs I had at not being able to eat any more! So, I badgered the caterer for the recipe, and here it is. I know it may sound not particularly appetizing to wrap frankfurters in puff pastry, but these pigs in blankets (or franks in blanks, as we call them in *casa mia*) along with their tangy dipping sauce provide an eating experience that is nothing short of rapturous. My gratitude to Jean Mackenzie and her Four Seasons catering company in Southampton, New York, is unbounded, as is my appetite for these little treasures.

Different brands of puff pastry can be rolled out to varying sizes, so what you have to know is that each frankfurter needs a pastry blanket to fit snugly. Each frankfurter will give you 4 little pigs.

Makes 72

1 x approx. 17.3-ounce package
ready-rolled puff-pastry sheets
(gives 2 sheets, each approx. 10 x
9½ inches), thawed if frozen
1 egg
3 x 12-ounce packages frankfurters
or hot dogs (gives 21, but you only
need 16)

for the mustard dipping sauce:
scant ½ cup wholegrain mustard
scant ½ cup Dijon mustard
2 tablespoons sour cream

♥ Preheat the oven to 425°F. Roll out one of the rectangular puff-pastry sheets to make it just a little bit thinner, stretching the long side rather than the short side as you roll. Cut the rectangle into quarters, then cut each rectangle in half lengthwise, to give 8 small pastry strips in total. (Stay with me!). You may need to roll each strip of pastry a little more to make sure it wraps snugly around your frankfurter.

♥ Beat the egg in a small bowl and paint each pastry section with the egg wash. Sit a frankfurter horizontally on the left-hand side of one of the pieces of pastry and roll it up until it just seals. Then do the same with the remaining 7 small pastry strips.

♥ Cut each rolled frank into 4 small pieces, pressing the pastry back around the sausage if it comes loose. Then place on a parchment paper–lined lipped baking sheet with the sealed bit down to prevent it springing open.

♥ Paint the franks in blankets with the egg wash, and put them in the oven for 15–20 minutes. The pastry should have puffed up a little and turned golden. You can get on with the other sheet of pastry while the first lot of franks are cooking and repeat the process with the remaining franks.

♥ Mix together the mustards and sour cream and put in little bowls.

♥ Put the cooked franks in blanks onto a plate and serve warm with the dipping sauce in the little bowls (for ease of eating and passing) on the side.

MAKE AHEAD NOTE

The frankfurters in their pastry can be assembled 1 day in advance. Put cut-up pigs in blankets on lined lipped baking sheets but do not glaze the outside. Cover with plastic wrap and refrigerate until needed; store egg wash in a separate, covered container in the refrigerator. Glaze and bake, following directions in recipe.

Coconutty crab cakes

Food obsession has its uses, not least that I am always thinking about how I could put any ingredients in the house to good service. I often put breadcrumbs in crab cakes, but it occurred to me one day that unsweetened shredded coconut might well do the same job, absorbing moisture and helping the cakes to set. It does, and rather better than the breadcrumbs: I like the faint tropical hint, like the memory of a Caribbean sky, and the less heavy, tender texture it lends the little patties.

You could serve lime wedges to squeeze over these crab cakes as you eat, and it certainly would look prettier, but for me, rice vinegar has the edge, to undercut the faint sweetness of the (albeit unsweetened) coconut.

427

Makes 14, *enough to serve 6–8*

7 ounces picked white crab meat
3 tablespoons all-purpose flour
3 tablespoons unsweetened
  shredded coconut
1 tablespoon chopped jalapeño
  peppers (drained from a can or
  jar)

1 tablespoon chopped fresh
  cilantro
2 teaspoons rice vinegar, plus
  more for serving
oil, for frying

♥ Put the crab meat in a bowl and check for any bits of stray shell which should be removed, then mix the crab meat, flour, and coconut in a bowl.

♥ Add the jalapeño, cilantro, and 2 teaspoons rice vinegar and mix well, patting down in the bowl to form a compact layer at the bottom.

♥ Cover and leave in the refrigerator to set for 1 hour.

♥ Heat enough oil in a frying pan to cover the bottom of the pan in a shallow layer.

♥ Take the crab mixture out of the refrigerator and scoop out tablespoonfuls – using a tablespoon measure with a rounded bowl shape – pressing the mixture into the measure and then easing out the mound into the hot oil.

♥ You will only be able to make 4 or 5 at a time comfortably, however big your pan, as the first crab cake to go down will need to be turned over just about the time you've added the fourth or fifth. Remember that the crab is already cooked, so really you're just cooking until the cakes are crisp and golden on the outside and heated right through inside. About 1 minute a side should be fine.

♥ Remove them to some sheets – double-thickness – of paper towels (lining a board, a cookie sheet, or a plate) and blot them as you go. To keep the cooked crab cakes warm, carefully transfer them to a wire rack, put the rack over a cookie sheet, and hold them in an oven preheated to 225°F for up to 20 minutes.

♥ Serve with a little more rice vinegar sprinkled on as you eat.

MAKE AHEAD NOTE
The crab mixture can be made up to 1 day ahead. Keep covered in the refrigerator until needed, then cook as instructed in recipe.

FREEZE NOTE
The crab cakes can be frozen for up to 1 month *but only* if the crab meat has not been previously frozen (check with fish seller or supermarket if you are not sure). Do not re-freeze previously frozen crabmeat. Spoon dollops of crab mixture onto cookie sheet lined with plastic wrap and flatten slightly. Cover with layer of plastic wrap and freeze until solid then transfer to airtight container. Fry directly from frozen, in about ½ inch depth oil, over medium heat and allowing 1–2 *extra* minutes' cooking time per side. Reduce heat if crab cakes are browning too quickly, and check they are hot right through. Blot and transfer to wire rack, and keep warm as directed in recipe.

Sherry-glazed chorizo

Chorizo cooked in red wine is a tapas-bar staple in Spain, but I don't feel too disrespectful using sherry in place of the wine; its provenance is, after all, the same as the chorizo. Any good sherry would do, but I always keep a bottle of amontillado in the house to splash into soups and stir-frys (as well as for drinking), though cream sherry actually works well, too.

This is great when you want to make a little something to go with cocktails, but have not much time to prepare. You can serve the chorizo alone, or add some Spanish marcona almonds, a choice of olives, and some Manchego cheese, broken up into rough chunks (or any local sharp hard cheese of your choice) to create, and quickly, an easily-got-together tapas table at home.

Serves 2 by itself, *or 4 with other picky bits*

10 ounces chorizo, sliced into ½-inch-thick coins
3 tablespoons amontillado or cream sherry

Spanish almonds, olives, Manchego cheese, to serve (optional)

♥ Heat a frying pan and cook the chorizo for a minute or so, until the slices color a little more deeply even, and their vibrant orange oil starts to collect in the pan.

♥ Pour in the sherry, let it bubble down for another minute or so, stirring all the while, until it is sticking to the coins of chorizo glossily. Transfer to a warmed plate, and serve.

Thai roasted scallops

There is something so beautiful about a sea scallop in its shell. It's true that you won't tend to find them at the supermarket, but a fish seller will be able to supply them, remove them from their shells, and then give them to you speedily cleaned and ready to go. They pretty well cook themselves, and yet to have them there, on the table, bronzed by the oven, makes everyone feel they are in for a treat. And they are. Being diver-caught, good scallops are also costly. But they really do feel like a precious accompaniment to a celebratory drink.

I've played around with Thai flavors and scallops elsewhere (see **p.72**) and love the contrast between the sweet, bouncy flesh and sharp heat of the curry paste, whichever way it comes. But if you can only get scallops in less majestic form, that's to say without their corals or their shells, you can still proceed here: double the number of scallops, since they will be smaller, toss them in the spice mixture below, and roast them – just their juicy near-naked selves – in the oven on an aluminum foil–lined sheet pan.

Serves 4–6

1 tablespoon red Thai curry paste
3 tablespoons lime juice
1 tablespoon fish sauce

12 sea scallops with corals (roe)
  and shells, or 24 large bay
  scallops without, preferably
  diver-caught

♥ Preheat your oven to 425°F.

♥ Whisk together the Thai curry paste, lime juice, and fish sauce, and pour into a wide, shallow dish.

♥ Put the scallops (with their corals, if you have them) into this mixture and swish the scallops about to cover them in the red paste. Leave for about 5 minutes.

♥ Set the scallop shells (if you are lucky enough to be using these) on a lipped baking sheet. Then put the scallops (and their corals, if using) back in their shells – or if shell-less, straight onto the baking sheet – keeping the scallops heavily coated in the marinade. When they are all on, drizzle over them any marinade that's left in the bowl.

♥ Roast the scallops in the oven for 15 minutes, until just cooked through, and serve in the shell; if you have shell-less scallops, 10 minutes should be fine. When cooked, the scallops will be just opaque in the center.

Avocado quesadillas

While I have no desire to be a short order chef, I rather like standing comfortably by my stove, a-grilling quesadillas, and handing out hot, seared tortillas, oozing with melted cheese, as I go. Since I buy the tortillas rather than make them myself (though I have plans in that direction), these are no harder to make than a grilled sandwich, which is, in effect, what they are.

If you want the grill marks to come through super-clearly, it will help if you weight the quesadilla down as it cooks; I used to use a saucepan with many canned things balanced on it, but my lovely handyman, Ken, kindly and unquestioningly gave me, at my request, a brick covered in aluminum foil, which does the trick perfectly. But for some reason, I seem to have lost my brick and don't dare ask for another, so I have resigned myself quite happily to cooking quesadillas freestyle, with no heavy weight to press them down.

Makes 24 slices/wedges

4 soft flour or corn tortillas
4 ounces Manchego cheese, sliced, or other cheese of your choice that melts well

1 avocado, pitted, skin removed, and cut into chunks
approx. 16 jalapeño rings, from a can or jar (or more, to taste)

♥ Get out 1 tortilla and lay it flat in front of you, then put about ¼ of the thinly sliced cheese on one half – not too near the edge, though, as you don't want the cheese to spill out as it cooks.

♥ Top the cheese with ¼ avocado, sliced in chunks, followed by about 4 jalapeño rings, or more to taste. Fold over the uncovered half of the tortilla, so you have a bulging semi-circle in front of you.

♥ Heat your grill pan – or use a dry frying pan if you don't have a grill pan – and slide the uncooked quesadilla on it. Squish down with a weight, or just press down briefly with a slotted spatula or similar, and cook for 1 minute, then flip the quesadilla and grill it for 1 minute on the other side.

♥ Tip the hot quesadilla out onto a cutting board and slice each folded semi-circle into 6 wedges, serving straightaway, and continue likewise with the remaining 3 tortillas.

Peanut butter hummus

Peanut butter hummus doesn't have an elegant ring to it, but elegant is exactly what this is. Rather than using tahini, which is in effect sesame butter, I use peanut butter. Is it dreadful to say I prefer this? It is gorgeously filling, but without the slight clagginess that tahini can give. I mean, in the right mood I adore the palate-thickening clay of tahini, but a little definitely goes a long way. Although I think this version possesses a certain manila-tinted chic (despite the kindergarten appeal of its title) that makes me happy to bring it out to eat with cocktails when I have people over, I am even happier to have a batch in the refrigerator to pick at, spreading it over spelt crispbread or a piece of rye toast, when the mood takes me.

Makes enough for a party of 10

2 x 15-ounce cans chickpeas
  (garbanzo beans)
1 garlic clove, peeled
3–5 tablespoons regular olive oil
⅓ cup creamy peanut butter
3 tablespoons lemon juice, or more
  as needed
2 teaspoons kosher salt or 1
  teaspoons table salt, or to taste

2 teaspoons ground cumin
¼–⅓ cup Greek yogurt
2 tablespoons peanuts, finely
  chopped, to serve (optional)
1 teaspoon smoked paprika, to
  serve (optional)
breadsticks, mini pitas, crackers,
  tortilla chips, to serve (optional)

♥ Drain and rinse the chickpeas. Put the garlic clove, chickpeas, 3 tablespoons oil, peanut butter, lemon juice, salt, and cumin into a food processor and blitz to a knobbly purée.

♥ Add ¼ cup of the Greek yogurt and process again; if the hummus is still very thick, add another 1–2 tablespoons yogurt and the same of oil. (This will often depend on the chickpeas, as different sorts make the hummus thicker or not.)

♥ Taste for seasoning, adding more lemon juice and salt if you feel it needs it.

♥ On serving, mix the chopped peanuts with the paprika and sprinkle on top if you wish, and put an array of bits and pieces to eat with or dip in, as you see fit.

MAKE AHEAD NOTE
The hummus can be made 1–2 days ahead. Transfer to non-metallic container, cover, and refrigerate until needed. Should be consumed within 2 days of making.

Churros
with chocolate dipping sauce

I have been desperate to find a churros recipe I can happily live with, and after much research and many churros – though overeating sugar-coated Spanish doughnuts is not in itself a hardship – I have found The One, in Thomasina Miers' *Mexican Food Made Simple*, a book of enormous charm and possessing that essential ingredient: it both induces and rewards greedy curiosity. This, my version of her churros, is slightly different; but then, we all, when we cook, tend to fiddle a bit.

I have never – sadly – been to Mexico, but I've eaten churros in Spain, grabbed from a bakery as I pass, in the morning or late at night, with a cup of sauce-thick hot chocolate on the side. At home, they are a sudden afternoon treat, an indulgent, late-morning weekend breakfast, or a gratifying finale to a meal of tapas-style offerings. The chocolate sauce that you dip each sugar-and-cinnamon-coated doughnut into is luscious and thick, and if it looks at first to be too much for the amount of churros you've made, bear in mind that it makes sense to give each person their own little bowl of chocolate sauce.

Enough: now get frying. I use a small saucepan, not just because it makes sense to do just 3 or 4 per batch, but because deep-frying in the kind of pan you'd boil an egg in is so much less daunting (in fact, not daunting at all) than having a great big bubbling vat of oil in front of you at the stove.

In Spain, and indeed in Ms. Miers' Mexican version, the churros are like long spindly ridged batter worms: mine are squatter, chunkier, altogether shorter and fatter, like pointy-corrugated puffs of doughnut, all the better for dipping and dunking.

Makes 16 churros, *which should be enough for 4–6, but . . .*

for the churros:
¼ cup superfine sugar
2 teaspoons ground cinnamon
⅔ cup plus 2 tablespoons all-purpose flour
1 teaspoon baking powder
1 tablespoon olive oil
1 cup freshly boiled water
approx. 2 cups corn (or vegetable) oil, for deep-frying

for the thick chocolate sauce:
4 ounces good-quality bittersweet chocolate (or ½ cup chips)
1 ounce milk chocolate (or 2 tablespoons chips)
1 tablespoon golden syrup (such as Lyle's), or corn syrup
⅔ cup heavy cream

437

♥ Mix the sugar and cinnamon for the churros in a wide, shallow dish: this is for coating the cooked churros later.

♥ Melt all the chocolate sauce ingredients in a heavy-based saucepan, really gently, and once the chocolate starts to melt, stir everything together, take off the heat, and leave in a warm place.

♥ To make the churros, put the flour into a bowl and stir in the baking powder, then beat in the olive oil and 1 cup freshly boiled water from a kettle. Keep mixing until you have a warm, sticky dough, and leave to rest for about 10 minutes, or for as long as it takes for the corn (or vegetable) oil to heat up.

♥ Heat the oil for frying in a smallish saucepan; it should come about a third of the way up the sides of the pan. When you think it's hot enough, toss in a cube of bread, and if it sizzles and browns in about 30 seconds, the oil's hot enough; or if you're using an electric deep-fat fryer or otherwise have the means to check the temperature, it should be at 325°F. Keep a watchful eye on your hot oil pan at all times.

♥ When you are ready, load up a piping bag with a large star-shaped piping tip and fill with the churros dough. Squeeze short lengths (approx. 1½–2 inches) of dough into the hot oil, snipping them off with a pair of scissors as you go. I love the squishy feel of this.

♥ Cook about 3 or 4 at a time and, once they turn a rich golden brown, fish them out of the oil with a perforated spoon or spatula, or with tongs, onto a cookie sheet lined with some paper towels. To keep the cooked churros warm while you fry the remaining dough, transfer them, after blotting with paper towels, to a parchment paper–lined lipped baking sheet and hold in a low oven (175°F). Even if you let them sit out of the oven, they do need 5–10 minutes to rest before you eat them, to allow them to set inside.

♥ Toss all the hot churros into the sugar and cinnamon and shake them about to get a good covering, just before serving.

♥ Once you have finished making the churros, pour the chocolate sauce into individual containers (to avoid the double-dipping dilemma) and dip'n'dunk away.

AND TO WASH IT ALL DOWN …

Note: My 1 shot measure is a 1-ounce one, though I often use 2 tablespoons for ease.

While there is a part of me that is bursting to clink around in camp cocktail mode, drinks-wise I tend to be more of a pourer than a shaker. When I'm cooking and talking to friends in the kitchen, fixing up barman-style beverages is not always possible, however desirable it may feel. I make exceptions: when there's a small group, or even just for a solitary snifter, I don't mind branching out, but on the whole I stick to the sort of cocktail you can mix sploshingly in a pitcher or a glass.

I have written before about my déclassé drinks cabinet; if anyone has a weakness for a kitsch tipple (more for the joy of the label than to drink, frankly) it's me. Still, any quickly thrown together party or even languorously planned kitchen gathering has to rely on a relatively restrained broth of bottles; a list of cocktails that calls upon a full bar is never going to make sense.

BLACK VELVET

When it comes to drinks-fixing, I take as my starting point, unsurprisingly, the bottles I keep in hand for general kitchen use. Well, it makes sense – to me, at any rate. Thus, as I keep some Guinness in store so that I can bake up a Guinness Gingerbread (see **p.305**) or a welcoming batch of Irish Oaten Rolls (**p.86**), I know I have half the makings of a weekend brunch pitcher of **Black Velvet**. I love this cocktail, but it is much misunderstood. That's to say, everyone falls for the drink-me glamour of the name, but it's – usually – impossible to sip without wincing. I'll tell you why. When the cocktail was invented (1861, so the saga goes, concocted by a steward at Brooks's Club to honor the passing of Victoria's Prince Consort), it was fashionable to drink sweet champagne. These days, sweet champagne is thought of as ultimately naff, and so Black Velvet is made up with equal quantities of dry champagne and Guinness, and is just as bitter as you'd think it would be. Make it instead by mixing 1 x 750ml bottle of sweet fizzy wine (I use Asti Spumante without embarrassment) with 3 cups Guinness and you'll have a drink that is (a) considerably cheaper than the chic champagne mix and (b) fantastically quaffable, making about 6–8 glasses. What's more, you could do worse than serve a dark, alluring pitcher with the oaten rolls that share its gorgeously bitter ingredient and with a plate of good smoked salmon. And if you do, consider goat's curd or cream cheese – or else just regular Philly – to spread on the manila-toned rolls before topping with the salmon. A small tangle of pickled red cabbage and a frond or two of fresh dill (as per my regular Christmas no-cook canapé) might be considered as a final, tangy flourish.

BABY GUINNESS

This brings me to the **Baby Guinness**. This has nothing to do with the ale in question, but is an after-dinner digestif that ends up looking exactly as the name suggests. You take a small shot glass (and I've got some that do look like teeny-tiny miniature beer glasses) and fill it almost to the top with coffee liqueur. I use Kahlúa in preference to Tia Maria here as it has more viscosity and therefore is fit for purpose, or Illy Espresso liqueur since it's a bit less sweet, which I like. Either way, into the nearly full shot glass of dark coffee liqueur, pour some Baileys over the humped back of a teaspoon (just to break its fall) so that you have a creamy white layer on top, to resemble the head on a glass

440

of Guinness. Good though this is to drink at the end of dinner, you could also consider serving a shot glass each for **dessert** to throw over a small bowl of vanilla ice cream. Or you could mix the coffee liqueur in equal parts with some Frangelico hazelnut liqueur (if you've made the tiramisu on **p.164** you should have some over).

Frangelico is also good added to coffee or **hot chocolate**: you can make a very superior hot chocolate if you melt 4 ounces good bittersweet chocolate, finely chopped, in 2 cups whole milk with a shot or two of Frangelico, over a medium heat. Pour into a couple of mugs and top, if you like, with squirty whipped cream and some chopped toasted hazelnuts. And I often make a **Frangelico Cream** just by softly whipping some heavy cream then whisking in a shot or so of Frangelico: 1 cup of heavy cream along with 1–3 tablespoons (or to taste) of Frangelico, should be enough to make a glorious accompaniment to any chocolate cake, turning it from teatime treat to dinner party dessert.

This is, in effect, along the lines of the Margarita Cream that accompanies my Flourless Chocolate Lime Cake (see **p.281**) and it is these ingredients that have given birth to a drink I am almost hysterically proud of.

Inspiration for this came in the wee small hours: truly this is sweet compensation, for insomnia. Folks, I bring you the **Lagarita**, a thirst-quenching lager beer sploshed with the makings of a Margarita plus some, or a kind of embellished version of the British favorite, lager'n'lime. So: take 1 x 12-ounce chilled bottle Mexican beer, add 2 tablespoons or 1 shot (whichever way is easiest for you to measure) each of tequila, Cointreau (or triple sec) and Rose's lime juice, then squeeze in fresh lime juice, to taste. Now, the beer doesn't absolutely have to be Mexican, but it does have to be (as always, in my book) so cold it hurts. This is just

the drink you want to wash down a quesadilla (see **p.433**) or a fiery plate of Dragon Chicken (**p.415**) and much else besides.

This leads me to another contender for quesadilla-accompaniment which, in turn, suggests brunch (and I wouldn't say no to the Coconutty Crab Cakes on **p.427** alongside, either) and that's a **Bloody Maria**. I told my friend Maria (see left) that this was a drink I'd created for her, but I'm afraid I was lying like a cheap rug. A Bloody Maria is regular barman's terminology for a Bloody Mary made with tequila in place of vodka. My recipe, such as it is, goes as follows: to 1 quart tomato juice, add 1 cup tequila, 2 tablespoons

LAGARITA

BLOODY MARIA

KITCHEN PICKINGS | KITCHEN COMFORTS

amontillado sherry, 1 tablespoon fresh lime juice (or more to taste, and you could serve a lime wedge per person after spritzing the mother-pitcher) plus 1 teaspoon Tabasco (or to taste). I also salt generously, tasting after each stirred-in sprinkle.

The above are serious hard cocktails, but I am a great believer in offering, on the other hand, the sort of stuff that can be knocked back without justified hesitation. I think I have told you before that – due to its mood-enhancing properties – prosecco is known *chez moi* as prozacco. Unsurprisingly, this is a drink that forms the foundation of my liquid entertaining. My favorite of all is a drink introduced to me by Anna Del Conte, called **Prosecco Sporco**, which involves pouring a glass of prosecco and then adding a dash or two of Campari. *Prosecco sporco* literally means "dirty prosecco" but somehow "Filthy Fizz" sounds better to me. I find it unutterably chic and absolutely gorgeous into the bargain. The bitterness of Campari is not to everyone's taste (though the bitterer the better, as far as I'm concerned), so if you are wanting to turn this into a cocktail for the sweeter toothed, I suggest a dash of Chambord black raspberry liqueur, instead, if you happen to have that in your cocktail cupboard.

However, while we're on the Campari – that you also, notionally, have in your cupboard – a Campari and soda says summer to me, but possibly one of the greatest cocktails of all time is an **Americano.** For that you need a squat, chunky tumbler which you cram with ice, before adding 2 shots each (or use ¼ cup) or just go by eye, of Campari and sweet red vermouth. Top with a little sparkling water (serving more on the side to be added as wished) and garnish with a slice or twist of orange. This is both rich and refreshing at the same time, and is a fantastically fiery red, as if terracotta had been turned into a stained glass window. It may interest you to know, if you don't already, that in the first of Ian Fleming's Bond books, *Casino Royale*, this was 007's cocktail of choice, before he moved into the martini, shaken not stirred, etc.

Another possible use for your Campari is a **Pink Margarita**. To make one of these, you need to shake together with ice, 3 tablespoons tequila (which may already be in your cocktail cabinet, see above) with 1 teaspoon Campari and 1 tablespoon each fresh lime juice and sugar syrup. (**Sugar syrup** is not hard to make – mix 1 cup water with 1¼ cups sugar and boil them together carefully until the sugar has dissolved, and then leave to cool – but it's a bore, so I buy it in a bottle: the easiest one to find is French and labelled "*gomme*.")

Now, it strikes me that if you've taken the Chambord route to your Filthy Fizz, you could also use the Chambord in place of Campari in your Pink Margarita, maybe upping the quantity a little, and doing without the sugar syrup.

FRENCH MARTINI

I don't go for sweet, sticky liqueurs, much, but I have a lot of time for Chambord. This may be in large part due to the prettiness of the bottle, which looks as though it were designed by Vivienne Westwood for Marie Antoinette; certainly, it looks as though it belongs more in the boudoir than the cocktail cabinet (especially in the smaller bottles). But its intense dark raspberry taste is worthy of attention, aesthetic considerations aside. As well as mixing it with fizz or adding it to tequila as above, you can make a classic cocktail and favorite of the knock-it-back nineties, a **French Martini**. Shake together with some ice (or mix in a more pedestrian way) 3 tablespoons of vodka with 1 tablespoon Chambord and 3 tablespoons pineapple juice. This is the drink to bear in mind when you're serving the spare ribs on **p.392**, since you'll be getting the pineapple juice in for those.

RASPBERRY COOLER

There's one last use I have for Chambord, which is in a **Raspberry Cooler**, another drink of my own wayward creation: in a long glass, I chuck in 1 shot each of raspberry vodka and Chambord, cram in ice, and then pour over some San Pellegrino limonata. I fear this is veering into the world of alcopops, as it doesn't taste nearly as alcoholic as something with vodka and liqueur should, but it is delicious and refreshing. As they are obliged to say on bottles and commercials these days, enjoy responsibly . . .

PETUNIA

443

If after everything we've downed since I first mentioned the Lagarita, you can still remember the ingredients, you will know that we had some Cointreau (or triple sec) in store . . . This can be added to a bottle of prosecco and some pink grapefruit juice to make a great party drink, a **Petunia**, so-called (by me) because it is a summery counterpart to my Christmas tipple, the Poinsettia. To make 8–9 glasses, pour 1 x 750ml bottle of dry white fizzy wine into a large pitcher and add ½ cup Cointreau (or triple sec) and 2 cups pink grapefruit juice – and because of the latter, you could also call this a **Florida Fizz**. When Barbara Castle, Labour's late great Red Queen, was asked whether she wanted to be called Chairman, Chairwoman, or Chair, she is said to have replied, "I don't care what I'm called so long as I'm in charge." Similarly, I don't care what you call this party piece, so long as you give it a go.

GRASSHOPPER

Now, as for crèmes de menthe and de cacao: I am more than aware that even a moderately well-stocked home cocktail cabinet could contain neither, but I've prevailed upon you already to think about buying both for the delectable Grasshopper Pie (see **p.182**), so feel our joint attention should be turned to them now. It's not a pretty prospect, I know. For, whereas I love the pie, I would gladly give the **Grasshopper** cocktail a miss. But we're here, the bottles are already opened, and you may as well give it a go; you may like it more than I do. In which case, shake 2 tablespoons each of green crème de menthe, white crème de cacao, heavy cream, and whole milk over ice before straining into a martini glass. Armed with this pair of liqueurs, I'd prefer an After Eight, which requires you to shake 1 tablespoon each of vodka, green crème de menthe, and the white crème de cacao over ice before pouring into a chilled shooter.

AFTER EIGHT

Still, a wise move might well be to unbracket the two drinks in your mind: 2 shots vodka, 1 each of white crème de cacao and dry vermouth shaken over ice make for a **Chocolate Martini**, and if you're feeling in fancy bartender mode, then dip the martini glass first in a splash of crème de cacao and then in a little sieved cocoa to provide a richly dusted rim. On the whole, though, I'd suggest the crème de cacao rather as I do the Frangelico: splosh it in hot chocolate, hot milk, or coffee to sweeten and strengthen, or use it in place of rum, where appropriate, in cooking – for example in the Chocolate Chip Bread Pudding on **p.142**.

But one last dash back to grab that crème de menthe. The best way of drinking this, and it has a retro pleasure all of its own for me, is simply poured over crushed ice, as in **crème de menthe frappé**. This was (I should be embarrassed but I'm just not) a favorite of mine when I was about fifteen, and I love, too, the lines it makes me remember from Harry Graham's *Ruthless Rhymes for Heartless Homes*:

"When Baby's cries grew hard to bear / I popped him in the Frigidaire. I never would have done so if / I'd known that he'd be frozen stiff. / My wife said 'George, I'm so unhappy! / Our darling's now completely frappé!'"

But back to the real world: I couldn't cook without some sake in the kitchen, and I felt it made sense to try and make a pourable cocktail out of it – the sake I keep on hand isn't generally high-toned or expensive enough to savor just as it is. I turn it into a cocktail known in my kitchen as a **Giddy Geisha**, though you might feel happier just calling it a **Sake and Tonic**. So, proceed as if you were making a G&T, but use sake in place of the gin, and add a dash of elderflower cordial at the end. If you're in garnishing mode, add a thin long tongue of cucumber. This is a fantastic refresher and Friday afternoon booster. (I'm particularly keen on some low-sugar, but aspartame-free, tonic water I've recently found.) I rather fancy ginger ale would be good with the sake, too, in which case dispense with the elderflower cordial.

For my own part, I could never dispense with elderflower, and it can be easily purchsed on-line. I have the cordial on hand for my Gooseberry and Elderflower Crumble (see **p.251**) and use it often to sweeten apples when I cook, too. An **Elderflower Spritzer** is a fabulously aromatic non-alcoholic drink to offer, so even if you don't plan to cook with it, it's worth having a bottle of the cordial in the house. Just dilute the elderflower cordial in a ratio of 1:4 or 1:5 with sparkling water (but some cordials are more concentrated, so check the instructions on the bottle). A sprig of mint in each glass is a good touch, too.

And I end with the elderflower because it makes for one of my favorite drinks, and what I mix myself when I need refreshment, succour, or Dutch courage. I call it an **Elderflower Gimlet** but that's what my children might call a random appellation, given that a gimlet has gin and Rose's lime juice in it and this has vodka and elderflower cordial. But I know what I mean. I don't bother to shake or any of that fandango. I just put ice in a small martini glass and add 3–4 tablespoons each of very good vodka and elderflower cordial. I had a dream recently in which I invented a beautifully clear cocktail called **Tears of a Clown** (don't ask). I do remember that at the very end, a tiny dot of rice vinegar was added. If you feel brave enough, do. But I am happy with my Elderflower Gimlet as it is. Bottoms up!

444

THE COOK'S CURE FOR SUNDAY-NIGHT-ITIS

It's all very straightforward really: I cook to suit my life; I write about the food I cook. There is certainly a Kitchen Constant in my life (and it seems right, come to think of it, that in physics the symbol for 'constant' is indeed k) and I don't believe the way I cook has essentially changed over the years. But life evolves, and so do recipes. How we cook, or how we eat, grows out of how we live.

This translates in my life into a whole new eating-entity: Sunday supper. When my children were little, I suddenly realized that there existed such a thing as the weekend lunch. I should rephrase this, for it was not just about lunch: when my children were little, I realized that clearing up one meal was nothing but a precursor to getting started on the next. Now that I have teenagers, rather than toddlers, the demands on the kitchen are different. For one thing, they're not up in time at the weekend to give lunch serious consideration and when they are up they seem to have some urgent but mysterious place to go to, called simply "out."

With Sunday lunch ruled out as a constant, I now concentrate my endeavors on Sunday supper. I am the most ineffectual of mothers, but even I can make a convincing argument as to why Sunday night is home time. I know that eating heavily in the evening is not on the dieticians' to-do list, but this is the time when I feel we all need bolstering. There is a certain gloom that threatens to descend, a dread, however unjustified, of the white-knuckle-ride of the week ahead: this my mother (who never really got over her own school-phobia) called Sunday-night-itis.

It's obviously important that your efforts to ease in the week don't ruin your weekend. But a little pottering in the kitchen gives me that feeling I find so crucial, of being in a fixed, familiar place in a whirling world. I do mean a little: while most of the recipes here may need a long time in the oven, that is what makes them easy – you are absolutely freed up while they cook. These are soothing suppers for the cook as well as the eaters.

And I don't think this particular cook is alone in deriving comfort from a sense of continuity. I have no attachment to my past other than in the kitchen, but here it matters deeply. All sentiment aside (it's my stomach not my soul speaking), I relish this unfancy and old-fashioned food that endures and helps you endure, that's passed down through the years and down the generations. It is my most cherished legacy. But I'm still happy to tweak a recipe here and there – we're talking cooking, not conservation, after all. And that's the evolution of eating: often a recipe has to adapt to survive. So here it is, from my kitchen to yours: cozy, cocooning food to fend off that Sunday-night feeling no matter what the day of the week.

446

Soup made with garlic and love
and pumpkin scones

Most of the recipes in this section come, if not from my childhood, then from someone else's and have consequently formed a part of my children's. This recipe, however, has an entirely literary provenance: the minute I read about Ezra's hopes for the restaurant in *Dinner at the Homesick Restaurant*, his plan for a soup made with garlic and love, I knew I had to eat it. Which meant, first, I had to come up with a recipe and cook it. I am not trying to replicate the recipe that the character had in mind, not that I could; but no matter, for this is the sort of soup that came into my head as I read. (I've spared you the gizzards – his dream, not mine – because I couldn't, in any case, get them past the home front.) With any other writer, there might be a danger of the title's being cloying or sentimental, but how – really – is that possible in an Anne Tyler novel? Your soul gets flayed on every page: I don't think any writer has managed to be so piercing and unrelentingly intense and plain downbeat at the same time.

There's not a sentence of hers I don't love, but after reading any of her books, a soup like this is what I need. I can't help feeling that this makes it perfect fodder for the low-energy, high-tension mood of a Monday-eve supper. I add the savory pumpkin scones (or biscuits), just because they go so well with it, and I like to have something to do as I wait for the soup, but you could just as easily make the Irish Oaten Rolls on **p.86**, or buy any bread you like to go with.

This kind of unflashy peasant soup does – there are no two ways about it – rather resemble dishwater, but it is delicious dishwater. Besides, it's exactly this sort of home food, the food that belongs in the kitchen, that I love and need.

Serves 4

1 head garlic
1 leek, cleaned and trimmed
3 tablespoons regular olive oil
1 heaping tablespoon chopped fresh
  thyme

2 baking potatoes, approx. 14
  ounces total
1½ quarts chicken broth,
  preferably organic
salt and pepper, to taste
few spoonfuls chopped fresh
  parsley, to serve

♥ Free each clove from the head of garlic, then peel, and slice them as thinly as possible.

♥ Halve the leek and also slice thinly. Heat the oil in a heavy-based saucepan which comes with a lid, and cook the leek gently for about 5 minutes with the lid off, stirring every now and again, until soft.

♥ Add the thyme leaves and sliced garlic, and cook gently for another 5 minutes, as above.

♥ Cut the potatoes (with skin on) into small dice, then add them to the pan, giving a good stir with your wooden spoon.

♥ Add the broth and bring the pan to a boil. Simmer for 20 minutes partially covered, then season with salt and pepper, to taste. Turn off the heat and let stand for a few minutes before serving, sprinkling with parsley as you hand out bowls.

MAKE AHEAD NOTE
The soup can be made up to 2 days ahead. Transfer to non-metallic bowl to cool, then cover and refrigerate as soon as possible. Reheat gently in a saucepan, stirring occasionally, until piping hot.

FREEZE NOTE
The cooled soup can be frozen, in airtight container, for up to 3 months. Thaw overnight in the refrigerator and reheat as above.

Pumpkin scones

I should confess up front that the pumpkin, which plays such a key part in these savory scones, comes out of a can. It is pretty much half a canful, and I suggest you freeze the remaining half in a resealable bag or airtight container (for up to 3 months) and bring it out the next time you want to charm with a batch of these beauties. Then again, you could just keep it in the refrigerator for up to 3 days (but take it out of the can) and use it as a sweet thickener in any meat sauce or vegetable soup, or stir it into any stew you might have a-bubbling away at the time. I sometimes add it to the Patara Lamb Shanks on **p.364**, for example.

But I love these scones: the sweetness of the pumpkin is well balanced by the saltiness of the Parmesan and the revving power of the chili oil. While I think they are best just smeared with butter, and generously, so you're left with a gloriously melted pool at the very center, I have to say they have an addictive draw for me when dabbed, too, with a spot of Vegemite: not so much that it darkens them, but enough to seep into the melted butter. Funnily enough, when I have them with this garlic soup (see opposite), I also adore them thickly spread with cream cheese. That tastes like Sunday evening to me.

They are gorgeous to make: the pumpkin gives them a supple and pliant texture that is lovely to work, and tints them with gusto: making them is like modeling with golden Play-Doh.

Makes 12 scones

¾ cup canned pumpkin purée
½ cup grated Parmesan cheese
1 egg
1 teaspoon Worcestershire sauce
  (such as Lea & Perrins)
½ teaspoon table salt
good grinding white pepper
2 teaspoons chili flavored oil

1⅔ cup all-purpose flour, plus more
  for rolling
2½ teaspoons baking powder
½ teaspoon baking soda
a little milk to glaze

1 x cookie sheet or lipped baking sheet
1 x 2 inch biscuit cutter

♥ Preheat the oven to 400°F. Put the pumpkin purée, Parmesan, egg, Worcestershire sauce, salt and pepper, and chili oil in a bowl. Beat well to mix.

♥ In another bowl, measure out the flour, baking powder, and baking soda, and mix together. Fold this into the pumpkin mixture and work it to form a dough.

♥ Flour your work surface, then tip the dough out of the bowl and pat down with your hands to make a slab about 2 inches thick. There's no need to roll it.

♥ Cut the dough into scones, using a round 2 inch biscuit cutter that you have first dipped in flour. Place the scones on a cookie sheet, about 1 inch apart.

♥ Re-form the dough so that you can keep cutting out rounds, and you should get 12 scones from this mixture.

♥ Brush the tops of the scones with milk to glaze them, and then bake for 15 minutes. Once out of the oven, let them cool a little and then eat warm or cold, though I think they're best warm. And you can always warm one up for yourself, should you want.

MAKE AHEAD NOTE
The scones are best the day they are made but day-old scones can be revived by warming in oven preheated to 300°F for 5–10 minutes.

FREEZE NOTE
Baked scones can be frozen in airtight containers or resealable bags for up to 1 month. Thaw for 1 hour at room temperature and warm as above. Unbaked scones can be put on parchment paper-lined cookie sheets and frozen until solid. Transfer to resealable bags and freeze for up to 3 months. Bake direct from frozen, as directed in recipe, but allowing extra 2–3 minutes' baking time. (Unused pumpkin purée can be frozen in airtight container for up to 3 months. Thaw overnight in the refrigerator. It can sometimes separate a bit, with a slight watery layer, on thawing but is still fine to cook with.)

Toad in the hole

Toad in the hole may sound like a strange name, but it is exactly what we Brits refer to in this beloved and old-fashioned dish, a nursery classic, which is best described as a giant popover baked with sausages. It is the platonic ideal of the Sunday night supper: undemanding and safe-making, it bolsters as it comforts. But while I love its British nursery charm, I have tweaked it a little from the traditional form, not least in that I don't leave the sausages whole, but squeeze them into little patties, which I fry on the stove before blanketing with batter and baking in a ferociously hot oven. I am not trying to create more work – not that squeezing sausages out of their skins is arduous (indeed, it is strangely satisfying) – but I really don't like the way that the sausages, when this is prepared in the traditional manner, go a spooky braised pink as they cook within the batter. Yes, you can give them a start in the hot oven so they sear first, but it never quite seems to do the trick, and this way one doesn't have to return to them. You just fry the little patties, pour the batter over them, chuck in the oven, and leave them to it.

Serves 4–6

1½ cups milk
4 eggs
pinch salt
1⅔ cups all-purpose flour
approx. 1 pound good pork
  sausages (6 in number)
1 tablespoon goose fat, vegetable
  shortening, or oil

4 sprigs fresh thyme, plus more for
  serving if wished

1 x round roasting pan approx.
  11 inches diameter, or small
  rectangular roasting pan approx.
  13 x 9 inches

♥ Preheat the oven to 425°F. Whisk the milk and eggs together with the salt, then whisk in the flour, beating to make a smooth batter. I find this way round makes for a lighter batter.

♥ Press the sausage meat out of its casing (you may need to nick the skin with a knife), half a sausage at a time, rolling it in your hands to form a ball, and then squash gently to make a little, fat patty. You should get 12 patties from the 6 sausages.

♥ Heat the fat or oil in a heavy-based, flame-safe roasting pan on the stove and brown the patties for about 1 minute each side: you need do no more than make them look enticingly brown.

♥ With the patties and oil still hot, pour in the batter and quickly drop in the sprigs of thyme. Absolutely immediately put into the oven for about 40 minutes or until the edges of the batter have risen and turned golden, and the eggy middle has set.

♥ Serve immediately, scattered with a thyme sprig or two or just a few leaves, and with gravy (either the onion one below, or the BBQ variant mooted on **p.458**), if you feel you can only properly enjoy your popovers when they are sauce-sogged.

MAKE AHEAD NOTE
The batter can be made 1 day ahead. Cover and refrigerate. The sausages can be formed into patties 1 day ahead. Cover and refrigerate until needed.

ONION
GRAVY

Warm 2 tablespoons fat or oil and then cook 2 onions, peeled, halved, and very finely sliced, until soft (about 10 minutes). Add 2 teaspoons sugar, and let the onions cook, caramelizing a little, for another 3 or so minutes, before stirring in 4 teaspoons flour, then 2 cups beef broth. When thickened and hot, add a glug of marsala to taste.

454

Finnan haddie my mother's way

My mother used to make this fairly often in my childhood, but mostly, I associate it with feeling under-the-weather: this is my idea – or rather my mother's – of hand-on-the-brow comfort food. My mother always used finnan haddie and put a tomato cut in half in the dish, but I once, unaccountably, found myself at home and tomato-less, so threw in some peas from the freezer, instead, and was very happy with the innovation. You could do either or both, as suits you; fresh bread, thickly sliced and buttered, is non-negotiable, however.

I put a fillet of finnan haddie in its own small ovenproof bowl or dish and pour milk over it, adding tomatoes or peas or both, most definitely an egg, and some tied parsley stalks if I have any around, and I give each person a bowl. So it makes sense to give quantities per bowl, and you can increase these to suit the number of people you're feeding.

Note: The egg should be soft, so don't give this to anyone with a weak or compromised immune system, such as pregnant women, the elderly, or infants.

Serves 1

3 tablespoons frozen peas
butter, for greasing
1 small fillet finnan haddie, or any
 firm, white fish
1 cup whole milk

few parsley stalks or sprigs, tied
1 tomato, halved
1 egg
freshly ground white pepper

♥ Preheat the oven to 400°F. Put the frozen peas into a bowl and pour some freshly boiled water over them.

♥ Grease a small ovenproof dish with butter and place the finnan haddie fillet in it.

♥ Pour the milk over, drop in the parsley stalks, and put in the 2 tomato halves, then find a space to crack in the egg.

♥ Drain the peas, add them, and give a good grinding of pepper before putting the dish into the oven. Cook for 10 minutes, if all your ingredients are at room temperature. If not, you may need 15–20 minutes. Do be careful, though, as you want the egg yolk to stay runny.

456

Ed's mother's meatloaf

I have a perfectly justifiable weakness for any recipe that comes to me having been passed on through someone else's family. This is not just sentimentality (I hope not *even* sentimentality, actually, since I'm somewhat contemptuously convinced that sentimentality is the refuge of those without genuine emotions). Yes, I do infer meaning from the food that has been passed down generations and then entrusted to me, but think about it: the recipes that last, do so for a reason.

And on top of all that, there is my entrancement with culinary Americana. I just hear the word meatloaf and feel the old-world, European irony and corruption seep from me, as I will myself into a Thomas Hart Benton painting. And then I take a bite: the dream is dispelled and I'm left with a mouthful of compacted, slab-shaped sawdust and major, major disappointment. So now you understand why I am so particularly excited about *this* recipe. It makes meatloaf taste like I always dreamed it should.

Even though this is, indeed, Ed's mother's meatloaf, the recipe as printed below is my adaptation. My father-in-law used to tell a story about asking his mother for instructions on making pickles. "How much vinegar do I need?" he asked. "Enough," she answered. Ed's mother's recipe takes a similar approach; I have added contemporary touches, such as being precise about measurements. But for all that, cooking can never be truly precise: bacon slices will weigh more or less, depending on how thickly or thinly the bacon is sliced, for example. And there are many other similar examples: no cookbook could ever be long enough to contain all possible variants for any one recipe. But what follows are reliable guidelines, you can be sure of that.

I do implore you, if you can, to get your meat for this from a butcher. I have made this recipe quite a few times, comparing ground beef that comes from the butcher and ground beef that comes from various supermarkets, and there is no getting round the fact that freshly ground butcher's meat is what makes the meatloaf melting (that, and the onions, but the onions alone can't do it). The difficulty with supermarket ground beef is not just the dryness as you eat, but the correlation, which is that the meatloaf has a crumblier texture, making it harder to slice.

As far as gravy goes, I am happy just to have the juices that drip from the meatloaf as it cooks, and not least because the whole point of this meatloaf for me is that I can count on a good half of it to eat cold in sandwiches for the rest of the week. (And you must be aware – it is my duty to make you aware – that a high-sided roasting pan makes for more juices than a shallow one.) But if you wanted to make enough gravy to cover the whole shebang hot, then either make an onion gravy, and pour the meat juices in at the end, or fashion a quick, stove-top BBQ gravy. By that, I mean get out a saucepan, put in it ¼ cup dark brown sugar, ½ cup beef broth, 4 tablespoons each of Dijon mustard, soy

QUICK BBQ
GRAVY

sauce, tomato paste, and red currant jelly, and 1 tablespoon red wine vinegar. Warm and whisk and pour into a jug to serve.

Ed instructed me to eat kasha with this, which is I imagine how his mother served it, but I really feel that if you haven't grown up on kasha – a kind of buckwheat polenta – then you will all too easily fail to see its charm. I can't see any argument against mashed potatoes, save the lazy one, but I don't mind going cross-cultural and making up a panful of polenta; I use the instant kind, as I've admitted (and see **p.336**), but replacing the water that the package instructions advise with chicken broth. And, as with the beef broth needed for the gravy suggested above, I am happy for this to be store-bought rather than home-made.

Serves 8–10, *but feed fewer and have leftovers*

4 eggs

4 onions, 1 pound total

5 tablespoons duck fat or butter

1 teaspoon kosher salt or ½ teaspoon table salt

1 teaspoon Worcestershire sauce (such as Lea & Perrins)

2 pounds ground beef, preferably organic

2 cups fresh breadcrumbs

10 ounces (approx. 20 slices) bacon

1 x large roasting pan

♥ Preheat the oven to 400°F. Bring a saucepan of water to a boil and then boil 3 of the eggs for 7 minutes. Refresh them in cold water.

♥ Peel and chop the onions, and heat the duck fat or butter in a thick-bottomed frying pan. Cook the onions gently, sprinkled with the salt, for about 20–25 minutes or until the onions are golden and catching in the fat. Remove to a bowl to cool.

♥ Put the Worcestershire sauce and ground beef into a bowl, and when the onion mixture is not hot to the touch, add it to the bowl and work everything together with your hands.

♥ Add the remaining raw egg and mix again before finally adding the breadcrumbs.

♥ Divide the mixture into 2, and in the pan make the bottom half of the meatloaf by patting half the beef mixture into a flattish ovoid shape approximately 9 inches long. Peel and place the 3 hard-boiled eggs in a row down the middle of the meatloaf.

♥ Shape the remaining mound over the top of the eggs and pat into a solid loaf shape. Compress the meatloaf to get rid of any holes, but don't overwork it.

♥ Cover the meatloaf with slices of bacon, as if it were a terrine, tucking the bacon ends underneath the meatloaf as best you can to avoid its curling up as it cooks.

♥ Bake for 1 hour, till the juices run clear, and once it's out of the oven let the meatloaf rest for 15 minutes. This should make it easier to slice. When slicing, do it generously, so everyone gets some egg. Pour meat juices over as you serve, or do what you will, gravy-wise.

MAKE AHEAD NOTE
The meatloaf can be assembled, covered, and kept in refrigerator one day ahead. Then bake as in recipe.

Making leftovers right

MEATLOAF SANDWICH

Without doubt a meatloaf sandwich is one of the most fabulous things anyone can eat ever, ever, ever. I don't want to be too bossy about this, but for me a meatloaf sandwich needs to be slathered with a mixture of wholegrain mustard and mayo, whatever bread you're using – and the bread I'm using (see previous page) is an Eastern-European-style dark rye, scented and studded with caraway seeds. (You should use up the leftovers within 2–3 days.)

460

Pork and apple hotpot

My maternal grandmother used to make a pork and apple hotpot, a slow-baked stew from the north of England, though it was years before I thought of making one myself. Why did I wait so long? There are few suppers so comforting, both to eat and, actually, to make.

It is a fiddly recipe, that I don't deny, and if Sunday afternoon finds you flat-out exhausted and (as my grandmother also used to say) rather on the top note, then perhaps this isn't ideal. But I sometimes find chopping and stirring, a bit of calm kitchen process, can restore some sanity to my frazzled brain. Not that my children would necessarily agree, since they are regular witnesses to my Sunday-night stoveside meltdowns.

Someone helping, a child perhaps, could make it an easier process; then again, a solo stint in the kitchen could be more emotionally restorative. But why I find recipes like this so helpful at the weekend is that they take long enough to cook for you to have a properly usable tranche of time between preparation and consumption.

Although I've specified boneless chops, I regularly ignore myself. On the plus side, having no bones makes greedy guzzling easier; on the other plus side, bones intensify the flavor. Either will do. Gloriously, I have also to report an overwhelming desire to add a layer of sliced black pudding (or blood sausage) to the cooked hotpot and return it to the oven, turned up to 425°F, for 10 or so uncovered minutes at the end.

I think the recipe that follows is pretty much traditional; my only failure in this regard is that I can't find my old-fashioned hotpot dish, the brown-glazed round pot that fans out at the top, which was exactly the same as the one my granny had. I did mind, and I still do, that I somehow have managed to lose it, though I have to report that the proper pot required a bit of fiddly covering with parchment paper and always bubbled over; so, now that necessity has made me move towards a round cast iron Dutch oven with a lid, it's all been easier.

I could suggest you start off cooking everything in this pot, but it will mean you are layering up in a hot greasy pan and you may prefer to add to the cleanup but work in less of a danger zone.

463

Serves 4–6

3 tablespoons oil
3 onions, peeled, halved, and cut
 into half-moons
9 ounces (18 slices) bacon
⅓ cup all-purpose flour
1 teaspoon apple pie spice
salt and pepper, to taste
6 boneless pork loin chops (6–8
 ounces each)

4 Granny Smith apples
3 cups sharp, pressed apple juice

1 x ovenproof dish, approx. 8
 inches diameter x 5 ½ inches
 deep, or 9 inch round Dutch oven
 with lid

♥ Preheat the oven to 325°F. Warm the oil in a wide, heavy-based frying pan, and fry the onion for about 10 minutes until soft, stirring occasionally. Remove to a bowl.

♥ Cut or scissor the bacon into small strips and fry in the oily onion pan for a few minutes; remove to the onion bowl and mix together.

♥ Put the flour, apple pie spice, and seasoning into a resealable bag and add 3 of the chops. Roll them around, and then shake off the excess flour. Sear the chops in the oily pan and remove them to a plate. Cook the other 3 chops in the same way, flouring and then searing.

♥ Peel and core the apples, cutting each one in half. Slice each half into fine segments and then arrange all the ingredients in the ovenproof dish or Dutch oven, as follows: a layer of onions and bacon, 3 pork chops, a layer of apple slices, onions, and bacon, another 3 pork chops, a layer of apple slices, onions, and bacon and, finally, a layer of apple slices.

♥ Tip the remaining spiced flour into the oily pan and stir around before whisking in the apple juice. Bring to a boil, then pour into the layered dish, letting it filter slowly through to the bottom.

♥ If necessary, make a snug lid for the dish with parchment paper and aluminum foil, and sit it in the oven on a lipped baking sheet, as it may leak. Otherwise, just pop the lid on your Dutch oven. Cook in the oven for 3 hours, until the pork is cooked through and the apples are tender.

MAKE AHEAD NOTE
The hotpot can be assembled 1 day ahead, though the apples will turn a bit brown but you won't notice when they're cooked. Cover tightly and refrigerate until needed. Cook as directed in recipe.

Slow roasted pork belly

There are a few meals I can say I'm making that will make my children excited (or pretend to be), and this is one of them. Alongside there must be Pie Insides (which is what my daughter has always called leeks in bechamel sauce, see **p.370**) and for ultimate gratification, roasted potatoes (for which, see **p.222**). Although I usually use goose fat for roasted potatoes, I feel the pork belly allows, indeed encourages, the substitution of lard. I'm not convinced that with all that fabulous crisp rind you do need roasted potatoes as well, but I like to provide what makes people happy. I actually prefer noodles or a bowl of plain, steamed brown basmati rice, and urge you to consider either; and I love to sprinkle a little rice vinegar on my own plate of pork as I eat.

This is another of those recipes that you can get done in advance and then have the afternoon off, unworried. I have advised an overnight marinade, but if I'm making this (as I tend to) for Sunday supper, I often prepare it in the morning and leave it in the refrigerator loosely covered with parchment paper, or midday-ish and leave it uncovered in a cold place (but not the refrigerator) for a few hours.

Serves 6–8

3¾ pounds pork belly, rind scored   juice 1 lemon
¼ cup tahini   juice 1 lime
¼ cup soy sauce

♥ Get out a shallow dish in which the scored pork will fit snugly and in it whisk together the tahini, soy sauce, lemon and lime juice.

♥ Sit the pork on top, skin-side up. You should find the marinade covers the underside and most of the sides, but doesn't touch the skin: that's what you want.

♥ Leave the pork in the refrigerator to marinate overnight, covered with aluminum foil, and then take out to return to room temperature before it goes into the oven. Preheat the oven to 300°F. Get out a shallow roasting pan and line with foil.

♥ Transfer the pork to the roasting pan and cook it uncovered for 3½ hours, then turn the oven up to 450°F and cook for a further 30 minutes to let the skin crisp to crunchy burnished perfection.

MAKE AHEAD NOTE
The pork can be marinated for up to 1 day. Cover and store in refrigerator until needed.

466

Making leftovers right

*Leftovers can be stored in the refrigerator, tightly wrapped in aluminum foil, for up to 3 days. If there's enough, I'd suggest cutting it into bite-sized pieces and reheating it in a mixture of soy sauce, sake, and mirin, and stirring it through some cooked rice with chopped cilantro and a few mixed seeds. However, I tend to find that not much gets left over, in which case I suggest you bag and mark it up, freeze it (for up to 2 months), and use it when needed in the Pantry Paella (**p.196**).*

Texas brisket

Brisket is one of those old-fashioned cuts, the very mention of which makes certain people dewy-eyed: this is the food of our grandmothers' grandmothers, cheap, flavorsome, substantial, in need of slow cooking and worthy of deep appreciation. Eating a plate of brisket, sliced and doused in its gravy, is to know you are safe in the warm embrace of the kitchen. With this under your belt, you enter the week fortified.

The most important thing you should know, though, is to ask for the brisket to be fresh: what you don't want is salt-beef, which is how brisket most commonly ends up – and not a bad ending it is, either. I'd also recommend you ask for it off the bone (although the chances are this will be done, anyway) and, though it may be wise to ask for the *excess* fat to be trimmed, what you most definitely do not want is for all the fat to be removed: you need the fat to give the meat flavor and keep it meltingly tender. Well, that and the slow roasting helps, too.

I don't roll my brisket: I just get a tapering sheet of it (well, that's how it comes: thicker on one end), sit it skin-side up on a bed of sliced onions, and cover it first in liquid and then in aluminum foil. I know there's a lot of it, but I can't tell you how good it is reheated, and I also freeze 2-person portions of the meat sliced in its gravy for future dates when greed outweighs energy. And I make no adjustment to the liquid measurements or cooking time, even when the weight of meat is less. In fact, I recently cooked this as a 1¾ pound rolled brisket, and the only changes I made were to put the rolled meat in the middle of a cast-iron Dutch oven, the onions on one side of it, a carrot, halved lengthwise, on the other, the liquid, then the lid, on top and cooked it exactly as for the flatter, immensely bigger cut below.

Curious though the ingredients for the cooking liquid sound, I cannot tell you how straightforwardly glorious it tastes. I'd defy you or anyone to be able to tell that there is coffee in it, but it is so good that I am not tempted to take it out, even once, just to tell the difference. I have some liquid smoke – a wonderfully poetic notion – and thrill to the legend on the label – "My life is in these bottles" – but I'm sure you could go ahead without. True, you'd miss that Texas barbecue flavor, but just double the amount of Worcestershire sauce, and the tang factor would be kept as it should.

I stay nearer home for the accompaniments. To me this says mashed potatoes, and the potato and parsnip, buttermilk-mixed version (minus the ginger) from **p.386** makes a pretty fantastic pardner, too. But there is no denying that some steamed potatoes, just cut up first and skins removed only after cooking, would be very much simpler and still do the essential job of absorbing the wonderful juices. Still, I have to say, I love this in a wide, low, shallow bowl with crunchy green beans and some bread for dipping, though the last of the juice I eat, like soup, with a spoon.

Serves approx. 12, *or many fewer with copious leftovers (the most desirable state of affairs)*

3 medium or 2 large onions
approx. 5½ pounds fresh (not
    salted) beef brisket
¼ cup apple cider vinegar
¼ cup soy sauce
¼ cup liquid smoke

¼ cup Worcestershire sauce (such
    as Lea & Perrins)
¼ cup steak sauce (such as A1)
¼ cup strong brewed black coffee
    or approx. 1 double espresso

♥ Preheat the oven to 300°F and get out a roasting pan that the oblong-shaped brisket will lie in snugly.

♥ Slice the onions, stripping away any skin that unwraps itself (it doesn't matter if the skin stays on) and arrange them largely in the center of the pan, to create an onion-platform for the brisket to lie on.

♥ Duly place the brisket on top, fat-topped side uppermost.

♥ Whisk together the remaining ingredients and pour them over the brisket, then cover the pan with aluminum foil, sealing it tightly – make a double layer if you want to feel secure – and place in the low oven for 3½ hours.

♥ Remove from the oven and transfer the meat to a board.

♥ Transfer the onions to a blender with a ladleful or two of the liquid from the pan and blend till smooth, then add back to the rest of the liquid in the pan and stir to mix.

♥ Slice the brisket in gentle diagonals across the grain and then, if you want, cut the slices in half across before plonking them into the onion-thickened gravy in the pan. I serve, happily and proudly, straight from the pan.

468

Making leftovers right

WARM
BRISKET
SANDWICH

There is no wrong way to eat these leftovers, and all I really do is reheat them, but it would be remiss of me not to add that a warm brisket sandwich, eaten messily and alone, is one of the truest pleasures available to mankind. The slices of beef can be stored in the refrigerator for up to 3 days: cover the surface with a thin layer of gravy and store on a plate covered tightly with plastic wrap or in an airtight container. You should store the remaining gravy separately in the refrigerator. (Leftovers can be frozen for up to 2 months in an airtight container: thaw overnight in the refrigerator and reheat as below.) When you're ready, proceed as follows: reheat meat in gravy, in an ovenproof dish covered tightly with foil, either in an oven preheated to 350°F, for 20– 30 minutes, or in the microwave in a bowl covered with plastic wrap, in 30-second bursts until piping hot; cut 2 thick slices of bread; dip 1 slice in gravy and sit wet-side up on plate; sit meat on top, then add dollop of horseradish sauce; using remaining piece of bread, wipe out gravy dish and sit the sopping slice of bread, wet-side down, on top of beef; lift up sandwich a little, crane forward so that you are hovering over plate, and eat sandwich before it falls utterly and damply to pieces.

469

Italian tomato and pasta soup

Think of this as a heavenly Italian version of Heinz tomato soup, made to comfort and delight and assure the eater that all manner of things shall be well. I rather think this is something we all need to feel – whether rightly or, alas, wrongly – on a Sunday night when the past week's failures and the coming week's obligations weigh heavy in the air. Actually, I'd go further than that: I'd say that if you go to bed on Sunday with this in your belly, Monday morning will be that bit more manageable.

You can add pasta or not, and blitz up or not, but my favorite way to eat this is the second option below: to pass the tomatoes and onions in their flavorsome liquid through a food mill and then cook the pasta in it. But the lovely thing about this soup, whichever way you eat it, is that it feels like something cozy on a tray that someone who loves you might bring you when you're down: the sort of comforting, undemanding food that cures whatever it is that ails you, from too much weekend carousing to the hysteria of undone school assignments.

Serves 4

6 large, ripe, fabulous tomatoes, approx. 1½ pounds
3 tablespoons olive oil
2 garlic cloves, peeled
1 large onion, peeled and finely chopped
1½ quarts cold water
1 teaspoon kosher salt or ½ teaspoon table salt
grind or two of pepper
2 teaspoons superfine sugar
1 cup ditalini or anelli rigati, or other soup pasta of your choice
sour cream, to serve (optional)
chopped fresh parsley, to serve (optional)

♥ Pour boiling water over the tomatoes in a bowl and leave to steep while you get on with a couple of other things.

♥ Namely: warm the oil in a thick-bottomed saucepan (one with a lid) and fry the garlic cloves until golden on both sides before discarding them and adding the chopped onion to the now garlicky oil. Stir a little and leave for a moment while you go back to the tomatoes.

♥ Drain the tomatoes and leave in the colander to cool slightly, before stripping off their skins. Halve the tomatoes – and get rid of seeds and white membrane – then roughly chop them and add to the onions in the pan. Stir well and leave to cook for 5 minutes or so, or until the onions have softened.

♥ Add the fresh cold water to the pan, let it come to a boil, adding salt, pepper and sugar, then turn down the heat, put the lid on and leave to simmer for **20 minutes**, if you want to eat the soup rough; **40 minutes** for smooth.

♥ **First option**: after 20 minutes remove the lid, bring back to a boil and add the pasta to cook till tender in the tomato and onion broth, then leave to stand for about 10 minutes before serving.

♥ **For the second, smooth option**, after the tomatoes and onions have had their 40-minute simmer, pass them through a vegetable mill, then pour back into the pan, bring to a boil, add the pasta and cook till it's tender, and let the soup stand for 10 minutes before serving.

♥ Sprinkle with chopped parsley to serve, as you like. If you wish to eat this without pasta, it will be runnier (the pasta starch thickens the soup) but still good, and you can add a retro squiggle of sour cream to each bowl on serving.

MAKE AHEAD NOTE
The soup can be made up to 2 days ahead. Transfer to non-metallic bowl to cool, then cover and refrigerate as quickly as possible. Best if made without pasta then, to reheat, bring to a boil in saucepan, add pasta and cook as directed in recipe. If made with pasta, you may need to add extra splash of water on reheating.

FREEZE NOTE
The cooled soup can be frozen in airtight container for up to 3 months. Thaw overnight in the refrigerator and reheat as above.

Acknowledgments

The clutter of my kitchen is not only the backdrop as I write and cook, but – fittingly enough – the backdrop of this book. Of course, many readers will recognize pots, pans, glasses, bowls, and other bits and pieces from previous books, and this is just how it should be. Familiarity is the cozy province of the home cook, and proudly so. But the needs of a kitchen and the needs of a photography shoot are not exactly the same, and many of the pictures that precede this page have been enormously aided by Ceramica Blue, The Conran Shop, David Mellor, Divertimenti, TheFrenchHouse.net, Few and Far, Heal's, John Lewis Partnership, littala, Lytton & Lily, NOM Living, Rice, Seeds of Italy, and Vintage Heaven. I am very grateful.

I am grateful, too, enduringly, to those who have worked so hard to make this the book I wanted it to be, even when I left them hardly any time to do so. Caroline Stearns, Jan Bowmer, Parisa Ebrahimi, Poppy Hampson, and Alison Samuel deserve more than thanks: they deserve some sort of medal of honor. Alison, in particular, I wish to thank for her patience, forbearance, and an attention to detail that verges on a state of grace (or medical condition). At Random House, too, I am, as ever, profoundly grateful for the huge good fortune that has provided me with a publisher as brilliant as Gail Rebuck.

I am similarly blessed beyond: I rely utterly on the guidance so generously given to me by Mark Hutchinson; and Ed Victor, I think, knows how eternally indebted I am to him. I can never truly get over my luck in having worked, over the years, with Caz Hildebrand. All my books, and especially this one, owe their existence greatly to her. As they benefit, too, from the dedicated attentions of my photographer, Lis Parsons.

But I have a special gratitude not just for those who have worked with me on this book, but who have spent so much time in the kitchen with me as it bubbled its way into being. Hettie Potter and Zoe Wales have devoted themselves particularly to the task in hand, as well as to me over the years, and Rose Murray, once again, helped bring a beautiful book into the world with them; but I give heartfelt thanks to all of them, my kitchen confidantes: Lisa and Francesco Grillo, Rose Murray, Hettie Potter, Zoe Wales, and Anzelle Wasserman.

Index

African drumsticks 46
After eight (cocktail) 443–4
agave nectare 22
almonds
  Raspberry almond bars 299–300
  Strawberry and almond crumble 131–2
aluminum foil pans 3, 19
Americano (cocktail) 442
anchovies 355
  Pepper, anchovy and egg salad 214–15
  Quick chick Caesar 230
  Slut's spaghetti 188–9
apples
  Apple and cinnamon muffins 128–30
  Apple and mustard sauce 414
  Apple pandowdy 144–5
  Pork and apple hotpot 463–4
arancini 354
arugula
  Arugula and lemon couscous 90
  Butternut, arugula and pine nut salad 92, 94–5
Asian braised beef shank with hot and sour shredded salad 382–5
asparagus
  Sweet potato supper 340
avocados
  Avocado quesadillas 433
  Avocado salsa 107
  Chicken, bacon, and avocado salad 226–7

Baby Guinness (cocktail) 440–41
bacon
  freezing bacon 15

Chicken, bacon, and avocado salad 226–7
  Egg and bacon salad 56–9
  see also lardons *and* pancetta
Baked egg custard 260–61
bakeware 4
baking 14–15, 236, 238
baking powder 15
baking, silicone liners for 14
bananas
  Banoffee cheesecake 133–4
  Chocolate banana muffins 138
  Coconut and cherry banana bread 136–7
Banoffee cheesecake 133–4
Barbecued ground beef 33–5
Bartholomew (Bartholomeus Anglicus): *On the Properties of Things* 362
BBQ gravy 458
beans *see* black beans; fava beans; green beans; Rice and peas
Beard, James 388
Beckett, Samuel 9
beef
  Asian braised beef shank with hot and sour shredded salad 382–5
  Barbecued ground beef 33–5
  Beer-braised beef Dutch oven 330–32
  Bolognese patties 358
  Carbonnade à la flamande 330–32
  Cheesy chili 31–2
  Date steak 321–2
  Ed's mother's meatloaf 458–60

Minetta marrowbones (veal) 400–1
  Risotto Bolognese 355–8
  Beef rib roast with wild mushrooms and Cheddar mashed potatoes 362, 402–7
  Texas brisket 467–8
  Venetian lasagne 336–8
  see also brisket
Beer-braised beef Dutch oven 330–32
Beer-braised pork knuckles with caraway, garlic, apples and potatoes 378–80
beets 17
  Halloumi with beets and lime 212–13
berries, mixed
  Jumbleberry jam 285–6
  No-fuss fruit tart 177–8, 318
baking soda 15
black beans
  Mexican lasagne 105–6
blackberries
  Blackberry vodka 292–4
  Drunken fool 295
  Orange and blackberry trifle 171, 271
  see also berries, mixed
Black velvet (cocktail) 440
blenders 6
Blondies 313–14
Bloody Maria (cocktail) 207, 441–2
blueberries
  Blueberry cornmeal muffins 243–4
  see also berries, mixed; Orange and blackberry trifle

476

477

483

484

Express Index

Recipes that take 30 minutes or under from first move to plate

487